Da

flying visits
CROATIA &
THE ADRIATIC

CADOGANguides

Contents

About the authors

James Stewart (*Croatia, Slovenia*) was born in Bangor, Northern Ireland, and, after studying music at London's City University and journalism as a postgraduate, he took to editing, travel and writing in a big way. He is also the author of *Flying Visits Germany* and co-author of *Flying Visits Central & Eastern Europe*; when not shackled to a computer in his London home, he flees to the coast.

Dana Facaros and **Michael Pauls** (*Italy*) have written over 30 books for Cadogan Guides. They have lived all over Europe with their son and daughter, and are currently ensconced in an old farmhouse in southwestern France with a large collection of tame and wild animals. In the *Flying Visits* series, they are authors of *Flying Visits Italy* and *Flying Visits Spain*, and co-authors of *Flying Visits France* and *Flying Visits Mediterranean*. Their text for this guide was updated 2005 by **Nicky Swallow**.

Cadogan Guides
Network House, 1 Ariel Way
London W12 7SL
info@cadoganguides.co.uk
www.cadoganguides.com

The Globe Pequot Press
246 Goose Lane, PO Box 480, Guilford,
Connecticut 06437–0480

Copyright © James Stewart, Dana Facaros and
Michael Pauls 2005

Cover design by Sarah Gardner
Book design by Andrew Barker
Cover photographs: © Pinimage/Alamy,
© imagebroker/Alamy, © Barry Mason/Alamy,
© DIOMEDIA/Alamy, © Jon Arnold Images/Alamy,
© Robert Mullan/Alamy, © Peter Adams
Photography/Alamy.
Maps © Cadogan Guides, drawn by Maidenhead
Cartographic Services Ltd
Managing Editor: Natalie Pomier
Flying Visits Series Editor: Linda McQueen
Editor: Linda McQueen
Proofreading: Alison Copland
Indexing: Isobel McLean

Printed in Italy by Legoprint
A catalogue record for this book is available
from the British Library
ISBN 1-86011-192-0

Introduction

Such was the ferocity of Croatia's five-year struggle for survival after the 1990 implosion of Communist Yugoslavia that travellers are only now rediscovering one of Europe's most complete all-rounders. Along nearly 1,800km of one of the continent's most outstanding coastlines, lapped by some of the cleanest seas on the planet, are daydreaming settlements casually studded with Roman antiquities, medieval small town-citadels, and cosy fishing villages where modernity is just a whisper; for every busy beach by a package hotel there is a clutch of quiet coves to discover or a wilderness park of limestone gorges to explore. Similarly, tourism is acknowledged only with a casual shrug on many of the islands in a constellation of nearly 1,200.

That stunning coastline is an easy ferry ride away from Italian ports neatly serviced by budget airline carriers, but, if you take this route, do explore before you sail across the Adriatic or nip south by bus: the salty old port of **Ancona** famed for seafood is the gateway to the Marches; prosperous **Pescara** has lofty Apennine peaks within easy reach of its miles of buzzy beach resort; neoclassical **Trieste** is a rich ethnic stew from neighbours Slovenia and Austria that sweetens Aquileia, a nearby feast of Roman antiquity, with delicious pastries; and then there's **Venice**, the former republic whose winged Lion of St Mark is stamped on the Croatian coastline it owned until the early 1800s and whose fairytale becomes more remarkable with every visit.

Summer catamarans also nip across from Venice to Istria in northern Croatia, a heart-shaped locket of land dangling in the sea. Its regional capital **Pula** is an intriguing mix of Roman antiquities and the no-nonsense grit of a working port, and gateway to ravishing Rovinj and a tour which explores Croatia's Tuscany, where rustic hill towns doze on their perches. Nearby **Rijeka** is the region's industrial dynamo, a noisy port easily escaped in Opatija, which retains a whiff of glamour from its heyday as the St-Tropez of Central Europe, or on Kvarner Gulf islands Krk, Cres and Lošinj.

Mountains march south as a backcloth to coastal Dalmatia and its northern capital **Zadar**, with a millennium-spanning mix of Roman remains, Croatia's jewel of Byzantium and a splendid *œuvre* of Romanesque churches. Even more intriguing is **Split**, whose inhabitants don't bat an eyelid at the UNESCO-listed retirement home of Roman emperor Diocletian in their midst, and take for granted the old town's fabulous medieval warren crammed with cafés. The nation's second city is also the jumping-off point for our tour around some of Croatia's most alluring islands. More unspoilt island idylls await further south, but first you'll have to prise yourself from gateway city **Dubrovnik**, a former proud merchant republic now saluted for its Baroque timewarp painted in clear light and cool stone within one of the world's best-preserved medieval citadels.

Counterbalancing the easygoing Mediterranean attitudes of the coast is inland Croatia, whose thrumming centre is capital city **Zagreb**, an enjoyable dollop of stuffy 19th-century Mitteleuropa softened with a Baroque old town. Step beyond its stylish café society, however, and you'll discover a fairytale landscape of hummocky hills and nestled bucolic villages in the Zagorje. There's more homespun sentimentality in Croatia's rustic neighbour Slovenia, whose 47km Adriatic coastline provides ample excuse to include **Ljubljana**, perhaps the most convivial capital in Europe, with, in its back garden, jagged Alps and one of the most magical cave systems you'll see.

Getting There

02

No budget flights currently fly to Croatia; you should always look for special deals with the scheduled airlines, however, and book online and early for the best prices.

However, there are many other more creative and perfectly feasible options. You can fly cheaply to Ljubljana, from where by train you can also reach Zagreb, and Rijeka on Croatia's Istrian Peninsula. You could fly to Trieste and take a bus over the border to visit the Istrian Peninsula (Pula and Rijeka). You could fly to Venice and take a ferry or catamaran to Pula or Rovinj on the Istrian Peninsula. Or, to get to the Dalmatian coastal resorts (Dubrovnik, Split, Zadar) and islands, you could fly to the towns on Italy's eastern Adriatic coast (Ancona, Pescara, Bari) and take a ferry. Note that travelling in winter (Nov–Mar) is always going to be extremely difficult, for both ferries and flights especially.

The best website for checking out the most current travel information, all explained extremely clearly and simply, with up-to-date timestables and contact details for all options, is *www.visit-croatia.co.uk/gettingthere/index.htm*.

By Air

From the UK and Ireland

The only airlines offering scheduled flights from the UK to Croatia are Croatia Airlines and British Airways, and most of the routes are summer-only. EasyJet and Slovenian national carrier Adria fly to Ljubljana, just over the border in Slovenia and a pleasure in its own right; and Ryanair will take you cheaply to all the towns along Italy's Adriatic Coast. EasyJet also flies to Venice, and unlike Ryanair they go to Marco Polo instead of Treviso some distance away. From Ireland you will have to travel via London; there are no direct flights. Journey times from London or Manchester and between two and three hours.

Many airlines fly indirectly to Croatia, especially Dubrovnik and Zagreb, via one stop at another European city. Check out the national airlines, e.g. Alitalia via Milan, Malev via Budapest, Austrian Arlines via Vienna, KLM via Amsterdam, Air France via Paris.

In the last few years the airline industry has undergone a revolution. Inspired by the success of Stelios Haji-Ioannou's easyJet

Who Goes Where?

	page	Croatia Airlines	British Airways	Adria Airlines	Ryanair	easyJet	Sky Europe	Germanwings
Zagreb (C)	29	●						▲
Dubrovnik (C)	121	★	●				▲	
Split (C)	97	★	★					▲
Zadar (C)	81	★						
Pula (C)	53	★						
Rijeka (C)	68	★						
Ljubljana (S)	161			●		●		
Venice (I)	208				●	●		
Trieste (I)	194				●			
Ancona (I)	226				●			
Pescara (I)	236				●			
Bari (I)	240				●			

C = Croatia, S = Slovenia, I = Italy   ● = direct, all year   ★ = direct, summer only   ▲ = not direct

Airlines

Adria Airways, t (00386) (0)1 36 91 010 (no UK tel), *www.adria-airways.com*. London Gatwick and Manchester to Ljubljana.
British Airways, t 0870 850 9850, *www.ba.com*. London Gatwick to Split (April–Oct) and Dubrovnik. Manchester to Dubrovnik (late Mar–Oct).
Croatia Airlines, t (020) 8563 0020, *www.croatiaairlines.hr*. London Heathrow to Zagreb, Rijeka (April–Oct), Zadar (April–Oct), Split (April–Oct). London Gatwick to Pula (April–Oct), Split (April–Oct), Dubrovnik (late Mar–Oct). Manchester to Pula (April–Oct), Split (April–Oct), Dubrovnik (late Mar–Oct).
easyJet, t 0905 821 0905 (reservations and changes to bookings; 65p/min) or t 0871 244 2366 (customer services; 10p/min), *www.easyjet.com*. London Stansted to Ljubljana and Venice (Marco Polo).
Germanwings, t (020) 8321 7255, *www.germanwings.com*. A low-cost German carrier: from London Stansted to Zagreb and Split via Cologne.
Ryanair, Irish Republic t 0818 30 30 30, UK t 0871 246 0000 (10p/min), *www.ryanair.com*. From London Stansted to Trieste, Venice (Treviso, some way from Venice), Pescara, Ancona, Bari. London Luton to Venice (Treviso). Liverpool to Venice (Treviso).
SkyEurope, t (020) 7365 0365, *www.skyeurope.com*. A low-cost carrier specializing in central Europe; London Stansted and Manchester to Dubrovnik via Bratislava or Budapest.

company, other airlines, especially Ryanair, flocked to join him in breaking all the conventions of air travel to offer fares at rock-bottom prices. Whereas in their first years no-frills airlines had an undoubted 'backpackerish' feel, this has become an increasingly mainstream way to travel. New airlines are still starting up all the time – and, most importantly, larger national airlines such as British Airways have got in on the act, copying some of the more attractive aspects of budget travel, such as Internet booking with discounts, flights from UK regional airports, and one-way fares.

It is important to note also that **no-frills airlines are not always the cheapest**, above all on the very popular routes at peak times. One of the benefits of the no-frills revolution that is not always appreciated is not so much their own prices as the concessions they have forced on the older, mainstream carriers. It is **always** worth comparing no-frills prices with those of the main airlines, and checking out what special offers are going. For flights and price comparisons on the Internet, *see www.skyscanner.net, www.whichbudget.com* (claims to include all routes flown by budget UK airlines on a single site), *www.traveljungle. co.uk, www.opodo.co.uk, www.travelocity. co.uk, www.expedia.co.uk* or *www.aboutflights.co.uk*.

From the USA and Canada

Because no scheduled airline currently operates direct routes from the United States and Canada to Croatia, Stateside travellers must fly to European travel hubs such as London, Frankfurt, Zürich or Paris, then connect with flights of European carriers.

Between June and August, direct charter flights from Chicago (O'Hare) and New York (JFK) to Split and Zagreb are operated by **Trans Meridian Airlines**, t 1 866 I FLY TMA, *www.transmeridian-airlines.com*, and can be booked through travel agencies **Croatia Travel**, 32–66 Steinway Street, Astoria, New York 11103, t (718) 726 6700; *www.croatiatravel.com*, or **Vega Travel**, 206 West Wacker Drive, Suite 616, Chicago, IL 60606, t 800 359 8437/t (312)332 7211, *www.vegatravel.net*.

Seasonal charter flights from Toronto to Zagreb and Split can be booked through travel agency **Maxxtours**, 6-966 Pantera Drive, Mississauga, ON L4W 2S1, t (866) 696 6299, *www.maxxtours.com*.

Various airlines do fly to Venice, from where you can easily get to northern Croatia (Zagreb and Istria) or Slovenia by train or ferry. The other option is to travel via London, *see pp.6–7*.

By Train

You can certainly get to Croatia by train, after crossing the Channel via the Eurostar, t 08705 186 186, *www.eurostar.com*, but the journey time is extremely long and costs around £360, about same as a scheduled flight to one of the Croatian city destinations.

Getting to Europe by Air from North America

You can fly directly to a few of the bigger cities in this guide from North America. But it is also possible for North Americans to take advantage of the explosion of cheap inter-European flights, by taking a charter flight to London, and booking a UK–Croatia/Slovenia/Italy budget flight in advance on a low-cost airline's website (*see* p.5). This will need careful planning: you're looking at an 8–14hr flight followed by a 3hr journey across London and another 2hr hop to Europe.

Direct to Europe

The main airports in this guide receiving transatlantic flights are the cities of **Venice** and **Zagreb**. The main carriers flying direct to these cities are **American Airlines, ČSA, Delta, LOT Polish Airlines, United, Air Canada** and **Trans Meridian**; *see* p.5 for details.

Since **prices** are constantly changing and there are numerous kinds of deals on offer, the first thing to do is find yourself a travel agent who is capable of laying the current options before you. The time of year can make a great difference to the price and availability; prices can range from around $350 for the best bargain deals to well over $1,000.

A number of companies offer cheaper **charter flights** to Europe – look in the Sunday travel sections of the *New York Times, Los Angeles Times, Chicago Tribune, Toronto Star* or other big-city papers. For fares, schedules and price comparisons on the **Internet**, see *www.traveljungle.us, www.lastminute.com, www.expedia.com, www.orbitz.com, www.travelocity.com* and *www.flyaow.com* (discounted fares and schedules on 500 worldwide airlines, also car hire and hotels).

Via London

Start by finding a charter or discounted scheduled flight to London. When you have the availability and arrival times for London flights, match up a convenient flight time on the website of the budget airline that flies to your chosen European city. *If you are flying to London, be careful to choose only flights from the airports near London: Luton, Gatwick, Heathrow, London City and Stansted.*

You will most likely be arriving at Heathrow terminals 3 or 4 (or possibly Gatwick), and may be flying out from Stansted, Luton, London City or Gatwick, all of which are in different directions and will mean travelling through central London, so leaving enough time is essential. Add together the journey times and prices for Heathrow into central London and back out again to your departure airport. You could mix and match – the Tube to Victoria and the Gatwick Express, or a taxi from Heathrow to St Pancras and a train to Luton – but don't even think of using a bus or taxi at rush hours (7–10am and 4–7pm); train and/or Underground (Tube) are the only sensible choices. Always add on waiting times and delays in London's notoriously creaky transport system; and finally, although the cheapest airline fares are early morning and late at night, make sure your chosen transport is still operating at that time (*see* below).

For travel information within London, call t (020) 7222 1234, *www.tfl.gov.uk*.

Airport to Airport Taxis

A taxi directly between airports might avoid central London, but is an expensive option: Heathrow–Gatwick: 1hr 30mins, £110–120. Heathrow–Stansted: 2hrs 15mins, £150–170. Heathrow–Luton: 1hr 15mins, £100–130.

For booking taxis in advance, try **Dial-A-Cab**, t (020) 7253 5000, **Taxi One-Number**, t 0871 871 8710 and **Data Cab, t** (020) 7432 1540, or see *www.londonblackcabs.co.uk* or *www.londontaxicabs.net*.

Heathrow

Heathrow is about 15 miles west of the centre. **Airport information: t** 0870 0000 123, *www.baa.co.uk*.

By train: The Heathrow Express (**t** 0845 600 1515) is the fastest option: trains every 15mins between 5.07am and midnight to Paddington station, which is on the Tube's Bakerloo, Circle and District Lines, taking 15mins, or 7–8mins more to Terminal 4. £14 single, £26 return.

By Tube to Terminals 1,2 and 3: Heathrow is on the Piccadilly Line. Tube trains from central London to Heathrow depart every 10mins from 6.32am (or 7.51am Sun) to 00.32am (or 11.38pm Sun) and the journey takes 55mins. Tube trains from Heathrow to central

London depart every 10mins from 5.13am (or 5.57am Sun) until 11.49pm (or 11.30pm Sun). Single fare to the centre: £3.80.

By Tube to Terminal 4: Owing to construction works on Terminal 5, the Tube service to Terminal 4 has been suspended until September 2006. Until then passengers can take a frequent bus shuttle from Hatton Cross Tube station on the Piccadilly Line; the journey takes an additional 5–10 minutes.

By coach: National Express 403 from Heathrow's Central Bus Station (CBS) terminates at Victoria Station and takes 30mins–1hr London–Heathrow or 45mins–1hr 25mins Heathrow–London, depending on traffic. £10 single, £15 return. You can book National Express tickets in advance, t 08705 808080, www.nationalexpress.com.

By bus: A vast network of local buses operates from Heathrow's Central Bus Station; some services also stop at Terminal 4. A single bus fare to anywhere in London costs £1.20.

By taxi: Black cab from or to central London: £45–60.

Gatwick

Gatwick is about 20 miles south of London. There are two terminals, North and South, linked by a fast shuttle service. **Airport information**: t 0870 000 2468.

By train: The fastest service is the Gatwick Express (t 0845 850 1530 or t 08457 48 49 50, www.gatwickexpress.com), which runs from Victoria Station to South Terminal every 15mins and takes about 30mins or 35mins on Sundays. £12 single, £23.50 return.

By taxi: Black cab from/to central London: £85.

Luton

30 miles north of London. **Airport information**: t (01582) 405 100, www.london-luton.co.uk.

By bus/coach: easyBus runs an express bus service from Luton Bus Station bay 4 to Baker Street/Gloucester Place, every 45mins–1hr from as little as £1 single; book at www.easybus.co.uk, or pay the driver. Alternatively, Green Line 757 (t 0870 608 7261) runs roughly every half-hour between Luton Airport and Buckingham Palace Road, Victoria, via Finchley Rd, Baker St and Marble Arch. £12.50 return, £9.00 single. 1hr 15mins.

By train: Between 8am and 10pm, Thameslink (t 08457 48 49 50, www.thameslink.co.uk)

runs frequent trains from St Pancras station to Luton Airport Parkway. Tickets cost from £10 if you buy online. At Luton Airport Parkway a free shuttle bus (10 mins) takes you on to the airport; in total the journey takes around 45–55mins.

By taxi: Black cab from/to central London: £80.

Stansted

Stansted is the furthest from London, about 35 miles to the northeast. **Airport information**: t 0870 000 0303.

By bus: Terravision Express Shuttle, t (01279) 662931, www.lowcostcoach.com, to London Victoria departs Stansted coach bay 26 every hour 7.15am–00.40am, and departs London Victoria every hour 3am–10.30pm; the journey takes around 75mins; £8.50 single or £14 return. The National Express A6 Victoria–Stansted and A7 Stansted–Victoria run 24hrs every 15–30mins from Victoria Station via Marble Arch, Hyde Park Corner, Baker Street, St John's Wood, Finchley Rd and Golders Green, taking 1hr 25mins–1hr 45mins in traffic; see www.nationalexpress.com, t 0870 5 747 777. £10 single or £15 return.

By train: The Stansted Express (www.stanstedexpress.com) runs every 15–30mins 5am–11pm Liverpool Street station–Stansted and 6am–11.45pm Stansted–Liverpool St station, taking 45mins. £14.50 single, £24 return.

By taxi: Black cab from/to central London: £85.

Sample Journeys

Heathrow–Luton: get to Heathrow Express from terminal 15mins; wait for train 10mins; journey 15mins; go from Paddington Station down into Tube 10mins; Tube to Farringdon 15mins; go up and buy Thameslink ticket 10mins including queueing; train and shuttle to Luton 55mins. **Total journey time** 2hrs 10mins, plus 45mins for delays and hitches, so 3hrs would be safest.

Heathrow–Stansted: get to Tube station from terminal 10mins, wait for Tube 5mins, Piccadilly Line to King's Cross 1hr 10mins, change to Circle Line and continue to Liverpool Street Tube station 15mins, up into main line station and buy Stansted Express ticket 10mins, wait for train 20mins, train journey 45mins. **Total journey time** 2hrs 55mins, plus 45mins for delays and hitches, so 3hrs 40mins would be safest.

If you want to check it out for yourself, or investigate the various **rail passes** available for UK, US or Canadian citizens travelling throgun Europe, see the **Rail Europe** website. Rail Europe handles bookings for all services, including Eurostar and Motorail, sells rail passes and acts for other continental rail companies. **UK**: 178 Piccadilly, London W1, t 08708 371371 *www.raileurope.co.uk.* **USA and Canada**: t 877 257 2887 (US), or t 800 361 RAIL (Canada), *www.raileurope.com.*

By Coach

Generally more expensive than a flight on a budget carrier to an Italian port and a ferry across the Adriatic, and certainly far longer, buses to Croatia or Slovenia are worth considering only by the most adamant non-flier and travel masochist. **Eurolines**, t 08705 808080; *www.eurolines. co.uk*, operates routes year-round from London to Zagreb and Varaždin. Buses take around 35hrs, plus you can expect a 3- or 4-hour wait when you change buses in Frankfurt, and a return fare costs around £179.

By Sea

Those with thinner wallets and time on their side can fly to Italian ports then catch ferries across the Adriatic, generally taking 8hrs, and overnight except in summer. Return tickets for overnight journeys are usually cheaper than two singles. Be aware that crossings may reduce considerably to one ferry a week in winter (company websites publish timetable details) and also that deck passage is just that – all but the most masochistic traveller should dig into pockets to find the few extra euros for a reclining seat, couchette or cabin.

Italy–Croatia Ferries

Jadrolinija, t +385 (0)51 666 111, *www. jadrolinija.hr.* Ancona–Split; Ancona–Split–Stari Grad (Hvar)–Korčula (summer only); Ancona–Zadar (summer only); Bari–Dubrovnik.
Adriatica di Navigazione, t +39 (0)41 781 611; *www.adriatica.it.* Ancona–Split; Bari–Dubrovnik.
SEM Maritime Company (SMC), t +385 (0)21 352 553; *www.sem-marina.hr.* Ancona–Split; Ancona–Stari Grad (Hvar) (summer only); Ancona–Vis (summer only).
SNAV, t +39 (0)71 207 6116; *www.snav.it.* Ancona–Split; Ancona–Zadar; Pescara–Split; Pescara–Stari Grad (Hvar); Cittanova–Zadar; Cittanova–Šibenik; Citanova–Mali Losinj. All routes summer only.
Venezia Lines, t +39 (0)41 2424 000; *www.venezialines.com.* Venice–Mali Losinj; Venice–Porec; Venice–Pula; Venice–Rabac; Venice–Rovinj; Venice–Umag; Rimini–Pula.

Slovenia and Italy to Croatia by Train or Bus

In addition to ferries, **buses** from Trieste trundle to Pula in two hours and also to Zagreb. From Slovenia, six direct **trains** a day (plus four trains requiring one change) blast from Ljubljana to Zagreb (c.2hrs 20mins) and two trains a day travel direct from Ljubljana to Rijeka ((via Opatija, 2hrs 30mins), although there are more trains which require one change.
Two trains a day travel direct from Venice (4hrs) and Trieste (3hrs 40mins) to Zagreb. Trieste is also linked to Koper in Slovenia, 20km southwest, by 13 buses a day, from where you can catch trains to Ljubljana.

Croatia:
Travel, Practical A–Z
and Language

03

Travel

Entry Formalities

Passports and Visas

Not yet a member of the EU, Croatia nevertheless harmonizes entry regulations with the continent, so holders of full, valid EU, US, Canadian, Australian and New Zealand passports can enter for a period of up to 90 days without a visa. If you decide to explore longer, the simplest visa extension is obtained by nipping across the Italian or Slovenian border then re-entering. Other nationals must apply to embassies or consulates for a visa, which costs 160Kn (£15) single transit; 200Kn (£19) double transit; 320Kn (£30) multiple-transit. In theory, new arrivals must register with the local police, a formality handled by hotels or private accommodation agencies which will require your passport. In practice, police turn a blind eye and are as relaxed about this as tourists. Pets can be brought into the country on presentation of an international certificate to testify the animal is rabies-free issued by an accredited vet at least 15 days earlier, but within six months.

Customs

Foreign travellers are exempted from customs duty for non-commercial goods carried as personal baggage up to the value of 30,000Kn, although it may be a good idea to declare flashy laptops on entry to save a brush with customs officials on departure. In addition, travellers are exempted from duty for: 200 cigarettes or 100 cigarillos or 50 cigars or 250g of tobacco; 1 litre of strong spirits; 2 litres of table wine; 2 litres of liqueurs (under 22%) sparkling wine or dessert wine; 500g of coffee; 50ml of perfume; 250ml of toilet water. In addition, you can only bring in and take out up to 15,000Kn.

A tortuous bureaucratic process reimburses foreign travellers with VAT paid on goods all bought in the same Croatian shop and whose value exceeds 500Kn if they complete a PDV-P form on purchase and present the goods to customs (*carina*) on departure; *see* 'Money and Banks', p.16. Official Croatian customs website *www.carina.hr* publishes full information on formalities.

Getting Around

By Train

The international rather than domestic priorities of the Habsburg rulers are revealed in Croatia's railway lines. A network pioneered in the 19th century centres on Slovenia-linked Zagreb and lays a mesh of track over the continental north and east of the country, but only snakes a single line down the country's spine to Split, off which branch lines potter to Rijeka and Zadar. A line from Rijeka threads north into Slovenia then Italy, to which a branch-line descends through Istria and pauses in Pazin on its way to Pula. Buses and ferries are the workhorses of a coast devoid of track. Worse, services on once-busy routes such as Zagreb–Rijeka have been slashed after Croatians discovered they could make the 4hr journey in just over half the time by car. National operator **Croatian Railways** (Hrvatske Željeznice) hopes an upgrade of track to accommodate go-fast trains which lean into the corners will woo back customers: by summer 2005 trains will blast from Zagreb to Split in 4hrs 40mins rather than the painful 8hrs previously.

Until then trains (*vlakov*, singular *vlak*), though clean and smooth, are slower than buses but around 10% cheaper. Fastest of the fleet are futuristic **InterCity** (IC) trains, which are air-conditioned and have first- and second-class (*prvi razred* and *drugi razred*) carriages. The drawback is they are also more expensive than **local passenger trains** (*putnički*), which dawdle through the countryside.

Tickets (*karte*, singular *karta*) are bought prior to travel from the booking office of the **train station** (*žljeznički kolodvor*), with a single ticket (*karta u jednom*) priced at exactly half that of a return (*povratna karta*) on all but some IC routes. High-end routes may also require a **seat reservation** (*rezervacije*), indicated on a **timetable** (*vozni red*) as *rezerviranje mjesta obvezatno*; **departures** are *odlazak*, **arrivals** are *dolazak*. Searchable timetable information is published in English on Croatian Railways' website, *www.hznet.hr*.

While **rail passes** such as the Euro Domino or InterRail are valid on Croatian Railways trains, they are not worth the expense if you intend to travel only within Croatia.

By Bus

The workhorses of Croatian travel, buses (*autobusni*) are operated by a bewildering profusion of private companies. The most comfortable are air-conditioned **intercity express buses**, which generally depart every hour. Since the price structure is by distance they may also work out cheaper (and certainly faster) than more frequent local buses, whose timetables are geared towards rush-hour needs of locals. Buses on islands are scheduled to co-ordinate with ferry arrivals; miss the one bus which waits at the dock then tours the island and you could be in trouble.

At large city **bus stations** (*autobusni kolodvor*) **tickets** are bought before boarding from the private companies which gather in a booking hall and display route lists in booth windows. Since companies frequently ply the same routes, check tickets to confirm the bus company and platform (*peron*). Be aware that some companies offer discounts on a return ticket, and advance purchase is a wise precaution in peak season. For local buses far less strict about timetables, simply pile on and pay the driver. Do the same on city runaround municipal buses and you will usually pay extra and be required to proffer the exact money – slightly cheaper tickets can be bought in advance from kiosks and newsagents – and all tickets must be validated on boarding in 'ticket cancellers'. The number of departures reduces at weekends – skeleton services are the norm on Sundays.

By Ferry

Ferries are the traveller's friend: cheap (at least for foot passengers) and with journeys often as enjoyable as the destination itself. Roll-on, roll-off ferries ply short hops on busy **mainland–island** routes such as Orebić–Dominče (Korčula) or Jablanac–Mišnjak (Rab) every 30mins–1hr, but most jaunts will be on scheduled ferries that link islands to each other and to hub ports Dubrovnik (Elafiti islands, Mljet), Split (Brač, Šolta, Hvar, Korčula, Vis and Lastovo) and Zadar (Ugljan and Dugi otok). In peak season, you can expect around 2–4 ferries a day, depending on popularity.

Be warned that locals' needs come before those of tourists – ferries to and from remote destinations can depart in the sort of early hours no holidaymaker should have to see.

National ferry company **Jadrolinija** (*see* p.8) claims most routes, bolstered by a clutch of private companies, especially in summer when hydrofoils and catamarans reward with faster travel times those foot-passengers prepared to pay a little extra. Whatever the company, **tickets** are bought before boarding from a company office or booth near the quay, or, for ports which are little more than a quay, from kiosks, approx 30mins before departure. Expect to pay around 10–30Kn for a foot passenger and 60–200Kn for a car according to journey distance and vehicle size. As ever, crowds can be a problem in a frequently chaotic peak season. Buy tickets in advance wherever possible and even then expect to have to arrive up to 2hrs before the departure time if you are driving; ferries operate on a first-come, first-served basis and protests about early purchase of tickets to a crew whose boat is full will be met with a stoic shrug. Seek advice from ticket sales staff about waiting times. Similarly, so heavy are August queues on short-hop routes to Rab or Korčula that drivers may have to wait for a ferry to make a return journey.

Jadrolinija also operates a **coastal service** which skips south from Rijeka to Dubrovnik in 22hrs and calls at Zadar, Split, Stari Grad (Hvar), Korčula and Sobra (Mljet). Departures are daily in July–Aug, four times a week in shoulder months and twice a week in winter. Prices vary depending on the level of comfort – slumming it in on deck or in the bar; a reclining seat; couchette-style bunk beds; or private cabin. Since deck passengers can linger in any destination for up to a week (validate ticket with the purser at each stop), this is an enticing option to tour Croatia's fabulous coastline. All ferries rustle up food – usually rather tired sandwiches – and drinks in a cafeteria or smoke-choked bar.

By Car

The day trips we propose in this guide are cherry-picked to be readily accessible by public transport, but a car is essential for all touring itineraries except those from Split and Dubrovnik. It also offers the freedom to combine otherwise tricky day trips such as Salona and Trogir, or Šibenik and the Krka National Park.

Conditions vary widely on Croatian roads. Well-maintained, three-lane **motorways** (*autocesta*), indicated by blue signs and an A prefix (green and E for international routes), thunder north, east and west of Zagreb and speed south through the country's centre to Zadar and on to Split – or should by summer 2005, when a snippet at Šibenik is scheduled for completion. Construction continues on an extension south to Dubrovnik and into Montenegro. All charge **tolls** for their use; collect tickets on joining, pay on exit and, as a gauge of costs, in 2004 Zagreb–Karlovac cost 16Kn, Zagreb–Rijeka 56Kn. Tolls are also payable for the Krk bridge (15Kn) and the Učka tunnel (25Kn) from inland Istria to Rijeka.

Croatia's only other major artery is the coastal **Adriatic Highway** (B8), a scenic treat which shows off to their best advantage Dalmatia's beautiful coastline and Croatia's anarchic driving – bumper-hanging and blind overtaking are standard practice. Fast it is not, however, especially in summer, when the single carriageway clogs with heavy traffic and tour coaches. Elsewhere, roads which have a casual disregard for numbers (and often signs) are generally passable.

Petrol stations (*benzinska stanica*) provide 95- and 98-octane unleaded and diesel from 7am to 7 or 8pm (till 10 summer), although those on motorways and at city fringes work longer hours and generally have an ATM. Although petrol stations punctuate motor-ways approx every 40–50km, chances to fill up evaporate alarmingly elsewhere.

Muscle your way into cities which have no time for timid drivers and **parking** is a headache. By all means follow the blue P to car parks located at the fringes of historic beauties such as Dubrovnik and Split, but accept that the wait will be long and the bill high, especially in summer. Side streets far from centres are good hunting grounds for free spaces, although cars parked illegally are swiftly removed.

The **Croatian Automobile Club** (Hrvatski Autoklub) is a good friend to the foreign driver – it provides roadside breakdown assistance (t 987) plus up-to-date information on road conditions and ferries in English either on t (01) 464 08 00 or its website *www.hak.hr*.

If you have an accident inform the police (t 92) immediately.

Rules and Regulations

Drivers are required to hold a full, valid licence and if driving their own vehicles must also keep to hand documents of registration and a certificate of third-party insurance (including a Green Card). Driving is on the right, overtaking on the left, and **seat belts** are obligatory for driver and passengers. Also compulsory is a reflective **hazard warning triangle**, and drivers are forbidden from using mobile phones while driving. Although it is not compulsory, Croatia recommends you drive with headlights on during the day.

Speed limits (generally ignored) are 130kph on motorways, 80kph outside built-up areas and 50kph in towns, and speeding fines rise according to the gravity of your offence. To wine-growers' and restaurateurs' prophecies of doom, the government in 2004 forbade drivers from touching a drop of alcohol. Double-check on arrival to see whether the hard-line policy remains in force.

Hiring a Car

Car hire is an expensive business in Croatia. Although prices of international players, which are represented in all major cities plus tourist destinations and operate bureaux in airports, fluctuate with the seasons, you can expect to stump up a hefty €65 per day for a basic two-door manual runaround, usually without air-conditioning, and a blanching €190 per day for a four-door estate with air conditioning. Longer-term hirers are rewarded with more favourable day-rates, and day-trippers can take advantage of cheap rates for limited mileage clauses. On the bright side, prices usually (but not always) include tax, personal accident insurance and collision damage waiver (CDW); be warned, the latter doesn't usually extend to tyres, wheels, the underside and the interior. Shopping around with major firms before you travel will turn up special deals (and is wise to secure a vehicle in peak season) and local companies are often cheaper if you are not overly concerned about cosmetics. Bargain-hunters may also discover cheap weekend deals. All hire companies require drivers to be over 21 (although some firms demand they must be older) and to have held an EU or international driving licence for (usually) one year. Also remember a passport, driving licence and credit card will be required.

Practical A–Z

Climate and When to Go

Croatia springs few surprises with its climate. The coast basks in Mediterranean-style hot summers cooled by balmy sea breezes and lit by brilliant sunshine, and mild, damp winters where locals talk about freak weather if temperatures drop below 6˚C, while the interior is continental, with sweltering summers and chilly winters when temperatures fluctuate around freezing.

Such is the climatic consistency, the prime issue for visitors is crowds. Peak season on the coast is July and especially August: café life is at its most effervescent in cities such as Split and Dubrovnik, which stage summer festival cultural extravaganzas (*see* 'Festivals', p.14), and the evening stroll (*korzo*) and alfresco nightlife at its most animated. The flip side to this popularity is, of course, crowds. Dubrovnik teeters on the chaotic, small towns such as Rovinj can be claustrophobic, and relaxing sightseeing is wishful thinking. In summer, too, hotel beds are at their most expensive and their hardest to find, and beaches vanish beneath a multicoloured patchwork of towels. Similarly, drivers can expect long queues for ferries and heavy traffic on the arterial coast road. Inland Croatia, however, dozes over summer, at its its quietest in a period when landlocked Croatians flee to the coast.

Croatia is at its best in spring and autumn. By early May you can dip a toe in the Adriatic and in June you can still expect smiles from restaurateurs and hoteliers. More enticing still is September, when the sea is at its warmest. October is a mite cooler but rewards gourmets with truffle season in Istria and walkers with pleasant midday temperatures and gorgeous colours in national parks and inland Istria.

Grey skies and spatters of rain fall in November to herald the beginning of a coastal winter season which lasts until April. Resorts pull down shutters for the season, especially on the islands, where you will have to source private accommodation, although there are bargains to be found in the hotels of Split, Dubrovnik and Zadar. Now, too, the chill *bura* wind blasts from the north-northeast for up to two weeks, interspersed by the warm *siroko*, which can bring rain squalls and high waves from the south. Inland, you can expect a dusting of snow from December to February, when Zagreb skiers take to slopes of Mount Medvednica. For sun-seekers, Hvar wears the laurels as sunniest spot in Croatia year-round, followed by Split, Korčula then Dubrovnik.

Crime and the Police

Police t 92

Maybe because of the newly independent nation's eagerness to show off its charms, Croatia is a tourist's delight. Foreigners are welcomed, hotel room theft unheard of and violent crime is a genuine shock. Although the petty crime rife on the other side of the Adriatic has not crossed the water, however, do exercise the usual precautions: leaving valuables unguarded in restaurants or bars is asking for trouble; lock cars, and hide valuables out of sight, and be aware that city pickpockets favour crowded public spaces such as rush-hour buses. In the unlikely event of a theft, report the loss to the police to receive your magic insurance number. Police are courteous and helpful, businesslike without being effusive, although their low level of English can overcomplicate brushes with the law. If possible, carry one official proof of identity to simplify matters. In the event of a lost passport, also inform your embassy, which will smile on those with the foresight to photocopy key information.

No-go areas do not exist in safe Croatia, except in isolated areas formerly on the 1991–5 front line – eastern Slavonia, border

Average temperatures ˚C												
	Jan	Feb	Mar	April	May	June	July	Aug	Sept	Oct	Nov	Dec
Dubrovnik	10	10	12	16	18	23	28	27	22	17	14	11
Split	9	9	12	15	19	24	29	28	23	18	13	10
Pula	7	7	10	14	17	22	27	25	21	16	12	8
Zagreb	0	1	7	131	17	21	25	24	19	12	7	2

regions of Bosnia-Herzegovina between Zadar and Split, and rural districts around Zadar – where land mines, though largely cleared, are an issue. Stick to footpaths and roads when exploring remote districts (in wilder reaches of the Krka national park towards Knin, for example) or shell-torn, deserted villages inland. Consider local sensitivities before blurting opinions on the Croat–Serb conflict.

Disabled Travellers

Disabled toilet facilities are provided in most major bus and train stations, which are generally wheelchair-friendly, and ramps are on the increase in cities. In Zagreb, the **Zagreb Electric Tram Company** (ZET, **t** (01) 66 00 443, *www.zet. hr*) provides a free vehicle for disabled visitors plus one passenger. Elsewhere, those in wheelchairs will struggle – access to public buildings is limited and public transport is not accessible without help from a usually sympathetic population. Ferries provide no ramps and you will have to rely on a steward or crew member. Similarly only high-end or modern hotels offer disabled rooms or a lift; seek local knowledge from tourist information agencies and confirm all advice before booking.

For country-wide information, consult Zagreb-based advice organization the **Association of Organizations of Disabled People in Croatia** (Savez Organizacija Invalida Hrvatske, **t** (01) 48 29 394) or, better, seek advice before travelling from UK disabled travel body **Tripscope** (helpline Mon–Fri 9.30–4.30, **t** (UK) 08457 585641; outside UK **t** +44 (117) 939 7782, *www.tripscope.org.uk*).

Electricity

Mains voltage is 220V, 50Hz. British and Irish appliances require a standard two-prong, round-pin adaptor; North American appliances require a transformer.

Embassies and Consulates

Croatian Embassies Abroad
UK: 21 Conway Street, London W1P 5HL, **t** (020) 7387 2022.

USA: 2343 Massachusetts Avenue NW, Washington DC, 20008-2853, **t** (202) 588 5899.
Canada: 229 Chapel Street, Ottawa, Ontario K1N 7Y6, **t** (613) 562 7820.

Foreign Embassies in Zagreb
UK: I Lučića 4, 10000 Zagreb, **t** (01) 66 09 100, *www.britishembassy.gov.uk/croatia*.
USA: Thomasa Jeffersona 2, 10010 Zagreb, **t** (01) 66 12 200, *www.usembassy.hr*.
Canada: Prilaz Gjure Deželića 4, 10000 Zagreb, **t** (01) 48 11 200.

Festivals and Events

Few national folk events unite the nation. Instead, as well as each town's impressive spread for the day of its own patron, staunch Roman Catholic Croatia uses its bewildering number of saints as excuses to host slap-up jamborees. Important ecclesiastical beanos on the Adriatic are **Holy Week** before Easter, when processions of Catholic pomp parade through Hvar and Korčula, and **Assumption** (15 August), when crowds of thousands say prayers at Marija Bistrica, Trsat (Rijeka) and Sinj.

The year's major inaugural event is *Karneval* (carnival), a pre-Lent indulgence of costumed parades usually on Shrove Tuesday or the preceding weekend which is at its most ebullient in Rijeka, where the week-long revels attract tens of thousands. A smaller event in Samobor lures half of Zagreb, cultured Dubrovnik holds a stylish bash, and effervescent Split, which seizes any excuse for a party, has recently joined in the fun. Some destinations such as Pag restage the events to take advantage of summer weather. Most bizarre and authentic event is that of *Lastovo*, whose festivities climax on Shrove Tuesday in the trials of a straw puppet, the *poklad*, led through the village while fireworks are set off, then ritually burned before the parish church.

In July and August a cultural jamboree of classical, folk and pop concerts and theatre is staged in almost every town on the Adriatic; the most prestigious is Dubrovnik's **Summer Festival**, which transforms historic courtyards and squares into beautiful venues for international acts, and second billing goes to Split. Not to be outdone, capital Zagreb hosts its own summer festival plus a programme of summer music events, but is more famous for the **International Folk Festival** over the last or penultimate weekend in July.

Health and Insurance

Ambulance (bolesnička kola) t 94; fire t 93

Croatia's reciprocal arrangement with the EU provides EU citizens with free consultation and emergency care on the presentation of a passport or stamped E111 (available from post offices); be aware the deal does not cover medical repatriation, private care or dental treatment. If you have to pay for any treatment, get a receipt for reimbursement later. Non-EU residents may enjoy the same deal; in any case, private **medical insurance** is a sensible precaution. Remember most policies levy a surcharge to cover 'dangerous sports' such as scuba-diving.

Accidents aside, Croatia is no health hazard. Standards of public health are high, tap water is drinkable everywhere and the most common complaint is sunburn. Having said that, swimmers should keep a wary eye for sea urchins on rocky shores of wild beaches and serious hikers of mountains woods should consider the vaccination for tick-borne encephalitis recommended by the US and British embassies. Inland, mosquitoes around lakes annoy rather than infect.

Medicines for minor illnesses plus first aid advice can be sourced at **pharmacies** (*ljekarna*), whose staff work shop hours and can match medicines from generic names if you proffer relevant packets. For more complicated medicines, bring a prescription (*recept*) signed by your doctor. In cities, one *ljekarna* works the night-shift and Sunday organized by rota; a list of the current incumbents is posted on all pharmacy windows.

More serious complaints are treated at a doctor's surgery best found through tourist information or a hotel concierge, or for emergencies and pressing health problems outside consultancy hours visit a hospital (*bolnica*) – only call an ambulance in a genuine emergency. Adequate English is spoken by many doctors, especially younger graduates; embassies hold lists of fluent English-speakers.

Internet

Whether in dedicated cafés, tourist agency rooms crammed with computers or simply a bar with a terminal in a corner, you will have little problem going online on the Adriatic coast – expect to pay around 20–30Kn/hr. Negotiating Croat keyboards is another matter. Fortunately, Croatia abandons letter accents in web addresses.

Executives in top-end hotels enjoy ISDN lines in their rooms, but an old-fashioned phone system means dial-up connections can be a headache. For boffins prepared to negotiate modem settings changes, modernized telephone sockets are standard US RJ-11.

Money and Banks

Until Croatia resolves its dithering over the euro, the official unit of currency is the **kuna**, whose translation as 'marten' recalls the pelts used for barter until the name was stamped on Slavonian coins in 1256. Notes printed on one side with aristocratic rulers and poets and on the other with national landmarks come in denominations of 5, 10, 20, 50, 100, 200 and 500Kn and coins bearing the inevitable mammal come in 1, 2 and 5Kn sums. Each kuna divides into 100 lipa, available as pocket-filling 1, 2, 5, 10, 20 and 50 lipa coins.

Current **exchange rates** (March 2005) are: £1 = 10.8Kn; $1 = 5.6Kn; €1 = 7.5Kn.

Though stable thanks to its being index-linked to the euro, the kuna is not a fully convertible currency, so currency cannot be bought in advance at home and must be exchanged or withdrawn on arrival. In addition, you can only take 2,000Kn out of the country (although because even banks of neighbour Slovenia groan when accepting them there's little reason you'd want to).

While it's a good idea to arrive with a fistful of notes (the most widely accepted non-Croat currency is the euro) to safeguard against failed ATM machines, carrying pocketfuls of cash is not the most prudent choice. Whether they come in dollars, sterling or euros, **travellers' cheques** (*putnički ček*) remain the most secure means of transporting money. These can be exchanged, like hard cash, at all major banks (*banka*) for a commission of 1% or at money exchanges (*mjenjačnica*) in larger post offices and major tourist agencies such as Atlas which typically levy 3% commission, and also at larger hotels which sting with commission of up to 5%.

More useful for flying visits (or when wallets lose weight) is to withdraw cash directly from **ATM cash dispensers**. These are ubiquitous on the Croatian coast and in major inland cities plus motorway petrol stations, but evaporate alarmingly in remote Slavonia. All have an English-language option. ATMs take major **credit cards** – Visa, MasterCard/EuroCard, Diner's Club and to a lesser extent American Express – with a PIN. However, remember that interest accrues as soon as those crisp notes emerge from the slot. Cheaper are **debit cards** affiliated to credit card operators and affiliates such as Plus, Cirrus and Maestro. Major credit cards are widely accepted in towns and tourist centres, but venture off-track and smaller *pensions* may just shrug and demand cash.

Value added tax (PDV) charged at 22% on most goods and 8.5% reduced rate for food, books and accommodation can be reclaimed by non-residents (except on alcohol and tobacco) if receipt/s on one day from one retailer exceed 500Kn; ask sales assistants to complete the relevant form, which is stamped by customs at departure then mailed back to the store and your refund will arrive within a year – probably.

Opening Hours

The winter season is usually Nov–Mar, but is often decided on a whim.

Shops: business hours are 8–7 or 8 on weekdays and 8–2 or 3 on Saturdays. City supermarkets operate longer hours on Saturday and sometimes open on Sunday mornings. During summer (June–Sept) most shops pull down shutters for a 12–4pm siesta, then operate later evening hours, some until 10pm in tourist locales, where many also open on Saturday afternoons. Large department stores usually work without a break. Private tourist agencies attempt to make a year's money in July–Aug by opening daily 8am–10pm. Croatia's wonderful markets are usually morning-only affairs, typically 8–1, Mon–Sat, though some open on Sundays.

> **National Holidays**
> **1 Jan** New Year's Day
> **6 Jan** Epiphany
> **Mar/April** Easter Sunday and Monday
> **1 May** Labour Day
> **Early–mid-June** Corpus Christi
> **22 June** Anti-Fascist Resistance Day
> **25 June** Statehood Day
> **5 Aug** National Thanksgiving Day
> **15 Aug** Assumption
> **8 Oct** Independence Day
> **1 Nov** All Saints' Day
> **25–26 Dec** Christmas

Banks and office hours: banks usually open Mon–Fri 8–5 and Sat 8–12 or 1, except on the coast where some follow shop hours. Offices and public services are strictly Mon–Fri 8–4.

Post offices: standard hours are Mon–Fri 7–7, Sat 8–1 or 2, but village and island offices usually open only Mon–Fri 7–2. The main office in large towns and tourist centres may open evenings until 9 or later.

Museum and galleries: cultural doyennes of cities such as Zagreb or Split operate strict hours, but elsewhere opening times are unpredictable; in peak season many open daily (with a long siesta), but don't be surprised if a place is closed. Many museums and hotels close for a winter season.

Churches: city churches open 7–7 are exceptions in a devout country where churches are for prayer. If you've come to see famous art, churches usually operate set opening hours, typically with a 12–4 pause. Wee ones in small towns and villages usually only open for mass, whose sanctity you should respect – if possible, slip in discreetly as the last of the congregation leave or ask neighbours for whereabouts of the key (*ključ*).

Post

You can buy stamps (*marke*, singular *marka*) at *pošta* of the **HPT Hravtska**, announced by a yellow spiral with a stripy triangle on its tail, but far easier is to purchase them from newsagents and tobacco kiosks, then pop postcards into canary-yellow post boxes: stamps for cards cost 4Kn for delivery within the EU, which takes around five days. Allow two weeks to send transatlantic (5Kn). Letters are priced according to weight, airmail (*avionska pošta*) costs extra, and staff must inspect parcels before you seal them. At some post offices, too, you can also buy telephone cards (*see* below) and make international calls, and change travellers' cheques and money.

Price Categories

Hotels

Hotel prices are quoted for the price of a double room with WC and bath or shower in July–Aug peak season. Not factored in is a 'tourist tax' levied per person per night.

expensive over 1,000Kn / €135
moderate 500–1,000Kn / €65–135
inexpensive under 500Kn / €65

Restaurants

Restaurants are quoted as the cost of a meal for one person, with an average-priced main course and a shared bottle of house wine.

expensive over 160Kn / €23
moderate 110–160Kn / €15–23
cheap under 110Kn / €15

Telephones

Telephone boxes only accept magnetic-strip telephone cards (*telekarta*) which are sold by post offices and newsagent kiosks in credit units (*impulsa*) of 25, 50, 100, 200 and 500. Credits fall at terrifying pace during peak rates between 7am and 10pm, when a 13Kn, 25-*impulsa* card will barely let you squawk hello and mention the weather before it cuts you off if dialling abroad. Rates are 5% lower from 4 to 10pm, and Sunday is deemed off-peak (50% off). For international calls head to phone booths of post offices, which reward with more favourable rates. Hotel telephones can raise a huge bill.

Croatia employs GSM 900/1800 standard for its **mobile phone network**, compatible with the rest of the Europe and US tri-band phones, but not with the North American GSM 1900/900. Coverage, which extends across most of the country, is excellent if phones are set to roam operators automatically to source the strongest signal. Your service provider will switch on international access on request free

or for a nominal charge. And no wonder – home operators charge vastly inflated prices for the privilege of tapping into affiliated networks and usually charge *you* for incoming calls as well as outgoing.

To **call Croatia from abroad**, dial the country code 385, omit the first zero of the area code, then dial the number.

To **call abroad from Croatia**, dial 00 then the country code (UK 44; Ireland 353; USA and Canada 1; Australia 61; New Zealand 64) then dial the number, again omitting the first zero of the area code.

Local directory enquiries: t 988
International directory enquiries: t 902
Weather and road conditions: t 902
Croatian Angels (state-operated tourist info, mid-Mar–mid-Oct): t 062 999 999.

Time

Croatia is within the Central European Time zone: one hour ahead of GMT, six hours ahead of Eastern Standard Time and nine ahead of Western Standard Time. Clocks go forward one hour on the last Sunday in March, back one hour on the last Sunday of October.

Tipping

Tips which are not included in the price of drinks or food are only expected for meals. As a rule of thumb, 10% is standard practice and bar bills are rounded up to a convenient figure if you are feeling benevolent. Taxi drivers will not expect a tip, but will obviously appreciate the sentiment.

Toilets

Public toilets are clean and hygienic, but few and far between. Train and bus stations have maintained public facilities (*zahodi* or *WC*) which charge c. 2Kn. Men should enter *Muški*, women *Ženski*, hence occasionally M and Z, but more commonly a twee picture of urinating toddlers or a shoe and stiletto. Bar and café owners will usually let you use their facilities, although it doesn't hurt to express your relief with an espresso.

Tourist Information

The quality of *turistički zajednica* varies hugely throughout the country; whereas offices in cities and popular resorts are goldmines of information, in some daydreaming idylls you are better off prospecting in a friendly private tourist agency whose hours are longer, its information more current. Private agencies also organize all-inclusive sightseeing trips to regional attractions; ubiquitous national player **Atlas** (*www.atlas-croatia.com*) is consistently reliable.

Both official and private agencies can proffer advice about hotel and private accommodation (though not always book) and public transport. Most also provide area maps free of charge or for a nominal fee.

Most towns and resorts publish a tourism **website**, with a database of current events, basic information and links to hotel accommodation. Almost all come in English, as do a laudable number of official government and organization sites. Dedicated city sites are provided in the text, but useful sites for pre-visit searches include: colourful Croatian National Tourist Board site *www.croatia.hr*, country portal and online magazine *www.croatica.net* and coastal tourism site *www.adriatica.net*; regional tourism sites *www.dalmacija.net*, *www.istria.com* and *www.tzzz.hr* (Zagreb region); Croatian Ministry of Foreign Affairs site *www.mvp.hr*, with links to national embassies; and *www.hr*, an excellent directory with a neural network of Croatian connections organized by theme. **Croatian National Tourist Board**, Iblerov trg 10/4, 10000 Zagreb, **t** (01) 4699 333; *www.croatia.hr*.

Croatian Tourist Offices Abroad

UK: 2 The Lanchesters, 162–4 Fulham Palace Road, London W6 9ER, **t** (020) 8563 7979.
USA: 350 Fifth Avenue, Suite 4003, 10118 New York, **t** 800 829 4416/**t** (212) 279 8672/8674.

Where to Stay

Fearful of the concrete vandalism which blighted Spanish and Grecian coastlines, Croatia outlawed new concrete monstrosities in 2004 and has pledged itself instead to smaller boutique-style hotels. But the décor of leftovers from Croatia's tourism boom of the 1970s and early 80s tends to be comfortable but bland and dated and frumpy, and hotels themselves are often sited in resort settlements 2–5km away from town centres. Grading is by a star system best ignored: one-stars might have a TV but otherwise barely rate above a hostel, four and five stars are comfy executives' choices or international-class residences of deep carpets and elegant furnishings. In between is a lottery, especially at three-star level. Neither is it cheap: prices for a modest room can shock in peak season.

More characterful, if a little frayed at the edges, are **rooms in private accommodation**; characterful homes-from-home in the houses – sometimes modern, occasionally refurbished stone cottages – of hospitable owners. Tourist offices and private tourist agencies, which hike prices to take their cut, hold lists of rooms or you can knock on doors of houses which advertise *sobe* (occasionally *zimmer*). A crack squad of silver-hairs meet buses or ferries in popular destinations; double-check locations before expressing an interest and confirm then reconfirm prices and length of stay. However you locate a room, don't be shy about asking to view before you commit. Again, rooms are graded: basic category I rooms share facilities; category II rooms are more comfy and are either en suite or share with one other guest; and top-of-the-range category III rooms are en suite, quietly plush and frequently preferable to a three-star hotel. Double room prices range between 140 and 300Kn and the only catch is a surcharge of 30–40% on stays of less than three nights. All accommodation is subject to a **tourist tax** of approx 7Kn per person per night.

For true escapism investigate so-called **Robinson Crusoe cottages**, back-to-basics dwellings without electricity or running water in the pristine Kornati archipelago. Source them through local agencies (*see* above left) or book a flights and week-long package through London agency **Croatia for Travellers**, **t** (020) 7226 4460, *www.croatiafortravellers. co.uk*. Similar isolated retreats are available in apartments of 11 restored lighthouses, most on islet specks which stretch the length of the Adriatic; Zagreb agency **Adriatica** (**t** +385 (01) 2415 611, *www.adriatica.net*) handles bookings.

Language

Even for confident linguists *au fait* with Indo-European languages rooted in Latin, Greek or Germanic, Slavonic-based Croatian is fiendishly complex. As if three genders (masculine, feminine and neuter), perplexing plural forms and slippery grammar rules which alter noun endings according to context were not sufficiently baffling, a polyglot of regional dialects will lead the inexperienced astray.

Perhaps for this reason, most Croatians speak another language – hotel staff and young Croats speak excellent English, the older generation prefers German, especially inland, and Italian is widely spoken on the Adriatic coast – and locals will not huff if you baulk at wrestling with their national tongue. However, they appreciate the effort made by those who learn basics – and all the rolled Rs are delicious. Food vocabulary is on pp.24–5.

Pronunciation

Although occasional parades of consonants strike fear, Croatian is not nearly as terrifying as it looks. Every letter is pronounced, and most are spoken as English except for those explained below. As a rule of thumb, the stress falls on the first syllable, and never on the last. Pre-trip tuition can be found on website *www.visit-croatia.co.uk*, which has online audio files of the basics.

C is pronounced as 'ts' as in 'cats', **č** is spoken as 'ch' as in 'church' and **ć** is softer, like the 'ch' of 'cheese'. **Đ/đ** is spoken as the 'j' of 'jam' and very occasionally is written as 'dj'.

G is always hard, as in 'get'. **J** is spoken as 'y' as in 'yacht' and looks a tongue-twister when combined with other consonants but is straightforward: **nj** is said as 'ny' as in 'canyon', like the Spanish ñ; **lj** as the 'li' of 'million'.

Rs are marvellous, rolled luxuriantly on the tongue and functioning as a vowel when placed between two consonants such as in 'Hrvatska' (Croatia).

Š is pronounced as the 'sh' of 'sheet', similar to **ž**, spoken as the 's' of 'leisure'.

Vowel sounds are short: **a** as in 'cat'; **e** as in 'met'; **i** is as the 'ee' of 'feet'; **o** as in 'dog'; and **u** as in 'oo' of 'hoot'.

Useful Vocabulary

Greetings and Courtesies

hello *dobar dan/zdravo*
goodbye *dovidjenja*
hi/bye! *bog!*
good morning *dobro jutro*
good evening *dobra večer*
goodnight *laku noć*
please *molim*
thank you (very much/for your help) *hvala (lijepo/ na pomoći)*
how are you? (formal)*kako ste?* **(informal)** *kako si?*
fine, thanks *dobra, hvala*
I am from England/Scotland/Wales/Ireland/ USA/Canada *ja sam iz Engleske/Škotske/ Velsa Irske/Amerike/Kanade*
pleased to meet you *drago mi je*
sorry (apology) *pardon*
excuse me *oprostite*

Basic Words and Phrases

yes/no/maybe *da/ne/možda*
do you speak English? *govorite li engleski?*
I (don't) understand *(ne) razumijem*
I don't speak Croatian *ne govorim hrvatski*
can I have... *mogu li dobiti...*
do you have... *imate li...*
how much is it? *koliko košta?*
that's cheap/too expensive *to je jeftino/ preskupo*
keep the change! *zadržite sitan novac!*
do you take credit cards? *primate li kreditne kartice?*
large/small *veliko/malo*
hot/cold *toplo/hladno*
why?/when?/where? *zašto?/kada?/gdje?*
rooms *sobe*
Can I reserve a room? *mogu li rezervirati sobu?*
Do you have a single/double room? *mate li jednokrevetu/dvokrevetnu sobu?*
No vacancies *nema slobodne*
Key/shower/sheets/toilet paper *ključ/tuš/ plahte/toaleti papir*
I am feeling ill (m/f) *osjećam se bolesnim/bolesnom*
ache/pain *bol*
I've a headache/earache/stomach ache *boli me glava/uho/želudac*
diarrhoea/toothache *zuboblja/proljev*
doctor/dentist *liječnik/zubar*

Around Town

open/closed *otvoreno/zatvoreno*
entrance/exit *ulaz/izlaz*
toilet *zahodi/ WC (pronounced 'vay-tsay')*
ladies/gents *ženski/muški*
bank *banka*
bureau de change *mjenjačnica*
to change *promijenti*
police/police station *policija/policijska stanica*
embassy *ambasada*
hospital *bolnica*
pharmacy *ljekarna*
post office *pošta*
airport *aerodrom*
(main) railway/bus station *(glavni)*
    željeznički/autobusni kolodvor
(ferry) port *(trajektna) luka*
market *tržnica*
tourist office *turistički ured, turistički informa-*
    tivni centar
travel agent *putnička agencija*
museum *muzej*
gallery *galerija*
cinema *kino*
church/cathedral *crkva/katedrala*
monastery *samostan*
old town *stari grad*
street/square *ulica/trg*
beach *plaža*

Getting Around and Driving

when is the next train/bus/boat for... *kada*
    polazi slijedeći vlak/autobus/trajekt za...
when does it arrive? *u koliko sati stiže?*
arrivals/departures *dolazak/odlazak*
platform *peron*
single/return ticket *karta u jednom/povratna*
    karta
where is (the nearest)... *gedje je (najbliža)...*
how far is it? *koliko je daleko?*
far/near *daleko/blizu*
left/right/straight on *lijevo/desno/pravo*
I am lost (m/f) *izgubio/izgubila sam se*
filling station *benzinska stanica*
petrol/diesel *benzin/diesel*
I want some petrol oil/water (m/f) *Želio/*
    željela bih gorivo/ulje/vodu
accident *slučaj*
car mechanic *automehaničar*
insurance *osiguranje*
Where can I park the car? *Gdje mogu parki-*
    rato auto?

Days, Months and Time

Monday *ponedjeljak*
Tuesday *utorak*
Wednesday *srijeda*
Thursday *četvrtak*
Friday *petak*
Saturday *subota*
Sunday *nedjelja*
what day is it today? *koli je danas dan?*

January *siječanj*
February *veljača*
March *ožujak*
April *travanj*
May *svibanj*
June *lipanj*
July *srpanj*
August *kolovoz*
September *rujan*
October *listopad*
November *studeni*
December *prosinac*

what time is it? *koliko je sati?*
early/late *rano/kasno*
in the morning *ujutro*
in the afternoon *popodne*
day/week/month *dan/tjedan/mjesec*
today/yesterday/tomorrow *danas/jučer/sutra*

Numbers

1 *jedan*	21 *dvadeset i jedan*	
2 *dva*	22 *dvadeset i dva*	
3 *tri*	30 *trideset*	
4 *četiri*	40 *četrdeset*	
5 *pet*	50 *petdeset*	
6 *šest*	100 *sto*	
7 *sedam*	101 *sto i jedan*	
8 *osam*	200 *dvjesto*	
9 *devet*	500 *petsto*	
10 *deset*	1,000 *tisuća*	
11 *jedanaest*		
12 *dvanaest*		
13 *trinaest*		
14 *četrnaest*		
15 *petnaest*		
16 *šesnaest*		
17 *sedamnaest*		
18 *osamnaest*		
19 *devetnaest*		
20 *dvadesets*		

Croatia:
Food and Drink

04

The Venetians may have retreated back across the Adriatic, and the Austrian Habsburgs slunk north, but both former rulers left behind a little piece of themselves in Croatia's contradictory cuisines. Pastas and risottos abound on coastal menus full of Mediterranean dishes, seafood is exquisite, and everything comes with a heady hit of herbs and garlic and soused in olive oil; but go inland, north and east, and instead tuck into rustic platters, where pork and paprika, goulash and beans nod to the rib-sticking fare of neighbours Hungary, Slovenia and Austria. Whatever you eat, however, the watchword of Croatian cuisine is honesty; some nations' chefs show off with algebraic recipies and high-falutin' sauces, but those of Croatia let good ingredients do the talking.

Eating Out

Wherever you are, **breakfast** (*doručak*) in Croatia is a wake-up call: a powerful hit of earthy Turkish coffee (*kava*) or Italian-style espresso, cappuccino or *bijela kava* (white coffee) in cafés and bars which open around 6am and will be busy with gossiping locals by 7. Few offer food, however, so visit bakeries (*pekarnica*) to find *burek*, an occasionally delicious, often stodgy snack of filo pastry stuffed with curd cheese (*sa sirom*) or minced meat (*sa mesom*). Do try it once – it's a Balkan favourite. *Pekarnica* usually bake jam-filled croissants for delicate morning stomachs, and hotels lay on the usual spread of bread rolls, jams, cheese and meats, usually ham and salami, plus cereal and scrambled eggs in more upmarket establishments. **Mid-morning** munchies in Dalmatia are sated by *merenda*, a bargain-priced spread of meat and fishy nibbles rustled up in a no-nonsense *gostiona* (*see* below), and so filling that it can serve as an early **lunch** (*ručak*), which is generally eaten at 1–2pm. What you have depends on where you are (*see* below), but in all but the simplest *gostiona* you will be offered simple starters (*predelo*) and occasionally *hors-d'œuvre* before a main course served with vegetables. Everything comes with a small bakery of bread. Croatians drink an aperitif of grape-based *rakija*, and wine and water wash everything down. **Dinner** (*večera*) is usually lighter, but restaurants offer the same lunchtime menu for foreigners. Thrown into the mix countrywide are Turkish delights as **snacks**.

Types of Restaurant

In title, the **restoran** is the aristocrat of Croatian dining, where smart waiters in black and whites present extensive menus. In truth, a **konoba** is just as skilled at traditional local dishes, and a term which originally referred to a wine cellar has been hijacked by any establishment with an eye for folksy, whimsical décor. Simple snacks for everyday eating are served in a **gostiona**, which leads a double life as a bar, and every town has its **pizzeria**: unpretentious and excellent on the coast, where you can get thin-crust pizzas and cut-price pastas to turn Italian heads and usually the best salad in town. In a nation only just succumbing to burger chains, **snack bars** are excellent – traditional Balkan fillers such as *ćevapi* (spicy meat rissoles), *pljeskavica* (a mixed-meat Croat hamburger) and *ražnjići* (shish kebab) served in pitta bread are tasty and high-quality.

Regional Specialities

Cuisine **on the coast** is typically Mediterranean – super-fresh and simple. Excellent first courses are *pršut*, similar to Italian prosciutto and whose slivers, smoked by family firms who jealously guard their secrets, dissolve in the mouth; and *Pakši sir* (Pag cheese), a tangy, hard sheep's cheese from Pag island . Both are pricey but worth it. *Salata od hobotnice* may also come as a starter, although this salad of octopus, potatoes and onion soaked with olive oil and a tang of vinegar is delicious as a light lunch, as is a list of appetizers bequeathed by the Venetians: pastas and simple but tasty risottos such as *crni rižot* (blackened with squid ink), *rižot sa škampi* (shrimp) and *rižot frutti di mare* (seafood, usually mussels, clams, prawns plus occasionally squid or octopus). Always worth investigating is the Adriatic catch of the day, brought fresh from the boat and priced by weight and category: gourmet's choice are *bijela riba* (white fish) such as John Dory, mullet and gilthead bream; hake is cheaper; and bargain fillers are *plava riba* (blue fish) such as tuna and mackerel. Pick from a platter brought to the table and your fish is grilled (*na žaru*) over wood and dashed with olive oil, baked (*pećnici*) or, if you really must, boiled (*lešo*). Connoisseurs can splash out on *jastog* (lobster), delicious when prepared simply, exquisite cooked *na buzaru*, tossed quickly in a pan with a splash of white wine and sprigs of fresh parsley. Mussels, shrimps and clams (*kucice*) are a treat with the same preparation. For a cheap eat, there's traditional fish stew *brodet*, served in the pan and best eaten with bread to mop up a rich sauce of tomatoes and onions. The classic fishy side dish is *blitva*, a filling medley of spinach-style Swiss chard, potatoes and garlic.

If you prefer meat, for a break from charcoal-grilled steaks, *kotlet* (pork chops) and *miješano meso* (mixed meats), seek out the **Dalmatia** speciality *pašticada*, a rich dish of beef slow-cooked in wine, or *janjetina*, spit-roast lamb popular on sheep-rearing islands Pag and Rab and in inland Dalmatia. Throughout Dalmatia menus include dishes cooked under a *peka*: octopus, lamb and veal (*teletina*) is covered with a metal lid then heaped with charcoals in a cooking style Illyrian tribes would still recognize. Desserts are simple: creamy *torta* (gâteaux) or *palacinke* (pancakes) with chocolate (*sa čokoladom*) or jam (*sa marmeladom*) to fill the corners, plus *sladoled* (ice cream) or seasonal *voće* (fruit). Around Dubrovnik, keep an eye open for *rozata*, a local crème caramel.

Tastes are similar north in **Istria**, although a region enthralled by neighbour Italy has stronger Latin accents in vegetable and bean soup *menestra*, filling *njoki* (gnocchi), twists of *fuži* pasta and *mar e monte* (literally, 'sea and mountains') dishes of shellfish and mushrooms. Explore just a few miles inland and you'll discover spicy, fat *kobasice* (sausages), fingers of wild *šparoga* (asparagus) in season, and thick *gulaš* (goulash) sauce in inland hill towns. More than anything, though, Istria is truffle (*tartufi*) country; highly prized by gourmets, they appear in autumn with everything from seafood to steaks.

Continental Croatians on the Hungarian and Slovenian borders prefer robust dishes of rustic portions. The classic **Zagorje** starter is *štrukli*, a doughy dumpling filled with curd cheese which deserves respect. Less filling is bean soup *grah*, often with hunks of

Croatian Menu Reader

Basic Terms

dobra tek bon appetit
živjeli! (or *na zdravlje*) cheers!
doručak breakfast
merenda brunch
ručak lunch
večera dinner
(imate li) stol? (do you have) a table?
Da li je uključena? Is service included?
jelovnik menu
konobaru/kanobarice waiter/waitress
račun, molim bill, please
vegetarijanskih vegetarian
viljuška fork
nož knife
žlica spoon
ploča plate
staklo glass
ubrus napkin

Cooking Terms

kiseli pickled
lešo boiled
na žaru grilled
na buzaru flash-fried with white wine, garlic
  and parsley
peka slow-baked under lid covered in
  hot coals
pečeno baked
prženo fried

Predjelo/Juhu Starters/Soups

fažol bean soup, Istria
grah bean soup
manestra Istrian bean and vegetable soup
pršut prosciutto ham
Paški sir sheep's cheese from Pag
štrukli baked or boiled cheese dumplings
šunka ham

Meso Meat

bubrezi kidneys
čevapčići/ćevapi spicy meat rissoles
govedina beef
gulaš goulash
janjetina lamb
jetra liver
kobasica sausage
koljenica roast pork knuckle
kotlet (*ombolo*, Istria) pork chop
kulen spicy paprika salami (Slavonia)
kunić rabbit
miješano meso mixed grill
pasticada beef stewed in wine (Dalmatia)
patka duck
peljeskavica mixed-meat patty (Croat
  hamburger)
piletina chicken
pršut smoked ham
punjene paprika peppers stuffed with meat
purica turkey
ramsteak rump steak
ražnjići shish kebab (usually pork)
salnina bacon
sarma cabbage leaves stuffed with meat
  and rice
svinjetina pork
teletina veal
zagrebački odrezak Zagreb Schnitzel (*cordon
  bleu* – stuffed with cheese and ham and
  fried in breadcrumbs)

Riba Fish

bakalar rehydrated salted cod
bijela riba white fish
brodet fish stew
crni rižot black (ink) risotto
dagnje/mušule mussels
fiš paprikaš spicy Slavonian fish stew
frutti de mare fruits of the sea (with risotto
  or pasta)
girice fried small fish (whitebait)
hobotnica octopus
inčun/srdele anchovies
jastog lobster
jegulja eel
kovač John Dory
kucice clams
lignje squid
lokarda/skuša mackerel
orada sea bream
ostrige oysters
pastrva trout
plava riba blue fish
rak crab
ribice whitebait
sardina sardines
sipa cuttlefish

škampi shrimps
školjke shells (i.e. shellfish)

Povrće Vegetables
ajvar red pepper and aubergine relish
blitva Swiss chard
gljiva/šampinjon mushrooms
grah beans
grašak peas
kiseli kupus sauerkraut
krastavac cucumber, gherkin
krumpir boiled potato
kupus cabbage
luk onion
paprika peppers or paprika
pomfrit chips
pura polenta
rajčica tomato
repa turnip
riža rice
rižot risotto
rukola rocket
salata (zelena, mješana) salad (green, mixed)
šparoga asparagus
špinat spinach
tartufi truffles

Desert Dessert
baklava syrupy Turkish pastry with walnuts
palacinke pancakes
pita od jabuka apple pie
rozata crème caramel (Dubrovnik area)
sa čokoladom with chocolate
sa marmeladom with jam
sladoled ice cream
torta gâteau

Voće/Orah Fruit/Nuts
ananas pineapple
badem almond
banana banana
breskva peach
dinja melon
grožde grapes
jabuka apple
jagoda strawberry
kajsija apricot
kruška pear
limun lemon
lješnjak hazelnut

lubenica watermelon
naranča orange
orah (ovina) walnut
šljiva plum
smokva fig
trešnja cherry

Miscellaneous
burek (sa sirom/sa mesom) filo pastry (filled
    with cheese/minced meat)
češnjak garlic
čokolada chocolate
jaje (na oko) egg (fried)
kajgana scrambled egg
kajmak clotted sour cream
kruha bread
marmeladom jam
maslac butter
maslina ulja olive oil
med honey
miljeko milk
octa vinegar
papra pepper
šećer sugar
sendvič sandwich
sir cheese
soli salt
ulja oil
vrhnje/krema cream

Pića Drinks
bevanda wine and water
čaj tea (herbal)
indijski čaj tea (Indian tea,
    i.e. British-style)
kava (sa mijlekom) coffee (with milk)
led ice
medovina honey brandy
pelinkovac juniper berry aperitif
pivo beer
rakija grape-based *eau de vie*
šljivovica plum brandy
špricer wine spritzer
sok/đus juice
topla čokolada hot chocolate
travarica herb liqueur
vino (crno, bijelo, roze, domaće) wine
    (red, white, rosé, house)
voda (mineralnu, negaziranu) water
    (sparkling, still)

sausage and far more appetizing than the standard repertoire of watery *juhu* (soups). For main courses Zagreb locals make a special trip to Samobor to eat *češnjovka* (garlic sausages), and **Slavonia** indulges its passion for paprika in *salami kulen*. Slavonians also pour the paprika into freshwater fish stew *fiš paprikaš*, but this is an exception in an inland with a taste for farmyard favourites: pork or a baffling variety of cuts and *gulaš*, duck (*patka*), *zagrebački odrezak* (Zagreb *Schnitzel*, actually *cordon bleu* and fried in breadcrumbs), and Zagreb and Zagorje institution turkey (*purica*) ubiquitously served with *mlinci*, thin baked noodles, as *purica z mlincima*. *Kupus* (cabbage) and *kiseli kupus* (*Sauerkraut*) are standard side dishes, as is *grah* (beans), but you may also find maize porridge polenta (*pura*) – just don't plan on fitting in the dessert of walnut or poppyseed cake as well.

Drinks

It is no surprise that **wine** (*vino*) is a part of everyday life in a country which basks in over 2,400 hours of sunshine in an average year and where vines have been tended as far back as Roman times. The Croatians keep tipples best drunk young for themselves, and no wonder: 70 per cent of the country's 620 wines are Quality standard and only two bottles in ten are plain old plonk.

There's an awful lot to explore. The finest tipples come from the Romans' former stomping ground, Dalmatia. Connoisseur's choice red wine (*crno vino*) is Dingač, luxurious and velvety and which just outranks rich Postup. Both are produced on the Pelješac peninsula by growers who will pour you a glass straight from the barrel. Less classy but just as drinkable reds include full-flavoured Plavac from Hvar and Vis; Babič from Primošten; and Istrian Teran, dangerously light and made for summer sipping. Istrian tourist authorities also gladly direct enthusiasts on tours of local wine-growers. Nobles among Dalmatian whites (*bijelo vino*) are Pošip and Grk from Korčula or Žlahtina from Krk. Faced with greater temperature extremes, continental Croatia prefers hardy white grapes: you'll find full-bodied dry Graševina, Chardonnays, and light, elegant Rizling (Riesling) with a floral nose in Slovenia and Zagorje. Croatians often dilute basic plonk to create *bevanda*, which slips down far too easily, as does soda water spritzer *špricer*. For a dessert tipple, look for sweet prosecco.

Croatia also turns its grape harvest into *rakija* or *loza*, a potent **eau de vie** tossed off as an aperitif with a salute of '*Živjeli!*' ('Cheers!'). It's also acceptable as a digestif, but better names on brandy bottles are *šljivovica* (plum), *travarica* (herbs), *medovina* (honey) and *pelinkovac* (flavoured with juniper berries). Keep an eye out for regional flavours, too: Istrian *biska* is a taste of mistletoe, Zadar maraschino cherry tipple Marska comes in a cabinet of flavours, and Samobor's *bermet* is aromatic and pleasantly bitter.

The Austro-Hungarian rulers who nurtured Croatia's taste for **beer** (*pivo*) instilled a taste for pale lagers, some with a hint of sweetness and all served chilled; ubiquitous national brands served in little (*malo*, 0.3cl) and large (*veliko*, 0.5cl) draughts or by the bottle are Ožujsko, Karlovačko and Laško. Zagreb's local brew is Tomislav, darker and rich in malt.

Croatia: Zagreb and the Zagorje

Around Zagreb

25 km
10 miles

N

Maribor

Ptuj

2

SLOVENIA

E59

9

Varaždin

Trakošćan

Đurmanec

Podčertrek
Veliki Tabor
Pregrada
Krapina

Desinić
Beženac

CROATIA

Krapinske Toplice

Kumrovec

Tuheljske Toplice

E59/A1

Gusakovec
Marija Bistrica

Donja Stubica

Medvednica

E65/E71/A4

Sljeme (1036m)
Medvedgrad

Popovec

E70/A4

Samobor

ZAGREB

E70/A4

After Italian influences and Mediterranean manners on the coast, continental Croatia assumes the bucolic sentimentality and robust platters of near-neighbours Austria and Hungary. Even Zagreb, a formal Mitteleuropa capital created on a human scale, occasionally takes a break from its role as national power-player and trend-setter and succumbs to nostalgia, a taste of the folksy homespun charms of the Zagorje, a cosy pocket of hummocky hills and nestled villages.

Zagreb

Few cities confess their multiple personalities as readily as Zagreb. Side by side in Croatia's contradictory capital are an easygoing Baroque kernel and a dollop of grandiose Mitteleuropa built on a human scale; walk 500 yards from the bucolic chatter of a farmers' market on Dolac and the air rings to the city-slicker gossip of a stylish (and dedicated) café society in Preradovićev trg and Bogovićeva.

Perhaps we should blame the schizophrenia on the Habsburgs, because it was the 19th-century Austrians who truly expanded Zagreb's horizons beyond the upper town kernel. Although a power-player by the 1700s, the city which made its debut as bishopric Kaptol, then merged with Hungarian garrison neighbour Gradec in the mid-1500s, tightened its grip on the national reins after the parliamentary capital of Varaždin (*see* pp.45 and 50) to the north went up in smoke in 1776. The Sabor (parliament) shifted south and Zagreb, swelled by success, let go its feisty adolescence and settled into maturity. As nationalist sentiment grew in the mid-1800s and Zagreb intellectuals furiously penned prose and poetry to fire Slavic pride, Zagreb's Austrian rulers dreamed onto the plain below the old city all the grand architecture and tree-lined boulevards requisite for a Central European power. The paint is peeling, exhaust fumes can choke you, but you can almost smell the pomade in the Austrians' parks flanked by stiff stalwart buildings, or in the foyers of their public showpieces. The cultural elevation which accompanied the architecture has also bequeathed some of Croatia's finest galleries and museums. But, for all the newcomers' swagger, it is the old-town kernel of Baroque squares and idle alleys that has all the charm.

The Upper Town (Gornji Grad): Kaptol and Gradec

Trg Bana Jelačića and Dolac

Zagreb relates that it was christened after a chance encounter between a viceroy and a local girl. '*Manduša, zagrabi!* (scoop)' ordered the thirsty noble, pointing to the stream that ran between them. Never mind the prosaic truth that '*zagreb*' probably refers to nothing more romantic than the city's location below Mount Medvednica, a fountain does indeed gush from the Manduševac spring now buried beneath the flagstones of **Trg bana Jelačića**, Zagreb's spiritual heart, set between the nostalgic upper town (Gornji grad) and grand lower town (Donji grad). The square, conceived in 1641 as a marketplace for an upper city where space was at a premium, was paved by 1765, then fringed with cutting-edge Viennese Secession show-offs a century later to create Zagreb's equivalent of Times Square; in this main theatre for public revels, trams on seven routes rumble backstage, locals rendezvous beneath a clock tower in the wings, and at centre stage national hero Ban Josip Jelačić charges into history.

Not that the history of the Croatian favourite is a tale of glory. Hoping to appease flickers of nationalist sentiment fanned by European revolution, the Viennese masters elevated the popular garrison commander Jelačić to *ban* (viceroy) in 1848, and the nation's new leader marched on anti-Habsburg forces in Hungary, hoping to

Zagreb

200 metres
200 yards

N

KAPTOL

Zagreb City Museum

Meštrović Studio

Natural History Museum

St Mark

Ban's Palace

Sabor

Croatian History Museum

GRADEC

Museum of Naïve Art

Lotrščak Tower

funicular

Stone Gate

Museum of Modern Art

St Catherine

Dolac

Cathedral

Archbishop's Palace

Ribnjak

ILICA

Gavella

Serbian Orthodox Church

TRG BANA JELAČIĆA

Archaeological Museum

DONJI GRAD

Museum of Arts and Crafts

Croatian National Theatre

Zrinjevac

Strossmayer Gallery of Old Masters

Modern Gallery

Mimara

Ethnographic Museum

Art Pavilion

Library

Botanical Gardens

Esplanade Hotel

Station

Technical Museum

To Vatroslav Linsinki Concert Hall

curry favour for Croatian independence. But his good turn for the Habsburgs was forgotten, his demands brushed aside, though the Austrians still felt able to unveil Viennese sculptor Antun Fernkorn's wonderfully pompous bronze in the capital's heart in 1866, just seven years after Jelačić died. Nearly a century later, Josep Broz Tito was suspicious of a figure he viewed as a rabble-rouser, and in 1947 the newly declared Yugoslav president demanded the statue be removed from a square he had rechristened Trg Republike. Croatians weren't so quick to forget their glorious failure, however. Amid a crescendo of calls for Croatian independence from Yugoslavia, President Franjo Tuđman pulled off a public relations coup when he opened the packing crates in 1991 and restored the statue to a square returned to its former title.

Addresses

Be aware that inconsistency between maps and street signs is the rule not the exception in Zagreb, whose casual disregard for a standard between colloquial names (on maps and postal addresses) and official names (on street signs) demands intuition from visitors; for example, eastern park Strossmayerov trg is interpreted on the ground as Trg Josipa Jurja Strossmayera, north–south street Gajeva is rendered on street signs as Ulica Ljudevita Gaja and Trg Nikole Šubića Zrinskog becomes, bewilderingly, Zrinjevac. Good luck.

Getting There

See **Getting There**, pp.3–8.

Getting from the Airport

A Croatia Airlines **bus** shuttles from Pleso International airport 17km southeast of the city to the bus station (25Kn) every 30mins between 5.30am and 7.30pm and at other times to co-ordinate with flights (bus information, **t** (01) 61 57 992). The bus station is southeast of the city centre on Držićeva, a long 15min walk west of the train station; you can take tram 6 to Trg bana Jelačić. Expect to pay 150–200Kn for a **taxi**.

Getting Around

The compact upper town (Gornji grad) doesn't demand top-grade shoe leather, but for rainy days and tired legs back to hotels catch **ZET trams** between 4am and 11.45pm; in theory **night trams** take over in the wee hours, in practice walking can be faster than waiting and night trams represent a new route map to grapple with, as the tourist information city maps feature only a day route map.

A single **ticket** bought from the driver costs 8Kn, from post offices and ZET kiosks located at major stops and termini 6.5Kn; and a **one-day ticket** which lasts till 4am is 18Kn. All tickets must be validated in ticket cancellers on boarding: inspectors have heard all the excuses and simply issue on-the-spot 150Kn fines; while baffled foreigners may receive a little leeway, they may also have their passport number taken to ensure a fine is paid within 8 days (after which it rises to 200Kn) or simply be marched to a police station via an ATM. Buy a **Zagreb Card** (60Kn, *see* below) and you won't reach into your pocket for 72hrs. Most trams trundle through transport hub Trg bana Jelačića, just below the old town, and location of the tourist office.

Fleets of **taxis** gather outside the bus and train stations and at central ranks at the north end of Gajeva, just south of Trg bana Jelačića, and by the National Theatre on Trg Maršala Tita. In theory, they charge a flat fee of 25Kn, plus 7Kn/km. Advance bookings can be made with **Taxi 970**, **t** (01) 66 82 505.

Car Hire

All the major players operate in the airport.
Hertz, Vukotinovićeva 4, **t** (01) 48 46 777.
Budget, Kneza Borne 2 (in hotel Sheraton), **t** (01) 45 54 943.
Europcar, Pierottijeva 5, **t** (01) 48 28 383.
Jameks90, Vlaška 58, **t** (01) 46 17 495.

Tourist Information

Zagreb: The helpful central tourist information office is on Trg bana Jelačića, **t** (01) 48 14 051/052/054, *www.zagreb-touristinfo.hr* (*open Mon–Fri 9–9, Sat 9–6, Sun 9–2*), and a smaller office is at Zrinjevac 14, **t** (01) 49 21 645 (*open Mon, Wed and Fri 9–5, Tues and Thurs 9–6*). Both provide excellent free city maps, can book hotels and entertainment tickets and sell the **Zagreb Card** (60Kn; also from most hotels), a three-day pass for public transport plus 50% discounts on museum entry and 10–20% reductions in selected shops and on car hire.

Guided Tours

The larger central tourist office operates a unashamedly touristy stroll around the sights led by a costumed guide for 95Kn, half-price with a Zagreb Card.

Festivals

Zagreb enjoys itself in summer. Trg bana Jelačića is centre stage of the **Folklore Festival** (*Međunarodna smotra folklora, www.msf.hr*), a five-day jamboree over the last or penultimate weekend in July, when Croatian folk groups, plus a few international acts, twirl and toot in colourful costume.

More highbrow music and dance are provided by: the **Contemporary Dance Week** in the first week of June; the **Summer Festival** which woos international stars of classical music between mid-July and mid-August; and the **Zagreb Biennial**, which celebrates contemporary classical music every odd-numbered year.

Shopping

Central high street **Ilica** lays out a window display of independents and chain stores in *fin-de-siècle* shop-fronts. Funky fashion boutiques plus the occasional antiques shop and gallery line **Radićeva**, which extends north off **Trg bana Jelačića**. For example, **Galerija Bil Ani**, Radićeva 37, pioneered in Croatia the Lilliputian ceramic models of streets and buildings of Zagreb, Dalmatia and Istria.

For more fashions, explore smart boutiques in yesteryear grand arcade the **Oktagon** off Ilica, or go to **Croata**, Kaptol 13, and pick up a silk tie from the country of its birth: inspired by the neckwear of a crack Croat regiment he inspected in 1635, fashion-conscious French king Louis XIV knotted bright silk handkerchiefs '*à la Hrvat* (Croat)', cravats caught on and the rest is history.

Foodies should sample Dalmatian *pršut* (prosciutto ham), sold by the slice (or leg), and browse a wonderland of tasty treats – fiery *raikija*, olive oils, sheep's cheeses from island Pag – at **Pršut Galerija**, Vlaška 7, and **Devin**, Hebrangova 23. **Zigante Tartufi**, Rotonda Centar, Jurišićeva 19, offers more of the same plus mysterious herbal liqueurs said to be aphrodisiac, but its heart is in Istrian truffles, which come fresh, sliced, minced and preserved in olive oil. The finest Croatian wines are available from exclusive *vinothek* **Bornstein**, Kaptol 19; grasiner, kraviner and chardonnay plonks of local vineyards come straight from the barrel at a cellar *vinarija* opposite (Kaptol 14) – bring an empty water bottle if you want to take some home.

Zagreb's whimsical souvenir pictured on every tourist board brochure is the *licitarsko srce*, a gingerbread love heart laced with icing frills – pick up yours at the Trg bana Jelačića tourist office and you'll realize the tough treat is intended as a decorative love token, not a snack. The tourist office also retails *paprenjak*, gingerbread pastries made with honey, walnuts and pepper and munched by Renaissance locals.

Markets

A daily market on **Dolac** (7–3) hides folksy traditional fabrics, wicker baskets and charming, naïve wooden toys beyond its fruit and veg, and a Sunday antique and flea market (8–2) on **Britanski trg**, off Ilica, is all tatty, cheerful fun. Early birds can even pick up a bargain.

Where to Stay

Zagreb **t** (01) –

Put this on the expense account, because Zagreb accommodation is not cheap. Budget hotels are in short supply and their few rooms are snapped up quickly in peak season. Hotels cluster south of the centre around the train station and unless you pay top rate are generally uninspiring, business-orientated ones.

Regent Esplanade, Mihanovićeva 1, **t** 45 66 666, *www.regenthotels.com* (*expensive*). A lengthy refurbishment has done nothing to dilute the glamour of this Zagreb *grande dame*, fashioned to serve the Orient Express and whose marble lobby is fit for an Agatha Christie whodunnit. Luxurious rooms (deluxe are worth the extra money) maintain the nostalgia: fabrics are delicious shades of plum and moss, and rich chocolate woods are lit with hints of gilt. Croatian-Mediterranean fusion food in restaurant Zinfandals is first-class and Zagreb locals say the *štrukli* of its bistro is the best in town. The connoisseur's choice.

Palace, Strossmayerov trg 10, **t** 48 14 611, *www.palace.hr* (*expensive*). You half expect to smell moustache wax in the oldest hotel in Central Europe, created from a central 1891 palace and whose lobby is reassuringly stuffy thanks to vintage walnut panelling, brass fittings and leather chairs. Elegant rooms were modernized in 2003 to boast four-star facilities and marble bathrooms.

Sheraton, Kneza Borne 2, **t** 45 53 535, *www. sheraton.com* (*expensive*). Five-star facilities in a hotel that's everything you expect of the American chain; it's pricey – almost two-thirds more than the Regent Esplanade, with cheaper rates online – but reliable.

Arcotel Allegra, Branimirova 29, **t** 46 96 000, *www.arcotel.at/allegra* (*expensive*). Streamlined minimalist design relaxes with the colourful fabrics of a hotel targeted at slick business suits who like high-tech toys – all the rooms boast vast TVs, DVD and CD players and ISDN lines for inveterate e-mail addicts.

Dubrovnik, Gajeva 1, **t** 48 18 499/446, *www. hotel-dubrovnik.htnet.hr* (*moderate*). The best of the mid-range hotels, with an unbeatable location in the thick of Zagreb's buzzy café scene and whose plush four-star rooms, with tubs for a post-sightseeing soak, are far more elegant than an unsightly shopping mall-style exterior suggests.

Central, Branimirova 3, **t** 48 41 122, *www. hotel-central.hr* (*moderate*). Unspectacular but competitively priced businessman's choice 50 yards east of the train station.

Jadran, Vlaška 50, **t** 45 53 777 (*moderate*). Clean and modern(ish) en suite rooms have satellite TV in a dated three-star worth considering for its central position 400 yards east of the cathedral.

Pansion Jägerhorn, Ilica 14, **t** 48 33 877, *www. hotel-pansion-jaegerhorn.hr* (*moderate*). Perhaps overpriced for the minimal facilities of its 13 chirpy rooms, but its location, two minutes' walk from the central square, is excellent.

Ilica, Ilica 102, **t** 37 77 522, *www.hotel-ilica.hr* (*inexpensive*). Chintzy glamour in en suite rooms where there's no room to swing a suitcase. Location is good, however, and the price – just 1Kn the right side of moderate (for now) – a bargain. Reserve ahead, then confirm and reconfirm all rooms, especially if you might be arriving later in the day.

Sliško, Supilova 13, **t** 61 94 210, *www.slisko.hr* (*inexpensive*). Spotless en suite rooms with simple furnishings, TV and air-conditioning in a friendly cheapie located in a quiet residential street two minutes from the bus station.

Eating Out

Zagreb **t** (01) –

Baltazar, Nova Ves 4, **t** 46 66 999 (*expensive*). High-end traditional dining from a Zagreb culinary king: the eponymous rustic tavern prepares a superb stuffed rump steak and a menu of perfectly grilled meats; and **Gašpar** is a classy fish restaurant furnished with antiques and palms. You may have to wait for a table in its wine bar christened – what else? – **Melkior**. *Closed Sun*.

Okrugljak, Mlinovi 28 (tram to Mihaljevac), **t** 46 74 112 (*expensive*). A star-studded clientele make the trek north for the acclaimed spit-roast lamb, choice dish on an upmarket menu of traditional dishes elevated with modern nuances. The rustic dining room is elegant, the wine list sensational. Book at weekends.

Paviljon, Tomislava trg 22, **t** 48 13 066 (*expensive*). Execs tuck into steak with truffles and gorgonzola and sea bass tinted with saffron and basil on a bed of fried rocket during high-powered business lunches in the ground floor of the 19th-century Arts Pavilion. *Closed Sun*.

Pod Gričkim Topem, Zakamarijeve stube 5, **t** 48 33 607 (*expensive–moderate*). Folksy charm – a cosy wood-panelled dining room and friendly, attentive service – meets top-notch Croatian cuisine of fresh fish and succulent slivers of beef at the top of the funicular; reserve a terrace table for a panorama which sweeps over Zagreb. Worth every kuna. *Closed Sun eve*.

Dubravkin put, Dubravkin Put 2, **t** 48 34 970 (*expensive–moderate*). A stylish and award-winning restaurant where fish is expertly grilled or flavoured with saffron or scampi sauces and seafood is exquisite; try Dalmatian favourite *jastog na buzara* (lobster in garlic, tomatoes and white wine).

Dida, Petrova 176, **t** 23 35 661 (*moderate*). A tiny piece of the Dalmatian coast wafted inland to Zagreb, 100 yards west of park Maksimir. Rustic charm abounds in a snug stone dining room of chunky beams and rustic knick-knacks, there is all sorts of interesting fish and seafood to explore, and its owners are liable to burst into song mid-evening. A gem. Book at weekends.

Maškin i Lota, A Hebranga 11a, t 48 18 273 (*moderate*). Just smart enough to feel like dinner but without any of the formalities, serving turkey or veal stuffed with *pršut* (prosciutto ham) and sheep's cheese, or tasty Dalmatian fish, in a candlelit cellar.

Stari Fijaker, Mesnička 6, t 48 33 829 (*moderate*). A taste of tradition continental Croatia-style – thick winter-warmer soups plus meat-feast plates of beef, pork, veal and venison – in an enjoyably old-fashioned dining of traditional tablecloths ruled by waiters in black-and-whites.

Vinodol, Teslina 10, t 48 11 427 (*moderate*). Spit-roast lamb and *peka* dishes are the choice in this reliable restaurant one block south of Trg bana Jelačića, with a candlelit courtyard for summer evenings.

Kereumph, Kaptol 3, t 48 19 000 (*cheap*). Lunching professionals and rustic market-goers alike salute the no-nonsense inland Croatian cuisine at this small restaurant whose lunch menu is a bargain. You'll need to move fast to claim a terrace table with a grandstand view over the Dolac market (*see* pp.32 and 35).

Leonardo, Skalinska 6, t 48 73 005 (*cheap*). Pastas in cream and truffle sauces, pizzas and good-value meats on a terrace adjacent to the crafts stalls of the Dolac market. Service can be slow when busy.

Boban, Gajeva 9, t 48 11 549 (*cheap*). Ever-popular cellar restaurant whose Italian dishes come in portions to make dieters weep; the resolute can deliberate over a large menu of salads.

Cafés and Bars

Zagreb takes its café society seriously and loses entire weekends to gossiping over a *kava* in café-bars of Bogovićeva and Preradovićev trg. Bar-hopping venue of choice is Tkalčićeva, northwest of Trg bana Jelačića.

Bulldog – Belgian Beer Café, Bogovićeva 6. Ever-busy café thronged at weekends and with a frequently boisterous bar inside at the centre of Bogovićeva.

Gradska kavana, Trg bana Jelačića 10. Reassuringly old-fashioned café where silver-hairs enjoy grandstand views of Zagreb's Times Square.

Charlie Brown's, Bogovićeva 1. Come rain, sun or snow, movers and shakers exchange politics and pose at the doyenne of Bogovićeva cafés.

K&K, Jurišićeva 3. A cosy bohemian retreat just off the main square, crammed with photos of prints of old and new Zagreb.

Kazališna Kavana, Trg maršala Tita. Zagreb's arty set once debated in this Viennese-style old-timer opposite the theatre.

Hemingway, Tuškanac 1. Dress to impress in this slick 'n' stylish cocktail bar favoured by Zagreb's fashion-conscious.

Kaptolska klet, Kaptol 5. A refined take on the beer hall, with stucco and heavy beams and a menu (*cheap*) of robust local fare.

Entertainment and Nightlife

Zagreb t (01) –
The visitors' cultural bible is monthly pamphlet *Events & Performances*, available free from the tourist office.

Croatian National Theatre (Hrvatsko Narodno Kazalište), Trg Maršala Tita 15, t 48 28 532. The Habsburgs' neoclassical *grande dame* is the prestigious venue for classical theatre, ballet and opera from Croatian big names plus international visitors.

Gavella, Frankopanska 8, t 48 48 552. Excellently staged and less stuffy theatre staged alongside visiting productions, occasionally in English.

Vatroslav Linsinski Concert Hall (Koncertana dvorana Vatroslav Linsinski), Trg Stjepana Radića 4, t 61 21 166/167/168. Orchestral extravaganzas in the main auditorium, home to the Zagreb Philharmonic, ensembles and jazz in the small hall.

Croatian Music Institute (Hrvatski glazbeni zavod), Gunduliceva 6, t 48 30 822. Chamber music recitals and virtuoso soloists.

BP Club, Nikole Tesle 7, t 48 14 444. A cosy, intimate jazz bar-club which swings on gig nights but is also a treat for a smart evening drink.

Sax, Palmotićeva 22, t 48 72 836. Blues, swing and occasional rock acts play to an enthusiastic crowd every night.

Keep your eyes high to spot a corner relief of figures with muscles like polished walnut by Croatia's finest 20th-century sculptor Ivan Mestrović as you walk north to **Dolac**. Moments from the grand airs of its main stage, Zagreb suddenly bursts out with a farmers' market that sprawls good-natured chaos across a piazza ringed by cafés and cheap-eat restaurants; fruit and vegetables, olives and nuts are piled on stalls, women in aprons hawk home-made cheeses wrapped in soggy cloths, and on a second tier stallholders tout chunky wooden toys, lacy tablecloths and embroidery.

Kaptol

The rustic sentimentality evaporates in stately Kaptol, northeast of Dolac. Zagreb made its 1094 debut as a bishopric of Hungarian king Ladislas on the hill named for Middle Ages canons of the cathedral chapter – Kaptol is a corruption of *Capitulum* – and the main street, still claimed by Catholic institutions, has an air of quiet formality thanks to a parade of Baroque erected after a fire reduced earlier buildings to ashes. Showpiece residences include Nos.9 and 28, and, at the south end, barely able to restrain its swagger, the 1730s **Archbishop's Palace**. The residence of Bishop Juraj Branjug rings the neo-Gothic **cathedral** (Katedrale Marijina Uznesenja) which follows to the letter Gothic's guiding principle of guiding eyes to heaven with two filigree spires that punctuate Zagreb's skyline like exclamation marks. Viennese architects Friedrich von Schmidt and Hermann Bollé sketched the 345ft-high steeples to crown a cathedral rebuilt after an 1880 earthquake reduced to rubble the Gothic original, itself a replacement for a Romanesque church levelled by marauding Mongols in 1242.

Scraps of medieval fresco in the south aisle, nearby Renaissance choir stalls inlaid with cartoony saints and plait motifs handed down from medieval style books (incorporated today on the bands of policemen's caps), and a Baroque pulpit like a pagoda, survive in a lofty interior whose scale reveals the Austrians' aspirations for their Central European acquisition. Look, too, at the rear of the south aisle for the Ten Commandments on a 1941 tablet that celebrates 1,300 years of Croatian Christianity in an alien-looking Glagolitic script scratched by 12th-century monks – and also in the north aisle for Archbishop Alojzije Stepinac, who kneels before Christ, ecstatic and awed, in a Mestrović relief which marks his tomb. In 1988 the late Pope John Paul II beatified the Croatian church leader, whose criticism of oppression under Tito's newly empowered partisans earned him 16 years' hard labour until his ill health forced the regime to shift him from a Stepinac prison to house arrest in Krasic in December 1951. His effigy reclines in a glass sarcophagus behind the altar. Far more cheerful are Fernkorn's gilded *Virgin and Child*, who swoon on a pillar before the cathedral.

Outside, walk around the former **ramparts** which abut Vlaška. A section of 15th-century **defence wall** that ringed a cathedral then on Christianity's ramparts as Europe's most easterly church borders Ribnjak to the northeast. Grassy scoops remember the fishponds that christened the leafy park; shame about the litter.

From Tkalčićeva into Gradec

When 1898 engineers filled a stream, Potok (brook) became **Tkalčićeva** and pickled an absurdly pretty street of 18th- and 19th-century houses to give camera shutter fingers cramp; you half-expect to see Mickey and Donald wave and beam as they parade between lovingly restored town houses once owned by workers in a street of textile mills. Today this is prime bar-hopping territory, and on warm summer evenings the Disney heroes would find almost no space to stroll. Off the south end of Tkalčićeva, **Blood Bridge** (Krvavi most) recalls the vicious border wars between chalk-and-cheese city founders Kaptol and Gradec (*see* below). Bloody skirmishes were commonplace as the sacred and secular rivals wrestled to be regional power player – in fits of pique, Middle Ages Kaptol frequently excommunicated its mercantile neighbour – and it took the newly elevated Habsburg king Ferdinand to knock together heads in 1527. The bitter enemies put to the sword by 13th-century Mongols agreed a sulky truce in the face of a new common enemy, ambitious Turks.

The street links Tkalčićeva to parallel **Radićeva**, at the northern end of which is the **stone gate** (Kamenita vrata). The sole survivor of a quartet of town wall gateways where guards kept a sharp eye on incoming traders has found its second wind as a shrine for a 16th-century statue of the Virgin, found without a singe among the ashes of a gate destroyed by a 1731 blaze, and who now quietly works miracles from a niche. Or so walls covered in plaques exclaiming '*Hvala Marija*' (Thank you, Mary) entreat you to believe; an ever-present congregation testifies to the locals' enduring affection.

Beyond is **Gradec**, a genteel district of Baroque alleys and squares that barely recalls its roots as the Hungarian garrison town King Béla IV of Hungary rebuilt after the 1240s Mongol rout, then fattened up into a royal free town. You can also enter its cosy pocket of lanes via a funicular off Ilica (*see* below). Just beyond the stone gate is Croatia's second-oldest **pharmacy** on the corner of Kamenita – Dante's grandson Niccolò Alighieri once dispensed cures from this mid-1300s chemist's shop.

Markov Trg

The physical and symbolic heart of Gradec, Markov trg seems far too charming to be Croatia's political power base. While other parliament buildings aspire to induce awe, the **Sabor** on the east flank reveals itself as a modest palace (1910); from its balcony, Croatia declared emancipation from Austro-Hungarian rule on 1 December 1918, and behind its stately neoclassical façade politicians ratified the 25 June 1991 split from the Socialist Yugoslav republic. Retaliation came on 7 October 1991, when Yugoslav jets dropped bombs on the **Ban's Palace** (Banski dvori) opposite, where political strategists now stride past armed police into the government administrative and reception building fashioned from two Baroque palaces for Habsburg-appointed Croatian viceroys. The Yugoslav republic's clumsy attempt to assert authority – and, say some observers, to assassinate Croatian president Franjo Tuđman – only prompted Croatia to sever all links with Belgrade, but then, the square has always been a venue for expressions of political might. Here in 1573 peasant revolutionary 'king' Matija Gubec was crowned with a band of white-hot iron before he was quartered; local lore claims the stone head which gazes mournfully from the corner of Ćirilometodska on the south side of Markov trg is his portrait.

For all the square's elegant Baroque buildings, none stands a chance beside the explosion of colour on centrepiece **St Mark's Church** (Crkva svete Marka). City tourist board and travel photographers alike probably whisper a votive prayer to the Austrians who unwittingly created a Zagreb icon when they patterned ceramic roof tiles into two coats of arms: a united shield of the Kingdom of Croatia (red and white check), Dalmatia (three lions) and Slavonia (a marten); and the city of Zagreb. Their shot of cultural adrenaline, injected during rigorous renovation in the 1880s, was just the latest in a history of home improvements which also added an awkward Baroque tower to the 13th-century parish church christened after St Mark's Day fairs in Gradec's main square; a snapshot of the Gothic original remains on a south portal crowded with biblical bigwigs. Inside, gloomy Croat kings strike a pose among biblical personalities in muscular 1930s frescoes by painter Jozo Kljakovic, and the ever-present Mestrović pens powerful lines for a *Crucifixion* and *Pietà* bronzes.

Around Katarinin Trg

Canvases fizz with character in the quirky **Museum of Naive Art** (Hrvatski muzej navine umjetnosti; *open Tues–Fri 10–6, Sat–Sun 10–1; closed Mon; adm*) south on Čirilometodska. Enthused by Rousseau-esque concepts of 'primitive' integrity, Professor Krsto Hegedušić seized upon self-taught daubers in the Slavonian village of Hlebine and moulded their raw talent into the 'Hlebine School', writing the first chapter of a style demeaned as 'peasant' then 'primitive' art until Croatian politicians proposed the more flattering 'naïve' in 1994. Although not the cerebral fare of expressionism or surrealism, despite the museum's protests, there is still much to admire in glass-on-oil works by Ivan Generalić, as vivid and fizzy as cartoon cell acetates. The Hegedušić *protégé*'s bucolic scenes of fairytale whimsy are far more charming than second-generation superstar Ivan Večenaj – thick globs of blood and tortured trees in *Evangelists on Calvary* are the stuff of which Grimm nightmares are made. Look, too, for works by Ivan Lacković Croata, a star among later Hlebine painters, whose lapses into twee melancholy are forgivable for his exquisite draughtsmanship.

Čirilometodska opens into **Katarinin trg**, guarded on the south by the **Lotršćak Tower** (Kula Lotršćak; *open Tues–Sun 11–8; adm*), a relic of 13th-century defences named for the 'Robber's' bell which rang to warn locals of city closing time. A fanciful tale relates that a cannonball loosed from the Romanesque tower at warlike Turks camped across the Sava river obliterated the pasha's chicken dinner and so demoralized the prince that he had second thoughts about raising his scimitar against Zagreb. Never mind that Ottoman forces never launched an assault on the capital (although they razed villages on the other side of the Sava during the mid-1500s), Zagreb locals have set their watches by the cannon, which has blasted above rooftops at midday sharp since 1876 – be warned, it's loud. Miss it, and the tower still offers temporary art exhibitions and superlative views over Donji grad from its turret, just topping those spread below hillside promenade **Strossmayerovo šetalište**, where weekend lovers moon beneath a canopy of chestnut trees. In front of the tower is the terminus of Zagreb's **funicular** from Ilica (*every 10mins 6.30am–9pm; 3Kn*); its dinky carriages first huffed up by steam in 1871.

The **Museum of Modern Art** (Muzej suvremene umjetnosti; *open Tues–Sat 11–7, Sun 10–1; adm*) tracks trends of home and international artists on the north side of

Katarinin trg, and, on the east, St Catherine feigns surprise like a starlet at the fuss in her honour on **St Catherine's Church** (Crkva svete Katarine). Jesuits looked to Rome's Il Gesù when they sketched a new church (1620) whose outward public decorum drops no hint of the bewitching interior; walls are iced with sugar-sweet pink and white stucco in intimation of spiritual ecstasy through decorative excess in Zagreb's Baroque treasure. Concerts of classical music here score high on the tingle factor. Almost overpowered by the candy walls, frescoes of Catherine with the pagan philosophers she dared to out-debate play witty *trompe l'œil* tricks behind the main altar; his war of words lost, furious Emperor Maxentius answered the patron saint's impudence by torturing her on the spiked wheel she holds outside, and which christened the spinning Catherine Wheel firework.

After nearly two centuries of being press-ganged into military service until 1945, Baroque **Jesuit monastery** the Klovićevi dvori on adjacent Jezuitski trg is enjoying its freedom as a **gallery** (*open Tues–Sun 10–8; closed Mon; adm*) for international block-busters and a lovely courtyard venue for concerts of the Zagreb Summer Festival.

North of Markov Trg

One block west of Gradec's central square, on Matoševa, the ritzy Baroque Rauch mansion is a suitably grand setting for questions of Croatian history posed by temporary exhibitions in the **Croatian History Museum** (Hrvastski povijesni muzej; *open Mon–Fri 10–5, Sat–Sun 10–1; adm*).

Doyenne of Gradec museums, however, is the **Mestrović Studio** (Altelje Mestrović; *Mletačka 8; open Tues–Fri 9–2, Sat 10–6; closed Sun and Mon; adm*). Flushed by the success of the first one-man show in the Victoria and Albert Museum in London, Croatia's finest modern sculptor treated himself to the Mletačka town house in which he crafted 20 years of bronzes – including the bronze Indians in Chicago's Grand Central Park – until persecution by Ustaše fascists forced him into exile in America in 1942. Even models of more swaggering public works relax in the house, which preserves Mestrović's dusky frescoes and furniture. The sculptor who shaped swaggering Croat icons such as bishop Grgur Ninski in Split, on show in miniature as a study, also reveals unexpected tenderness in a lovely bronze of his second wife Olga breastfeeding their son Tvrtko. It's a treat – not something which can always be said of the stuffed mammals and geology displays in the **Croatian Natural History Museum** (Hrvatski prirodoslovni muzej; *open Tues–Fri 10–5, Sat–Sun 10–1; closed Mon; adm*) a block north on Demetrova; enthusiasts can investigate a nostalgic corridor of *fin-de-siècle* specimen jars and the world's largest haul of Neanderthal finds, unearthed in Krapina (*see p.46*).

Last up in this cultural quarter, squirrelled away in the back streets, is the **Zagreb City Museum** (Muzej grada Zagreba; Opatička 20; *open Tues–Fri 10–6, Sat–Sun 10–1; adm*), which chronicles local history from days when Zagreb was a twinkle in the eye of 7th-century BC settlers to modern triumph in the Homeland War, in the 17th-century Convent of the Poor Clares. Rejoice – for once, captions that describe artworks and weapons, costumes and city models are also provided in English.

The Lower Town (Donji Grad)

After the *rubato* of winding alleys in the upper town, Donji grad beats strict four-four time in a grid of streets drawn by late-19th-century Habsburgs, one element in their aspiration to elevate Zagreb into the sort of cultured duchess who could hold her own among European grandees, a sort of metropolitan *My Fair Lady*. The pencil of urban architect Milan Lenuci didn't stray far from the ruler, but he softened his formal plan with a U of leafy squares dubbed, inevitably, Lenuci's Green Horseshoe.

From Trg Bana Jelačića to Zrinjevac

The Romans would have approved of the architect's grid, and the east–west road which marched past their *municipium*, laid waste by AD 600 Slavs, blazed a trail now followed by **Ilica**, Zagreb's longest street and shopping parade. Dive south as it blasts west from Trg bana Jelačića and you reach **Preradovićev trg**, christened in honour of romantic poet Petar Preradović at its centre but nicknamed Cvijetni trg (flower square). A few lonely florists' stalls recall the now-banished market in a square abuzz with the gossip of a dedicated café society – visit at weekends and it seems all Zagreb has descended to sup and pose here and in adjacent Bogovićeva. On the north side is the **Serbian Orthodox Church**, its congregation seriously depleted by recent history, its interior scented by incense and full of shimmering icons steeped in mystery.

Lenuci confesses his hankering after the elegant parks of European *grandes dames* in his first green creation, **Zrinjevac**, two or three blocks to the southeast. *Fin-de-siècle* strollers who took the air and doffed hats probably marvelled at the reinvention of a cattle fairground into a handsome park (1872) where you can almost hear the swish of Sunday-best silk skirts or click of ebony walking canes. Structure in late-19th-century Zagreb's favourite promenade comes from busts of Croatian luminaries, a wrought-iron bandstand and a bizarre fountain like stacked gyroscopes, a whim of a Hermann Bollé, freed from the architectural straitjacket of the neo-Gothic cathedral. A daffodil-yellow paint-job highlights the **Archaeological Museum** (Arheološki muzej; *Trg Nicole Subića Zrinjskog 19; open Tues–Fri 10–5, Sat–Sun 10–1; closed Mon; adm*) among the late-1800s stalwarts on the park's west flank. Despite impressive national artefacts which start at prehistory and peter out at invasion by medieval Tartars, the crowds clot the two rooms of Egyptian mummies, one prized for the world's longest script of Etruscan text, inked on bands that cocooned the body. The star exhibit is far more modest: so highly does Croatia treasure the *Vučedol Dove*, a tubby bird-shaped vessel crafted by Bronze Age settlers near Vukovar, Slavonia, that it is celebrated on the 20Kn note. Rest in a courtyard café that leads a double life as a Roman lapidarium.

Strossmayer Trg and Tomislavov Trg

Bishop Juraj Strossmayer found time between denouncing papal infallibility (in the end he grudgingly commended the pope's 'remarkably good Latin') and promoting Croatian nationalism (he argued that its tinder box of resentments was preferable to foreign rule) to found the brick pile Academy of Science and Art in 1884; Mestrović portrays the benefactor behind his creation, his head crowned by hair tufts like

Mercurial wings. Later acquisitions have expanded the bishop's private gallery to 120 canvases and turned it into the **Strossmayer Gallery of Old Masters** (Strossmayerova galerija starih majstora; *open Tues 10–1 and 5–7, Wed–Sun 10–1; closed Mon; adm*), whose star players are Venetians such as Tintoretto, Bellini and Carpaccio. Brueghel and van Dyck fly the flag for the Flemish, and El Greco adds a dainty *Mary Magdalene*. Security guards will permit you to ponder for free the *Baška tablet* (*c.*1100) in the foyer; Croatia's most celebrated slab, etched with bizarre liturgical script Glagolitic, was discovered on the island of Krk.

Zig-zag west and the **Modern Gallery** (Moderna galerija; *open Tues–Sat 10–6, Sun 10–1; adm*) on the corner of Hebrangova may have flung open doors after protracted renovation to showcase the cream of Croatian art from 1850–1950 in 16 rooms. If not, try the **Art Pavilion** (Umjetnički paviljon; *open Mon–Sat 11–7, Sun 10–1; adm*). One of the pioneers among European prefab buildings, moved brick by iron girder to Zagreb two years after it was showcased at the Budapest Millennium Exhibition in 1896, it now hosts passing exhibitions. You can't miss it – it's canary-yellow.

South is the manicured lawn of **Tomislavov trg**, named in salute to the first king of the fledgling Croatian state. The 10th-century ruler brandishes his sceptre south-wards at the neoclassical train station, which was briefly in Europe's spotlight when royalty, diplomats and the bourgeoisie en route to Istanbul disembarked from the Orient Express. Those high rollers bedded down in the **Hotel Regent Esplanade** (*see* p.32) moments west of the station, whose luxurious Art Deco foyer remains the 'triumph of architecture and crafts' it was lauded as when doors opened in April 1923. Appropriately, the hotel's first registered guest was a Herr Glück (Mr Luck).

Botanical Gardens, Technical Museum and Ethnographic Museum

For an intermission in the lower town's symphony of high culture, flee to the **Botanical Gardens** (Botansički vrt; *Mihanovićeva; open Tues, Wed and Fri–Sun 9–7, Mon and Thurs 9–2.30*). The base section of Lenuci's horticultural horseshoe (*see* p.39) is a lovely place to amble along paths which meander through naturalistic gardens, or laze by pea-green ponds speckled with waterlilies. State archives now fill the former **university library** opposite, an architectural hotch-potch, with window stripes and stern owls shouldering globes, toys with Viennese Secession. **Marulićev trg**, behind, honours Split Renaissance poet Marko Marulić, who penned the first epic in Croatian, *Judita*. Not that you'd guess from the bronze by Mestrović – the author slumps in an armchair as if dozing after a weighty lunch.

Never mind official opening hours, the **Technical Museum** (Tehnički muzej; *open Tues–Fri 9–5, Sat–Sun 9–1; closed Mon; adm*), on Savska, a detour southwest, is all about timing. Plan carefully and you can explore historic fire engines, central Europe's oldest driving machines and a hall crammed with the usual modes of transport – automobiles, aeroplanes, a dinky submarine swiped from careless Italians in 1942 – before you join tours which: burrow into a 1,000ft mine shaft (*Tues–Fri 3, Sat–Sun 11; adm*); conduct electricity experiments in a mock-up study of Nikola Tesla (*Tues–Fri 3.30, Sat–Sun 11.30; adm*), the Serbian inventor who pioneered alternating current (Tesla coils still power many radio sets) and whose dark mutterings about being able to split the Earth like an apple or a ray capable of obliterating a 10,000-strong squadron at 250 miles made him a favourite with sensationalist editors; or star-gaze in a planetarium (*Tues–Fri 4, Sat–Sun 12; adm*). A dry section on geology is highly miss-able if you're pushed for time.

North, the penultimate building block of Lenuci's horseshoe Trg braće Mažuranić is home to the **Ethnographic Museum** (Etnografski muzej; *open Tues–Thurs 10–6, Fri–Sun 10–1; closed Mon; adm*), with African sculptures and sleepy Buddhas brought home as holiday souvenirs of late-1800s explorers, but best visited for displays which rummage into Croatia's own corners: lace like spider webs from the island of Pag; Sunday-best folk costumes which celebrate the country's cultural mishmash; and ritzy Slavonian scarves threaded with gold.

Mimara Museum, Art and Crafts Museum and Trg Maršala Tita

If the small fleet of school group coaches on Rooseveltov trg doesn't give the game away, the imposing neo-Renaissance building declares the **Mimara** (*open Tues, Wed, Fri and Sat 10–5, Thurs 10–7, Sun 10–2; adm*) the heavyweight of Zagreb (and Croatian) museums, stuffed with the private treasures amassed by Ante Topić Mimara. Possibly. Intrigue and plot still surround not only the art collector's identity – some claim the Dalmatian peasant-farmer's son adopted 'Mimara' as a *nom de plume* while studying under Italian portrait painter Antonio Mancini, others that Mirko Maratović stole the identity of First World War battlefield victim Ante Topić, then tagged on Mimara as a sly nod to his own name – but also how the shadowy art collector acquired such a rich century-spanning collection. 'The master swindler of Yugoslavia', hiss critics, alluding to allegations that Mimara used a post-war ruse of Yugoslav repatriation to swipe art snatched by the Nazi élite. Other art detectives list forgery alongside theft on Mimara's crime sheet. Either way, the flamboyant collector donated his hoard to the nation and was paid royally by a government convinced it had struck a bargain for a 3,600-strong *œuvre* of canvases and *objets d'art* it valued at a billion dollars. In 1987, the ribbon was snipped, champagne corks flew and the Zagreb Louvre opened its doors, only for critics to denounce as fakes many of its Michelangelos, Rembrandts and Botticellis. Croatian authorities are reluctantly addressing the claims, and many canvases have been downgraded to 'School of...' to be on the safe side. Of course, the museum holds no truck with such slanders, and sets aside a top-floor homage to its benefactor, who smiles from his death mask (and no wonder since the government threw into the deal a Zagreb penthouse), and, whatever the truth, there's an astonishing range of art and objects here. Ancient Egyptian glass, Persian rugs and Far East objects spice the ground floor with exotica while above china and fiddly ivory reliquary boxes feature in a millennium of European applied arts. Those disputed artworks are on the second floor; big-name canvases which span from almond-eyed Byzantine icons to French Impressionists such as Renoir and Manet, genuine or otherwise.

There are no authenticity problems in the **Museum of Arts and Crafts** (Muzej za umjetnost i obrit; *open Tues–Sat 10–7, Sun 10–2; closed Mon; adm*) a block north. Its stylistic tour through the decorative arts begins in the 1400s with stolid Gothic furniture, then perks up in rooms crammed with frothy Renaissance objects. Don't miss a Mary altar from the village of Remetinec in a room of devotional sculpture – statuettes of the willowy Virgin are a press release of her good deeds; building cathedrals, protecting lambs, etc. – before you inspect heavy historicism inspired by Austria and Italy above. Arts and Crafts furniture and elegant Tiffany lamps, plus a gallery of Sixties poster art, provide light relief. Worth a peek in their own right are the atrium and staircase of the museum's ritzy neo-Renaissance palace, a vision of the ever-industrious Hermann Bollé. The museum flanks the west side of **Trg maršala Tita**, western tip of Lenuci's horseshoe and a square with a swaggering centrepiece, the **Croatian National Theatre**. Viennese architects sketched its columns and cupolas in 1894, then knocked up the neo-Baroque pile at lightning pace to impress Emperor Franz Josef, who cut the ribbons at the 1895 opening. Overlooked but more enchanting before it is Mestrović's sculpture *Well of Life* (1905) – it's no surprise that its luxurious eroticism came from the imagination of a 22-year-old student.

Outside the Centre

Maksimir Park

3km east of the centre; trams 12 and 7 (to Dubrava), 11 and 12 (to Dubec) from Trg bana Jelačića.

Ask about the easiest escape from summer crowds and most locals will point you to Maksimir Park. Zagreb archbishop Maksimilijan Vrhovac is honoured with his name on the map for seeding a modest French-style garden in 1784 to create the first public promenade in southeast Europe, but the real debt of gratitude is owed to his successor. Enamoured by naturalistic English-style gardens, archbishop Jurjaj Haulik incorporated an existing oak wood and expanded the 45-acre progenitor into today's 780-acre expanse of meadows, woods and lakes perfect for a lazy Sunday stroll. If there are better places for a summer picnic, Zagreb is keeping them secret.

An avenue of trees channels arrow-straight alleys past Croatia's largest **zoo** (*open daily 9–5; adm*) and adjacent 19th-century whimsy the **Echo Pavilion** towards romantic belvedere building the **Vivikovac** (1843), now a café with a view – expect to wait for a table at weekends. A contemporary **Swiss chalet** nestles among woods nearby, but the real escapist treats – thicker woods, less-populated meadows – are revealed to those who indulge the more meandering paths north of the belvedere.

Mirogoj Cemetery

2km northeast of the centre; bus 106 from the cathedral or tram 14 east (to Mihaljevac) from Trg bana Jelačića, then 10min walk from Gupčeva zvijezda (stop four).

So beautiful is one of Europe's finest cemeteries, goes the quip, its occupants fare better than some of the living. Hermann Bollé would be quietly thrilled. The industrious architect who designed much of Zagreb's Habsburg-era cityscape turned his attentions to a burial ground for the expanding city in 1876 and created a fortress-like necropolis whose walls are crowned with cupolas and pierced by a gateway which tempers sombre stolidity with grace. Don't be put off – Mirogoj's leafy park cocooned in hush is a serene spot to hunt out mixed-denomination tombs; Communist partisans honoured with five-pointed stars lie beside Orthodox Jews named in Cyrillic, and Muslim headstones like obelisks lie next to Christian. Ponderous family mausoleums beneath evocative colonnades on either side of the entrance draw a late-19th-century stylebook of funerary sculpture carved by some of Croatia's finest: Ivan Rendić's 1872 mourner in billowing skirts, who lays a flower on the simple sarcophagus of Slavophile poet Petar Preradović (he of the central square); or the stooped Jewish patriarchs that Robert Franges Mihanović shaped for the Mayer family vault. Famous deceased include Stjepan Radić, Croatian Peasant Party founder whose demands for national independence were silenced by an assassin's bullet in the Belgrade parliament, and Croatia's first non-aristocrat *ban* (viceroy), Ivan Mazuranic. And then there's Franjo Tuđman; church bells tolled countrywide and jets flew over Mirogoj in December 1999 when Croatia's first president was entombed in a black granite crypt on the doorstep of the Christ the King Church.

Day Trips from Zagreb

Mount Medvednica

Nature-loving 19th-century strollers knew what they were talking about when they extolled jaunts on 'Bear Mountain', because 'Zagrebačka gora' (Zagreb's Mountain) is now treasured as a city playground. On summer Sundays, an army of Zagreb silverhairs dons walking boots to tramp thickly wooded slopes while families idle in meadows over a picnic, and in winter skiers swish down slopes (ski hire available at Sljeme summit). Be warned: the nature park, protected by parliamentary decree since 1981, is also Croatia's busiest at weekends.

Getting There

Tram 14 from Trg bana Jelačića terminates at Mihaljevac, where tram 15 begins for the four-stop hop to Dolje. A subway and woodland path leads to the **cable car** (signposted Žičara) for the ascent to Sljeme. A **footpath** from Zagreb street Dubravkin put (northwest of Gornji grad) also ambles north through wooded suburbs to Medvedgrad (*c.* 1hr 40mins).

Tourist Information

Bliznec bb, Zagreb, **t** (01) 45 86 317; *open Mon–Fri 8–4*. Zagreb tourist offices also stock free maps which mark footpaths and mountain bike trails through the park.

Eating Out

Okrugljak, Mlinovi 28 (left fork just before Mihaljevac terminus), **t** (01) 46 74 112 (*expensive*). A member of Zagreb's culinary élite; *see* p.33; book at weekends.

Šestinski Lagvić, Šestinska cesta bb, **t** (01) 46 74 417 (*moderate*). North Croatian specialities served on a wonderful terrace or dining room which oozes bucolic charm in a restaurant downhill from the Medvedgrad fortress.

Zlatni Medved, Sljeme; no tel (*cheap*). A busy and cheerful Alpine-style chalet at the summit which rustles up no-nonsense fillers: bean soup *grah*, sturdy pork cutlets and thick stews.

For once, the journey itself (*see* 'Getting There', p.43) to the uplands just free of Zagreb's northern suburbs (easily combined with a visit to Mirogoj cemetery) is part of the attraction, because the **cable car** (*daily 8–8; 10Kn single, return 17Kn*) which glides 4km up to Sljeme, the giant of the range of hills which limit Zagreb, also offers the best views there are over its urban sprawl. Keen walkers can also reach the 3,400ft summit on a footpath from the lower cable car terminus (approx 2hrs). A TV tower spikes the summit despite the best efforts of the Yugoslavian People's Army in 1991, and an adjacent belvedere provides a sensational panorama north over the Zagorje, a fairytale carpet of villages and forest which on gin-clear days stretches to the Slovenian Alps.

Turn right from the cable car's upper terminus and cross a steep meadow and the boxy **Shrine of Our Lady of Sljeme** (Sljemenska kapelina; *open Tues, Thurs, Sat, Sun 11–3*) quotes from Byzantine, Romanesque and Gothic, an academic's 1932 salute to a millennium of Croatian Christianity.

Fortress Medvedgrad (*open daily 7–10; adm free*) provides different views over Zagreb and a goal for exploration 5km southwest of Sljeme. If the thick walls and chunky towers of a fortification erected by mid-1300s Zagreb bishops seem a mite immaculate it's because Croatia celebrated its emancipation from the Yugoslav republic by rebuilding the stronghold against Mongol raids to support the Shrine of the Homeland; a modern glass-and-stone altar where a flame burns to heroes who fell for Croatian liberty. To save a return to Sljeme, a road threads downhill to suburb Šestine, from where bus 102 trundles back to Zagreb centre.

Samobor

Officially, Samobor is under the jurisdiction of Zagreb. Thankfully, you'd never know it. Though just 22km west of her big sister, the intimate town snuggled among wooded slopes hums with a provincial prosperity that's a world away in atmosphere; in the central square alone, old-fashioned grocers display tins in exact rows and the Gradna brook chuckles contentedly in a corner. Small wonder that Samobor, home-spun and quietly sentimental, is a favourite weekend jaunt for Zagrebers.

The earliest relic of the settlement saluted as a royal free market town in a 1242 charter is 13th-century castle **Stari grad** (literally, 'old town') isolated on a western spur. The heart of the town which blossomed beneath alongside the Gradna is **Trg kralja Tomislava**, lined by the smart Baroque town houses – plus one Art Nouveau newcomer topped by blasé angels – which replaced a townscape reduced to ashes in 1797. If you want to sample local delicacy *Samoborske kremšnite*, a thick slab of custard which quivers between flaky pastry, this is the place to do it. For intellectual nourishment there's the **Samobor Museum** (Samoborski muzej; *open Tues–Fri 9–3, Sat–Sun 9–1; closed Mon; adm*) west of the square. Its streamside villa was formerly the home of composer Ferdinand Livadićev, and musty displays of town documents, hunting weapons and gloomy local dignitaries perk up (slightly) in period rooms where the advocate of Slavic independence and promoter of the national tongue composed 1883 rallying cry 'Croatia Has Not Yet Fallen'.

Getting There

Buses from Zagreb main bus station every 20–30mins take 40mins and cost 23Kn single.

Tourist Information

Samobor: Trg kralja Tomislava 5, **t** (01) 33 60 050, *www.samobor.com. Open Mon–Fri 8–7, Sat 9–7, Sun 10–7.*

Festivals

Sedate Samobor is anything but during Carnival (*Samoborksi fašnik*) held since 1827 on the weekend before Shrove Tuesday.

Eating Out

Samobor sausages (*češjovke*), acclaimed by connoisseurs, are best munched with local mustard then washed down with *bermet*, an aromatic, slightly bitter local tipple whose wine-based recipe is guarded by a family firm. Develop a taste for it and you can buy a bottle (plus jars of mustard) from a factory outlet at Stražnička 1a (off Trg kralja Tomislava).

Pri Staroj Vuri, Giznik 2, **t** (01) 33 50 548 (*expensive–moderate*). A charming dining room cluttered with the 'old clocks' of its name sets the tone for a traditional menu. Fat smoked sausages are served with sauerkraut, baked pork comes in a spicy red wine sauce and local trout is laced with Riesling wine and garlic.

Samoborska Pivnica, Šmedhenova 3, **t** (01) 33 61 623 (*moderate*). Every cut of a pig is fried, smoked and grilled in this old-fashioned cellar restaurant with a platter of sausages.

U Prolazu, Trg krala Tomislava 6 (*cheap*). Terrace tables to people-watch and Samobor's best *Samoborske kremšnite* on the showpiece square.

Look, too, for a large model of 1764 Samobor as a cosy village before the blaze, barely recognizable were it not for the Baroque parish church of **St Anastasia** (Crkva svete Anastazije) whose pastel-yellow hulk still lords it over the east end of Trg kralja Tomislava. Amble beside it up street **Svete Ane** and a path just beyond the cemetery picks through woods towards the diminutive 16th-century chapel of **St Anne** (Kapela svete Ana). Stations of the cross count down the ascent to a sister chapel of **St George** (Kapela svete Jurjan), beyond which a path threads through the trees to Stari grad. Or does in theory. To guarantee you are not left pathless and stranded above a castle mailed in ivy and whose shell (*no access*) is crumbling into a romantic ruin after abandonment by 18th-century feudal counts, instead take the gravel path which potters along the hillside west of St Anne's.

Varaždin

*You can visit Varaždin by car, but it is also accessible by public transport: hourly buses (54Kn) from the main bus station journey northeast in 1hr 40mins (tourist office at Vana Padovca 3, **t** (042) 210 987, www. varazdin.hr).*

The old parliamentary capital of Varaždin, razed to the ground by fire in 1776 and gloriously rebuilt, is Croatia's most perfectly preserved Baroque townscape, a spacious charmer shaded duck-egg blue, cream and saffron. Music-lovers should not hesitate to visit in September, when international orchestras visit during three-week classical music beano Varaždin Baroque Evenings. For more on the sights of Varaždin, and suggestions on how to spend a day here, or where to sleep if you wish to stay overnight, *see* 'Touring from Zagreb', 'Day 5', p.50.

Touring from Zagreb: North into the Zagorje

Day 1: Marian Miracles and Croatian Beginnings

Morning: Head north towards Varaždin on the E71 but take the Popovec exit and turn left at Soblinec for **Marija Bistrica**, Croatia's most venerable pilgrimage site. A divine beam of light revealed a black Madonna lost in the parish church after it was hidden from Turks in 1545, then on 15 July 1684 a mystical woman in blue beseeched the priest to liberate the statue bricked into a niche to protect it from a new assault. His faith paid off – restored to the altar the next day, the Madonna cured a noblewoman's paralysed daughter and confirmed its credentials by surviving an 1880 blaze. Pay respects to the 1400s statue in a Baroque church aggrandized by the light-hearted neo-Gothic of Zagreb cathedral architect Hermann Bollé.

Lunch: In Marija Bistrica, *see* below.

Afternoon: Drive west through Donja Stubica until, just beyond the motorway, you turn north to spa town **Krapinske Toplice**; four outdoor pools in a park are ideal for a dip on hot days. Refreshed, continue north to pick up signs to **Krapina**, 17km northeast. In 1899, Dragutin Gorjanović Kramberger unearthed the 30,000-year-old bones and tools of Krapina Man in a cave north of the town. The world's richest Neanderthal finds were snaffled by Zagreb, but Krapina salutes its first settlers with a museum (*open April–Sept daily 9–5; Oct–Mar Tues–Sun 9–3; adm*) of fossils, and early skulls, and bronzes strike action-poses in the hillside cave opposite (signposted Nalazište pračovjeka).

Dinner and Sleeping: In Krapinske Toplice, Krapina or Bežanec, *see* below.

Day 1

Lunch in Marija Bistrica

Dioniz, Trg Pape Ivanan Paval II, t (049) 469 103 (*cheap*). If *kobasice* (sausages) and pork cutlets sound heavy-going, pizzas and pastas are passable in the central square – Zagorje speciality *štrukli sa sirom* (doughy cheese dumplings) will fill the corners.

Mladost, Zagrebačka 9, t (049) 469 099 (*cheap*). More substantial fare – grilled pork chops, squid and fish – is prepared by a bistro on the Zagreb road.

Loljzekova hiža, 6km west of Marija Bistrica, signposted off Gusakovec road, t (049) 469 325 (*cheap*). A rustic charmer which hits all the right buttons: a menu of home-cooking – delicious fat sausages and steaks in rich mushroom sauces – and a peaceful setting.

Sleeping in Krapinske Toplice

Aquae Vivae, Antuna Mihanovića 2, t (049) 202 202 (*inexpensive*). Comfortable but bland, this modern three-star has a pool and pampers guests with spa treatments.

Dinner and Sleeping in Krapina

Pod Starim krovovima, Trg Ljudevita Gaja 15, t (049) 370 536 (*inexpensive*). A friendly central *pension* with modest en-suite rooms: fork out an extra 100Kn to upgrade to a suite-sized three-bed. Locals tuck into strange cuts of pig in its restaurant; culinary cowards will be relieved to see cutlets and schnitzels in belly-busting country portions.

Pizzeria Picikato, Magistratska 2, no tel (*cheap*). Pizzas and pastas in a courtyard.

Dinner and Sleeping in Bežanec

Dvorac Bežanec, Valentinovo bb, Pregrada (13km north of Krapinske Toplice), t (049) 376 800 (*moderate*). Croatia's only five-star manor house hotel is carved from the Count of Keglević's 17th-century home. The chef is first-class and its wine list is 500-strong – unbeatable for a romantic splurge.

Day 2: Over the Border to Slovenia

Morning: Return to Krapinske Toplice, follow signs to Pregrada and at the junction shimmy left (to Zagreb) then right (Tuheljske Toplice) to reach **Kumrovec**. When local couple Franjo and Marija Tito celebrated the birth of their son Josip Broz in 1892, the Zagorje hamlet could never have imagined it would later be buffed up then plopped in a specimen jar as the Old Village Museum (Muzej staro selo; *open daily 8–4; adm*). Trace the Yugoslav father's rise from Second World War partisan leader to world statesman in his boyhood home – the president strides into history in front – before you follow a stream which chuckles through Croatia's largest open-air museum, full of immaculate cottages which spin idealized tales of late-1800s lifestyles; the village granddaddy is reinvented as a toymaker's, the buntings are up and an ample spread laid for a traditional wedding in another.

Lunch: In Kumrovec, *see* below.

Afternoon: Go west just into Slovenia – a Customs *bureau de change* converts kunas to tolars – head north to Podčertrek then enjoy a lovely drive to the **Olimje Monastery**. Mid-17th-century Pauline monks celebrated the bequest of a 1550 castle by adding a Baroque church with one of Slovenia's most jaw-dropping altars: a three-tier extravaganza of gilt and black marble dedicated to the Virgin. Its razzmatazz almost drowns out a charming St Francis Xavier altar in a side-chapel ablaze with frescoes. More paintings, these of healing heroes, charm in a hidey-hole 1780s pharmacy (*adm*), one of Europe's oldest. Devilish temptation comes from the goodies on sale in a *chocolateria* east of the monastery.

Dinner and Sleeping: In Olimje, *see* below.

Day 2

Lunch in Kumrovec

Stara Vura, Josipa Broza 13, **t** (049) 553 137 (*cheap*). Hearty Zagorje cooking is prepared in country portions in the village's best restaurant, located 100 yds right of the entrance; pick from a small menu of trout for a light lunch. Be warned: the dining room can be swamped by jolly coach groups, so wait for a terrace table in peak season.

Kod starog, Josipa Broza 24, no tel (*cheap*). Light bites for a summer's day opposite Tito's house – cold platters of meats and cheeses are served with hunks of bread, there are fat local sausages to sample and Zagorje favourite *štrukli* (baked cheese dumplings) all washed down with a cheerful home-made wine.

Zagorsko Klet, Staro selo, no tel (*cheap*). Home-made cakes, doughy *štrukli*, cheese and wine are served in the cellar of a buffed-up 1887 farmhouse in the village. Touristy, but charming nonetheless.

Dinner and Sleeping in Olimje

Amon, Olimje 24, **t** (00 386) (0)3 818 2480 (*moderate*). Upmarket rusticity in this country retreat near the monastery, with a handful of rooms and a golf course (hire available) – reservation essential. Its regional acclaim is as a winery of Smarje-Virstajn tipples (Modra Frankinja and Zametna Crnina) served in a restaurant whose master chef elevates traditional fare to exquisite level: there's roast duck, steak and venison in rich sauces and kebabs of pork and bacon dipped in rosemary.

Haler, Olimje 6, **t** (00 386) (0)3 812 1200 (*inexpensive*). Pine furniture and cheerful modern fabrics in simple but homely en-suite rooms in a friendly hotel, and a reliable menu of pork and trout dishes plus beer brewed on site in the adjacent tavern.

Day 3: A Brace of Castles

Morning: Take the Miljarla border crossing back into Croatia, then potter east towards Desinić. You'll spot **Veliki Tabor** (*open daily 10–5; adm*) before you see the signposts because the Zagorje's mightiest castle hunkers down on a hilltop above the village it spawned. Close up, the oldest residential building in continental Croatia – a 12th-century fortress onto which sturdy Gothic bastions were grafted at lightning pace in 1502 as Turkish troops drew on – is showing its age. Rummage through the rooms where Second World War orphans wept, to uncover odds and ends for all tastes – there are business-like pikes and maces, homages to residents past, farming tools – then swoon to views of hummocky Zagorje countryside from the upper gallery.

Lunch: In Desinić, *see* below.

Afternoon: Allow an hour to wriggle east through hills to **Trakošćan**: in Pregrada turn off the Zagreb road to reach Putkovec and at Đurmanec head north as if for Slovenian town Maribor, then follow signposts. The set-square-perfect castellations of the region's most visited castle (*open summer 9–6; winter 9–4; adm*) betray its origins as the conscious antiquarianism of 19th-century count Juraj Drašković, who buffed up a 13th-century ruin into a fashionable neo-baronial residence. His banqueting hall of faux-Gothic vaults and show-off heraldic mantelpiece is a paean to Germanic medieval chivalry; more relaxed are living quarters furnished with heirlooms and wistful portraits of locals by Croatia's first trained female painter, Julijana Erdödy Drašković. For picture-postcard views of the castle, scull a rowing boat across the count's ornamental lake or walk a 5km circuit through woods.

Dinner and Sleeping: In Trakošćan or **Ptuj**, Slovenia, 35km north (take the B9/E59).

Day 3

Lunch in Desinić

Grešna gornica, Taborgradska 3, **t** (049) 343 001 (*cheap*). Desinić has just one address for lunch (east of the castle signposted off main road) but it's a charmer in which to take your time; a snug wooden dining room decorated with embroidery tablecloths and dried flowers oozes bucolic jollity and the garden gazes across to the silhouette of Veliki Tabor. The menu of regional dishes is prepared from the freshest local farm produce: start with Grandpa Eduarda's Zagorje cheese, then try pork steaks stuffed with ham and home-made cheese or veal 'prepared the old-fashioned way'.

Dinner and Sleeping in Trakošćan

Coning, Trakošćan 5, **t** (042) 796 495 (*inexpensive*). A comfy if characterless two-star of the Coning chain, bland but well located bang opposite the castle. Its restaurant (*cheap*) is a carnivore's heaven; try roast duck stuffed with wheat and liver instead of steak.

Dinner and Sleeping in Ptuj

Blast north on the Slovenia road (B9/E59) to locate historic Ptuj. *See* 'Day 4' opposite for more eating out options.

Mitra, Prešernova 6, **t** (00 386) (0)2 787 74 55 (*inexpensive*). Spacious proportions reflect the 1870 vintage of this super-central hotel. Superior rooms (*moderate*) of old-fashioned luxury are worth the extra €10; standard rooms are small and frumpy by comparison.

Poetovio, Trstenjakova 13, **t** (00 386) (0)2 779 82 01 (*inexpensive*). The only other hotel in town; small rooms are a bit institutional.

Ribič, Dravska 9, **t** (00 386) (0)2 749 06 35 (*moderate*). Escape Zagorje's pork obsession in a classy fish restaurant. The riverside terrace is a delight for balmy evenings, a creative chef adds simple modern tastes.

Day 4: Back into Slovenia: Ptuj

Morning: Begin your exploration of pretty Ptuj's two millennia of architectural hand-me-downs at central square Mestni trg, in awe of a neo-Gothic town hall which obliterates its Renaissance predecessor; St Florian atop his Baroque plague column never gets a look-in. South on Krempljeva ulica is the **Minorite monastery** (Minortiski samostan; *adm free, by appt*). Book a time to see its Baroque summer refectory with thick stucco icing and frescoes of saints Peter and Paul, then peek into the saints' church next door; this prize of Slovenia is nearly rebuilt after it took a bomb on the nose in 1945. Northeast on Slovenski trg is the marble **Orpheus Monument**, carved for a 2nd-century Roman mayor but used as a Middle Ages pillory, and a 1500s **bell-tower-turned-gallery**. Here, too, you'll find **St George's Church** (Cerkev svete Jurija), a Romanesque gem stuffed with exquisite Gothic and Baroque altars in the half-light.

Lunch: In Ptuj, *see* below.

Afternoon: A bug-eyed 1400s mask at No.1 and Ptuj's oldest house (No.4) inaugurate arterial traders' street **Prešernova**. Go west, past portals through which Renaissance merchants clattered, to the Dominican monastery, home to the **Archaeological Museum** (*open mid April–Dec daily 10–5; adm*) with its rambling celebration of Ptuj's Celtic and Roman roots. Both founded settlements on the hilltop now claimed by the castle, once a stern 12th-century stronghold, now a Baroque dandy; as the regional museum (Pokrajinski muzej Ptuj; *open May–mid-Oct daily 9–6; mid-Oct–April daily 9–5; adm*) it contains period furnishings, *objets d'art* and musical instruments, and its belvedere (*free*) allows fairytale views over Ptuj's roofscape.

Dinner and Sleeping: In Ptuj (*see* 'Day 3') or Varaždin, back in Croatia (take the B228).

Day 4

Lunch and/or Dinner in Ptuj

Ribič, Dravska 9, **t** (00 386) (0)2 779 (*moderate*). The classiest restaurant in town is a stylish fish specialist by the river which nuances local freshwater and Adriatic fishes with delicate marinades, sauces and beds of fresh veggies. The best bite in town.

Amadeus, Prešernova 36, **t** (00 386) (0)2 771 70 51 (*cheap*). A cheerful modern rustic with a large menu of tasty Slovene standards: trout and salmon in creamy sauces or for large appetites the 'Figaro' feast – pork, chicken, liver, bacon and a frankfurter. Good luck.

Perutnina Ptuj (PP), Novi trg 2, **t** (00 386) (0)2 749 06 22 (*cheap*). No-nonsense pub-grub in a modern tavern a block north of Mestni trg.

Cafe Europa, Mestni trg, no tel (*cheap*). While Ptuj's café society people-watches on the main square outside, its teenagers tuck into huge pizzas and bowls of pasta within.

Dinner and Sleeping in Varaždin

Habsburg-era beauty Varaždin is 34km east of Ptuj; the B228 blasts over the border and continues direct to the town.

Pansion Maltar, Prešernova 1, **t** (042) 311 100 (*inexpensive*). Good-value rooms in this friendly *pension* are modest but more than adequate, all en suite and with satellite TV.

Turist, Aleja kralja Zvonimira 1, **t** (042) 395 394 (*inexpensive*). The three-star businessman's favourite is 100m west. Skip dowdy standard rooms which are poor value compared with the Maltar and upgrade to comfy business class (*moderate*); modern if a mite bland.

Zlatna Guska, J Habdelića 4, **t** (042) 213 393 (*moderate*). Combine a barrel-vaulted cellar which strives for medieval splendour and a talented chef who does magic things with freshwater fish and tasty meat-feasts and you have the local culinary highlight which sits with the best in Croatia's top 100.

For more dining options, *see* 'Day 5', over.

Day 5: Varaždin

Morning: Greatness nipped in the bud characterizes Varaždin. The wealthy merchant town lost its brief status as parliamentary capital after a 1776 fire: its reinvention in elegant Baroque just couldn't lure the Croat viceroy back from Zagreb. But atrophy made this Croatia's most perfectly preserved Baroque town, at its grandest around main square **Trg kralja Tomislava**, whose tubby **town hall** (1523) was spiked with a jaunty clock tower after the blaze. Just east is the **cathedral**, the first building to wear Baroque fashion in the mid-1600s, with a glorious altar on which saints preach from niches like fairground showmen. More Baroque show-offs put on the Ritz west on **Franjevački trg** – hub of 1700s high life the **Patačić Palace** still swaggers despite demotion as a bank and the **Herzer Palace** west is now home to the **Entomology Museum** (Entomološki muzej; open Tues–Fri 10–5, Sat–Sun 10–1; adm), with beautiful displays of insects like a Victorian naturalist's sketch book.

Lunch: In Varaždin, see below.

Afternoon: Pause at the Baroque **Ursuline church** which blushes on Ursulinska as you thread north to the **castle**; the town founder's stolid Gothic was overhauled by Renaissance owners wary of raiding Turks and its **museum** (open May–Sept Tues–Sun 10–6; Oct–April Tues–Fri 10–5, Sat–Sun 10–1; adm) rambles through local history and interior décor styles. Then stroll west on Hallerova aleja. Bewailing the 'lugubrious-ness' of European cemeteries, **town cemetery** overseer Hermann Heller strove for 'a park of the living' and in 1905 created a lovely spot for a stroll. You can return directly to Zagreb in the morning on the motorway south from Varaždin.

Dinner and Sleeping: In Varaždin, see below.

Day 5

Lunch and Dinner in Varaždin

Dominico, Trg slobode 7, **t** (042) 212 017 (cheap). Fifteen styles of pizza plus tasty home-made pastas beside the park.

Grenadir, Kranjčevićeva 12, **t** (042) 211 131 (cheap). A traditional dining room of starched white tablecloths and antique dressers sets the tone for a good-value menu of continental Croatian fare: pork chops and trout dishes.

Kavana Korzo, Trg Kralja Tomir 2, **t** (042) 320 914 (cheap). Auntie's favourite café for a gossip over elevenses coffee and gâteaux. Tear yourself from a terrace perfect for people-watching to revel in a nostalgic interior of dark woods and red upholstery, a timewarp into the yesteryear Varaždin pictured on the walls.

Park, J Habdelića 6, **t** (042) 211 499 (moderate–cheap). Another timewarp, this time into the stiff formality of a 1970s dining room; a terrace beside the eponymous park is more relaxed. It's no surprise that the traditional menu is solid and reliable, with lots of pork chops and tasty charcoal-grilled meats.

Zlatna Guska, J Habdelića 4, **t** (042) 213 393 (moderate). Combine a barrel-vaulted cellar which strives for medieval splendour and a talented chef who does magic things with freshwater fish and baronial meat-feasts and you have a restaurant in Croatia's top 100. The 'Golden Goose' is the place for a last-night splurge, no question.

Sleeping in Varaždin

Turist, Aleja kralja Zvonimira 1, **t** (042) 395 394 (inexpensive). The three-star businessman's favourite. Upgrade to comfy business class (moderate), a mite bland but with mod cons.

Pansion Maltar, Prešernova 1, **t** (042) 311 100 (inexpensive). Good-value rooms in a friendly pension, all en suite and with satellite TV.

Croatia: Pula, Rijeka and the Istrian Peninsula

Istria

TRIESTE — ITALY
Škocjan

SLOVENIA

Piran
Koper
Portorož

CROATIA

Buje
Buzet
Roč
Groźnjan
Hum
Motovun
Vološko
Opatija
RIJEKA
Novigrad
Lovran
Kraljevica
Poreč
Jama
Baredine
Pazin
Sv Nikola
Medveja
Krk
E65/8
Gradina
Crikvenica
Vrsar
Dvigrad
Žminj
Brestova
Porozina
Vrbnik
Rovinj
Kanfanar
Labin
Beli
Sveta Katarina
Cres
Krk
Crveni Otok
Valbiska
Punat
Bale
Baška
Mali Brijun
Fažana
Vodnjan
Cres
Prvić
Brijuni National Park
Plavnik
Veli Brijun
Valun
Cres
Lopar
To Venice
San Marino
PULA
Supetarska Draga
Rab
Kalifront
Peninsula
Rab
Cape Kamenjak
Jablanac
Osor
E65/8

N

Lošinj
Prizna
Novalja
Žigljen
Mali Lošinj
Veli Lošinj
Pag
Susak

25 km
10 miles

From the Romans who founded regional capital Pula to the between-war Fascists who snatched port Rijeka, the Italians have influenced Istria, the heart-shaped locket at the Adriatic's throat. Explore from our gateway duo and Rovinj seems wafted over the Adriatic on balmy zephyrs while inland, Vodnjan retains a staunch Italian population and hilltowns doze in Croatia's answer to Tuscany (without the crowds). And on menus everywhere there are delicious Latin accents: gnocchi, pasta and prize truffles.

Pula

Even if the tale that Colchians, pursuing Jason and his Golden Fleece, founded the town rather than return to King Aeëtes empty-handed is just swords-and-sandals bluster, Pula has good reason to pride itself on its ancient history. Crowds still roar in the world's sixth largest Roman amphitheatre, the prize of Croatian antiquity, during prestigious concerts; locals potter to market beneath a classical monumental gateway whose grand proportions feature in Michelangelo's sketchbook; and one of the finest Roman temples you'll see lends antique elegance to the showpiece Forum.

For such antique treasures, Istria's capital can thank 1st-century BC Italians. They destroyed a sleepy Illyrian hillfort to give Pula its big break and within 200 years the new star on the Adriatic stage, Colonia Julia Pollentia Herculanea, was a sensation as a thriving commercial and administrative centre. Success proved short-lived after the wane of its first manager, however. Signed up with the Venetian Republic from 1150, Pula atrophied, devastated by plague, its port neglected as Italian ambitions turned elsewhere, and a population reduced to just 600 probably breathed a sigh of relief when their town was claimed in 1797 by the Austro-Hungarians, who wrote the last chapter in the rags-to-riches story by masterminding Pula's second golden age as the Habsburgs' naval powerhouse on the Adriatic. Shipbuilding and a commercial harbour still fill local pockets and bring no-nonsense, workaday grit to a city which encouraged industry under Tito. But the reason to visit is those relics of earlier glory in the historic kernel.

The Amphitheatre (Amfiteatar)

Open daily summer 8–9, winter 9–5; adm.

No monument symbolizes Roman Pula like its amphitheatre. The 430ft ellipse expanded over the course of a century from a modest arena under 1st-century BC Emperor Augustus to an awe-inspiring gladiatorial stadium under Emperor Vespasian, badgered, the story goes, by his Pula-born girlfriend Cenida to build a 23,000-seater north of the ancient Italians' town walls despite the fact that Pula's population never topped 5,000. The stadium, which shaded its togaed spectators with *velarii* (canvas sails) strung across 100ft-high walls, was the sixth largest Roman stadium in the world, but after the 7th century, when wild animal bouts followed gladiator fights into the imperial statute books as criminal offences, it was looted as a quarry of pre-cut limestone by pragmatic locals. Although most of the stone terraces have therefore morphed into local houses, the outer shell of arches still stamps its authority on the shoreline, and for that Pula owes a debt to Gabriele Emo. In 1583, the senator put the brakes on the plans of a Venetian senate hankering after its own antiquities to ship the amphitheatre across the Adriatic stone by stone; the enlightened local son is honoured with a plaque inside. Circle its rhythmic tiers of arches before you enter to gawp at gladiator's-eye views from the floor of an amphitheatre which now fills for blockbuster concerts not bloody contests. A musty **museum** of wine and olive presses and barnacle-encrusted amphorae, displayed in the cellars where animals were caged and gladiators prepared, is a disappointment by comparison.

Getting There

From April–Oct, Croatian Airlines **flies** from Gatwick to Pula airport, and Venezialines **catamarans** nip across the Adriatic from Venice in 3hrs mid-May–mid-Sept. *See pp.3–8.*

Getting from the Airport

Pick up a fistful of kunas at airport exchanges, because **taxis** are the only means of transport from the airport to Pula 10km southwest; expect to pay 60Kn.

Getting Around

The pedestrianized city centre is compact and a delight to wander. **Buses** 1 (to Stoja), 2 and 3 to southern suburbs (2a and 3a continue to package hotels on the Verudela peninsula) start from the main bus station at 43 Istarska, although stops in central street Giardini are more convenient. A single zone 1 ticket to Verudela costs 6Kn from the driver or 10Kn for a two-journey ticket bought from kiosks.

Car Hire

Major players also operate at the airport. **Hertz**, Hotel Histria, Verudela, **t** (052) 210 868. **Avis**, Starih Statuta 4, **t** (052) 223 739. **Budget**, Carrarina 4, **t** (052) 218 252. **Tref**, Splitska 1, **t** (052) 223 124.

Festivals

Even if not the celebrity honeypot which lured stars such as Richard Burton, Elizabeth Taylor and Sophia Loren, the highlight of Pula's social calendar remains the **July Film Festival**, when the amphitheatre terraces fill and Croatian plus a smattering of international releases are premiered beneath the stars.

Tourist Information

Pula: Forum 3, **t** (052) 219 197, *www.pulainfo.hr. Open June–mid-Sept daily 8am–10pm; mid-Sept–May Mon–Sat 8–7, Sun 9–6.* Offers advice about accommodation, and city maps which mark bus routes and major hotels and extend south to the Verudela peninsula. The office also enthuses about its wine routes that tour Istrian vineyards, worth picking up to detour from our suggested tour (*see* pp.63–7).

Shopping

Central high street **Sergijevaca** offers a mixed bag of shops, which, though meagre, are more interesting than the chain stores in the streets east of Giardini.

Foodies will uncover a wonderland of Istrian treats – olive oils and truffles, wines, *rakija* and fruit brandies – in **Saxa**, Kandlerova 28, and **Zigante Tartufi**, Smareglina 7; the latter is one in a quartet of truffle-obsessed outlets of entrepreneur Giancarlo Zigante, who stumbled upon the world's biggest truffle while walking his dog in November 1999 and, after casting it in bronze to convince doubters, treated 100 lucky guests to a dinner of the 1.31kg monster. Less refined, equally tasty, are olive oils, cheeses, seasonal fruit and sticky pastries – sold at the market in **Narodni trg**.

Where to Stay

Pula t (052) –

Compared with other Croatian towns, Pula is well stocked with interesting hotels, boasting a handful of characterful central options and a couple of classy boutique numbers to the south. However, most beds are in concrete package hotels by the beaches of the Verudela peninsula, 4km south of the centre; book through **Arenaturist**, Splitska 1, **t** 529 400.

Histria, Verudela, **t** 590 000, *www.arenaturist. hr* (*moderate*). The best of the package holiday hotels on the Verudela peninsula and the only one open year-round. Proximity to beaches (plus a pool) and large four-star rooms with panoramic balconies compensate for an anonymous sprawling complex.

Valsabbion, Pješćana IX/26, **t** 218 033, *www. valsabbion.hr* (*moderate*). Four spacious suites (*expensive*) enjoy sea views – no.2 is a knock-out – but double rooms in this family-run boutique hotel near the Marina Veruda are still homey and there is a beauty centre and sensational restaurant (*see below*).

Milan, Stoja 4, **t** 210 200, *www.milan1967.hr* (*moderate*). Another classy family-run number with an excellent restaurant (*see below*), 2km south of the centre and with an eye for designer style in its 12 rooms, all en suite, with air-conditioning and satellite TV.

Scaletta, Flavijevska 26, **t** 541 599, *www.hotel-scaletta.com* (*moderate*). Bright, cheery fabrics lend charm to stylish modern rooms of pale woods and stainless steel fittings in a friendly family hotel with a gourmet restaurant (*see below*) and a central location near the amphitheatre – book in advance.

Riviera, Splitska 1, **t** 211 166, *www.arenaturist.hr* (*moderate*). A 1908 *grande dame* from Pula's Austro-Hungarian past opposite the amphitheatre, a little tired, but atmospheric nevertheless. Faded glories are recalled in the public areas; dated one-star rooms make up for in space what they lack in mod cons; ask for a balcony and harbour view.

Omir, Dobrićeva 6, **t** 210 614/218 186 (*inexpensive*). Nineteen compact but comfy rooms of flowery fabrics in an old-fashioned family-run two-star, in a side street off Giardini.

Galia, Epulonova 3, **t** 383 602, *www.hotel-galija-pula.com* (*inexpensive*). Book ahead to claim one of ten modest, modern rooms, all en suite, in this hotel-restaurant, a three-star bargain near Giardini.

Eating Out

Pula **t** (052) –

Istria is truffle country, and in autumn chefs create delicacies in the first-class restaurants of Pula's small hotels. Whatever the time of year, gourmets should make the pilgrimage to sample their cuisine, which ranks among the finest in Croatia – central restaurants are disappointing by comparison.

Valsabbion, Pješćana IX/26, **t** 218 033 (*expensive*). Crowned king of Croatian restaurants twice and consistently voted Istria's number one, the 'slow food' advocate is a gourmet treat. A classy dining room effortlessly unites antiques and modern style, the super-fresh menu changes with the seasons to feature dishes such as frogfish in vine leaves or a sensational scampi *carpaccio*, and service is immaculate and personal. A treat.

Milan, Stoja 4, **t** 210 200 (*expensive–moderate*). One of Istria's top three does magic things with fish in a stylish modern dining room

lifted by the soft tinkle of live jazz piano. Good luck with the 150 choices of Istria's finest wine list.

Vela Nera, Veruda Marina, Pješćana uvala bb, **t** 219 209 (*expensive–moderate*). A fellow member of Croatian dining royalty, with an expert *sommelier*, just around the corner from Valsabbion. Claim a terrace table above the yachts to dine on Adriatic fish grilled or roasted to perfection; try chef's special baked sea bass with chickpeas and tomatoes. Delightful on lazy summer evenings.

Kažun, Vrtlarska 1 (off Mutilska from Trg Republike), **t** 223 184 (*moderate*). Pula's finest *konoba*, named after a country barn, prepares a menu of filling rustic dishes as authentic as it gets. Try home-made *kobasice u vinu* (sausages in wine) or thick goulashes and ragoûts of game or beef, all washed down with an Istrian Merlot or Teran.

Caffe degli Spechhi, Flacijusova 20, **t** 210 663 (*moderate*). Stained glass, marble pillars and stately dimensions lend a *fin-de-siècle* air to the 'Cafe of Mirrors'. Whether past patrons James Joyce or Thomas Mann could have sampled a wide-ranging menu that includes veal medallions laced with a herb sauce or noodles with Istrian truffles is doubtful.

Scaletta, Flavijevska 26, **t** 541 599 (*moderate*). Try a renowned ravioli stuffed with scampi in a creamy truffle sauce or a seafood risotto delicately nuanced with saffron and dried grapes in this central hotel gourmet restaurant that's smart without being stuffy. *Closed Jan, and Sun Dec and Feb.*

Barbara, Kandlerova 5, **t** 219 317 (*cheap*). Grilled squid stuffed with ham, mackerel and slabs of pork rustled up in a no-frills locals' caff.

Dva Ferala, Kandlerova 32, no tel (*cheap*). Gruff working men's bar that's a credit to its breed (though not nearly as intimidating as its patrons would have you believe). Solid *kotlet* (pork cutlets), simple fish dishes such as *girice* (whitebait) and snacks such as *čevapi* are on the menu and there's a bargain *marenda* (lunch menu).

Café Cvajner, Forum 2, **t** 216 502 (*cheap*). Sticky pastries and coffee served in an arty café perfect for people-watching. Prise yourself from the terrace and there are scraps of Renaissance fresco in a grand interior where medieval municipal council officers toiled.

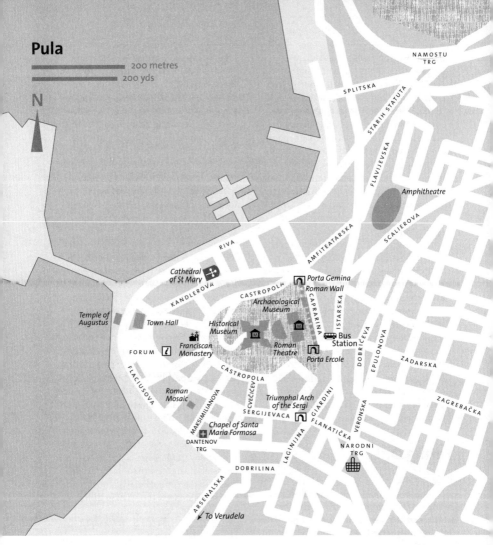

From the Amphitheatre to Giardini

Antique Italians padded out to sate their blood-lust through the AD 2 city gateway **Porta Gemina** (Dvojna vrata) on Carrarina, called the Twin Gate for its double arches and which punctuates a section of Roman wall patched up over the centuries with whatever came to hand; hunt among its bricks and you'll uncover lozenges of Roman column and chunks of carved tablet. The 1st-century BC fortification is matched at the other end by the contemporary **Porta Ercole** (Herkulova vrata) – but it takes a keen imagination to conjure the giant hero Hercules's head and raised club from the weathered blobs of stone at the apex.

The rest of the city walls fell to the modernization plans of the brisk Austro-Hungarians, who merged two streets to create leafy boulevard **Giardini**, a favourite place to promenade and exchange gossip over a coffee. Their 19th-century rulers' city update also freed from its stone vice late-Hellenistic gateway the **Triumphal Arch of** the Sergi (Slavoluk Sergijevaca; 30 BC). And it certainly is triumphal. On the far side of the monumental gateway, towards the Forum, one Slavia Posthuma Sergii crows over her family's role in the Battle of Actium (a 31 BC Roman-on-Roman spat which Octavian, later Emperor Augustus, won after Cleopatra left the fray trailed by Mark Antony) with a vainglorious boast and wealth of reliefs. Small wonder the gate appeared in the sketchbooks of Michelangelo and Inigo Jones.

James Joyce also pondered its chariots and winged goddesses Nika and Victoria, and now reclines in bronze outside opposite Café Uliks (Ulysses), a few steps from the building in which he received £2 a week for drumming tenses and grammar into Austrian naval officers. Not that the literary colossus, who arrived with future wife Nora Barnacle in October 1904, enjoyed his stint as an English teacher at the Berlitz school. Pula, he sniffed, was 'a naval Siberia', one he suffered for just five months before demanding a transfer to Trieste. On the bright side, with so little to divert his eclectic intellect, by December the Irish author had completed chapters 12 and 13 of *Stephen Hero* and formulated the aesthetic principles for its successor, *Portrait of the Artist as a Young Man*, which he set down in the 'Pola Notebook'. No wonder, then, that his associate Tatjana Arambašin Slišković mused, 'He did not forget Dublin, he was often there in his thoughts.'

Along Sergijevaca to the Forum

Sidetrack east of the arch on Flanatička and in Pula's buzzy market on Narodni trg sprawls a counter of fresh local produce beneath chestnut trees that's far more charming than the adjacent Austro-Hungarian market hall, like a hangar for a small blimp and whose glass and steel construction wowed architects in 1903.

West along Roman spine street Sergijevaca then left into Maksimilianova is Dantenov trg. The *Divine Comedy* poet Dante saw 13th-century Pula, 'near Quarnaro's bay/That fences Italy with its washing tides', racked by plague, a scourge which made a deep impression: the Italian placed the former Roman graveyard outside the Sergi arch, 'uneven with the array, on every hand, of countless sepulchres', in his fifth circle of Hell (Canto IX). Architectural buffs should peer into the square's post office (*open Mon–Fri 7–8, Sat 7–2*) where a mosaic-clad spiral staircase by Bologna architect Angiolo Mazzoni dabbles with Futurism. Others can continue a block west. Marooned in a small park, former choir side chapel and part-time gallery Chapel of Santa Maria Formosa (Kapela Marije Formoze; *times vary*) is all that remains intact of the basilica of a 6th-century Benedictine abbey whose walls, in ruin by the late 1500s, are incorporated into adjacent houses. The marble ornamentation and columns of the Byzantine basilica which christened the church the 'Magnificent' (*formosa*) were snaffled by the Venetians for the San Marco basilica, but a snapshot of its mosaic *luxe* is on display in the Archaeological Museum (*see* overleaf).

Somehow still *in situ* across a wasteland car park north is a Roman mosaic (Rimski mozaik) revealed after an apartment took a bomb on the nose during the Second World War. Beaming brothers Amphion and Zethus tie Dirce to the horns of an enraged bull in revenge for maltreating their mother, Zeus's wife Antiphone, in the 3rd-century floor which pepped up an aristocrat's villa.

The Forum and Cathedral

At the end of Sergijevaca is the **Forum**, handsome centre stage of Pula ever since Roman city planners pegged out a piazza here. The flanking arcades of that antique showpiece have long gone, but the **Temple of Augustus** (Augustov hram) remains and imposes architectural authority on the square through a parade of powerful Corinthian columns as thrusting as redwood trunks, and an emphatic gable crown. The founder of the Roman Empire would be delighted that the AD 2–14 homage erected during his lifetime still stands proud as one of the world's finest Roman temples (rebuilt post-1945) – but less so that it was reinvented as a Christian church and later a granary. Today it houses a **lapidarium** of Roman sculpture (*open May–Sept Mon–Fri 9.30–9, Sat–Sun 9.30–1; adm*). Its lost twin, the Temple of Diana, is just visible as a sketch on the back wall of the adjacent **town hall** (Gradska palača) built from those Roman blocks in the 13th century and tinkered with by Renaissance architects, who tacked on a loggia, and Baroque, who stripped their fancies away again.

Hunt for a Gothic staircase remembered like a scar on the north end wall before you walk down Kandlerova to the **Cathedral of St Mary** (Katedrala svete Marija). A progenitor 4th-century church sprouted symbolically over a Roman temple and laid the foundations for today's architectural encyclopaedia: the core Romanesque basilica was tweaked by Gothic architects and the grandiose Renaissance façade was added in 1660 after Pula peered across the Adriatic and swooned at Italian fashions. A 3rd-century AD Roman sarcophagus used for a high altar peps up the otherwise disappointingly ascetic three-nave interior.

The Archaeological Museum and Fortress

Pula made its Illyrian debut on the conical hill which rises at its centre and which every ruler since has shaped into a defensive stronghold after their own tastes: a Roman *castrum* replaced the Illyrians' 1000 BC hill fort; medieval feudal rulers lorded it over town from a castle at the summit; and 1630s Venetians gazed across the bay from a spanking new fortress, drawn by French defence supremo Antoine de Vile and modernized by succeeding Austro-Hungarians (*see p.59*).

From the buzzy Forum, ascend the hill via the 13th-century **Monastery of the Franciscan Order** (Franjevački samostan; *open June–mid-Oct daily 10–12 and 2–4; adm*), whose vows of poverty meant that anything other than a hulking barn was far too great an extravagance. A charmingly haphazard lapidarium rambles through the Roman and medieval finds in its cloister, but Pula's real sculptural prizes are in the **Archaeological Museum** (Arheološki muzej Istre; *open May–Sept Mon–Sat 9–8, Sun 10–3; Oct–Mar Mon–Fri 9–2; adm*) on the other side of the hill. Staircases and corridors stuffed with Roman sculpture entreat you to embark on a treasure hunt for cavorting cherubs and grinning dolphins, furiously bearded gods and sombre funeral snapshots carved on slabs which once lined the amphitheatre road. All are more appealing than worthy but musty display cases of 4th-century BC spiral jewellery and weapons exhumed from Illyrian graves on hill fort Nesactium, 7km from Pula, near the airport. More Roman exhibits are on the top floor: a 1st-century alabaster funerary urn to make stylists swoon, a marble bust of Agrippina Minor, mother of Nero, and saucy picture-postcards on terracotta oil lamps, all speaking volumes about Roman high life. Behind the museum are remnants of a 2nd-century **Roman theatre** (Malo Rimsko kazalište) – with the right eyes you can conjure from its crumbling walls a crescent of seating, orchestra space and pit from which scenery was hoisted.

The Venetians shifted limestone blocks from a larger Roman theatre to create their hilltop **battery** (kaštel), from which they lobbed cannonballs into the bay and which was tweaked by Austro-Hungarians as a link in the 12-strong chain of defences whose sights crisscrossed the Habsburg naval stronghold and secured Pula as one of the best-protected towns in 19th-century Europe. As the **Historical Museum of Istria** (Povijesni muzej Istre; *open daily May–Sept 8–8; Oct–April 9–5; adm*) the fortification has little to recommend it: meagre exhibits of the Habsburg port teased out over three rooms which perk up briefly in jaunty commemorative mugs of a magnificently mustachioed Emperor Franz Josef I. For the best views over Pula, however, its bastions are unbeatable.

South of the Centre: The Verudela Peninsula

Clad in a coat of pine forest, its shingle beaches lapped by clear seas and boasting a clutch of splendid restaurants, the Verudela peninsula is a favourite weekend playground, especially on Sunday afternoons when locals idle in cafés or stroll along shady paths. A headland track loops around an Austro-Hungarian fort which houses a lacklustre **aquarium** of Adriatic sealife (*open April–Oct daily 9–9; Nov–Mar Sat–Sun 11–5; adm*) and ambles past the best town beaches. Proximity to the resort hotels also makes them the busiest, however; escapist locals and in-the-know visitors with their own wheels drive 10km south to cherrypick a pristine cove from the many which notch **Cape Kamenjak**, which pokes a finger of land into the Adriatic from the tip of Istria. Explore paths through a **nature reserve** speckled in spring by white and yellow heather flowers and aromatic Aleppo pines year-round and you understand why its *terra magica* was prime real estate for rustic villas of moneyed Romans.

Day Trips and Overnighters from Pula

Brijuni National Park

In 1885, accompanied by his children, a retired Pula naval officer and a hamper of roast chicken, peaches and wine, Paul Kupelwieser hired a Fažana fishing boat to reach uninhabited island Veli Brijun for a picnic. The Austrian industrial magnate clearly liked what he found, because eight years later he signed the title deeds and began to transform an island abandoned due to malarial mosquitoes into a resort. While the winged pests fell victim to the Nobel Prize-winning know-how of German bacteriologist Robert Koch, Kupelwieser busied himself clearing scrub to create a nine-hole golf course (today expanded to 18) and fashioned villas and luxury hotels to entice the cream of European high society. And lured they were: Austro-Hungarian heir Franz Ferdinand, German emperor Wilhelm II and author Thomas Mann all lazed in the name of recuperation at his élite health resort.

Getting There

Frequent **buses** shuttle 9km north of Pula to village Fažana (12Kn), departure point for ferries to Veli Brijun, which can only be visited on tours organized by the National Par; some larger hotels offer packages (c. 260Kn) which include coach transport to Fažana and often lunch. In addition, private **boats** from Pula harbour operate 5hr sprees to the national park (c. 160Kn), either for a picnic on little sister Mali Brijun or a panoramic jaunt around the archipelago, but do not land on Veli Brijun.

The only way to explore at leisure an island perfect for idle strolling is by an overnight stay in one of three hotels booked through the National Park office (*moderate*).

Tourist Information

Brijuni National Park: Brijunska 10 (harbour-front), Fažana, **t** (052) 521 880, *www.np-brijuni.hr. Open Mon–Sat 8–8, Sun 8–3.*
Fažana: Riva 2, **t** (052) 383 727. *Open summer daily 8–8.*

The war which condemned the era's idle aristocracy also doomed the Austrian's playground – in 1930 his son Karl committed suicide on an island he bankrupted himself trying to revive – and Veli Brijun slumbered until it caught the eye of Yugoslavian president Tito. Two years after his victory parade into Zagreb in 1945, the Partisan leader commandeered the island for Communism, treated himself to official residence the **Bijela Vila** (White Villa) and, when not tending the vegetable plots of his summer retreat, entertained heads of state to slot together the multi-nation economic and political jigsaw of the Non-Aligned Nations movement, or bathed in the limelight of celebrity guests such as Sophia Loren, Gina Lollobrigida or Elizabeth Taylor and Richard Burton. If future leaders have seemed less enthusiastic about a residence still in government hands, at least they have good reason: Veli Brijun flung open its doors to the hoi polloi as a national park three years after Tito's death in 1980.

Two of Kupelwieser's hotels overlook the harbour, from where little trains on national park tours (*available in English; five per day July–Aug 180Kn, June and Sept 170Kn, April–May and Oct 140Kn; one per day Nov–Mar 90Kn; tickets from Fažana park office, includes ferry; advance booking essential in peak season*) potter north through parks whose manicured lawns are clipped by the descendants of the Austrians' deer to reach a **safari park**, created in 1978 for the menagerie of animals gifted to Tito by world leaders. Queen Elizabeth II's Shetland ponies are poor show compared with elephants Sonny and Lanka presented by Indira Gandhi. The tours then head south past Tito's White Villa (still guarded) to pause at the remains of a 2 BC Byzantine castle whose walls enclose the foundations of a 15th-century settlement that was abandoned because of plague.

Back at the harbour, you embark on a whistlestop tour of Istrian ecclesiastical art through Kupelwieser's reproductions of medieval frescoes housed in his rebuilt **St Germaine** church (Crka sveti Germana). Far more intriguing, however, is nearby exhibition '**Tito on Brijuni**'. A floor of stuffed animals, deceased gifts from world leaders, is highly missable, but there's much to enjoy in a quirky photo album of the republic's father-figure beaming when dressed in swimming trunks or pootling in his garden in casuals, then attired in state regalia to greet the jet-set and political leaders. Poor Kupelwieser is all but forgotten in a room that chronicles Veli Brijun's 19th-century creation.

Rovinj

Lovely and uncomplicated, Rovinj is Istria's pin-up. The allure of a medieval port back in bloom after a stormy marriage to the Venetian Republic (1283–1797) is not her intellect – there's little to tick off in the way of high culture – but head-turning looks. Shoehorned into an old town huddled into an oval, as if still constrained on the island engineers linked to the mainland in 1763, is an absurdly picturesque medieval warren and harbour. Visit islet Svete Katarina (*see* p.62) opposite and look back, and the town appears like the vision of a romantic artist made actual: houses in rich shades which seem to have ripened in the sun jostle on the seafront, and a dappled jumble of terra-cotta roofs climbs to a mighty church. Of course, being everyone's favourite It girl has its downsides – too many people and too high prices in August – but even when Rovinj's enchantment is more manic *Sorcerer's Apprentice* than romantic *Cinderella* there's an certain fizz in the air. Visit late in the season and ravishing Rovinj encourages more intimate exploration.

Start at main harbourside square **Trg Maršala Tita**, lined with cafés in which to see and be seen. The counts of Califfi would splutter in disgust that their Baroque palace at the back of the triangular square has been gutted to house the **Town Museum** (Gradska muzej; *open June–Sept Tues–Sun 9–12 and 7–10; Oct–May Tues–Sat 9–1; adm*) and small wonder, considering the musty displays of Roman odds and ends plus scraps of stone rescued from 9th-century Carolingian church St Thomas's on the ground floor. The 17th- and 18th-century aristocrats might feel more comfortable with a small gallery of largely Italian Old Masters upstairs; the pure simplicity of Giovanni Bellini's 15th-century *Madonna and Child with Saints* puts Renaissance show-off neighbours to shame. Look, too, for a lovely contemporary *Adoration of the Magi* by Bonifazio de Pitati.

Getting There

Hourly **buses** trundle north to Rovinj in 1hr 10mins and cost 26Kn.

Tourist Information

Rovinj: Obala Pina Budicina 12, **t** (052) 811 566, *www.tzgrovinj.hr. Open June–Sept daily 8–10; Oct–May daily 8–4.*

Eating Out

Rovinj t (052) –
Tear yourself from the lovely views claimed by the touristy restaurants round the harbour and the best cuisine is found in Rovinj's back streets. For more options and accommodation, *see* 'Touring from Pula', pp.63–5.

Veli Jože, Sveti Križa 1, **t** (052) 816 337 (*moderate*). A little more pricey than the average *konoba*, but more upmarket, too, with a marvellously cluttered bosun's locker of an interior. *Janjetina pečana* (roast lamb) served with potato is delicious (better still with an Istrian red) or try *bakalar in bianco* (dried cod in white wine sauce).

Giannio, Via A. Ferri 38, **t** (052) 813 402 (*moderate*). Don't be fooled by a modest dining room of benches and stone walls, this is an acclaimed seafood address, where sole comes with truffles, and conger and scorpion fish feature alongside bream and bass. *Closed Mon.*

Viecia Batana, Trg Maršala Tita 8; no tel (*cheap*). Pastries and coffees in a locals'-choice café, the most characterful on a central square, and perfect for inexpensive people-watching.

Off the square, the Baroque **Balbi arch** is christened for the noble family whose coat of arms features in the pecking order beneath a growling Lion of St Mark, emblem of the Venetian Republic. Beyond is old town spine-street **Grisia**, thronged in summer and almost impassable when it becomes a free-for-all al fresco art gallery during a mid-August art fair (*usually second Sat*). Follow it uphill and you reach Rovinj's crowning glory, **St Euphemia** (Crkva svete Eufemije; *open July–Aug 8am–10pm; April–June and Sept–Nov 10–6*). Facts – or at least Christian records – say Rovinj's patron saint was thrown to the lions of Constantinople amphitheatre in 304 for daring to denounce the pagan gods of Emperor Diocletian. Local lore claims that Euphemia's stone sarcophagus washed up miraculously at Rovinj's harbour on 13 July 800 and was hauled uphill to then-humble church St George's by a boy and some oxen strengthened through divine intervention when the town's horses proved too feeble. Prosaic academics suggest that fishermen smuggled the marble sarcophagus out of Constantinople during purges of iconoclast emperor Nicefor. Either way, the 6th-century marble box, surrounded by frescoes of the saint's legend, lies in state behind the right altar of the hulking Baroque pile erected in 1725. She also enjoys the best views in town as a wind vane from the summit of a 200ft campanile modelled on St Mark's, Venice, and whose **belvedere** (*adm*) provides the best views in Rovinj.

Away from these showpieces, Rovinj reveals her charms to those willing to get to know her properly. Simply follow your instincts in the streets that spread beneath the church and you'll discover a medieval and Renaissance beauty which seems wafted over from the other side of the Adriatic: cobbled alleys trickle like tributaries down to the harbour, winding through tightly packed houses whose speciality chimneys thrust skywards during a population explosion that converted every spare room into living quarters. East of its cosy pocket, at Obala Giordano Paliaga 5, the **Aquarium** (Akvarij; *open daily mid-April–Oct 9–8; adm*) has brought Adriatic aquatics onto dry land since 1891. For a glimpse of the real thing, take a dip at the shingle beaches of pine-shaded islets **Svete Katarina** (St Katherine) and **Crveni Otok** (Red Island), reached by a half-hourly ferry from the harbour and marina opposite the town.

Venice

Venezialines catamarans zip to Venice mid-May–mid-Sept.

La Serenissima, a Canaletto cityscape where time has held its breath, Pula's beautiful former owner needs no introduction and is achingly close to her former charge, just a three-hour blast across the Adriatic. Timetables may enforce a stay of three days, but since when has that been a hardship? *See* pp.208–18.

Touring from Pula: Note
Those with time on their hands can extend the five-day itinerary of coastal and inland Istria (*see* following pages) by hooking up to the three-day jaunt around islands Krk and Cres from Rijeka (*see* pp.76–8). Otherwise, the tour ends at Rijeka with a straight run back to Pula on the E751.

Touring from Pula: The Istrian Peninsula

Day 1: A Trio of Saints and an Enchantress

Morning: Take the main road north of Pula to **Vodnjan**. Never mind a defiantly Italian community, forget a Gothic warren which crumbles quietly around Narodni trg – the town's fame is for its mummified saints, Leon Bembo, Giovanni Olini and Nicholas Bursa. Peer behind the altar of the Church of St Blaise (Crkva svetog Blaža; *open June–Sept daily 9–7; Oct–May by request to priest*) to venerate the medieval trio quietly working miracle cures on the devout and needy from their glass boxes, then enter the sacristy – the Collection of Sacral Art (*adm*) treasures its 1321 polyptych of Bembo in action which served as his coffin lid, plus an anatomy of holy body parts. Flee 10km north to warm chilled blood in enchanting **Bale**. Follow the cobbled streets which spiral up to neo-Baroque hilltop church of St Elizabeth and you'll pass the Soardo-Bembo Palace, boast of a 15th-century Venetian beside a main town gate stamped with the republic's Lion of St Mark. Continue 10km west to **Rovinj** for lunch.

Lunch: In Rovinj, *see* below.

Afternoon: Explore the alleys which burrow like woodworm holes through an architectural-encyclopedia old town shoehorned on to a peninsula and you'll understand why artists sigh over Rovinj. Old Masters can be seen in the Town Museum (*see* p.61); picture-postcard images are available from the 200ft-high campanile of hilltop church St Euphemia; and enchantment is everywhere. For full information on Rovinj, *see* pp.61–2.

Dinner and Sleeping: In Rovinj, *see* below.

Day 1

Lunch and Dinner in Rovinj

Veli Jože, Sveti Križa 1, **t** (052) 816 337 (*moderate*). A little more pricey than the average *konoba*, but more upmarket, too, with a marvellously cluttered of an interior. *Janjetina pečana* (roast lamb) served with spuds is delicious (best with an Istrian red).

Toni, Driovier 3, **t** (052) 815 303 (*moderate*). Good-value pastas such as fusilli with scampi and truffles or a tasty tagliatelle with scampi and mushrooms, plus fillers like sheep-milk cheese in a charming trattoria.

Giannio, Via A. Ferri 38, **t** (052) 813 402 (*moderate*). Don't be fooled by a modest dining room of benches and stone walls; this is an acclaimed seafood address. *Closed Mon.*

Viecia Batana, Trg Maršala Tita 8; no tel (*cheap*). Pastries and coffees in the most characterful café on the central square.

Sleeping in Rovinj

Angelo d'Oro, Vladimir Švalba 38–42, **t** (052) 840 502 (*expensive*). Booking is essential to claim one of 23 rooms in this luxury hotel, an effortless marriage of four-star facilities, 1600s features and antiques. Breakfast comes on a garden terrace and its classy restaurant (*expensive*) is Rovinj's gourmet treat; the sea bass in a salt crust is exquisite.

Katarina, Sveta Katarina, **t** (052) 804 100 (*expensive*). Pricey, but oh, the romance of a staying on a wooded island which boasts Rovinj's best beaches. Superior doubles in the modern four-star are worth the extra €9.

Adriatic, Trg Maršala Tita, **t** (052) 815 088 (*moderate*). Fabulously located on the main square beside the harbour, although it has just 27 rooms so reservations are a must.

Source **private rooms** at **Natale-Lokva**, Carducci 4, **t** (052) 813 365, by the bus station.

Day 2: North Up the Coast

Morning: Drag yourself from Rovinj inland towards **Kanfanar**, then, before it, turn to Dvigrad (signposted). Sieges by Uskok pirates were the final blow of a battalion of sorrows – plague, taxes and clashes between Austrians and the Venetian Republic – which assaulted the town and prompted the last citizens to pack their bags in 1630. Follow a path around defence walls and watchtowers mailed in ivy to explore streets lined with the shells of houses; with the right eyes you can trace the layout of three-nave early Christian basilica St Sophia at the town rear. Backtrack west, go through Gradina towards Vrsar, then follow the coast north to **Poreč**. Although its street map retains their Dekumanus spine-street, its Roman founders wouldn't recognize Istria's largest tourist resort, whose shameless tack is rescued by a shimmering skin of exquisite Byzantine mosaics comparable to those of Ravenna in the 6th-century Basilica of Euphrasius (Eurfrazijeva basilika; *open daily 7–7*). Ponder rooftop views from the campanile (*adm*) or early Christian mosaics in an adjacent museum (*adm*).
Lunch: In Poreč, *see* below.
Afternoon: Drive 8km east towards Višnjan to the **Baredine Cave** (Jama Baredine; *open July–Aug 9.30–6; May–June and Sept 10–5; April and 1–15 Oct 10–4; adm*); during the 40min tours, guides revel in the yarn of a 13th-century milkmaid cast into the caves and calcified after the mother of local lord disapproved of her son's sweet-heart. Alternatively catch a ferry (*daily 7–11, every 30mins; 14Kn*) from Poreč to laze on island **Sveti Nikola** which has the town's best beaches – just don't expect to have them to yourself. Spend the night in **Novigrad**, 20km north of Poreč.
Dinner and Sleeping: In Novigrad, *see* below.

Day 2

Lunch in Poreč

Dvi Murve, Grožnjanska 17, Vranići, **t** (052) 434 115 (*expensive*). In the top five of Istrian gourmet addresses, signposted off the road to Vrs, 3km north of the centre. The style is elegant rustic, the cuisine exquisite, with fish dishes such as a carpaccio of sea bass and frogfish on the menu alongside game, and the wine list is sensational.
Peterokutna Kula, Dekomanska 1, **t** (0 52) 451 378 (*expensive–moderate*). Classy dining in the most atmospheric restaurant in the centre, whose terrace claims a 15th-century Venetian tower. For a lunchtime splurge, tuck into a thick steak in truffles.
Istra, Bože Milanovica 30, **t** (0 52) 434 636 (*moderate*). *Jastog sa rezancima* (lobster with tagliatelle) and a house special fish plate feature in this fish restaurant whose ordinary looks belie a good reputation.

Dinner in Novigrad

For cheaper eats, *see* lunch,' Day 3'.
Mandrač, Mandrač 6, **t** (052) 757 120 (*expensive–moderate*). The smartest option in town boasts a large terrace by the inner harbour and a talented chef who prepares fresh fish and grilled steaks. *Closed Mon–Fri in winter*.
Damir & Ornella, Zidine 5, **t** (052) 758 134, (*expensive–moderate*). An upmarket *konoba* with a stone dining room. Culinary adventurers should try Istria-renowned dishes of sushi-style raw fish. *Closed Mon*.

Sleeping in Novigrad

Cittar, Prolaz Venecija 1, **t** (0 52) 757 737 (*moderate*). Understated but tasteful rooms of modern fabrics and parquet floors in a cosy three-star hidden behind town walls.
Rotonda, Rotonda, **t** (0 52) 757 736 (*moderate*) A bland second best nearby, with a pool.

Source **private rooms** via agency **Montakso**, **t** (052) 757 603, in the bus station on Murvi.

Day 3: Novigrad and Buje

Morning: Begin your exploration of friendly **Novigrad**, which, unlike Poreč, refuses to bow to tourist hordes at its heart, Veliki trg. Locals insist on acclaiming its Baroque church of St Pelagius (Crkva svete Pelagija) as the Katedrala (cathedral) despite its demotion in 1831. See why inside – there's ecclesiastical swagger about the Baroque altarpieces and a contemporary altar on which cherubs pout and shamelessly steal attention from Istria's only Romanesque crypt. Streets south lead to most extant sections of the 13th-century castellated walls, which survived the 1687 Turkish raid that obliterated much of Novigrad. For a dip, however, choose a private cove backed by pines among notches in the rocky coastline north of town; the desperate (or lazy) can suffer the concrete platforms before large resort hotels 1km south.

Lunch: In Novigrad, *see* below.

Afternoon: Head 20km northeast from Novigrad to quietly bustling rustic **Buje**, which earned its nickname as the 'Guard of Istria' by watching over trade routes from its defensive hilltop; from aptly named street Belvedere, admire the panorama over the countryside. The crowning glory of a gently crumbling medieval town where there are picture-postcard images everywhere is the Baroque church of St Servolo (Crkva svetog Servula), studded with the pillars and a funerary slab of an earlier Roman temple. Beneath the town, the Ethnographic Museum (*open June–Sept Mon–Sat 9–12 and 5–8; adm*) has rustic handicrafts, and dinky church the Madonna of Mercy (Crka majke milosrdja) opposite hides Baroque altarpieces. There are no hotels in Buje; find a bed by driving northwest on the Slovenia road (to Koper).

Dinner and Sleeping: In Buje, Volpia or Plovanija, *see* below.

Day 3

Lunch in Novigrad

Cok, Sv Antona 2, **t** (052) 757 643 (*moderate*). Lobster with noodles or home-made fusilli pasta thick with truffles come from an extensive menu of excellent Istrian dishes prepared in this old-fashioned *konoba* that's a cut above the usual. Find it near the round-about before the inner harbour.

Sidro, Mandrač 5, **t** (052) 757 604 (*moderate*). The same terrace views of fishing boats as its upmarket neighbour Mandrač (*see* Day 2) come at lower prices, in a restaurant whose chef prepares a catch of fresh fish plus a herd of charcoal-barbecued meats.

Pivinca Park, Mandrač 24, **t** (052) 757 775 (*cheap*). A lovely lunch spot where al fresco tables are screened by a small park. Fishy pastas and risottos are perfect for a light lunch, chef specials slow-cooked under a *peka* (*moderate*) sate larger hungers.

Dinner in Buje

Olivia, Via Giuseppe Verde 9, **t** (052) 772 050 (*moderate*). Just downhill and a little more upmarket, this prepares good seafood and pastas with local speciality truffles.

Pod Voltum, Ante Bibić, **t** (052) 772 232 (*cheap*). Sturdy Istrian rustic fillers such as *njoki sa gulaš* (gnocchi with goulash) plus the usual steaks in a no-nonsense locals' choice *konoba* near the museum.

Dinner and Sleeping in Volpia

Volpia, Volpia 3, **t** (052) 777 425 (*moderate*). Beg for a room in Croatia's first agrotourism hotel, a friendly, family-run treat carved from granny's stone house and which oozes modern-rustic charm. It also prepares super seasonal dishes from all-local produce.

Sleeping in Plovanija

Miro, **t** (052) 777 050 (*moderate*). A rather flashy casino-hotel before the border, with modest business-style accommodation.

Day 4: Piran

Morning: Continue north and cross the border at Plovanija to reach Slovenian coastal jewel Piran, signposted off the E751 near Portorož; a *bureau de change* at Customs exchanges kunas for tolars (euros from 2007). Begin your tour of Slovenia's Rovinj, stuffed with Gothic-Venetian beauties by former Italian rulers, at lovely marble oval **Tartinijev trg**, named after dapper 18th-century violinist Giuseppe Tartini at its centre. He's honoured in his former home, **Tartini's House** (Tartinijeva Hiša; *open daily June–Aug 9–12 and 6–9; Sept–May 11–12 and 5–6; adm*), unlike the merchant who fell for a local beauty and inscribed '*Lassa pur dir*' (let them talk) on his nearby Gothic mansion, **Venetian House**. On a ridge north, the **Cathedral of St George** (Stolna Cerkev sv. Jurija) is slowly revealing Baroque altars and a splendid organ during its extended restoration, but always shows church treasures and statuary in its **museum** (Župnijski muzej; *open Mon–Fri 10–1 and 4–7, Sat and Sun 10–8; adm*) and fabulous views from a 1609 **campanile** (*adm*) modelled on St Mark's in Venice.

Lunch: In Piran, *see* below.

Afternoon: Other ecclesiastical charmers are south: **St Mary of the Snows** (Sv Marija Snežne), with a salute to the miracle of snow, and, opposite, the Minorite Monastery (Minortitski samostan) with a lovely cloister (*both open through tourist board; Tartinjev trg 2*). While waiting, thread south to the **Sergej Mašera Maritime Museum** (*open Tues–Sun June–Sept 9–12 and 3–6; July-Aug 6–9; adm*), a salute to local Piran salt and shipping in an 1800s palace. For a shot of metropolitan vim, continue north to nip across the Italian border into **Trieste**, *see* pp.194–9.

Dinner and Sleeping: In Piran or Trieste, *see* below.

Day 4

Lunch and Dinner in Piran

Identikit fish restaurants on seafront Prešernovo narbreže claim the best views.

Galeb, Pusterla ulica 5, **t** (05) 673 32 35 (*moderate*). It's worth booking ahead to secure one of only five tables in this friendly locals' choice east of the lighthouse at the peninsula tip. A friendly husband-and-wife team offer grilled catch of the day; exquisite *brancin* (sea bass) in olive oil and garlic or fat and succulent *škampi*. A gem.

Stara Gostilna, Savudrijska 2, **t** (05) 673 31 65 (*cheap*). A charming inn with a pavement terrace for al fresco dining on a side street close to the seafront gaggle, but a world away in attitude. Start with a treat of Karst *pršut* ham, then choose from a menu of sturdy meats and Adriatic fish.

Tartini Café, Tartinijev trg 3, **t** (05) 673 33 81 (*cheap*). On the main square, with powerful hits of coffee and sticky, sweet treats to revive after a hard morning's sightseeing.

Teater Café, Stjenkova ulica 1, no tel (*cheap*). Buzzy and hugely popular café with a water-front terrace, a sprinkling of antiques and surly waiters. Marvellous, but pricey.

Sleeping in Piran

Tartini, Tartinijev trg 15 **t** (05) 671 10 00 (*moderate*). A class act with an eye for stylish modern décor and a location on the central square; pay an extra €12 for sea views and a balcony. It has a pool and parking, too.

Piran, Stjenkova 1, **t** (05) 676 25 02 (*moderate*). Smack on the waterfront, with 80 modern en-suite rooms, plus a good restaurant and panorama bar.

Source private accommodation through tourist agencies **Turist Biro**, Tomažičeva ulica 3, **t** (05) 673 25 09, or **Maona**, Cankarjevo nabrežje 7, **t** (05) 673 45 20.

See pp.198–9 for eating/sleeping in **Trieste**.

Day 5: Inland Istria

Morning: Backtrack south to Buje to continue your exploration of inland Istria in
Grožnjan, the region's most enchanting hilltown 8km east of Buje on the Buzet
road. 1960s artists restored a village crumbling into ruin to create an idyllic '*grad
umjetnika*' ('town of artists') full of galleries and workshops. So glorious are today's
flower-filled alleys that it's forgivable to overlook the older glories: the Baroque
church of saints Vitus, Modestus and Crescentia with folksy decorated pews; a
Renaissance loggia (1557) where Venetian Republic judges deliberated; and, through
a town gate, the church (1554) of Sts Cosimo and Damian.

Lunch: Tear yourself 6km east to Motovun for lunch, *see below*.

Afternoon: Jolly coach tours blight the most famous hill town in Istria, but there's no
denying the appeal of **Motovun**'s medieval charm, at its grandest around central
Renaissance church St Stephen's, or that of the views from ramparts built by 1300s
Venetians: the republic stamped its winged lion on the main gate. Past hilltop
Buzet, care-worn truffle capital of Istria, dosy village **Roč** encircled by 16th-century
stone walls studs a main gate with a lapidarium of Roman tombstones. Just before
it, a road bears right to **Hum**. Concrete sculptures celebrate Byzantine Glagolitic
script, more alien than ecclesiastical, en route to theis 'smallest town in the world',
a Lilliput city of walls, with watchtowers enjoyed by a population of 17. If it's open
ponder 12th-century frescoes in the cemetery church of St Jerome or pick up
souvenir Glagolitic penned by local schoolchildren in a gallery-*vinotech*. Back on the
main road, drive to Rijeka then Opatija (*see* pp.68–75).

Dinner and Sleeping: In Hum or Opatija, *see below*.

Day 5

Lunch in Motovun

Barbacan, Barbakan 1, no tel (*expensive*).
Truffles with everything in a *konoba* before
the city gates which unites rustic charm and
style. Beef and lamb have a twang of New
World and Mediterranean accents.

Pod Voltun, Trg Josefa Ressala 6, no tel
(*moderate*). Touristy but atmospheric dining
'under the vaults' of the Venetian inner gate.
Its chef has a truffle infatuation.

Kastel, Trg Andrea Antico 7, t (052) 681 607
(*moderate*). Istrian speciality *manestra*, a
spicy soup of beans, spuds and noodles, plus
pasta thick with jugged venison rustled up
in a hotel restaurant – be prepared to wait
for a table on the showpiece square.

Dinner in Hum

Humska Konoba, Hum 2 t (052) 660 005
(*moderate*). It's worth lingering in Hum to
dine in this lovely *konoba* with a menu of fat

home-made *kobasice* (sausages) and idyllic
country views from its terrace. *Closed Mon
Oct–Nov and April–May; Mon–Fri Jan–Feb*.

Dinner and Sleeping in Opatija

For more Opatija options, *see* pp.74–5.

Villa Ariston, Maršala Tita 179, t (051) 271 379
(*expensive*). Book ahead to claim a room in
this reassuringly old-style villa. Unbeatable
for a romantic last-night splurge.

Kvarner, Park 1, t (051) 271 233 (*moderate*). The
outer proportions are grander than the
modest rooms, which are nevertheless
comfy and quietly tasteful, but the *grande
dame* which kickstarted Opatija's trajectory
retains a whiff of *fin-de-siècle* elegance.

Amfora, Vl Josip Tariba, Volosko, t (051) 701 222
(*expensive*). Excellent lobster and some of
Croatia's finest seafood in a renowned
address in Opatija neighbour Volosko. Classy
sister **Plavi Podrum** (t (051) 701 223; *expensive*) has an almost exclusively fishy menu
and unbeatable location by the harbour.

Rijeka

On Croatia's fairytale coastline, Rijeka is something of an ugly sister. While Split or Zadar boast kernels of creamy stone mansions and idling streets, the *lietmotifs* of the industrious city which stops northern Croatia nodding off in a surfeit of sunshine and Istrian red wine are the cargo hulks and cranes of the country's largest port; and while most Istrian or Dalmatian cities daydream, dynamo Rijeka thrums as the country's third largest city. For that we can thank Austria. Ambitious Austrians snatched up the dozy 15th-century port as an Adriatic base before the Venetian Republic could add yet another name to its list of acquisitions on Croatia's coastline. They certainly looked after their city, though. Fostering 1700s trade routes and elevating Rijeka to a free port, the rulers drip-fed money into their prize to transform it into a powerhouse of

Getting There

Between April and Oct Croatian Airlines **flies** from Heathrow in 2hrs 25mins. From Slovenia, two **trains** a day travel direct from Ljubljana to Rijeka (2hrs 30mins).

Getting from the Airport

Croatian Airlines **buses** co-ordinate with flights to shuttle arrivals from Rijeka's airport 25km south on island Krk to Jelačićev trg (25Kn) and leave from the same stop 1hr 30mins before departures. Expect to pay around 280Kn for a **taxi**.

Getting Around

Central Rijeka is eminently walkable. **Buses** for Opatija (see 'Where to Stay' and pp.74–5) and Trsat leave from the local bus station on Jelačićev trg.

Car Hire

Hertz, Riva 6, **t** (051) 311 098.
Avis, Riva 22, **t** (051) 337 917.
Budget, Dolac 4, **t** (051) 214 742.
AGO, Trg Republike Hrvatske 4, **t** (051) 337 547.

Tourist Information

Rijeka: Korzo 33, **t** (051) 335 882, *www.tz-rijeka.hr*. Open Mon–Sat 8–8, Sun 8–2. An enthusiastic office at the hub of pedestrianized high street Korzo provides free detailed maps and city tourist information booklets.

Festivals

As if to compensate for a largely faceless cityscape, Rijeka lets rip during Croatia's biggest **carnival** (*karneval*). A week of boisterous bonhomie climaxes on the Sunday before Shrove Tuesday with the International Carnival Procession, a noisy, 5km parade of costumes, floats and, bringing up the rear, traditional *zvončari* – young bucks from surrounding villages, costumed in sheepskins, who clang bells to frighten evil spirits.

Shopping

Rijeka carries out everyday sessions of retail therapy on **Korzo**, although you'll need to hunt away from its parade of high street stores to find the city's most famous souvenir, jewellery of city mascot the *morčići*, a moorish figure with a white turban. Aristocratic 19th-century Austrians – including Empress Maria-Anna, who should have known better – popularized as jewellery Rijeka's take on the Venetian *moretto*, and **Mala Galerija**, Užarska 25, retails enamel and gold brooches and earrings of the figure crafted in Rijeka since the 17th century. For folksy sculptures and *objets d'art*, try **Pokon galerija**, Strossmayerova 6c.

Where to Stay

Rijeka t (051) –
Rijeka assumes that its visitors hurry to the hotels and restaurants of the Opatija Riviera

shipbuilding, an industry which still fills local coffers. And even though the wartime occupation by Italian fascists put Rijeka in the sights of Allied bombadiers, who reduced it to a woebegone widow of the Adriatic, the city retains treasured heirlooms from her past as a grand lady under the protectorate of Austria's 19th-century partner, Hungary. Yes, Rijeka has more than its fair share of dreary apartment blocks, but in streets such as Korzo or showpiece public buildings you can almost sense ghosts in the smart tweed suits and stiff leather brogues of 19th-century Budapest.

Around the Korzo

Fattened with late-1700s prosperity, Rijeka burst beyond the stone girdle of its defence walls and erased from the map its moat, today traced by spacious high street **Korzo**, where locals window-shop or exchange news over coffee and whose peeling

15km west and offers just three central hotels; unless your wallet is fat enough for the four-star Bonavia or you're visiting for carnival, better beds are available in the nearby resort town of Opatija (*see* pp.74–5).

Bonavia, Dolac 4, **t** 357 100, *www.bonavia.hr* (*moderate*). A modern and luxurious four-star in the heart of Rijeka, which exudes relaxed comfort in classy rooms of tasteful fabrics and deep carpets to please the toes.

Kontinental, Šetalište A Kačića-Miošića 1, **t** 372 008 (*moderate*). High-ceilinged rooms are a Seventies timewarp of patterned wallpaper and polystyrene ceiling tiles in this rather pricey two-star opposite the stairway to Trsat. Spacious and adequate but frumpy.

Neboder, Strossmayerova 1, **t** 373 538 (*inexpensive*). Five minutes' walk east is this grubby tower block. Fearfully basic rooms of tatty carpets, peeling wallpaper and youth hostel-style furnishings barely deserve their one-star status; a renovation is promised.

Eating Out

Rijeka **t** (051) –

For a gourmet splurge, do as Rijeka locals do for and reserve a table in Opatija (*see* p.75).

Feral, Matje Gupa 5b, **t** 212 274 (*expensive–moderate*). The freshest fish and seafood prepared by Rijeka's most talented chef consistently affords this lovely cellar-style *konoba* hung with fishing nets a place among Croatia's top 100 restaurants. House speciality shellfish are worth investigating, including delicious *gratinirane jakopske*,

gratinated scallops prepared with white wine, tomato and cheese.

Zlatna Školka, Kružna 12, **t** 213 782 (*moderate*). A semi-smart address with a nautical theme secreted off the Korzo; try a rich *jastog na buzaru* (lobster flash-fried in white wine, garlic and parsley). A sister restaurant opposite (*cheap*) serves pizza and pasta in a cosy nook decorated with fishing knick-knacks.

Brun, Ivana Zajca 2, **t** 212 544 (*moderate*). A theatre-goers' favourite with good fish that's smart enough to feel like a proper dinner but without the fussy formalities.

Trsatika, Šetalište Joakima Rakovca 33, Trsat, **t** 217 455 (*moderate*). Lovely lunch spot opposite the pilgrimage church, with a large menu which covers all bases and a large terrace that affords a panorama over Rijeka and the Kvarner Gulf.

Pod Voltun, Pod Voltun 15, **t** 330 806 (*cheap*). A menu of tasty simple dishes such as *bakalar gulaš* (cod goulash) or winter-warmer bean and beef soups ensure a steady stream of locals to this snug, friendly choice beside a car park west of St Vitus's church. Ask about daily specials, always a good bet.

Hemingway Bar, Korzo 28, **t** 212 696 (*cheap*). Rijeka's style slaves nibble croissants and sticky pastries and people-watch or sip evening cocktails beneath grand chandeliers in this homage to streamlined design carved from a Hungarian-era mansion.

Captiano Bar, Riva 10, no tel (*cheap*). Best of the Riva bars, where café society lazes over a *kava* and studiously ignores the cars which thunder past beyond a screen of trees.

Viennese Secession-era grandees and Art Nouveau mansions bequeathed by the Hungarians soften the heart among newcomers with all the style of a breeze block. Those early defence fortifications ended up as filler for the moat, but Rijeka could not bare to part with the **City Tower**, the seafront gateway that greeted medieval sailors. Austrian emperors Leopold I and Charles VI pout like shameless drama queens above a double-headed Imperial eagle on the arch of its rebuilt Baroque upper sections, although the fabulously mustachioed Charles has good reason to look smug – his 1719 elevation of Rijeka to free port catapulted the city into the economic big league.

Pass like the merchants of old through an arch once manned by hawk-eyed guards and you enter the **Stari Grad** (old town), a rather optimistic description for the tatty hotch-potch of patched-up old-timers, swaying derelicts and ugly glass and concrete post-war additions on **Trg Ivana Koblerov**. Were it not for a chunky stone arch secreted in an alley off the square's north side, you'd never guess that you now stand in the military command post which marked Rijeka's début – Roman legionnaires stomped through the portal into Tarsatica.

Northeast is square **Grivica**, in awe of **St Vitus's Church** (Crka sv. Vida). Eager to reclaim a congregation wooed by the Reformation with a more magnificent church, 17th-century Jesuits revived the legend of one Petar Lončarić, a gambler so frustrated at his luck during a hand of cards in 1296 that he is said to have hurled a stone at the order's crucifix. The wooden effigy of Jesus bled, the 13th-century player was swallowed whole into the ground and Rijeka Jesuits proclaimed their Gothic crucifix miraculous, a dubious tale which nevertheless so impressed Countess Ursula von Thanhausen that in 1638 she pledged funds for architect Giacomo Briani to lay the first brick of today's church, modelled on Santa Maria della Salute in Venice. The money-spinning Gothic crucifix hangs in pride of place in the rotunda.

Around Jadranski Trg

Architecture aficionados should sidetrack west of the Korzo to **Jadranski trg**, dominated by a pair of Rijeka landmarks: on the south flank, the late-1800s **Adriatic Palace** is the Historicist boast of a shipping company – a quartet of sailors strike preposterous heroic poses on the Riva (*see* below) side; and on the west rises lone survivor of 1930s Italian occupation the **Rijeka Skyscraper**, a stack of cubes cruelly (but understandably) mocked by locals as a 'chest of drawers'. Explore north up Erazma Barčića, past protomodernist **Teatro Fenice** (1913) which dithers between geometrical Secession and early Futurism and lives in reduced circumstances as a scruffy cinema, to reach **Dolac**. Here the university library hosts occasional exhibitions of challenging work in the **Modern Art Gallery** (Moderna galerija; *open Tues–Sun 10–1 and 5–8; adm*). In theory, you can also ponder the library's room of manuscripts inked in Glagolitic, not extraterrestrial for all its looks, but actually the Greek-based alphabet of medieval Croatian ecclesiastics; in practice the **Glagolitic Exhibition** (Izložba glagoljice; *open Mon–Fri 8–3; adm*) is often closed. A block west of Jadranski trg, looming over the bus station, the Capuchin church of **Our Lady of Lourdes** is a neo-Gothic surprise in Rijeka's modern cityscape. Inspired by a visit to France, Superior of the Capuchin monastery Bernardin Škrivanić nurtured visions of Rijeka as a pilgrimage centre when his homage to Lourdes began to rise in 1900. His enthusiasm wasn't matched by his funds, however, and the project stalled until a 'St Jochanza' loosened locals' purse strings by miraculously sweating blood. The church finally stood in all its Venetian neo-Gothic glory by 1929, 16 years after the showman saint was arrested for fraud.

The Museums

Northwest of St Vitus, past the overbearing Palace of Justice and across Žrtava fašizma, the **Govenor's Palace** is a wonderfully stocky neo-Renaissance 1869 pile erected by new arrivals the Hungarians to awe locals. They weren't the only ones who whistled in appreciation. So impressed by its declaration of authority was Italian Gabriele D'Annunzio that he commandeered the palace after his few hundred black-shirted *arditi* took Fiume (literally 'river', the Italian translation of Rijeka) unopposed on 12 September 1919, deeming it a suitable personal headquarters for the self-proclaimed leader of 'the Italian Regency of Carnaro'. For a heady year during his occupation, the First World War pilot, poet and unrepentant fascist stood on his balcony to deliver orations and watch nightly fireworks displays while the *arditi* silenced dissenters of his pioneer totalitarian state with overdoses of castor oil. It was only after D'Annunzio went too far and declared war on Italy's spineless leaders – it was their sulky withdrawal from the Paris Peace Conference, which had snubbed Italian ambitions on Fiume, that had spurred the warrior-poet into action – that premier Giovanni Giolitti tired of diplomacy and ordered battleship *Andrea Doria* to attack Rijeka. The mini-dictator ousted in December 1920, Fiume was declared a free state – but not for long. Inspired by D'Annunzio, Il Duce goose-stepped into town in 1922, then consolidated his smash-and-grab raid through the 1924 Treaty of Rome.

The formal atrium of the Hungarian palace and sumptuous interiors of gloriously over-the-top Historicism are as Hungarian governors knew them, today on show as the **History and Marine Museum** (Pomorski i povijesni muzej; *open winter Tues–Fri 9–6, Sat 9–1; summer Tues–Fri 9–8, Sat 9–1; adm*). The exhibits – a salute to Rijeka's port above, with nautical knick-knacks such as model ships, navigation equipment and oils of barques, and a ground-floor display of rustic regional crafts – are overawed by such decorative splendour. More museums are at the palace's shoulders: on the left, the **Rijeka City Museum** (Muzek grade Rijeka; *open Mon–Fri 10–1 and 5–8, Sat 10–1; adm*) hosts temporary exhibitions of local history; and behind the palace to the northeast there are so-so displays of Adriatic geology and sealife in the **Natural History Museum** (Prirodoslovni muzej; *open Mon–Sat 9–7, Sun 9–3; adm*).

Along the Riva

Lined by the grand offices of Hungarian shipping magnates, the **Riva** is a missed opportunity where café society might laze to drink in port views and lattes. Instead, industrious Rijeka has no time for the sort of unproductive frippery favoured by other Croatian cities – yes, there are a handful of cafés, but oh, the traffic: four lanes, cease-less. Suffer the fumes as you walk east into **Ivana Zajca** for the main **market**, where a wonderland of cheeses and pastries, breads and meats is crammed into two 1880s pavilions; a sister pavilion (1914) stocks fresh fish beneath a frieze of Adriatic sea life.

On the far side of an adjacent scruffy park, the **Croatian National Theatre** (1885) keeps up appearances as the *grande dame* of cultural life under the Hungarian rulers. Its formal public airs relax inside a concert hall (*viewing by appointment or during concerts*) adorned with dreamy frescoes by Gustav and Ernst Klimt, one of the first commissions for the brothers' short-lived company before Gustav flew solo.

Trsat

Between the world wars, Rijeka stagnated at the farthest reaches of the Italian kingdom and glowered at rival **Sušak**, a cheeky 19th-century upstart then flourishing as a Yugoslav border town, today a mere suburb. Between 1924 and 1941, visitors had to show passports as they crossed the grubby river Rječina, as it demarcated the Italy-Yugoslavia border; today you can follow unimpeded the adjunct Mrtvi Kanal to reach **Titov trg**. Here, a Baroque gateway crowned with a relief of the Virgin leads to a **staircase** to quell the stoutest heart. Good pilgrims who puff up the 538 steps beyond, instigated as an act of devotion by a 1531 military captain, will climb to pilgrimage centre **Trsat** – spare a thought for devout believers who ascend on their knees during holy of holy days 10 May as you climb past votive chapels. Agnostics can catch bus 1 or 1a from the stop on Fiumara.

On 10 May 1291, puffed angels charged with spiriting the Nazareth Tabernacle away from invading heathens paused for a breather in hilltop village Trsat, now swallowed in Rijeka's sprawl. Believe the hype and the angelic removal men whisked the house of the Virgin and Joseph to Loreto, near Ancona, Italy, three years later and Rijeka could only commemorate the spot with the **Church of Our Lady of Trsat** (Gospa Tratske). Not that it did too badly out of the event. In the hushed sanctuary of a largely Biedermeier replacement for that 13th-century progenitor church, an icon of Mary hung with votive beads has been quietly working miracles ever since its donation in 1367, Pope Urban V's gift to console Trsat for its loss.

Evidence of its power fills the **Chapel of Votive Gifts** (Kapela zavjetnih darova), squirrelled away off the Baroque cloister of the adjacent **Franciscan monastery** and which makes up in personality for what it lacks in ecclesiastical pomp. Paintings of doe-eyed Madonnas who interceded for accident victims or recent Homelands War casualties, embroideries of storm-tossed ships, even crutches presumably tossed aside after a miracle cure hang on walls inked with grateful graffiti .

Roman guards first kept a keen eye out for marauding barbarians from a frontier watchtower here; then medieval Frankopan counts, Croatian aristocracy from island Krk, spied the strategic potential of the hilltop location and wrote the next chapter of **Trsat Castle** (Tratska gradina; *open June–Sept daily 9–8; April–June and Oct daily 9–5; Nov–Mar 9–3; adm free*) reached via a lane opposite the church. Tramp its walkways and towers, which offer Rijeka's finest views across the Kvarner Gulf to the humps of Krk and Cres, and you can understand why Irish-born Austrian Field-Marshal Count Laval Nugent fell for its charms and determined to restore sections of the crumbling castle in neo-Gothic as a museum for his war booty and prize paintings. The eccentric commander also created the dumpy Doric temple at its centre; his '*mir junaka*' (haven for heroes) family mausoleum is now a gallery space.

Overnighters from Rijeka: The Opatija Riviera

Never mind that it was christened after a 1420s Benedictine abbey (*opatija*), hidden as the kernel of the seafront **St James's Church** (Crkva Sveti Jakov), **Opatija** dates its birth to 1844. Seeking a retreat from totting up balance sheets, Rijeka tycoon Iginio Scarpa fell in love with the nearby sleepy fishing village huddled around its ecclesiastical founding father and treated himself to Villa Angiolina, a grand holiday home named in lament for his deceased wife and screened in a park of leafy exotics. Here he softened up business partners with aristocratic luxury and cultivated relations with élite Habsburgs such as Austro-Hungarian Empress Marie Anne, wife of Ferdinand I. However, it was railways not regents which elevated Opatija to the St-Tropez of Central Europe. In 1882 the Society of Southern Railways pioneered a link from Rijeka to Budapest and Vienna, snapped up Scarpa's villa and in two years knocked up the eastern Adriatic's first hotel, today **Hotel Kvarner**. Life in Opatija was never the same again. Lured by the microclimate of a resort protected from blasts of cold north wind the bura, a *Who's Who* of Central Europe flocked to play and promenade in the fashionable winter playground: Gustav Mahler recuperated from an operation to toil over the reorchestration of his fourth symphony; Anton Chekhov escaped his Russian gloom to stroll in sunshine; dancer Isadora Duncan found inspiration in Opatija's fluttering palm leaves; and James Joyce idled over coffee in the Hotel Imperial (and did precious little else during his stay, apparently).

Just a decade after its debut, Opatija was knighted an aristocrat among resorts when Austrian emperor Franz Josef staged a historic 1894 meeting with German emperor Wilhelm II, a trip he must have enjoyed, since he returned ten years later to salute Swedish king Oscar. Even though war nipped in the bud such heady *fin-de-siècle* glamour and today's Italian, German and, increasingly, American silver-hairs have swapped tweed suits for cashmere cardigans, there remains a hint of old-fashioned gentility about Croatia's oldest resort. Showy Viennese Secession hotels erected at lightning pace during 1885–94 and villas of the moneyed élite line parts of arterial **Maršala Tita**, although it's a steady stream of traffic rather than carriages which now fills the arterial road. Fortunately Scarpa's **Villa Angiolina** remains at peace in its park of specimens from Japan, South America, Australia and China seeded by Viennese architect Carl Schubert; the stately pile of sugary stucco frills is fronted by neo-Renaissance parterre hedge geometry, and its manicured lawn fringed with exuberant palms begs for a picnic party in boaters and blazers. Check with the tourist board to discover if the tycoon's neoclassical interior – a joy of frescoed ceilings, Corinthian capitals and marble floors – is open to view over summer. If not, you can admire its luxury by attending one of the classical music concerts held here.

Opatija's favourite attraction, though, is seafront promenade the **Lungomare**. The 12km footpath completed by Southern Railways to coincide with the glamorous débutante's 1889 coming-out party, when she was presented as a spa and recuperation resort before a European élite crazy for seawater bathing, is a treat which ambles past lush Mediterranean planting and a string of enticing swimming spots which end at the last (or lazy) choice for swimmng, Opatija's concrete Lido, before the villa.

Getting There and Around

Every 20 minutes, **bus** 32 from Rijeka follows the coastline through Volosko to Opatija in approx 25mins, then trundles on to Lovran. A single ticket to Opatija and Volosko costs 12Kn from the driver or 18.70Kn for a double ticket bought from kiosks, and to Lovran costs 16Kn or 22Kn.

Tourist Information

Opatija: Maršala Tita 101, **t** (051) 271 310, *www.opatija-tourism.hr. Open May–Sept daily 8am–10pm, otherwise Mon–Sat 8–3.*
Lovran: beside harbour, **t** (051) 291 740, *www.tz-lovran.hr. Open May–Sept Mon–Sat 8am–8pm, Sun 8–12, otherwise Mon–Fri 9–4.*

Where to Stay

Opatija **t** (051) –

Far from cheap perhaps, Opatija is neverthe-less awash with accommodation and boasts the best beds in the Rijeka region. Those on a budget can source **rooms in private houses** (*cheap*) through central tourist agency **Katarina Line**, Maršala Tita 71/1, **t** 272 110.

Villa Ariston, Maršala Tita 179, **t** 271 379, *www.villa-ariston.hr* (*expensive*). Book ahead to secure one of six plush rooms or two suites in this reassuringly old-fashioned villa 1km west of Opatija and you can enjoy breakfast on a seafront terrace which has hosted a *Who's Who* of Habsburgs, assorted Kennedys and Coco Chanel. Every bit as enticing is its gourmet restaurant whose master chef dreams up exquisite Croat-international crossover dishes in an elegant Biedermeier dining room. The connoisseur's choice.
Milenij, Maršala Tita 109, **t** 202 000, *www.ugohoteli.hr* (*expensive*). A five-star in the centre of Opatija; choose from tasteful modern rooms in the main hotel or enjoyably old-fashioned luxury rooms and suites in an adjacent villa.
Kvarner, Park 1, **t** 271 233, *www.liburnia.hr* (*moderate*). Admittedly, proportions are grander than the rather dated rooms, which are comfy and tasteful, but the *grande dame* which kickstarted Opatija's trajectory in 1884 retains a whiff of *fin-de-siècle* elegance and service is friendly and exact.
Palace-Bellevue, Maršala Tita 144–6, **t** 271 811, *www.liburnia.hr* (*moderate*). Two competi-tively priced old-timers under one banner, both with a comfy mish-mash of *fin-de-siècle* pomp in public areas – the Palace foyer

Volosko and Lovran

Follow the main coastal path 1.5km north past parks of cypresses, pines, magnolias and palms and you reach enchanting **Volosko**, which remembers its past as a fishing village despite being swallowed into Opatija's sprawl. This little sister of showy Opatija is actually more charming, a cosy pocket of alleys which trickle down past villas whose flowerboxes burst with blooms to an inner harbour crammed with fishing boats.

Just as delightful is lovely **Lovran**, an easy 5km stroll south of Opatija through villages Ičiči and Ika, beyond which you'll pass the palatial retreats of Austro-Hungarian aristocrats; Viennese Secession architect Carl Siedl sketched much of their flowery Venetian neo-Gothic at the turn of the century. Bays and notches in the coast provide opportunities for a dip on the way, although the best beach of the riviera is 2km beyond Lovran in **Medveja**, a crescent of shingle backed by restaurants and cafés. Recuperating German Wehrmacht soldiers probably couldn't believe their luck when posted to Lovran for R&R between 1943 and 1945.

Leafy Lovran is christened after laurel trees, and poetry is wholly appropriate for the medieval kernel, a charming kasbah-like warren of alleys and houses huddled is a marvel – and flowery fabrics in spacious, old-fashioned rooms. Those of the Palace are a mite smarter, a touch more modern. **Opatija**, Trg V Gortana 2/1, **t** 271 388, *www. hotel-opatija.hr* (*inexpensive*). A little bland, perhaps, this is a good-value cheapie, with compact but perfectly comfortable modern rooms, plus tennis courts and a small pool.

Eating Out

Opatija and Around **t** (051) –

Gourmets rate Opatija's seafood establishments as among the country's best.

Bevanda, Zert 8, Opatija, **t** 712 769 (*expensive*). All sorts of strange Adriatic fishes plus exquisite *jastog* (lobster) and *škampi* (prawns) served by exact waiters wearing cropped nautical jackets in a consistently award-winning seafront restaurant; reservations are a must for a terrace table.

Amfora, Vl Josip Tariba, Volosko, **t** 051 701 222 (*expensive*). Another flagship seafood restaurant, perched above a cove and offering romantic views over Volosko stacked behind its harbour and a menu of consistently excellent specials such as lobster and *buzara od rakova i školjki* (shellfish and crab in tomato, garlic and wine).

Plavi Podrum, harbour, Volosko, **t** 701 223 (*expensive*). The sister restaurant to the Amfora is a quietly classy charmer with a marvellous location beside fishing boats that nod in the inner harbour. The chef peps up shrimp risottos with Istrian truffles and fizzes of champagne on an almost exclusively fishy menu.

Bistro Yacht Club, Zert 1, Opatija, **t** 272 345 (*moderate*). An easy-going eaterie with views over yachts in the little harbour and a cookbook of squid and scampi on the menu.

Kvarner, Maršala Tita 68, Lovran, **t** 291 118 (*moderate*). Grilled fish and succulent meats are served on a terrace overlooking the Lovran harbour.

Buffet Stubica, Stari Grad 25, Lovran, **t** 293 412 (*cheap*). Almost opposite is this chirpy little *konoba*, crammed with the national champion trophies of its fishermen owner, who rustles up a small menu of simple fish – *girice* (whitebait) and *lignje* (squid) – plus seasonal treats. A chirpy little terrace is a delight, though suffers from the traffic.

Madonnina, Pava Tomašica 3, Opatija, **t** 272 579 (*cheap*). A cosy pizzeria opposite the Kvarner Hotel, with a small menu of tasty pizzas and pastas.

tight as if still girdled by the removed defensive wall. On Trg sv. Jurja, Romanesque parish church **St George's** (Crkva sv. Jurja) was rebuilt in the 15th century, when the chancel received its Gothic frescoes by local painters. The village's patron saint spears his dragon in an early-1800s tympanum of the Renaissance mansion opposite the church, upstaged by the century-older Mustaćon on the same square, whose fearsome looks and fabulous moustache were intended to scare sprites intent on evil.

Touring from Rijeka: Note

The defensive hilltowns and sturdy goulashes of inland Istria form a rustic counterpoint to the harbours and seafood of our island tour from Rijeka (following pages). Those with time on their hands might therefore extend their tour with the five-day itinerary on pp.63–7 which explores the cosy towns of the Istrian (and Slovenian) coast, then tracks inland; begin your exploration either with Roman antiquities in **Pula** (p.53) 62km south of mainland ferry terminal Brestova, or ghoulish mummies in Vodnjan, signposted from **Marčana**, 46km south of the terminal.

Touring from Rijeka: Islands in the Kvarner Gulf

Day 1: A Circuit of Krk

Morning: Go east of Rijeka across the bridge which has transformed Krk from isolated medieval powerbase of regional overlords the Frankopan dukes into the most go-ahead of Croatia's islands. East of its eponymous capital, relaxed resort **Punat** overlooks an almost landlocked bay where a 15th-century Franciscan monastery (*open Mon–Sat 9–6, Sun 9–12; adm*) is hushed in isolation on islet **Košljun** (*taxi boats, 15Kn*). Ponder a kinetic *Last Judgment* (1653) which swirls above the church altar and rummage through an eclectic museum whose prize is a rare *Ptolemy Atlas* from the late 1500s, then explore footpaths through the islet's pine woods. Continue on the road from Krk to **Baška**. Only cosy lanes around the harbour recall the fishing village expanded by a straggle of development to serve one of Croatia's finest shingle beaches. On the way, sidetrack east to medieval huddle **Vrbnik**, perched on cliffs.
Lunch: In Punat or Baška, *see* below.

Afternoon: Return to **Krk**, expanding at frightening pace but whose isolated chunks of medieval defence walls protect from modernity a kernel of terracotta-roofed houses and the Cathedral of the Assumption on Trg Sv Kvirina. Its nave parades a catwalk of multicoloured columns looted from Roman palaces bar an early Christian pair – birds peck at a fish on their capitals in an allegory of the Eucharist. Check to see if the belltower treasury of Romanesque church St Quirinus is open; otherwise walk the city walls to the 15th-century castle, stamped with the Lion of St Mark.
Dinner and Sleeping: In Krk, *see* below.

Day 1

Lunch in Punat
Kostarika, Obala 94, **t** (051) 855 284 (*moderate*). Forgive a leafy but rather bland square and sample the impressive range of grilled meats and fresh fish for a slap-up lunch.

Lunch in Baška
Cicibela, Emila Geistlicha bb, **t** (051) 856 013 (*moderate*). Succulent seafood in a modern restaurant with stone walls and a penchant for ropework behind the famous beach.
Pirun, Palada 92, **t** (051) 864 061 (*moderate*). At the farthest end of the harbour, so this friendly restaurant is quieter. Die-hard carnivores should resist a reliable catch of the day and gorge on a chef's special mixed grill.

Dinner in Krk
Frankopan, Trg sv. Kvirina bb, **t** (051) 221 437 (*moderate*). The full Adriatic menu – fresh fish and seafood, grilled steaks and tasty spaghettis – offered at keen prices beneath the campanile of St Quirinus.
Nono, Krčkih iseljenika 8, **t** (051) 222 221 (*moderate*). Walk east beyond the city walls to locate this rustic-themed *konoba* which prepares hearty goulashes and lamb stews.
Šime, Obala Hrvatske Mornarice bb, **t** (051) 222 426 (*moderate*). A small menu of fishy delights plus rich pastas in the most intimate of the harbour-front restaurants.

Sleeping in Krk
When package-orientated hotels fill up in summer, source private accommodation (*inexpensive*) through **Autotrans**, **t** (051) 222 661, in the Trg bana Jelačića bus station.
Marina, Obala Hrvatske Mornarice bb, **t** (051) 221 128 (*moderate*). Modest rooms, but what a location – in Krk centre, on the harbour.
Koralj, Vlade Tomašića bb, **t** (051) 221 044 (*moderate*). A little bland, but the best of Krk's package hotels, which overlooks a bay east of town and is nestled among pines.

Day 2: Down to the Tip of Lošinj

Morning: Go north of Krk as if returning to Rijeka but turn left to **Valbiska**, quay for the hop to **Cres** and **Lošinj**; Medea is said to have hacked limbs off her brother pursuing Jason and his Golden Fleece to create these lovely island slivers. Austrian holidaymakers in the 19th century would recognize the colourful mosaic of houses which dresses the harbour of **Veli Lošinj** at the far tip of Lošinj. At its side, barn-like Baroque (1774) church St Anthony (Crkva sveti Antun) hangs a masterclass of Italian art – Venetian Bartolmeo Vivarini dabbles with Renaissance in its prize *Madonna with Child and Saints* (1475) left of the portal. The Venetians also erected the 1455 defence tower opposite so Uskok pirates from Senj might think twice before raids; gen up on its museum of local history to prepare for your afternoon in Mali Lošinj.

Lunch: In Veli Lošinj, *see* below.

Afternoon: Hard to believe, but **Mali Lošinj** was the 'Little' to Veli Lošinj's 'Large' until ships outgrew the sister town 3km south and transformed into a thriving 19th-century port. Tourism not tall ships is the modern money-spinner; boats now pootle on day trips to isolated sandy islet Susak. Behind palm-fringed promenade Riva Lošinjskih Kapetana, at Vladimira Gortana 35, the Art Collections (Umjetničke zbirke; *open June–Sept daily 9–12 and 7–9; Oct–May Mon–Fri 10–12; adm*) hang 20th-century Croatian and swooning Baroque canvases bequeathed by two private local collectors, Cres-born Zagreb Academy of Arts professor Andro Vid Mihičić and physician Giuseppe Piperata. Afterwards, drive south for a swim from pebble beaches of Čikat Bay, the town's best but ever-busy due to a cluster of resort hotels.

Dinner and Sleeping: In Mali Lošinj, *see* below.

Day 2

Lunch in Veli Lošinj
Villa San, Garina 15, **t** (051) 236 527 (*moderate*). Grilled fish and island lamb served among garden palms on a terrace. Fall in love with the village and Villa 'Dream' also offers a clutch of basic but clean rooms (*cheap*); request no.8 and you can wake up slowly on a balcony overlooking the harbour.

Marina, Obala Maršala Tita 38, **t** (051) 236 178 (*moderate*). A lovely spot for a lazy al fresco lunch at the far end of the harbour – terrace tables look down into the village and there's a tasty haul of super-fresh fish on the menu.

Dinner in Mali Lošinj
Corrado, Sv Marije 1, **t** (051) 232 487 (*expensive–moderate*). Lošinj lamb goulash and stuffed squid prepared in a garden *konoba*.

Bonito, Spiridona Gopčevića 37; no tel (*moderate*). A modern restaurant behind the Riva; try gnocchi with shrimps and truffles for a light meal or a gastro-tour of starters and fishy mains for a blow-out (*expensive*).

Lanterna, Sv Martin 71, **t** (051) 233 625 (*cheap*). Just a simple *konoba* on a bay 1km east of the centre, perhaps, but this is a romantic gem. Chef rustles up simple fresh fish dishes and meaty snacks at bargain prices.

Sleeping in Mali Lošinj
Lošinjska Plovidba, Riva Lošinjskih Kapetana 8, **t** (051) 231 077, can source private rooms.

Villa Anna, Velopin 31, **t** (051) 233 223 (*moderate*). Blond wood furnishings and thick white cotton sheets in a small and quietly stylish modern hotel with views across the harbour to the Riva.

Bellevue, Čikat Bay, **t** (051) 231 222 (*moderate*). A little anonymous, but the best of the package hotels and perfect for the beach.

Villa Margarita, Bočac 64, **t** (051) 233 837 (*moderate*). Simple but adequate *pension* in a side street moments from the harbour.

Day 3: Cres

Morning: Either Illyrians or Romans carved the Kavuada channel that separates Cres and Lošinj and made museum-hamlet **Osor** into a thriving port. The grand proportions and stately early-Renaissance trefoil façade of the Church of the Assumption recall centuries before the island power-player withered on the vine, its life-blood trade leached by sea routes to the Americas. The church, demoted from cathedral in 1828, also retains relics of St Gaudencius in its Baroque altar; the coffin of the local 11th-century bishop is said to have drifted home across the Adriatic from Rome. Osor's early years are on display in the Archaeological Museum (*open summer daily 10–12 and 7–9; adm*) in the 15th-century Venetian town hall, and the Bishop's Palace (*times erratic; adm*), down a side street, with Roman reliefs and medieval carving.

Lunch: In Osor or **Loznati**, *see* below.

Afternoon: Drive north to island capital **Cres**, breaking the journey in blissful **Valun**, famous for a Glagolitic script tablet in its church. Start your tour of the mazy lanes of the capital at its harbourside heart, Trg Frane Petrića, with a 16th-century loggia. Beyond the contemporary Main Gate, Gothic-Renaissance hybrid St Mary of the Snows is shoehorned into square Pod Urom and recalls a legend of local snowfall. Less fanciful history is on display in the Gothic Petrić Palace behind Hotel Cres on the harbour, and there are ecclesiastical goodies in the museum of a Franciscan monastery (*open Mon–Sat 9–12 and 4–6.30; adm*) southeast of the centre.

Dinner and Sleeping: In Cres, *see* below. In the morning return to Rijeka from Porozina; nature-lovers might pause in pretty **Beli** for nature trails and griffon vulture sanctuary Caput Insulae (*open daily 9–11 and 5–9; adm*).

Day 3

Lunch in Osor

Bonifačić, Osor 64, **t** (051) 237 413 (*moderate*). Interesting fresh Adriatic fish plus creamy tagliatelle and spaghetti are on the menu in a surprisingly stylish garden *konoba* buried behind the main square.

Livio, Osor 30, **t** (051) 237 242 (*moderate*). The décor gives away a hunting infatuation, so no surprise that this *konoba* prepares thick game-fest *gulaš Lovačk* (hunter's goulash) and a rich dish of Dalmatian-style rabbit.

Lunch in Loznati

Bukaleta, Loznati, signposted 4km south of Cres, **t** (051) 571 606 (*moderate*). The island specialist of famous Cres lamb; *Janječi zgvacet* (lamb stew) or *janjetina u krušnoj peći* (lamb slow-cooked in a *peka*) is served with hunks of home-made bread and a passable local red wine. *Closed Nov–April.*

Dinner in Cres

Riva, Riva Creskih Kapetana 13, **t** (051) 571 107 (*expensive–moderate*). Semi-smart; platters of Adriatic fish are presented for inspection, then cooked to perfection.

Al Buon Gusto, Sveti Sidar 14, **t** (051) 571 878 (*cheap*). Squirrelled away in the old town is this charming snug *konoba*, with a passion for bygone days and a wide-ranging menu.

Bleona, Šetaliste 20 Aprila 24, **t** (051) 571 203 (*cheap*). Portions are large and prices low in an old-fashioned locals' choice.

Sleeping in Cres

Private rooms (*inexpensive*) via **Putnička Agencia Croatia**, Cons 10, **t** (051) 573 053.

Kimen, Varozina 25, **t** (051) 571 161 (*moderate*). Simple but acceptable rooms in Cres's only hotel, a bloated package holiday favourite overlooking a bay 1km north of the centre.

Cres, Creskih kapetana bb, **t** (051) 571 108 (*moderate*). Simple rooms above a central restaurant, some offering harbour views.

Croatia: Zadar, Split and the Dalmatian Coast

The Dalmatian Coast

Lopar • San Marino
• Supetarska Draga
Kalifront
Peninsula *Rab* • Jablanac

Plitvice
Lakes
National
Park

Žigljen • Prizna
Novalja •

Pag

BOSNIA-HERZEGOVINA

Gospić

Pag
• Pag

Paklenica
National
Park

To Ancona
Starigrad-
Paklenica

Gračac

Nin • Vrsi
Seline

Veli Rat • Božava
Dragove •
Bribinj Ugljan
Zaglav

ZADAR

Benkovac

Knin

Dugi Otok Pašman

Manojlovački
slapovi

Guli

Krka
National
Park

Roški slap

Telašćica
Nature Park Žut
Kornat
Jadra Murter
Kaprije Kornati
National
Park Žirje

Visovac
Skradin
Skradinski buk
Lozovac

Šibenik

Sinj

Trogir Salona

SPLIT Dugi Rat

Imotski

Supetar
Šolta • Škrip
Milna

Makarska

Bol *Brač*

Stari Grad Vboska
Hvar Jelsa *Hvar* Sućaraj

To Ancona &
Pescara

Pelješac Peninsula

Komiža Vis Kut
Vis

Kučište Orebić
Vela Luka Korčula

Biševo

Blato Pupnatska
Luka Lumbarda

Korčula

N

Lastovo

Ubli *Lastovo*

50 km

20 miles

Croatia's restless, endearingly scatty second-city Split and quieter little sister Zadar
are the urban powerhouses of the Dalmatian coast, their wardrobes stuffed with
architectural hand-me-downs that span a millennium, their bar and café scenes
fizzing with life. But the real draws of Croatia's central strip are some of the nation's
most alluring islands: we take you to gorgeous glamour girls as well as humble
rustics who acknowledge tourism only with a casual shrug.

Zadar

Zadar's fate has been to attract trouble. The Romans were the first to disturb the peace when they set their imperial stamp on an early Illyrian settlement and laid the foundations for a city which blossomed into the Croat capital of Byzantine Dalmatia. Next were the Venetians, who swooped on the medieval port during two centuries of raids until they stumped up 100,000 ducats and scratched the republic's signature on to Zadar title deeds in 1409, only to suffer Turkish raids and strangled economics during their four-century tenure. Nor has recent history been kind. In the Second World War the Allies obliterated two-thirds of the old town in their determination to evict the Germans who replaced Mussolini's capitulated Fascists, and no sooner was the architectural fabric carefully darned and patched than Zadar found itself back on the front line of the inland Serbian Krajina hinterland. In 1991 Yugoslav army forces gripped the city in a stranglehold that forced locals underground for three months, and artillery units embedded in neighbouring hillsides continued to lob rockets until routed in 1995 by Croatian army offensive Operation Storm.

The wonder, then, is that northern Dalmatia's largest city is still so beguiling. Although post-war reconstruction could never recapture the medieval show of other coastal towns, with wounds largely healed, the historic kernel packs in an intriguing millennium-spanning mishmash: Roman relics stand beside Croatia's prize jewel of Byzantium, and a splendid *œuvre* of Romanesque churches graces the lanes of a compact centre crowded onto a peninsula. And as if to balance out the cerebral allure, Zadar boasts an effervescent café and bar scene, a leftover, perhaps, of its 26 years under the Italian flag until it was reclaimed for Yugoslavia in 1947.

The Forum and the Church of St Donatus

Its official title is Zeleni trg, but a millennium's habitual use guarantees that Zadar's central square will forever be the **Forum**. Only a casual litter of sarcophagi and chunks of carved pediment betray the Roman roots of what was the largest public space in the eastern Adriatic, a 95m by 45m Times Square ordered by Emperor Augustus to aggrandize his 1 BC–AD 3 Roman settlement. The flanking porticoes, temples and shops fell victim to fire, earthquake and the declining fortunes of the Roman colony, but a lone decorative column stands guard today where it always stood, saved from destruction by centuries of use as a pillory. The miscreants chained and shamed in public until 1840 probably cared little about the Corinthian capital which flowers on its stem, nor the trio of Roman god masquerons that pull faces on a wall that demarcates the position of the Capitolium temple on the Forum's west flank.

Much of the Forum's masonry was seized by 9th-century Christians as a pre-cut quarry during the building of the church of **St Donatus** (Crkva sv. Donat; *open April–June and Sept–Oct 9–8; July–Aug 9am–11pm; closed Nov–Mar; adm*), a powerful, austere cylinder celebrated as a city icon. Hunt the inscriptions to 'Augustate' carved on sacrificial altars embedded alongside Roman columns as the foundations of the largest Byzantine church in Croatia, then admire Roman relics in an impressively ascetic interior; a pair of Corinthian columns helps support the upper gallery, and

Zadar

(map labels)

LIBURNSKA OBALA

ISTARSKA OBALA · IVANA BRČIĆA

OBALA KNEZA BRANIMIRA

TRG TRI BUNARA

Our Lady of Health · Arsenal · POLJANA NATKA NODILA · Harbour Gate

LIBURNSKA OBALA

BEDEMI

ZADARSKIH POBUNA

BRAĆE BILIŠIĆ · JURJA BIJANKINIJA

City Museum

JERONIMA VIDULICA · TRG SV. STOŠIJE · St Thomas (Ruined)

OBALA KNEZA BRANIMIRA

Franciscan Monastery

Cathedral · BENIE · St Chrysogonus

St Donatus · TRG SV. KRŠEVANA

FORUM (ZELENI TRG) · Archaeological Museum

St Mary · ŠIROKA

OBALA KRALJA PETRA KREŠIMIRA IV

JURJA DALMATINCA

MADIJEVACA · JURJA BARAKOVIĆA

Guardhouse · Ghirardini Palace

NARODNI TRG · Loggia · DON IVE PRODANA

ELIZABETE KOTROMANIĆ

MIHOVILA PAVLINOVIĆA

BORELLI · Narodnog Lista

STORNORICA · VAROŠKA · SPIRE BRUSINE · MIHE & ALI ROMANIĆ · St Simeon

Roman Old Town Gate and Capital

TRG PETRA ZERANIĆA · Captain's Tower

KOVAČKA · ŠIME LJUBICA · SIRAC · TRG PET BUNARA

VAROŠ · Land Gate

FOSA

ZVONIMIRA

RAVNICE

OBALA KRALJA TOMISLAVA

N

200 metres
200 yds

---

slabs of tablet from the Roman temple evoke deities Juno and Jupiter. Dedicated to wandering Irish saint and local bishop St Donatus, the church, deconsecrated in 1798, has found a second wind as Zadar's favourite concert hall thanks to superb acoustics.

Southwest of the Forum is waterfront boulevard **Obala kralja Petra Krešimira IV**, a mouthful locals dismiss for the more manageable title **Riva**. Sixty years after they stomped into Zadar in 1813, Austro-Hungarian modernizers ripped down sea wall defences to gift Zadar its favourite promenade, now with trees and flowerbeds in ballgown colours that heal scars from the Second World War. It's a lovely spot for a stroll and the best in town to test the truth of film director Alfred Hitchcock's sigh, 'The sunset is more beautiful in Zadar than in California!'

The Archaeological Museum and Church Art Exhibition

Zadar's sculptural prizes are all in the **Archaeological Museum** (Arheološki muzej; *open Mon–Sat 9–12 and 5–8; July–Aug Mon–Sat 9–12 and 5–10; adm*) on the east side of the Forum. Breeze through musty Neolithic displays on the top floor to pore over spiral jewellery and ceramics brought home by merchant Liburnians as souvenirs from Greece and Italy, or finds from Roman Zadar displayed on the first floor below:

Getting There

Between April and Oct, Croatia Airlines **flies** from London in 2hrs 30mins. Year-round, Jadrolinija **ferries** chug across the Adriatic overnight from Ancona, Italy, in 8hrs and fast SNAV ferries zip from Ancona (3hrs) and Cittanova (3hrs 45mins) July–Sept.

Getting from the Airport

Croatia Airlines **buses** meet incoming flights and shuttle new arrivals 9km northwest to Zadar (20Kn). Return buses leave from the same bay, on Liburnska obala one block west of the port gate, 1hr 20mins before flight departures.

Getting Around

Although the small historic kernel of Zadar is a joy to stroll, most of the hotel beds are 5km away to the northwest on the **Puntamika peninsula**; **bus** 5 trundles there, via stops on Obala kneza Branimira on the far side of the harbour, for 6Kn (single from driver) or 10Kn (two journeys, tokens from tobacconists or newsagents). If you decide to walk there, a **rowing boat taxi** (*barkarijoli*, 3Kn) from the northern breakwater dodges between ferries across the harbour to trim journey times by 15mins and continue an 800-year tradition.

The main **bus station** is 1km east of the town centre at Ante Starčevića 1.

Car Hire

The major players also operate bureaux in Zadar airport.

Dollar/Thrifty, Hotel Kolovare, Bože Peričića 14, **t** (023) 315 733.

Hertz, Vrata Svete Krševana bb, **t** (023) 254 301.

Budget, Obala kneza Branimira 1 (in Generalturist agency), **t** (023) 313 681.

Sidro, Jadranska cesta bb, **t** (023) 343 916 .

Tourist Information

Zadar: Corner of Narodni trg and Mihe Klaića, **t** (023) 316 166, *www.zadar.hr*. Open Oct–May daily 8–10; June–Sept daily 8–12. The helpful tourist office offers free maps of the Zadar and locale which extend to the Puntamika peninsula, and proffers advice on regional day trips.

Shopping

Spine-street **Široka** has a parade of high street shopping, and interesting small clothes and jewellery boutiques line alleys of the **Varoš** quarter to the southeast.

Framed samplers of Pag lace and folksy embroidery are among touristy regional handicrafts in **Studio Lik**, Don Ive Prodana 7, which also has glassware and ceramics.

Foodies and wine buffs should browse bottles of Croatian vintners' finest, plus honeys, truffles and potted anchovies, in

grave slabs and an elegant 1st-century statue of Roman overlord Augustus. Look, too, for a model of the Forum which makes sense of today's remnants before you examine ground-floor eye-catchers chiselled by medieval sculptors of the fledgling Croatian nation. Highlights among a stylebook of national wicker and plait motifs like Celtic knotwork (still on the band of policemen's caps) are a cartoon-strip of Christ's early life carved for 11th-century illiterates and swiped from nearby chapel St Nedilice (*see* p.84), and a 10th-century *ciborium* with caricature lions, griffins and peacocks.

For all the museum's efforts, the doyenne of Zadar museums and pride of the city is ecclesiastical treasure chest the **Permanent Exhibition of Church Art** (Stalna izložba crkvene umjetnosti; *open summer Mon–Sat 10–1 and 6–8; winter Mon–Sat 10–12.30 and 5–6.30; adm*) in the adjacent Benedictine convent of the church of St Mary. An 11th-century reliquary of St Isidore's arm spiralled with gold filigree catches the eye among sensitively lit gold and silver, studded with outrageous gems like booty from a vintage swashbuckler, as does a quirky reliquary which looks like a model piano for

Vinoteka Mauris, Jakše Čedomila Čuke 5, which also operates as a gallery. Develop a taste for Marska maraschino cherry brandies, distilled in Zadar for over 250 years, and there's a head-spinning range on sale in a distillery outlet at Mate Karamana 3.

Where to Stay

Zadar t (023) –

Bar a few exceptions, Zadar's hotels are on the **Puntamika peninsula** 5km northwest of the centre. Most beds are in package resort giants the Adriana, Donat and Puntamika, owned by the Falkensteiner chain and located in the Borik complex, an antiseptic tourist enclave low on character but big on amenities such as pools and tennis courts and located before a shabby scrap of shingle beach.

Private rooms in the historic kernel can be sourced through tourist agencies **Aquarius**, Nova Vrata (gateway at top of Jurja Barakovića), t 212 919, and **Miatours**, Vrata Svete Krševana, t 254 300/400.

President, Vladana Desnice 16, Puntamika, t 333 696, www.hotel-president.hr (expensive). Impeccable manners and taste characterize a small four-star long hailed Zadar's premier address. Rich tones of mustard and ruby are set off by walnut and rosewood in rooms with deep carpets and marble bathrooms; those on the third floor boast coastal views. Its restaurant, **Vivaldi**,

prepares an international menu in Croatia's top ten and has the best cellar in Zadar.

Niko, Obala kneza Domagoja 9, Puntamika, t 337 880, www.hotel-niko.hr (moderate). Not quite as luxurious, but still a good-value family-run number above Puntamika's finest restaurant (see 'Eating Out'), whose stylish accommodation takes on the President in the main building; a new wing is due to open in 2005.

Villa Hrešc, Obala kneza Trpimira 28, t 337 570, www.villa-hrsec.hr (moderate). All three rooms and six suites (expensive) have parquet floors and tasteful shades; the best come with views across the harbour to the old town in a design-led seafront hotel which prides itself on personal service and an excellent restaurant. Better still is its location, just a 15min walk to the centre.

Kolovare, Bože Peričića 14, t 211 017 (moderate). Above the beaches of the same name and perhaps a little pricey, but the closest hotel to the old town provides spacious and now comfy three-star accommodation after a 2004 revamp; a limited number of basic rooms which recall Communist-era origins are available at bargain prices on request.

Adriana Select, Mastora Radovana 7, Puntamika, t 206 637, www.falkensteiner.com (moderate). Revamped in 2004, the best of the Boriks has 48 junior suites dressed in understated style; think rattan furnishings, sea rass matting and neutral shades of calico and café au lait.

Liberace, but is actually a receptacle for St Mark's shoulderblade. There are paintings upstairs: look for prized Adriatic icon the *Benedictine Madonna* (c. 1300); Lorenzo Luzzo's wonderful *Assumption of the Virgin* (1520), in which she fixes the viewer with a steely gaze as she is hoisted heavenwards by a flutter of angels; and an elegant polyptych of St Martin donning his cloak to the beggar, the vision of 15th-century Venetian Vittore Carpaccio. Sculpture includes a crowd of bashful Gothic saints, who once evaded the eyes of the Zadar cathedral congregation atop a rood screen – and don't leave without exploring the nook of the **Chapel of St Nedilice** (Crkvica sv. Neđelica) hidden away beyond Romanesque-Byzantine sculpture on the ground floor.

Though founded two centuries after St Donat's (1066), centuries of improvements have added chapters to the adjacent church of **St Mary** (Crkva sv. Marije) to create an encyclopaedia of styles, erudite stuff for the architecturally literate – behind a swoopy Venetian Renaissance façade, Roman pillars march down a nave frothed with rococo plaster but which preserves original Romanesque lines.

Mediteran, Matje Gupaca 19, Puntamika, **t** 337 500, *www.hotelmediteran-zd.hr* (*moderate*). Modest but pleasant three-star accommodation keenly priced just the wrong side of cheap from a small family-run hotel north of the Borik package enclave.

Venera, Šime Ljubića 4a (off Kovačka), **t** 214 098 (*inexpensive*). Forgive the basic quality of the tiny en-suite rooms of this *pension* above a tourist agency and this is a bargain, located in the old town's Varoš district.

Eating Out

Zadar **t** (023) –

Kornat, Liburnska obala 6, **t** 254 101 (*expensive–moderate*). A talented chef prepares gourmet dishes without ever showing off – succulent lamb in a rosemary sauce, monkfish laced with Istrian truffles – in the smartest restaurant in central Zadar. Round it off with a sniffter of local cherry liqueur Marska.

Roko, Put Dikla 74, **t** 331 000 (*expensive–moderate*). Super-fresh seafood that is immaculately cooked elevated this restaurant on the road to Puntamika into Croatia's top 100 in 2003.

Niko, Obala kneza Domagoja 9, Puntamika, **t** 337 888 (*expensive–moderate*). A Zadar institution before the Puntamika marina and locals' choice for a Sunday slap-up. Choose from a changing catch-of-the-day platter or indulge in a seafood menu of favourites such as *jastog* (lobster) and *škampi na buzaru* (scampi cooked in garlic and white wine).

Foša, Kralja Dmitra Zvonimira 2, **t** 314 421 (*moderate*). More highly rated seafood and fish, this time in a former guard and customs house beside the Land Gate. Move fast to claim a seat on a charming terrace beside the Foša harbour.

Zadar, Obala kralja Petra Krešimira IV bb, **t** 212 182 (*moderate*). The small menu of seafoods, steaks and pastas is unremarkable, but the terrace on Zadar's favourite promenade is a delight, offering the best views in town across the bay to Ugljan.

Trata, Jerolima Vidulića 5, no tel (*moderate*). Rummage through the back streets west of the Forum to find this friendly *konoba* with a lovely garden and traditional tastebuds: rich *brodet* (Dalmatian fish stew) is served in old-fashioned clay bowls and local tipples are on the wine list.

Stomorica, Stomorica 12, **t** 315 946 (*cheap*). Simple snacks such as *giri* (small fried fish), *lignje* (squid) and *bakala* (cod) in a simple *konoba* whose patrons are liable to burst into song as an impromptu *klapa* (a Dalmatian barbershop quartet) after a few glasses of home-made plonk. A gem.

Dva Ribara, Blaža Jurjeva bb, **t** 213 445 (*cheap*). An unpretentious favourite which serves delicious thin-crust pizzas plus home-made pastas in portions to make dieters give up.

The Cathedral and Southwest Zadar

Picture-postcard views over the Forum – and Zadar – are available from the belvedere of the **campanile** (*open summer Mon–Sat 10–1 and 5.30–8; adm*) which spikes the piazza's north side. For all its looks, the cathedral bell tower is a relative newcomer to the Zadar skyline; until a Vienna committee agreed the plans of T.G. Jackson in the 1890s, the 15th-century original was stalled as a single stumpy storey. Small wonder that the conservative Austro-Hungarians approved of the design of the English architect – he modelled it on the cathedral in Rab.

The campanile stands behind a cathedral which replaces a founding Christian basilica dealt a body blow in 1202, when ambitious Venetians sacked Zadar with the force of Crusaders en route to Palestine; explaining his excommunication order, Pope Innocent III scolded that blind Venetian Doge Henrique Dandolo had 'bloodied [his] hands, plundered a city, ruined churches, pulled down altars'. The pontiff would have been thrilled at its replacement, the 13th-century **cathedral of St Anastasia**

(Katedrala sv. Stošije). Admire the perfectly balanced Romanesque **façade** of blind arcades punched with rose windows, pure Romanesque and glorious Gothic, and the vines around the central portal – birds and animals pick at grapes, an angel climbs a ladder to swipe eggs from a nest and a cat stalks a mouse on the lintel – before you enter a lofty **nave** whose alternating capitals and neat arcades look almost Tuscan, and parade down to a Gothic *ciborium* (1332) and medieval choir stalls. The cathedral's prize possession, secreted away in the left aisle as if for devout eyes only, is a simple marble casket that holds the bones of its patron. The remains of the 4th-century martyr beheaded by Emperor Diocletian were presented to Bishop Donatus in the 9th century, a vote of thanks, perhaps, for his canny diplomacy in quelling a spat between Frankish Emperor Charlemagne and the Byzantine Empire.

West of the cathedral, Jurja Bijankinija culminates in the **Church of Our Lady of Health** (Crkva Gospe od zdravilja), a dainty Baroque nave tacked onto a 1582 circular chapel like a grotto on one side of triangular park **Trg Tri bunara**, named for the three wells on its north side. Explore south on alley Braće Bilišić to discover the 13th-century **Franciscan monastery** (Franjevaca samostan). The story goes that construction of the Order's oldest monastery in the eastern Adriatic was inspired by a visit of St Francis himself and while the Baroque-renovated church is nothing special – a barn-like space seemingly not recovered from a 1798 incarnation as a military hospital – its lovely cloister lined with epitaphs of Zadar nobles is an oasis of peace.

Along the City Walls

Zadar, saluted 13th-century Frenchman M. Villeharduin, 'is a city surrounded with tall walls and high towers. It is useless,' he declared with finality, 'to look for a greater and richer city.' The medieval defences admired by the chronicler of the Fourth Crusade were beefed up in the 1560s by Venetians nervous of fractious Ottomans to create the largest city-fortress in their republic. And just in the nick of time, too – the final brick had not long been laid when the stone girdle was tested by a two-year Turkish siege during the 1570–71 Cyprus Wars. Having withstood the Ottomans, the walls' stolid bulk still guards the city's northern flank. Before you enjoy guard's-eye views over the port from a road which marches along those city ramparts, pause in Trg sv. Krševana for the lovely Romanesque **St Chrysogonus** (Crkva sv. Krševana); its exterior is lined with twisted columns like old-fashioned candy sticks and a sash of blind arcade wraps around the apse. If it's open, scraps of 12th-century fresco in two side apses enliven a stark interior in awe of a Baroque high altar (1701) which demands the attention as if in apology for the congregation's 70-year delay in honouring a desperate pledge made during a plague in 1632. **St Thomas's** opposite fared less well – tellers from the Zagrebačka banka sit among its late-5th-century columns.

Just before the walls is the so-so **City Museum** (Narodni muzej Zadar; *open Mon–Fri 9–12 and 5–8, Sat 9–1; adm*), at its best with its models of medieval, 18th-century and early-20th-century Zadar which offer a perspective of the city's development. Beyond is the **Harbour Gate**, erected in 1573 to celebrate the Christian fleet's knockout blow to the Turks in the 1571 Battle of Lepanto. Travellers departing from Zadar are blessed by principal city protector St Chrysogonus on horseback above a section of ceremonial

Roman arch; and a growling Venetian Lion of St Mark informs arrivals from the port just whose town they're in.

A happy upshot of the Allied bombs that obliterated housing was that they cleared space for Zadar's wonderful daily **market**, which spreads produce from the agricul-tural hinterland across a small square hard against the walls. Walk southeast along the defences (ascend via steps on Poljana Natka Nodila a block west) or follow them east on Pod bedemom and a crack squad of silver-haired *bakice* tout cheeses and fruits, decant home-made olive oils, wines and *rakija* into old water bottles, or pause from their clacking knitting needles to offer up crocheted dollies and tablecloths.

Narodni Trg, Varoš Quarter and St Simeon's Church

As Zadar's purse fattened up through medieval trade, the city fathers created **Narodni trg** as a mercantile reply to the ecclesiastical Forum – a stage for municipal and merchant life where proclamations were read, committees debated and traders wheeled and dealt. Relaxed now after its days at the epicentre of secular life, 'People's Square' nevertheless remains the main venue for a gossip after Sunday service. Glass has filled the formerly open arches of the municipal courthouse to transform the sturdy 1565 city **loggia** into a space for art and photography exhibitions (*open Mon–Fri 9–12 and 5–8, Sat 9–1*). Opposite is the former city **guardhouse** (1562); the Venetians' delicately trilling scrolls and *pizzicato* obelisks are drowned out by the *sforzando* Austro-Hungarian trump card of a clock tower (1798). No wonder 1608 Venetian governor G.G .Zane, with a beard like a doormat, frowns in a niche.

Dive south off Narodni trg on Mihe Klaića and you plunge into **Varoš**, a cat's-cradle of atmospheric medieval alleys stuffed with boutiques and bars where you should throw away the map and simply be led by your eyes. Otherwise, pause to inspect the Renaissance carvings which frame a balconied window begging for a Shakespeare love scene on the **Ghirardini Palace** – the Romanesque mansion on the corner of Jurja Barakovića is a rare survivor of the hail of Allied bombs – then thread southeast off Narodni trg along Don Ive Prodana to the church of **St Simeon** (Crkva sv. Šimuna), rebuilt in fashionable Baroque in the 17th century. To explain the adoption as city patron of an apostle said to have held Christ in the Temple, a suspect tale relates how a dying Venetian merchant, storm-bound in Zadar, confided to monks that he had buried St Simeon's relics nearby for safe keeping, and the brothers were wowed by visions as they exhumed the relics intended for Venice. On the saint's gilded casket, a no-expense-spared extravaganza that Queen Elizabeth of Hungary commissioned from a Milanese silversmith in 1381, the monks dig furiously and St Simeon displays the Christ child (a scene pinched from a Giotto fresco in the Arena Chapel, Padua). Another story claims that she ordered the casket to atone for stealing a finger of the saint, although, if so, she took the same opportunity to remind locals about the triumphant entry her husband Louis I[er] of Anjou made into Zadar 23 years earlier; the Hungarian-Croat King swaggers in style on the right-hand panel, probably a canny piece of sloganeering on behalf of a king who was waging a losing battle against Venetian ambitions on Zadar. Visit on the feast day, 8 October, and the saint's mummified remains attempt to impress the locals who shuffle past in homage.

Around Trg Pet Bunara

A hotch-potch of Roman columns swiped from the Forum and patched into a whole stands as antique sentry over the Romans' longitudinal artery the **decumanus**, still arrow-straight, still marching through central Zadar as streets Elizabete Kotromanić, Široka and Jurja Bijankinija. An echo of the Roman city can also be seen in the remains of their **gateway**, forgotten behind nearby railings on Trg Petra Zoranića and reduced to an antique Lego brick as opposed to the original impressive triumphal arch.

Behind it, **Trg Pet bunara** is christened for its five wells (*pet bunara*) which tapped a new cistern from 1574 and supplied the city with water until the mid-19th century, when the square enjoyed a fleeting heyday as fashionable promenade of smart Zadar. Doubtless its surprise elevation was aided by General Welden – the whimsical Austro-Hungarian officer seized on a rare outbreak of peace in 1829 to seed the first public park in Dalmatia atop the pentagonal bastion which abuts the square. Earlier defences – a chunk of crenellated 13th-century defence wall – hang on the shoulder of medieval watchtower the **Captain's Tower** (Kapitanova Kula; *open Mon–Sat 10–1 and 5–8; adm*) opposite. View its exhibitions of art or photography or simply marvel at the views across Zadar's roofscape from the lookout, then head south to admire the swaggering **Land Gate** (Kopnena vrata). If the Venetian rulers of 1543 wanted first impressions to count, they must have been delighted with the stocky gateway created by fellow countryman Michele Sanmicheli, with a pediment of cattle skulls and flower buds and muscular dimensions, a strictly symmetrical triple arch which apes the crumbled entry before Trg Pet bunara. Its fierce Lion of St Mark represents the most forceful stamp of Venetian rule on the Dalmatian coast; mounted city patron St Chrysogonus on the keystone doesn't stand a chance.

More relaxed is the adjacent **Foša harbour**, shaped from the former city moat and crammed with nodding fishing boats. From here, coast road **Zvonimira** continues southeast, and central Zadar eases into genteel residential district **Kolovare**, fronted by a thin strip of beach, restaurants and cafés which reveals more of its charms to those prepared to walk that little bit further.

Day Trips and Overnighters from Zadar

Šibenik and Krka National Park

Šibenik likes to set itself apart as an 11th-century Croatian thoroughbred on a coast-line of antique Greeks and Romans, and points out its charming cat's-cradle of Gothic and Renaissance streets, its strings picked out by Venetian rulers and lovely to explore. But really there's only one reason to visit. And fortunately for an industrial modern town which all but smothers its historic kernel, it's a good one. Not only is **St James's Cathedral** (Katedrala svetog Jakova) a jewel of Croatia, UNESOCO inked the Gothic-Renaissance masterpiece on to its World Heritage list in 2000.

The Venetians instigated the building of the cathedral in 1402, which stalled almost immediately for want of funds, but established a Gothic core enlivened with Italian gusto at its liveliest around the **main portal**. Gloomy apostles glower from within a gloriously frothy arch of twisted barley-stick columns and verdant reliefs flow like rapids. Before you enter, look, too, at the **north portal**, where a pair of lions beam at each other and a shamefaced Adam and Eve try to retain their modesty opposite the Venetians' town hall (now a restaurant; *see* box, below).

Bursting with the ambition of new funds, city fathers proclaimed Gothic passé in 1441, appointed Venice-trained Juraj Dalmatinac, and Šibenik's ecclesiastical show-piece inched into the skyline in ritzy Renaissance. The Croatian architect's superb **nave** is an architectural history lesson: those first Gothic arches submit to Renaissance proportions that power to a high barrel-vault **roof**, nowhere more spectacular than at the crossing. If the cathedral inspires all the awe, Dalmatinac's intimate **baptistry** to the right of the altar has all the charm; wait till tour groups leave to fall for his enchanting masterpiece, a grotto-like nook whose low roof carved with swooning angels and a furiously bearded Creator is caught between Gothic and Renaissance.

Dalmatinac never saw his creation in its full glory – it was left to Italian pupil Nikola Firentinac to mount the Florentine cupola and wow contemporaries with an innovative roof of stone slabs. However, Dalmatia's most revered Renaissance architect must have chuckled when his 71 carved heads wrapped their none-too-flattering character study of local personalities around the exterior of the three apses. Don't miss them.

Apart from hunting out relics of nobility in the 15–17th-century stone mansions in the medieval streets, or gazing across a bay dotted with islands from a Venetian fortress (*trvđava*) above the old town where Šibenik made its Byzantine debut, there's not much else to keep you in town. Fortunately the waterfalls, plunging gorges and lakes of the river valley known as the **Krka National Park** (*open daily, July–Aug 60Kn;*

Getting There and Around

Hourly **buses** (1hr 30mins; 44Kn) trundle south from Zadar to Šibenik, which is linked to Krka embarkation village Skradin by five buses a day (25mins, 14Kn). To avoid the early start needed to do the pair justice in one day, it is worth considering your own transport.

Tourist Information

Šibenik: Obala Dr Franje Tuđmana 5, **t** (022) 214 411/448. *Open Mar–Oct daily 8–8; Nov–Feb 8–12.* Fausta Vrančića 18, **t** (022) 212 075. *Open Mon–Fri 7.30–3.*
Krka National Park: Trg Ivana Pavla II 5, Šibenik, **t** (022) 217 720/730/740. *Open Mon–Fri 7–3.*

Eating Out

Vijećnica, Trg Republike Hrvatske 1, Šibenik, **t** (022) 213 605 (*expensive–moderate*). Semi-smart and priced just the right side of expensive, the restaurant in the Venetian town hall opposite the cathedral prepares a menu of grilled fish and seafood, with pastas and risottos for thinner wallets. You'll have to be quick to snaffle an outside table beneath the town loggia.
Uzorita, Bana Jelačića 50, Šibenik, **t** (022) 213 660 (*expensive–moderate*). An 1898-vintage charmer of stone walls, chunky beams and rustic décor 20 minutes' walk northeast of the centre, famous for *hobotnica ispod peke* (octopus slow-baked under a *peka*) and super-fresh seafood harvested from the bay.
Bonaca, Rokovačka 5, Skradin, **t** (022) 771 444 (*moderate*). Traditional cooking in a yachties' favourite above the ACI marina at the Krka Park entry village. Try fat local mussels or chef's special Skradin grey mullet (*cipal*), or for adventures *à la carte* there's thick eel broth (*brodet od jegulja*).

April–June and Sept–Oct 50Kn; Nov–Mar 20Kn) are just 13km inland. Tour boats (*included in ticket*) chug upstream every hour from village **Skradin** to the **Skradinksi buk waterfalls**, 17 cascades which tumble over travertine (tufa) stone into a natural (and usually busy) paddling pool. If you can bear to leave the adjacent meadows perfect for a summer picnic, footbridges criss-cross between idyllic islets and a path explores to a huddle of stone watermills which can trace their lineage back to 1251.

Those with strong legs can take to well-marked footpaths which amble north 10km; everyone else can walk 20 minutes to **Lozovac** to embark on a boat upstream to a second fall, **Roški slap**, whose 90ft waters plunge into a lake where the Krk valley relaxes from steep gorge into gentle slopes. For once laziness is rewarded, because the tour boats pause at islet **Visovac**, where a 15th-century Franciscan monastery hushed behind a veil of trees treasures in its valuable library a contemporary, illustrated *Aesop's Fables*.

Explore the remote wilderness regions north to make a day of the national park and escape the day-trippers – the Krka gorge is at its most spectacular at the **Manojlovački slapovi**, a set of four cascades which tumble (*winter and spring only*) at an elbow. The views are sensational, once admired by 5,000 Roman soldiers stationed in military camp Burnistarum, recalled in arches above. Good maps are a must, however – buy yours and a national park guidebook from the park tourist office in Šibenik (*see* 'Tourist Information', p.89) – and the officials insist you stick to the footpaths in a hinterland that was formerly on the frontline of the Homelands War and may conceal uncleared landmines.

Kornati National Park

Boat captains run day trips from Zadar and Sali (Dugi Otok) for 250Kn, which includes lunch, wine and the 50Kn entry into the park. Book through Zadar travel agencies or directly at the boats which tout for custom on the port.

Even if George Bernard Shaw's sigh that 'on the last day of the Creation, God desired to crown His work and thus created the Kornati islands out of tears, stars and breath' is a mite hyperbolic, few Croatian landscapes compare with the archipelago southeast of Zadar. Modernity is still just a rumour on the 39 limestone islands and numerous islets which hump from a turquoise sea like pumice stones dropped by careless angels, largely stripped of vegetation after 17th-century Venetian aristocrats gave the nod to shepherds from island **Murter** to strip for pasture a thick coat of Mediterranean oak and pine. Parched without freshwater streams, scoured by greedy sheep, the islands withered. The Venetians shrugged and handed over 90 per cent ownership to the Murterians, some of whom continue to eke out a living in summer grazing sheep, keeping bees and cultivating olives, figs and grapes. Many, however, have reinvented their 300 cottages which shelter in coves as Robinson Crusoe retreats, baffled that city-slickers will pay handsome sums to roll up trouser legs and potter around a humble stone house which lacks electricity and running water; book your visit through Murter-based agencies Coronata (*Zrtava ratova 17*, **t** *(022) 435 933, www.coronata.hr*) or Kornatturist (*Hrvatskih vladara 2*, **t** *(022) 435 854, www.kornat-*

turist.hr). Not that the week of pure escapism which lures stressed executives is the only reason to visit – their pristine bays make the Kornatis day trip heaven, too.

Nin

*Frequent buses go 14km north from Zadar in 45mins and cost 11Kn each way; get times of return buses from Nin tourist information (Trg braće Radić, before bridge to old gate, **t** (023) 265 247; open May–Sept Mon–Sat 8–8, Sun 9–12).*

Forget Zagreb, roll over Split. If any settlement can stake its claim to be cradle of Croatia it is Nin (*see* 'Touring from Zadar', p.93). The village slumbering quietly on an island in soupy marshes dimly recalls glory years as the royal seat of the nation's first kings in its **Archaeology Museum**, and there's a faint echo of its years as Croatian powerbase in an inscription which salutes 9th-century ruler Župan on the lintel of diminutive **Church of the Holy Cross** (Crkva sv. Križa), the first church Croatia ever built – small wonder that poet Vinko Nikolić acclaimed Nin the 'Croatian Bethlehem'. Not that Nin is all history – after a morning spent poring over snapshots of the infant Croatia, a rare sandy **beach** entreats you to ease, like Nin, into daydreams.

Dugi Otok

A sliver of land 43km long, never more than 4.6km wide and coated in a thick fuzz of scrubby pine, 'Long Island' seems to have drifted through the centuries untrammelled by the events which raged on the mainland. Without freshwater springs, civilization – from Romans to Zadar Venetians who fled Turkish raiders – established little more than a fingerhold on the largest island of the Zadar archipelago; indeed, its modern worry is depopulation. And, while Zadar inhabitants were sheltering underground from the hail of Serbian shells in 1991, Dugi Otok's 1,800 inhabitants busied themselves with the Mediterranean mainstays of fishing, sheep-farming and vineyards. Even tourism, wooed in Zadar since the late 1800s, is a newcomer – and that, alongside the wild Telašćica Nature Park, is reason enough to visit.

Nearly half of Dugi Otok's population call main port **Sali** home, but don't let that put you off, because this is a quietly handsome Mediterranean harbour which slumbers in the afternoon sunshine until the evening cool encourages a gentle *korzo* (stroll). The medieval salt-pans which christened the island's largest village fell in importance compared to fishing, and in summer some Sali locals pause from their nets to catch tourists keen to embark on a spree to the neighbouring moonscape of the Kornati National Park (*see* p.90).

Most boats also wriggle through islets before the Kornati to the **Telašćica National Park**, but you can also reach this pristine 8km inlet scattered casually with islets by walking 3km south of Sali through olive groves (signposted before Sali if driving). Arrive by car and for once there's no need to explore off-track, because the views are sensational – the road wraps around the bay's east end, then cuts across to vertiginous cliffs on the park's wild south shore; their vantage point, up to 525ft high and 10km (6 miles) long, offers spectacular views of an Adriatic speckled by sails. A

Getting There and Around

Regular Jadrolinija **ferries** weave through the Zadar archipelago to Bribinj, Sali and Zaglav (*1hr 30mins; foot passenger 14Kn, car (Bribinj only) 60kn*) and a summer-only Miatours **hydrofoil** speeds to Božava (*40mins, 30Kn*).

A **bus** meets ferries at Bribinj and trundles north to Božava and Veli Rat; another meets arrivals at either Sali and Zaglav to connect the two villages. Apart from that, only one bus a week links north and south Dugi Otok, so your own **car** (hire one in Zadar) is essential to really explore – a single, spectacular road traces the island's spine. The island petrol station is at Zaglav, 5km north of Sali.

Tourist Information

Sali: harbour, **t** (023) 377 094. *Open May–Oct daily 8–12 and 5–8; Nov–April Mon–Fri 8–2.*
Božava: **t** (023) 377 607. *Open daily June–Sept 8–12 and 6–8.*

Where to Stay

Dugi Otok **t** (023) –

Both tourist offices can advise about **rooms** (*inexpensive*) in private houses – true escapists should investigate daydreaming villages such as Dragove or Luka.

Both hotels operate May–Oct only.
Sali, Sali, **t** 377 049, *www.hotel-sali.hr* (*moderate*). Air-conditioning, fridges and balcony views over a quiet bay come as standard in the 52 modest but comfy en-suite rooms of this friendly hotel five minutes' walk from the harbour.
Božava, Božava, **t** 377 618 (*inexpensive*). Standard package fare in a complex of hotels screened by pine woods by the harbour; adequate but unspectacular.

Eating Out

Kod Sipe, Sali, **t** 377 137 (*moderate*). *Hobotnica ispod peke* (octopus baked under a *peka*) is a chef special of this lovely *konoba*; locate the stairs which ascend off the harbourside to find its cosy wood interior where locals put the world to rights, or the spacious al fresco dining area.
Boxavia, Božava, **t** 377 614 (*moderate*). Simple bench seating and prime views over the harbour to accompany a house-special fish platter and tasty seafood delights, from simple grilled squid to rich *škampi na buzara*.
Marin, Sali, **t** 377 500 (*moderate*). This charming back street *konoba* just off the harbour end prepares a small menu of tasty grilled meats, served in a snug dining room hung with nets or a small terrace.

number of nearby bays tempt you to pause for a dip; alternatively, the **Jezero Mir** lake rewards those who explore further east. Even if you refuse to believe local tales about the salt water's curative properties, the lake is a few degrees warmer than the bay.

From **Bribinj**, just a dock and lone restaurant-*pension*, the island's only road idles north past hilltop village **Dragove**, which shimmers in the heat-haze like a water-colour of terracottas and greens, to dozy fishing village **Božava**, whose stone houses huddle around a pretty harbour lined with seasonal *konobe* and cafés. Beyond it, a path rambles around a rocky, pine-cloaked headland to swimming spots off rocks.

The best beach on Dugi Otok, however, is **Sakarun**, a double-bill treat of aromatic pine woods behind and spectacular views down the island's rugged spine in front. Its fine-shingle crescent is signposted northwest of Božava on the road towards village **Veli Rat**, a string of houses on a bay with Roman roots. Continue northwest and the road peters out at an 1849 Austro-Hungarian **lighthouse**, whose bricks were mortared with 100,000 egg yolks (and a considerable dollop of faith) and which overlooks a handful of notches for a dip.

Touring from Zadar

Day 1: North to Nin and Pag

Morning: Head north to **Nin**, cradle of Croatia. At the heart of an islet village which dozes after years as seat of the nation's first kings is the diminutive Church of the Holy Cross. Its lintel inscription salutes 9th-century ruler Godežav, who commissioned the first church Croatia ever built. To peek into its bare and usually locked interior, consult the Archaeological Museum (Arheološka Muzej; *open June–Aug Mon–Sat 9–12 and 6–8, Sept–May 9–12; adm*), with a century-spanning gallery of early Croatian and Roman finds. Look for remains of the Italians' temple of Diana behind, then admire the treasury of nearby St Anselmo (*open May–Aug Mon–Sat 9–1 and 5–9; adm*). Then walk to dinky 11th-century St Nicholas on a defensive blister off the Zadar road, or amble 3km north to Kraljičina, one of Croatia's best beaches.

Lunch: In Nin, *see* below.

Afternoon: Drive east of Nin towards Vrsi then follow signs to island **Pag**, grazed to a moonscape and famous for its tangy sheep's cheese. Dalmatian Renaissance superstar Juraj Dalmatinac drew the neat grid of its eponymous, intimate capital and crowned his main square with grand parish church St Mary's. Its doily-like rose window is an apt flourish for an island with a lace obsession: Austro-Hungarian Empress Maria Theresia prized it so highly that she retained a Pag lace-maker at the Viennese court. Admire samplers in the nearby lace museum (*open daily July–Aug 8–10; adm free*) then pick up a souvenir piece in Tomislava or Zvonimira.

Dinner and Sleeping: In Pag town, *see* below.

Day 1

Lunch in Nin

Branimir, Trg Višeslavov, **t** (023) 284 866 (*expensive–moderate*). Nin's finest *konoba* is classy-rustic in style, with a terrace which overlooks the Church of the Holy Cross and a menu of top-notch local cuisine. Try a platter of white fish and crab cooked under a *peka*.

Sokol, Hrvatskog Sabora, **t** (023) 234 442 (*moderate*). Charcoal-grilled meats are served in a courtyard restaurant near the lower bridge (Donji most).

Buffet Branimir, Trg Kraljevac bb, no tel (*cheap*). Sandwiches, salads and light bites in a café on Nin's sweetest square, located before the Archaeological Museum and perfect for people-watching.

Dinner in Pag Town

Smokva, Golija bb, **t** (023) 611 095 (*moderate*). Start with the freshest island cheese then tuck into *Paška janjetina* (Pag lamb) on a terrace littered with rustic knick-knacks and which gazes out across the bay.

Bodulo, Van Grade 19, no tel (*cheap*). An old-fashioned Dalmatia *konoba* that's a credit to the name: snug, simple and with a small menu of basic meat and fish dishes.

Sleeping in Pag Town

Source **private rooms** (*cheap*) at **Mediteran**, Nazora 12, **t** (023) 611 238, or **Sunturist**, Šetalište Gradac Carbonere 1, **t** (023) 612 060.

Pagus, A Starčevica 1, **t** (023) 611 309 (*moderate*). The closest hotel to the old town, just a 5-minute walk from the town centre, is a brisk and efficient number before a strip of beach, with modern, spacious rooms and three-star facilities.

Biser, AG Matoša 8, **t** (023) 611 333 (*inexpensive*). Rather dated décor of lacy net curtains and 1980s pastel shades, but with air-conditioning and satellite TV in 20 en-suite rooms, the best with views across the bay to the old town, and an excellent restaurant.

Day 2: On to Rab

Morning: Twist 20km north to **Novalja**. Romans would stare at the settlement they established on a notch in the coast, today the busiest of Pag's resorts. However, their engineers would recognize the kilometre-long 1st-century underground aqueduct aerated by nine vents, a technical feat which locals slight as the Talijanova buža ('Italians' hole'). Don a miner's helmet then squeeze along a section open as part of the town museum (*on Kralja Zvonimira; open Mon–Sat 10–12 and 5–7; adm*). Then breathe freely at shingle beach Straško south of the centre or smaller sand coves in Babe north. Afterwards drive to **Žigljen** through the bare 'Pag Triangle' – islanders swear it's a honeypot for extraterrestrials – to catch a boat to mainland port **Prizna**. Drive 10km north to **Jablanac** before you hop back across the water to **Rab** island.

Lunch: In Novalja or Rab town, *see* below.

Afternoon: Explore ravishing **Rab town**, a medieval beauty of creamy stone and terracotta which made its fortune as a silk trader and enjoyed a golden age as self-governing city-state until its ambitions were shackled by Venice in 1409. Get your bearings and admire Rab's roofscape from the belvedere of the Great Bell Tower (Veli zvonik; *open May–Sept daily 10–1 and 7.30–10; adm*), campanile of the adjacent Church of St Mary whose crescendo of 12th-century arches rests on Roman foundations. East along the same sacred spine street, aloof from the mercantile old town, there are more views from a chunk of medieval town wall and from the campanile of the ruined 7th-century Basilica of St John the Evangelist, with a small lapidarium of assorted headstones and carvings (*open summer daily 9–1 and 6–8; adm*).

Dinner and Sleeping: In Rab town, *see* below.

Day 2

Lunch in Novalja

Steffani, Petra Krešimira IV 28, **t** (023) 661 697 (*moderate*). The best of the otherwise bland choice of eateries, this centrally located restaurant rustles up catch of the day and in season its chef prepares a thick lamb stew.

Lunch or Dinner in Rab Town

For more restaurant choices, *see* 'Day 3'.
Ana, Palit 80, **t** (051) 724 376 (*expensive–moderate*). A talented chef peps up old faves such as grilled Rab lamb or Adriatic fish in a salt crust with subtle flavours in this smart new town restaurant which locals salute as one of the island's finest addresses.
Rab, Kneza Branimira 3, **t** (051) 725 666 (*moderate*). A little touristy, perhaps, but still a charming *konoba* which oozes homespun rusticity in a balconied interior full of cosy nooks and decorated with rough-plastered walls, heavy beams and tiled roofs. Try island lamb or veal slow-cooked under a *peka*.
Paradiso, Stjepana Radića 2, **t** (051) 771 109 (*cheap*). A long-standing tourist favourite thanks to its courtyard setting, this offers a large menu of tasty pizzas and pastas.

Sleeping in Rab Town

Ros Maris, Obala Petra Krešimira IV, **t** (051) 778 899 (*expensive*). Designer style and rich tones of chocolate, ruby and calico from a stylish newcomer (2004) on the harbour with a good restaurant and a spa, too.
Istria, M de Dominisa bb, **t** (051) 742 276 (*moderate*). A keenly priced small hotel on the harbour – the best simple but comfortable en suite rooms boast harbour views from their balconies.
Imperial, Palit bb, **t** (051) 724 544 (*moderate*). Rather frumpy and tired, but this large old-timer is rescued by a price just the wrong side of inexpensive and a location among the pines and palms of a verdant park.

Day 3: A Relaxed Island Idyll

Morning: Continue your exploration of Rab in Trg Municipium Arbe, a café-society favourite dominated by the Gothic Rector's Palace – Venetian-appointed overlords proclaimed dictates from the leonine balcony. Then return uphill to the church of St Justine (Crkva sv. Justina) near the Great Bell Tower. Its nuns having been evicted by Napoleon in 1808, the 1572 convent church now hosts the Museum of Sacred Art (Muzej Sakralne Umjetnosti; *open daily June–Sept 10–12 and 6–8; adm*), a treasury of ecclesiastica with vestments like tapestries, a 1350s *Crucifixion* polyptych by Paolo Veneziano and a box reliquary which holds the skull of St Christopher and depicts scenes of his martyrdom. Work up an appetite for lunch on a 3km stroll west to the monastery of St Euphemia (Samostan sv. Fumije; *open June–Sept Mon–Sat 9–12 and 4–6; adm*); its Gothic church juxtaposes an ethereal ceiling and tortured crucifix.

Lunch: In Rab town or Supetarska Draga, *see* below.

Afternoon: In 1936 British king Edward VIII scandalized Britons (and titillated Europe and America) when he chose the belle of the Kvarner Gulf islands to laze with Wallis Simpson. Visit the rare sand beaches which notch the **Lopar peninsula** northwest and you understand why. Resort **San Marino** is fronted by family-favourite Rajska Plaža (Paradise Beach). For the more secluded Sahara and Stolac bays, take the path which loops around the headland – crowd numbers and swimming costumes lower the further you go. Alternatively, pull on hiking boots and explore the footpaths of the rugged southwest **Kalifront peninsula** to locate a rocky cove backed by pine forest – the best line the south coast.

Dinner and Sleeping: In Rab town or Supetarska Draga, *see* below.

Day 3

Lunch, Dinner or Sleeping in Supetarska Draga

Zlatni Zalaz, Supetarska Draga 379, **t** (051) 775 150 (*expensive–moderate*). Rather a dignitary among Rab eateries, located just a few kilometres before Lopar. Savour the sweeping panoramas over the coast and fresh fish or, with luck, leg of lamb. It also offers 14 rooms (*moderate*).

Lunch or Dinner in Rab Town

For more restaurant choices, *see* 'Day 2'.

Santa Maria, Dinka Dokule 6, **t** (0 51) 724 196 (*moderate*). Fish and seafood – *škampi na buzaru* (shrimps tossed in white wine and garlic) is a lunchtime treat – plus the restaurant offers a world tour of grilled steaks in a classy establishment which claims the courtyard of a merchant's 14th-century mansion in the old town.

Riva, Biskupa Draga bb, no tel (*cheap*). A down-to-earth *konoba* snuggled off main square Trg Municipium Arbe, with a cosy stone interior. Expect a changing menu of simple tasty fare: *girice* (small fish, like whitebait) or *lignje na žaru* (grilled squid).

Kod Kineza, Kneza Domagoja bb, no tel (*cheap*). It's no surprise that the chef of this cellar *konoba* hung with fishing nets and decorated with folksy clutter prepares his dishes straight up and simple – tasty Adriatic fish and squid, grilled and soused in olive oil, and country fillers such as roast lamb and roast knuckle of veal.

Sleeping in Rab Town

Ros Maris, Obala Petra Krešimira IV, **t** (051) 778 899 (*expensive*). See 'Day 2'.

Istria, M de Dominisa bb, **t** (051) 742 276 (*moderate*). See 'Day 2'.

Imperial, Palit bb, **t** (051) 724 544 (*moderate*). See 'Day 2'.

Day 4: Climbing Clefts in Paklenica National Park

Morning: Catch a ferry back to the mainland then drive south to **Starigrad-Paklenica** and the sensational **Paklenica National Park** (*adm 30Kn*). Even reluctant walkers should pull on trainers to view stunning little-and-large limestone gorges Mala and Velika Paklenica, cut like giant axe clefts in 1,300ft cliffs. From a car park beyond the park ticket booth, a cement path ascends into narrow karst **Velika Paklenica**, at some points only 30m wide beneath the cliffs. After 40 minutes, catch your breath before a sweaty ascent (signposted right) around the back of Anića Kuk to stand on the top of a 2,350ft face scaled by daredevil climbers and be rewarded with spectacular views. Alternatively, press on for 1km through lush forest, past a right-hand fork which loops through Mala Paklenica, for a stiff zigzag up to cave **Manite peći** (*open July–Aug daily 10–1; June and Sept Mon, Wed, Sat 10–1; adm*) hung with stalactites. A path rewards those who ascend for an hour east with a view over neighbouring islands from **Vidakov kuk** (806m/2,644ft). Otherwise, continue 2km beyond the cave fork for lunch at Lugarnica; allow a 2hr walk from the car park directly to lunch.

Lunch: In Paklenica National Park, *see below.*

Afternoon: Lightweights can return through Velika Paklenica to **Starigrad-Paklenica**'s best beach, on a headland south of Hotel Alan. Explorers as sturdy as their footwear should venture into the rugged wilderness of southern sister gorge **Mala Paklenica**, which loops back to coastal village **Seline** 2.5km south of Starigrad-Paklenica; allow 8hrs for a full circuit from the car park and consider carefully buying a map (44Kn) in the park office (*open Mon–Fri 8–3*) in the centre of Starigrad-Paklenica.

Dinner and Sleeping: In Starigrad-Paklenica, *see below.* Zadar is a short drive south.

Day 4

Lunch in Paklenica National Park

Lugarnica, a 2hr walk from car park, no tel (*cheap*). Stock up on hearty grilled sausages, sandwiches, water and coffee for the return journey in a former forester's hut, a charmer snuggled among woods and located beside a chuckling stream. *Closed Oct–May.*

Dinner in Starigrad-Paklenica

As well as these, a string of establishments on the main road throw open doors in season and all the hotels have good restaurants.
Roli, Stipana Bušljete 1, **t** (023) 369 018 (*moderate*). A good choice for a relaxed evening meal, with a haul of fresh fish snapped up that morning at the harbour and a pleasant terrace sheltered from the main road. Also has rooms (*inexpensive*).
Dalmacija, Sv. Jurja 9 **t** (023) 369 018 (*cheap*). Follow a track south from the central market to hunt out this laid-back, modern café-restaurant with a peaceful seafront location. Chef's special *Pladanj Dalmacija* (*moderate*) rewards ravenous walkers with a mixed meat-feast for two, plus there are the usual Adriatic fish, risottos and pastas.

Sleeping in Starigrad-Paklenica

Vicko, Jose Dokoze 20, **t** (0 23) 369 304 (*moderate*). The décor dates as you move upstairs from simple modern to traditional, but all rooms in this quietly swish, family three-star are spacious and comfy. Seafront sister hotel **Depandanse** has slick modern style and bright spacious rooms (*expensive*).
Alan, Dr Franje Tudmana 14, **t** (023) 369 236 (*moderate*). Comfy if a little bland modern rooms in a large package three-star before the beach and with a swimming pool.
Ranja, Dr Franje Tudmana 105, **t** (023) 359 105 (*inexpensive*). Modest rooms in a trekkers' choice near the park entrance which offers year-round park jeep tours.

Split

Fizzing with metropolitan vim and endearingly scatty, Split is not nearly as well known as it deserves. Dubrovnik may steal all the international limelight, but this, the nation's second city, may have the more intriguing personality, because, whereas its southern rival protects its Baroque timewarp so fiercely that shop signs are outlawed in its showpiece streets, Split just shrugs and dons as everyday wear architectural hand-me-downs that span nearly a millennium. Locals queue for a teller without batting an eye at the UNESCO-listed Roman columns which march across the bank, and stylish boutiques display high-fashion handbags in medieval aristocrats' mansions. Even Split's Sunday best, the cathedral, is allowed to show signs of age.

Split emerged from the AD 295 seaside retirement home Roman emperor Diocletian built to live out his dotage in, an easy trot from regional capital Salona (*see* p.107). Despite a few centuries' use as an imperial holiday home after Diocletian's death, the magnificent *castrum*-cum-villa fell into ruin until 7th-century refugees, fleeing sacked

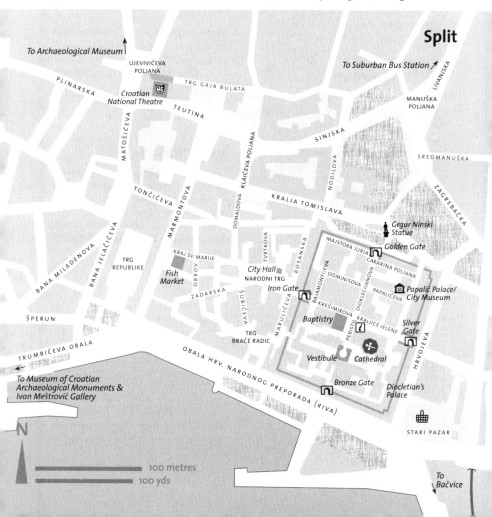

Getting There

From April to October, Croatia Airlines **flies** from Heathrow and Gatwick and British Airways flies from Gatwick in 2hrs 35mins. **Ferry** companies Adriatica di Navigazione, SMC and Jadrolinija sail year-round from Ancona, Italy, in around 9hrs, with up to five or six ferries a week in July and August. From June to Sept SNAV operates a fast, 4hr **catamaran** service from Ancona. *See pp.3–8.*

Getting from the Airport

A scheduled Croatia Airlines **bus** (30Kn) shuttles new arrivals and departees 1hr 30mins before take-off to and from a bus stop at the east end of the Riva. Miss that and Trogir-Split bus 37 (14Kn) runs to the suburban bus stop on Domoviniskog rata 15mins walk north of the centre. Expect to pay around 250Kn for a **taxi** from the airport.

Getting Around

The pedestrianized historic centre is a strollers' paradise, riddled with interesting alleys which you will still be exploring after a week. Bus 12 (stop opposite Trg Republike) is a godsend to reach museums west of the centre and the beaches of the Marjan peninsula: a single costs 7Kn from the driver, a return 10Kn when bought from a tobacconist or newsstand (*tisak*). Buses to Trogir and Salona depart from the **suburban bus station** 1km north of the centre on Domovinskog rata. **Taxis** congregate at either end of the Riva.

Car Hire

All agencies also operate bureaux at the airport.
Hertz, Tomića stine 9, **t** (021) 360 455.
ABC and **ADEX**, Obala Lazareta 3, **t** (021) 342 364 and **t** (021) 344 344 respectively.
Avis, Obala kneza Branimira 8 (in Hotel Marjan), **t** (021) 399 000.
ITR, Obala Lazareta 2, **t** (021) 343 264.

Tourist Information

Split: Adjacent to the cathedral on the Peristil, **t** (021) 347 100, *www.visitsplit.com*. *Open*
Mon–Fri 8–8, Sat 8–1, Sun 9–1. Ever-helpful though often beleagured, the tourist information office provides free sketch maps of the city, lists of departure times for all Split ferries and a contacts sheet of every telephone number and address you'll need, from diving and sailing schools to the usual car hire and consolates. It also sells the superb **Split Card** (35Kn; free if staying over 72hrs) which allows free or 50% discounts for all museums and galleries, 20% discounts on car hire and cheap deals on hotels and restaurants. Private agencies (*see* 'Where to Stay', p.99) also stock the card and can book jaunts to neighbouring towns and sports activities.

Festivals

The Peristyle and squares of the old town ring to top-notch opera and classical music and host dance and theatre during mid-July to mid-Aug arts extravaganza the **Split Summer Festival**, and the Peristyle fills with religious theatre on **7 May** for the feast of patron saint St Domnius.

Shopping

Forget uninspiring shopping high street **Marmontova** and explore instead the boutiques of innovative independent designers in the old town warren; the **Get**, the northeastern quadrant of Diocletian's palace christened for its former Jewish ghetto, is a good hunting ground.

Touristy crafts and handicrafts are on sale in the market which fills the **cellars of Diocletian's Palace** between the Peristyle and Riva. Antique-lovers should rummage through **Antikvarnica**, Cosmija 1, near Sarajevo restaurant, or **Antik Shop & Galerija** on Trg Cararina Poliana.

Foodies will delight at **Vinoteka sv. Martin**, Majstora Jurja 17, stockist of high-quality Croatian wines, honeys, olive oils and truffles. More tipples fill shelves of **Vinoteka Bouquet**, Riva 3, west of Trg Republike. For rustic authenticity, however, explore home-made food, wine and *rakija* sold at the daily market east of the Silver Gate.

Where to Stay

Split **t** (021) –

Bargains are rare in Split. The major port assumes its visitors are passing through on their way to the islands and the few hotels there hike prices. Most are in the dull new town: for rooms inside the historic warren, try the modest but good-value trio listed or source **rooms** (*inexpensive*) in private houses through tourist agencies: the most convenient are **Turistički Biro**, Riva 12, **t** 347 100, and **Atlas**, Trg Braće Radić 6, **t** 343 055.

Park, Hatzeov perivoj 3, **t** 406 400, *www.hotel-park-split.hr* (*expensive*). A touch of class from Split's premier address, located in a stone 1700s building and with a pedigree it traces to 1921. Marble floors and hushed waiters lend an air of yesteryear elegance in public areas, continued in silk cushions and soft tones of plush rooms, all with ISDN lines for e-mail junkies and doubles with a view over Bačvice beach 50m away.

Marjan, Obala Kneza Branimira 8, **t** 302 111, *www.hotel-marjan.com* (*moderate*). Not nearly as dismal as its semi-derelict exterior suggests, but a dated and rather pricey offering for the modest rooms of the one-time city flagship. Concentrate instead on harbour views from some and a location an easy stroll from the buzzy Riva.

Bellevue, Bana Jelačića 2, **t** 345 644, *www.hotel-bellevue-split.hr* (*moderate*). Better still is the excellent position of this old-timer overlooking Trg Republike. Spacious rooms boast 1979-vintage high ceilings and authentically frumpy heavy wood décor.

Globo, Lovretska 18, **t** 481 111 (*moderate*). Four-star mod cons and quietly plush rooms for businessmen, one block west of the bus station and 10mins walk north of the centre.

Adriana, Riva 8, **t** 340 000, *www.hotel-adriana.hr* (*moderate*). Comfy accommodation is decent without being remarkable, but this is all about an unbeatable location smack on the Riva – all but two rooms are with a view over the harbour.

Jadran, Sustipanski put 23, **t** 398 622, *www.hoteljadran.hr* (*moderate*). A bright and breezy small hotel with a peaceful location behind the ACI marina of Sustipan. En-suite accommodation is modest though adequate and there are tennis courts, a pool and access to the sea for a dip.

Consul, Tršćanska 34, **t** 340 130, *www.hotel-consul.net* (*moderate*). Nothing special but a small, friendly three-star in a leafy residential street north of the centre; all rooms are spacious, some boast a Jacuzzi.

Slavija, Buvinina 2, **t** 323 840 (*moderate–inexpensive*). Simple but modern en suite rooms priced just the wrong side of cheap are the biggest bargain in Split; cheaper rooms share facilities and have basic pine décor. Either way, location one block east of Braće Radica is excellent. Breakfast not included.

Jupiter, Grabovčeva širina 1, **t** 344 081, *www.hotel-jupiter.info* (*inexpensive*). A family-run *pension* with the cheapest beds in Split. Tatty rooms, although spotless, verge on hostel-esque, but no quibbles about a location moments south of the Jupiter Palace. Breakfast not included.

Eating Out

Split **t** (021) –

Stuffed with boutiques it may be, but Split's old town lacks a glut of restaurants. A good hunting ground is on the western edge of the old town, in lanes west of Trg Republike at the fringe of residential district Veli Varoš. For a quick snack on the go, join the queue of locals waiting for *čevapčići* (spicy meat rissoles) from Kantun Paulina, opposite Pizzeria Galija.

Boban, Hektorovićeva 49 (parallel to Bačvice beach road Put Firula), **t** 543 300 (*expensive*). The gourmet's choice, visited by prime ministers and luminaries such as Placido Domingo. A well-priced menu of Croatian dishes adds Italian accents – *grob grdobine* (monkfish) grilled with bacon in a cream sauce; spicy lobster and tomato stew *jastog na brudet* pepped up with white wine and herbs; or a superb sushi-style fish carpaccio – and the cellar is sensational.

Šumica, Put Firla 6, **t** 389 897 (*expensive*). The freshest fish and shellfish plus a good choice of meats – try two-person house special meat-feast Plata Šumica – in a classy place just west of Bačvice beach with a terrace.

Noštromo, Kraj svete Marije 10, **t** 091 405 6666 (*expensive–moderate*). Chef's special *riblja* *plata*, a mixed plate of fishy treats, plus super-fresh catch of the day and seafood in a designer number of blonde wood and gleaming aluminium beside the fish market. Tables are limited: reserve or wait.

Sarajevo, Domaldova 6, **t** 347 454 (*moderate*). A bastion of traditional dining off Narodni trg, ruled by waiters in black-and-whites and with dark wood décor and Gothic arches. Dalmation dishes – fish and meats in creamy sauces – are on the menu.

Kod Joze, Sredmanuška 4 (off Zagrebačka), **t** 347 397 (*moderate*). Hardly the secret it once was and tourists often outnumber locals, but this charming *konoba* is a gem nonetheless, its snug stone dining rooms unbeatable for cosy atmosphere. A large menu covers all bases and risottos and pastas come at bargain prices.

Varoš, Ban Mladenova 7, **t** 396 138 (*moderate*) Highly rated by locals for a slap-up dinner of speciality *peka* dishes – veal, lamb, octopus or squid slow-cooked beneath a lid heaped with charcoal. Visit at lunchtime and there are bargains to be had.

Šperun, Šperun 3, **t** 346 999 (*cheap*). A taste of Dalmatia – chef specials include *tripice* (tripe), *bakalar* (cod) and fish stew *brodet* – in a small family restaurant. Start with a Capri-style Dalmatian cheese, spiced with tomato, basil, pepper and olive oil.

Zlata Ribica, Krav Svete Marije 8, no tel (*cheap*). No airs or graces and precious few smiles in a snack bar beside the fish market. Daily specials on the blackboard bolster a short menu of small plates of *prezzne lignje* (fried squid) or *mijessana riba* (mixed fish platter). Closes 9pm weekdays, 2pm weekends.

Pizzeria Galija, Tončićeva 12, **t** 347 932 (*cheap*). Split's finest pizzas cooked in a charcoal oven, plus tasty antipasti and pastas in sauces laced with cream and brandy, a block north of Trg Republike.

Zlatna Vrata Pizzeria, Mastorja Jurja, **t** 341 834 (*cheap*). If Galija has the reputation, this has the atmosphere, thanks to tables scattered in a Renaissance courtyard.

Cafés and Bars

The Riva is crammed with cafés; it's a mite smarter at the western end, probably why locals favour east-end café Bobis for a gossip after market. Young, funky bars spill out on to the street in Dosud, a block east of Mihovilova Širina; more poised are al fresco bars on Majstora Jurja, arty and relaxed by day, hip and stylish by night.

Porta and Dante, Majstora Jurja 4. In a small courtyard, the Twenties, brasserie-style former has over 100 cocktails in its recipe book, the latter has a chunk of Gothic arch in a snug interior and a larger terrace. Both serve Elevenses coffee and late-night drinks to Split's 30-something fashion cognoscenti.

Getto, Dosud 10. Arty bar with occasional exhibitions secreted away in a courtyard away from its noisy neighbours.

Gradska kavana, Narodni trg. Wicker seats and grandstand views for people-watching in one of Split's smarter cafés.

Žbirac, Bačvice beach. Daytime beach bar, where the beautiful people meet for a morning kava wake-up call. Nearby **Equador** bar lacks the escapist charm but boasts better views from its raised bar.

Vidilica, Prilaz Vladimira Nazora. Deep chairs in which to enjoy fine views over Split from a belvedere on the Marjan peninsula path.

Entertainment

What's-on information is sourced from municipal posters displayed on billboards throughout the old town (there's one before the Silver Gate, another north before the theatre) or from newspaper *Slobodna Dalmacija*.

For folk dancing and music; informal lunchtime concerts of *klapa* (Dalmatian male-voice choirs) and folksy quartets are staged in the Peristil and Nadroni trg in peak season; check with tourist information for current times.

Croatian National Theatre (Hrvatsko Narodno Kazalište, or HNK), Trg Gaja Bulata, **t** 344 999. Theatre, classical concerts and opera from the bastion of Split cultural life which co-ordinates the Summer Festival.

Shakespeare, Uvala Zente 3. An eclectic mix of pop and house plus occasional live concerts in the pick of Bačvice's nightspots, with a terrace that overlooks the sea.

Salona, patched up the fabric of their adopted home, then safeguarded it in statute by accepting Byzantine authority. Nurtured by the stability of the fledgling Croat kingdom, early medieval Split fleshed out its Roman skeleton into a warren of alleys and sudden squares which beg you to explore by instinct; and three centuries under Venetian rule introduced elegant Italian mansions and handsome piazzas.

Despite a forgettable modern town that has bloated Split into the post-Second World War giant of the Adriatic, that old-town mish-mash intrigues today as it did when it lured 18th-century architect Robert Adam to study Diocletian's palace, a role model he looked to when he designed Georgian London and Edinburgh and set the benchmark for British neoclassical design. And as if to balance the cerebral appeal of a palace included on UNESCO's World Heritage list in 1979, and Dalmatia's best museums, Split boasts a lazy café scene, buzzy bars and streets chock full of shops which untie purse strings as if by magic.

Around the Peristyle

Nowhere displays Split's early history so cleanly as the area around the **Peristyle** (Peristil), Diocletian's ceremonial courtyard at the crossroads of the east–west *decumanus* and north–south *cardo* which carved the palace into quadrants and are still hinted at by the modern street map. Corinthian columns and noble arches march along its sides – a grateful Renaissance architect incorporated them into the Gisogono-Cipci nobleman's palace on the northwest side – to frame the *protiron* at its south end. Even a pair of Renaissance chapels stuffed beneath the gable cannot hush the declaration of authority made by the front door to Diocletian's palace building, and if it impresses today it must have positively swaggered when crowned by a sculpture of four horses. It doesn't stretch the imagination too far to visualize the retired emperor in bright silks on his public balcony, gazing with haughty disdain over subjects prostrate before the self-declared son of Jupiter. The Peristyle is the main stage of celebrations for city patron St Dominus on 7 May and operatic extrava- ganzas of the Split Summer Festival. Admire a black granite sphinx before the *protiron*, a spoil of war from Diocletian's AD 297–9 campaigns in Egypt and the only one of 11 not ritually smashed after his death, then ascend beneath its mighty loggia to reach the domed **vestibule**, once coated in mosaics and marble. The waiting room for anxious ambassadors is the only room of Diocletian's palace intact above ground; you have to imagine the rest, and piece it together from the shape of the modern streets in its place and cellars below (*see* p.103).

The streets and squares beyond offer respite from Peristyle crowds in a shabby district overlooked by tourism, as if forever tainted by the down-at-heel and disgraced Romans who settled the southern quadrants after Diocletian's death.

The Cathedral and Baptistry

Sidekick to the Peristyle and holy of holies ever since Split made its début is the **Cathedral of St Domnius** (Katedral sveti Duje; *open 7–12 and 5–7*). The vainglorious Diocletian pooh-poohed the Roman custom of burial outside city walls as stuff for mere mortals and demanded instead a central, octagonal mausoleum attended by an arcade of columns looted from Grecian and Egyptian temples. Unwisely as it turns out, because, nearly 200 years after his death in AD 313, his mortal remains vanished from their final resting place in mysterious circumstances. That was a minor slight compared with the final insult, however – 7th-century refugees from Salona hijacked the tomb of an emperor who spent his final years feverishly persecuting Christians and transformed it into a church to venerate the bones of St Domnius. With delicious irony, Diocletian himself had demanded the head of Salona's first bishop in AD 304.

Ascend the cathedral's steps, guarded by a pair of snarling Romanesque lions, to magnificent walnut **doors**, a 28-panel Bible cartoon strip for 13th-century illiterates by local son Andrija Buvina which must have dazzled when painted and gold-plated, and enter an intimate **interior** whose nooks are crammed with ecclesiastical clutter. Diocletian's tomb in all its imperial pomp probably stood at the centre of the octagon beneath a shimmering skin of mosaics which coated the domed roof. A purge of pagan iconography stripped the mausoleum of both – a 13th-century Split archdeacon noted sagely an 'exorcism' of pagan spirits – but the Christians could not eradicate the dome's sash of Roman chariot-racing or hunting scenes, nor, wreathed by garlands and lauded by cupids, the reliefs of Diocletian and wife Empress Priscia.

One story claims that fragments of the emperor's ruby-coloured porphyry sarcophagus ended up in the 13th-century **pulpit**, whose slender columns bud into fabulous Romanesque capitals of tangled thickets where dragons and serpents lurk. Eclipsing even these is the 1448 **altar of St Anastasius**, on the cusp between Gothic and Renaissance and created by Croatian superstar architect Juraj Dalmatinac, whose exquisite pen drew the UNESCO-listed cathedral in Šibenik (*see* pp.88–9). Its patron reclines with the millstone with which he was drowned by Diocletian after the clothdyer, newly arrived from Aquileia in Italy and an innocent in Salona, daubed a cross on his front door. As if penitent for the sins of its founding father, Split has adopted the Chrsitian martyr as a second patron and venerates his bones behind reliefs of saints and a vicious relief of the scourging of Christ. Dalmatinac modelled his work on the 1427 **sarcophagus of St Domnius** on the opposite side of the cathedral; its dozing bishop and late-Gothic baldachin are the vision of Milanese master Bonino, the saint's sarcophagus before it was the devotional labour of an AD 2 Christian stonemason. The saint's holy remains are now in a whimsical Baroque altar by Venetian artist Giovan Maria Morlaiter stuffed into a chapel beside the St Anastasius altar.

Pause at a **choir** tacked awkwardly on to the original building in the 17th century only to look for 13th-century hunters and craftsmen who hide on the oldest choir stalls in Dalmatia, before investigating the **treasury** (*adm*) crammed with the cathedral's glittering goodies: reliquaries of saints Domnius and Anastasius, shimmering vestments and, in pride of place, the *Evangelarium Spalatenese* gospel brought to Split with the first Christian refugees and the oldest manuscript Croatia owns. Return outside the cathedral and you can descend to a missable **crypt** (*adm*), or pick out the palace ground plan (or simply admire a superb roofscape) from a belvedere of the 200ft-high **campanile** (*in theory, open daily summer 8–8, winter times erratic; adm*) – its slender stacks, rebuilt to the original Romanesque-Gothic blueprint, stood complete in 1908 and were promptly denounced as charmless by locals.

A passage opposite the cathedral steps threads to the cathedral **baptistry** (Jupiterov hram; *open same hours as campanile; adm*), actually more recognizable as the Jupiter Temple that Diocletian erected to his adopted father. Roman gods Jupiter, Hercules, Sol and Nike as well as dogs and cherubs ornament its emphatic portal and, inside, a barrel vault is studded with flower buds and heads. For a period during Venetian rule (1420–1797) this was the ritziest prison imaginable. In better condition are Romanesque interwoven knots and plaits carved on the cross-shaped 11th-century baptismal font, on which an enthroned Croat king, possibly Krešimir IV, brandishes his orb and crucifix over either a prostrate citizen or vanquished foe. The lanky *St John the Baptist* behind is a late work by Croatia's finest modern sculptor, Ivan Meštrović.

From the Peristyle to the Riva

Largely razed above ground, the palace floorplan is fossilized underground in mirror-image as brick **cellars** (*podrum*) whose architectural integrity is intact thanks to centuries of use as a rubbish dump until cleared in the 1950s. Descend steps from the Peristyle and arts and crafts stalls huddle in the cellars, which reflect the vestibule and connecting central hall. At the latter's end stretched the *cryptoporticus*, a promenade which wafted cool sea breezes into palace rooms and doubled as Diocletian's seafront promenade, interpreted below ground as a long corridor. If it's open for intermittent antiques markets, the eastern arm allows a glimpse into cellars beneath the *triclinium* (dining hall). Otherwise, you can explore mazy Roman substructures off the *cryptoporticus*'s western arm (*open Mon–Sat 9–8, Sun 10–6; adm*) which illustrate the imperial reception hall (possibly a throne room) and a cluster of living quarters.

Exit the vaulted nether world of the central hall through the **Bronze Gate**, the southern entrance of the palace's quartet of gates. Rather than the galleon dock sketched on Roman plans, it now emerges on to a harbourside boulevard finalized in the 19th century after the infill of a swampy ditch and officially titled Obala hrvatskog naradnog preporoda (Croatian National Revival Embankment). Even tourist authorities baulk at that mouthful and sensibly dub their palm-fringed promenade the **Riva**. Do as Split locals do: study the papers over morning coffee, people-watch with a sundowner or join a vivacious *korzo* (evening stroll) – then step back from the parade for a tantalising glimpse of the seafront south wall of Diocletian's palace, a rhythmic parade of Corinthian columns and arches etched into Renaissance houses and punctuated with the definitive full-stop of a solid defence bastion at its southeast corner.

East and North of the Peristyle

Its flagstones buffed smooth by millions of feet – from Roman sandals to trainers – the *decumanus* (aka Poljana Kraljice Jelene) parades east past the cathedral and exits the former palace through the **Silver Gate**. Not that locals notice Diocletian's former east gate, nor the arches which skip along the eastern flank of the palace, in an area which twangs with life beside Split's superb **market**, a wonderland of juicy seasonal fruits and home produce – cheese and honey, olive oil and wine.

Tracing the north–south Roman *cardo* which marched briskly from Salona to the Peristyle and divided the palace's east and west quadrants, **Dioklecijanova** excavates through doddery Gothic and Renaissance houses dotted with the occasional court-yard mansion of the medieval élite. None is finer than the **Papalić Palace**, an aristocratic 15th-century pile on side street Papalićeva from the drawing board of Renaissance supremo and St Anastasius altar architect Juraj Dalmatinac. Look for its owner's star-and-feathers coat of arms in a frothy plaque before the courtyard portal before you sigh at a lovely courtyard with a well and tasteful loggia, then enter the **City Museum** (Muzej grada; *open summer Tues–Fri 9–9, Sat–Sun 9–1; winter Tues–Fri 9–4, Sat–Sun 9–1; closed Mon; adm*), whose narrative of city history, told in Roman coins stamped with a bearded Diocletian, sculpture rescued from the cathedral exterior and medieval weapons, perks up in the first-floor festive hall. Beneath its ceiling of fashionable colours and floral trim, Split's Renaissance intellectuals enthused about exciting new philosophies drifting from the other side of the Adriatic, which explains the salute to Marko Marulić – fired by the humanist ideal, the local poet renounced Latin to pen the first literary work in Croatian, *Judita* (1521).

Dioklecijanova culminates in the **Golden Gate** (Zlatna vrata) – though architectural aficionados should sidetrack right before the before the north gateway to Cararina poljane, where Split's best-preserved early-medieval house (*c.* 10th century) hides in a corner, its exterior staircase erected to preserve space inside. Even if it has lost the statuary in its niches, the stocky monumental gate retains a hint of the swagger with which Diocletian made a lasting first impression on new arrivals from Salona, with his statue and those of his tetrarchs on four column bases atop the wall.

The grave wizard who hurls a spell from fingers like spiders' legs before the gate is actually **Grgur Ninski**, 10th-century bishop of Nin (*see* p.91). who campaigned for the use of Slav over Latin in the liturgy. If the 1929 colossus cast by Ivan Meštrović to celebrate the millennium anniversary of the Synod of Split seems impressive here, it must have astounded in the Peristyle, which is probably why the occupying Italian Fascists exiled the symbol of Croatian nationalism in 1941. Rub his lucky big toe worn gold by hopeful locals as you pass to the star-shaped fortification beyond a small park, the best-preserved **bastion** of five erected by mid-17th century Venetians.

The Rest of the Old Town

Feeling the pinch of its antique girdle, a medieval city fattened through free-city status burst beyond the palace walls and by the 14th century had sprawled west to Marmontova (*see* p.105). Follow main trade route the *decumanus* through west palace entrance the **Iron Gate** to emerge in **Narodni trg**, a square clad in white marble with cafés perfect for a break from sightseeing, enjoying its dotage after centuries as the epicentre of medieval government. For an aerial perspective of 'People's Square', dubbed simply Pjaca (piazza) by locals, ascend the steps just north of the Iron Gate and follow a route trodden by expectant mothers who prayed before a 13th-century icon in **Our Lady of the Belfry** church, named after the 1090 tower which caps the gate. The square would have been more lovely still had 19th-century modernizers not razed jaded Gothic-Renaissance mansions in the name of progress. A few old-timers remain on the east flank: a Romanesque belfry with a 24-hour Renaissance clock; a Romanesque palace carved with a cartoony relief of St Anthony, a devotee hiding in his skirts; and a High Renaissance balconied mansion living in reduced circumstances as a shop. The Austro-Hungarians also spared the loggia of the Gothic **City Hall** (Gradska vijećina), which displays a traditional wardrobe of Dalmatian party frocks and Sunday best as the **Ethnographic Museum** (Etnografski Muzej; *open Mon–Fri 9–2, Sat 10–1; closed Sun; adm*).

Sweet little sister of Narodni trg, **Trg Braće Radić** is commonly nicknamed Voćni trg ('Fruit Square') in memory of an earlier market, and stars a bronze of local hero Marulić poring over his poetry by the ever-dramatic Meštrović. The octagonal tower on its south side is a leftover of a 1453 garrison citadel Venetian rulers erected to safe-guard the seafront from Turkish raids and awe Split's unruly citizens. West, there's a cosy medieval warren to explore before modernity returns with a jolt on old town border **Marmontova**. Split's shopping high street is christened in honour of French marshal Marmont, in acknowledgement of the Napoleonic governor of Dalmatia who modernized the city and carved out the Riva during his 1806–13 tenure. Reinvented in the mid-19th century, his park became **Trg Republike**, flanked on three sides with neo-Renaissance buildings and dubbed the **Prokurative** in optimistic allu-sion to its Venetian role model, although it's a rather forlorn space next to the buzzy old town. More enjoyable is a lively morning **fish market** on Krav sv. Marije opposite.

Museums North and East of the Old Centre

Away from the historic centre, a missable modern city littered with apartment blocks and carved up by heavy traffic is rescued from anonymity by Split's finest museums. Croatia's oldest, the **Archaeological Museum** (Arheološki muzej; *open June–Sept Mon–Fri 9–1 and 5–8, Sat 9–1; Oct–May Mon–Fri 9–2, Sat 9–1; adm*) 10 minutes' walk north of the centre on Zrinsko-Frankopanska, hoards rich Roman pickings unearthed at Salona. Overlook the musty didacticism of its display cases and there are exquisite gold jewellery, glassware and votive statuettes of preening gods to discover. However, the fun is in an arcaded courtyard with a treasure hunt of sculp-ture to rummage through: Roman and early Christian sarcophagi, grave slabs carved with gloomy snapshots of their interred, and crowds of decapitated statues. Don't miss, in a roadside corner tower, an immaculate 3rd-century marble sarcophagus of *Phaedra and Hippolytus*; the hero displays a love letter from the amorous stepmother he spurned, who spreads gossip with her attendants stage left, while his troubled father Theseus waits in the wings musing on accusations that his son made a move on his wife. Just as famous is a 4th-century sarcophagus in the opposite tower dubbed the *Good Shepherd* for its central relief and whose bet-hedging muddle of early-Christian with Roman images such as the gates of Hades has baffled scholars.

Reached through alleys of stone cottages in residential district Radunica east of the old town, the **Maritime Museum** (Pomorski muzej; *open Tues–Sun 9–1 and 6–8, adm*) has pressganged into service another 17th-century Venetian fortress to salute Croatian maritime heritage. More enticing is Split's most central beach, **Bačvice**, 10 minutes' walk east of the port, whose shallow waters are heaven for hesitant swimmers. Just don't expect them to yourself. Locals favour quieter nearby islands or the beaches of the Marjan peninsula (*see* p.106).

West of the Old Centre: Museum of Croatian Archaeological Monuments and Ivan Meštrović Gallery

The dignitaries of Split's museums are a 20-minute stroll west of the old centre on Marjan peninsula road Supilova; on the way, take a breather from the traffic in cemetery gardens **Sustipan** behind the ACI Marina, with a seafront promenade 'under the pine trees' of the area's name. A giant sword thrust into the earth to the hilt is the dramatic overture to the **Museum of Croatian Archaeological Monuments** (Muzej hrvatskih arheoloških spomenika; *open Tues–Fri 10–1 and 5–8, Sat 10–1, Sun 10–12; closed Mon; adm*), which has no time for the Roman infatuation elsewhere and instead dedicates its spacious halls to pre-Romanesque *ciboria* and 7–12th-century plaques of plaits and geometric knots that were the favourite designs for centuries of Croat craftsmen despite their Celtic looks – police caps still feature the design.

Little is likely to appeal to the heart, but for that there's the **Ivan Meštrović Gallery** (Galerija Ivana Meštrović; *open mid-May to Sept Tues–Sat 9–9, Sun 12–9; Oct–mid-May Tues–Sat 9–2, Sun 10–3; closed Mon; adm*) five minutes further west. Family portraits charm among bronzes of nude beauties who pose in the 1930s house and gardens of Croatia's most celebrated modern sculptor, and reveal a tender side to the artist associated with muscular public works such as Grgur Ninski. The sculptor who gave Chicago Grand Park its equestrian Indians also turns in a taut *Job* (1946), as if racked by the traumas of the Second World War; opposition to the Fascist Ustaše and support for Yugoslav nationalism put Meštrović behind bars for five months until the entreaties of high-ranking Italian friends secured his release and allowed the sculptor to flee and settle in America.

For all its career-spanning *œuvre*, the gallery's prize is secreted a little way down the road in the Holy Cross Chapel of the **Kaštelet** (*open Tues–Sun 10–5; same ticket*). Meštrović nursed back to health a dilapidated 16th-century residence in order to create a gallery for his *Life of Christ* cycle (1950), a stylized New Testament chiselled over nearly 40 years and lauded by critics as his finest work.

Marjan Hill

Locals' choice for a lazy Sunday stroll, the **Marjan peninsula nature reserve** is a delight when summer crowds clot the old town alleys. Flee the Riva's hordes west through residential district Veli Varoš – you won't believe you're still in Croatia's second largest city in its cobbled alleys – to café Vidilica. From here an asphalt footpath with sweeping panoramas of the coast ambles past the humble 13th-century chapel of **St Nicholas** (Sv. Nikola) to the 15th-century church of **St Jerome** (Sv. Jere), pressed hard against a cliff face in which medieval hermits pondered their faith in caves.

Split saves the finest views over the rugged coastline and islands for those who puff up to the peninsula's highest peak, **Telegrin**, reached on a right-hand fork off the main path. Climb to its 178m (584ft) summit then descend (also on paths from St Jerome) for a dip and a snack in **Bene Bay** at the western tip of the peninsula – those with strong legs will discover more secluded coves further north – after which you'll be grateful that bus 12 makes the return trip back to central Split.

Day Trips and Overnighters from Split

Salona

Bus 1 trundles to and from the site entrance and bus 37 returns to Split on the motorway below the amphitheatre (cross via an underpass). Both trips take around 20mins and cost 10Kn. Open May–Sept Mon–Fri 7–7, Sat 10–7, Sun 4–7; Oct–April Mon–Fri 7–3; adm.

When Split was just a daydream in Emperor Diocletian's idle hours, Colonia Martia Iulia Salona was the thriving capital of Dalmatia, a 60,000-strong metropolis on the Jadro delta that developed into a cosmopolitan, multi-faith community. And then came Avar and Slavic tribes. In their AD 614 raid along the coast, refugees fled to the shell of Diocletian's palace and Salona, in ruins, was left to crumble to dust. The prize finds of the ancient city unearthed by amateur archaeologist Father Frane Bulić can be seen in Split's Archaeological Museum (*see* p.105), but the foundation walls sketch the self-declared 'Cradle of Croatia' in fields which still seem half-forgotten. Keep your eyes peeled and you'll even spot Roman cart tracks in the flagstones.

Your tour of the most important site of Croatian antiquity begins on the bus: en route to the site you'll see sections of a 9km aqueduct which channelled fresh water to Diocletian's retirement home, still in use thanks to 19th-century ingenuity. Beyond the site car park, crumbling walls outline the **Manastirine**, surrounded by a litter of sarcophagi showing its origins as an early Christian necropolis. A kernel chapel built as a requiem for first Salona bishop Dominus, martyred in Diocletian's amphitheatre in AD 304, sprouted private chapels of élite Salona Christians, then flowered into the ruins of a 5th-century basilica, whose columns still punctuate one of three naves. Behind it the **Villa Bulić**, erected as a base for excavations, is aggrandized with Roman grave slabs and statutory. The good father gazes across the site in photos inside, and snaffled ancient columns to support the rose and honeysuckle bushes in his garden.

Salona begins downhill, as walls which trace eastern suburb Urbs Nova Orientalis, episcopal centre of a city which kept alive the flame of Christianity despite furious persecution by Diocletian. The AD 313 Edict of Milan which forced pagan Romans to practise religious tolerance also emboldened Christians here to create a confident 5th-century **basilica**, a far cry from the cellar baths of a private house located below the site access stairs, in which they previously sang clandestine liturgies. Directly east of the basilica are ruins of the **public baths**, still with paths for their hot-water pipes.

Tramp south along flagstones like early Romans, then turn right at the five arches of a Roman bridge to find the *decumanus maximus*, or take to the walls for a guard's-eye view as you march south to reach the **Porta Caesarea**, an east gate that demarcates the Urbs Novas (new town) from the Urbs Vetus (old town). Olive groves and vineyards have swallowed the old city on the other side of the Augustinian gate. Follow the walls past the outline of the **Kapulić basilica**, Salona's oldest cathedral, which honours four imperial guard martyrs, and you reach the 2nd-century **amphitheatre** in what was the northwest of the city. It may be stripped of its terraces, but stand at the centre and you can almost hear the whisper of an 18,000-strong crowd.

Trogir

Tiny, uncomplicated and shoehorned onto an islet, Trogir has picture-postcard images everywhere you look. Yes, one of Dalmatia's most seductive small towns suffers from more than its fair share of jolly tour groups, but explore the back streets or stay till dusk and there's magic in the air. If there's also a whiff of Venice about a warren where cobbles tumble through alleys of medieval houses or pool in quiet squares strung with buntings of washing, it's because the Italian republic snatched the prosperous Mediterranean trader in 1420 and stamped its authority until 1797, an occupation that rankled even in the 1930s.

The Venetians would point out that they protected their prize from Turkish raiders with 15th-century town walls, pierced on the mainland side by late-Renaissance arch the **Land Gate**, from which 12th-century bishop and town protector St John of Trogir salutes visitors. Just inside it, a noble dynasty's Baroque palace houses the rather dull **town museum** (Gradski muzej; *open summer daily 9–12 and 6–9; winter in theory Mon–Fri 8–3; adm*), with Greek and Roman finds and 18th-century furnishings.

You're better off reading the 1240 calendar of locals busy at seasonal chores or dressed in their Sunday best that Slavic master Radovan carved on the main portal of the Romanesque **Cathedral of St Lawrence** (Katedrala sveti Lovre). Don't miss the baptistry (1467) left of the portal by Andrija Aleši, pupil of Croatian supremo Juraj Dalmatinac, before you enter the three-nave interior of a church largely completed in the 13th century, but whose belfry inched up over a further three centuries, a history neatly summed up by its transition through first-storey Gothic to flowery Venetian Gothic then Renaissance. Climb it for lovely views (*adm*) across Trogir's jumbled roofs-cape. But, for all its Romanesque dignity, the main reason to enter the church is the beautiful Renaissance **chapel of St John of Trogir** (1480) in the east nave, by fellow Dalmatinac pupil Nikola Firentinac, which blazes with light like a revelation in the gloom. The sacristy **treasury** (*adm*) is a disappointment by comparison.

Firentinac also carved the relief of *Justice* flanked by St Lawrence and St John of Trogir in the **loggia** opposite the cathedral, a 15th-century, open-air courtroom still with the rusty chains to which miscreants were shackled. The sculptor's Lion of St Mark – a conspicuous blank in the loggia – fared less well after citizens bristled at Mussolini's declaration that 'whichever place bears the sign of a lion with wings should belong to Italy' and in 1932 hacked out the Venetian Republic icon. Il Duce raged at their impertinence and the Yugoslav government was forced to issue a formal apology. If Trogir hoped to restore local pride with the relief of local son Petar Berislavić, 16th-century Croatian *ban* (viceroy) and Zagreb bishop who battled against Italian rule, it must have been sorely disappointed with an uncharacteristically flaccid relief by 20th-century superstar sculptor Ivan Meštrović. Before you leave the main square, admire the town's ritziest **mansion** opposite the cathedral portal.

Southeast of the square, the church of St John the Baptist hoards the pick of Trogir's ecclesiastical artworks as the **Pinakoteka** (*open July–Aug Mon–Sat 9.30–1.30 and 4.30–7; adm*); and there are icons of *Madonnas* plus a superb 3rd-century BC relief of Kairos, Greek god of opportunity who must be seized or lost forever – dither and you'll only scrabble on his bald pate – in the **Convent of St Nicholas** (Samostan sv. Nikole;

Getting There

Bus 37 takes 40mins to reach Trogir, departs every 30mins and and costs 18Kn.

Tourist Information

Trogir: Trg Ivanan Pavla II, **t** (021) 885 628, *www.dalmacija.net/trogir.htm. Open June–Aug daily 8–9, otherwise Mon–Sat 8–7.*

Festivals

The highlight of Trogir's calendar is the **Summer Festival**, with performances of classical and folk music from early July to the end of August. Also worth investigating is the religious pomp that celebrates patron saint **St John** on 16 November.

Eating Out

Alka, Augustina Kažotića 15, **t** (021) 881 856 (*expensive–moderate*). Top-notch fishy specials plus a polyglot of steak styles or chicken with *pršut* in an award-winning restaurant which gets the nod from locals for a formal meal. Wait for a table in a nearby terrace rather than suffer its stuffy interior.

Fontana, Obrov 1, **t** (021) 884 811 (*expensive–moderate*). Less formal than the Alka but just as pricey thanks to an unbeatable location before the Riva, a lovely spot for a lazy al fresco lunch of high-quality seafood.

Škrapa, Hrvatskih Mučenika 9 (*cheap*). Don't be fooled by the chunky bench seating and checked tablecloths of this chirpy café at the top of Trogir's north–south spine – the mixed fish plate (*mješana riba*) is delicious.

open summer Mon–Sat 10–12 and 4–6; in winter consult tourist information; adm). Find it northwest of the square on **Gradska**, which emerges from the old town's intimacy on to harbourside promenade **Riva**. At its end the dumpy **Kamerlengo Fortress** (*open April–May and Sept–Oct daily 10–6; June–Aug 10–12; adm*) is the creation of 15th-century Venetians; subsequent foreign ruler Napoleonic marshal Marmont demanded the waterside gazebo (1808) at its shoulder to glorify France.

Brač

Locals may grumble at a loss of identity during a summer invasion from the mainland, but after decades of depopulation Brač is finally looking forward. Before it accepted the tourist kuna (and an airport) in the 1960s, Dalmatia's third largest island was more famous for the creamy-white marble of its quarries: Brač masons carved blocks for Diocletian's imperial palace in Split, and the Brač stone which created the high altar of Liverpool's cathedral also put the white into America's White House. A minor trade continues in an island interior that's heaven for explorers: circular *bunja* (shepherds' shelters) are dotted among scrubby pine; houses and vineyards go gently to seed, abandoned in the early 20th century by farmers ruined by phylloxera; and hamlets doze free from the visitors who stampede to the famous beach in Bol.

Supetar's palm-lined harbour flanked by honey and cream mansions is christened after a 6th-century basilica to St Peter; scraps of its mosaic paint geometric patterns before the replacement Baroque parish church near a **museum of town history** (Gradski muzej; *open summer daily 10–12 and 5–7; adm*). Supetar's artistic prizes are the funerary sculptures that Ivan Rendić (1849–1932) created for the élite families of his home town in a **cemetery** beyond the harbour. Admire the eclectic tastes of one of the era's leading sculptors – a tender *Pietà* on the tomb of Mihovil Frasnovic, quirky Art Nouveau for that of Rinaldo Culić by the entrance, and a stolid Byzantine-inspired

Getting There and Around

Jadrolinija **ferries** which travel hourly in summer (otherwise every 2½hrs) take 50mins to reach Supetar and cost 19Kn. A peak-season SEM **hydrofoil** plies between Split and Milna.

A **bus** from Supetar to Bol meets ferries, but, to truly explore, hire a **car** (*c.300Kn/6hrs*) or **scooter** (*c. 120Kn*) from Mjenjačnica, **t** (021) 630 709, or Atlas, **t** (021) 631 105, at the Supetar harbour; pre-booking is a must in summer.

Tourist Information

Supetar: Porat 1 (opposite ferry dock), **t** (021) 630 551, *www.supetar.hr*. *Open July–Aug daily 8am–10pm; Sept–June Mon–Sat 8–4*.
Bol: far end of harbour, **t** (021) 635 638, *www.bol.hr*. *Open July–Aug daily 8–10; Sept–June Mon–Sat 8.30–2 and 4–8, Sun 8.30–12*.

Eating Out

Gušt, Frane Radic 14, Bol, **t** (021) 635 911 (*expensive–moderate*). A rustic charmer decorated with bygones and sepia photos of yesteryear Bol and whose chef prepares the full Dalmatian kitchen. Be prepared to queue for an outside table in summer.
Vinotoka, Jobova 6, Supetar, **t** (021) 630 969 (*moderate*). A *konoba* hailed by locals as one of the premier addresses in Brač is a joy, with a snug folksy interior, a lovely terrace and platters of strange Adriatic fishes on a largely seafood menu.
Palute, Porat 4, Supetar, **t** (021) 631 730 (*cheap*). There's green pasta with mussels or crab for starters and speciality meats prepared on a wood grill from a long-standing favourite with Supetar's largest harbour terrace.

mausoleum of the Radnić family – before you succumb to Toma Rosandić's centre-piece **Petrinović mausoleum**, shaped like a bell and crowned by a mourning angel. If it's open (*in theory, summer daily 9–2 and 4–7; adm*), the Split sculptor's intensely personal ode to Resurrection and life related in a hushed Art Nouveau interior is a joy, otherwise there are more Rendić bronzes in the **library** (Knjižnica; *open Mon, Wed and Fri 2.30–7.30, Tues, Thurs and Sat 8.30–1.30*) located off Jobova behind the harbour.

If you have your own transport, pretty fishing village **Milna** 20km southwest of Supetar is an enjoyable spot to idle among a tangle of alleys at the end of a deep natural bay. For culture, there's **Škrip** (*three buses a day from Supetar*), a haphazard sprawl of stone houses which drifts at yesteryear pace 3km south of charming Splitska, itself retired and dozy after years as the export port of Brač stone. The island's oldest settlement, founded by ancient Ilyrians, Škrip is at its most nostalgic around the Baroque church of **St Helena** (Sv. Jelena) – the village is said to be the birthplace of St Helena, mother of Constantine the Great – beyond which a 16th-century tower, fortified to withstand Turkish raids, houses a junkshop of island odds and ends plus a relief of Hercules as the **Museum of Brač** (Brački muzej; *open summer daily 8–8; key next-door if locked; adm*). Apparently, Diocletian's wife and daughter were laid in the museum's incorporated Roman mausoleum, a new arrival compared with the 5,000 BC Cyclopean wall on which it stands.

And so to **Bol**. This quiet fishing village daydreaming on the south coast was reinvented practically overnight when tourists discovered **Zlatni rat** (Golden Cape). There's no denying the allure of Croatia's most famous beach, star of every glossy tourist brochure, which pokes a shingle finger into turquoise seas; finding space to lay a towel in July and August is another matter. Coves north are quieter. A promenade between the beach and harbour is the launch point for boat tours to 1588 hermitage **Pustinja Blaca** perched dramatically beneath a vertiginous cliff face (*approx 70Kn per* *person*). Also at Bol harbour, the **Branislav Dešković Gallery** (*open July–Aug daily 9–12, other times vary; adm free*) showcases works by Croatian sculptors such as Ivan Meštrović and Rendić plus noisy Expressionist canvases. There's more art – a treasured Tintoretto *Madonna with Child* – plus ancient Greek coins and amphorae in the museum of the **Dominican monastery** (Dominikanski samostan; *open May–Sept 10–12 and 5–9; adm*), screened by gardens on a knuckle of rock beyond the harbour.

Šibenik and Krka National Park

Although local buses from Split take two hours to reach Šibenik, Croatia's finest Renaissance cathedral is an easy drive away for those with a hire car. Better still, it is within easy striking distance of the idyllic waterfalls, meadows and lakes of the Krka National Park – few nicer spots to escape Split's August crowds. *See pp.88–90.*

Vis and Biševo

Few islands in Croatia seize the imagination like idyllic Vis. Captivating villages Vis town and Komiža drift at yesteryear pace and use dialects which baffle even their fellow countrymen; semi-abandoned villages crumble in a rugged interior where vineyards produce acclaimed white Vugava and red Viški Plavac wines; and some of the Adriatic's cleanest seas lap its beaches. A siren call of adventure can be heard even on the approach, when Vis rises on the horizon like some lost treasure island – which, in a sense, it was. The Yugoslav naval base that put Croatia's most isolated island off-limits to foreigners until 1989 also sheltered it from modernity and the excesses of package tourism. Croatians acclaim it as a retreat for those in the know; now foreigners are finding it out – catch it while you can.

The isolated location which entices today also saw Vis prized as a central Adriatic stronghold squabbled over by a succession of rulers – Venetian, British, then Austrian – and enlisted as a 1944 base for Tito's fledgling partisan struggle. First to arrive, however, were the Greeks. They founded 4th-century BC town Issa on the slopes above main port **Vis**, which straggles along the bay between the once-separate villages of portside Luka and residential Kut. Under the Romans, Issa matured into a town that Julius Caesar hailed as 'the most distinguished city in the area'; it can be glimpsed through the lens of Greek and Roman finds in a **town museum** (Gradski muzej; *open June–Sept Tues–Sat 10–1 and 6–9, Sun 10–1, otherwise on demand via tourist agencies; adm*) housed in Austrian fortification Our Lady's Battery east of the port (*left from ferry dock*). A superb collection of antique ceramics and a prize bust of Artemis are on the top floor; handicrafts and 19th-century furnishings are below.

Backtrack past the barn-like Renaissance **Church of our Lady** (Gospa od Spilica) which united Kut and Luka. Right of the port, a few tombstones of the ancient **Greek cemetery** (*times vary*) are forgotten ignominiously behind municipal tennis courts, and further around the bay are the scrappy remains of 1st-century **Roman baths** (*times vary*), worth a visit for mosaic dolphins (at the rear) and swastikas, an ancient good luck symbol until hijacked by Hitler. Exhibit B of Roman Issa is the peninsula **Franciscan monastery** (Franjevački samostan), whose 16th-century arc recalls terraces of the amphitheatre on which it is founded. That arena was located outside city walls

Getting There and Around

Two or three Jadrolinija **ferries** (28Kn, 2hrs) and one SEM **catamaran** (28Kn, 1hr 30mins) per day shuttle between Split and Vis. Five **buses** go between Vis and Komiža, with buses scheduled to coincide with ferry arrivals.

Tourist Information

Vis: opposite ferry dock in Jadrolinija office, **t** (021) 717 017; *http://www.tz-vis.hr*. Open *summer daily 8–8; winter Mon–Fri 8–2*.

Private Tourist Agencies

Vis (both near ferry dock): Ionios, Obala sv. Jurja 37, **t** (021) 711 532; or Navigator, Šetalište stare Isse 1, **t** (021) 717 786.
Komiža (on harbour): Darlić & Darlić, Riva 13, **t** (021) 717 025.

All can arrange private accommodation and organize tours to Biševo and diving trips in Vis's gin-clear seas. Navigator can also rustle up vineyard and farm tours on request.

Where to Stay

Vis t (021) –

Private tourist agencies co-ordinate accommodation in **private houses** (*inexpensive*).
Tamaris, Obala sv. Jurja 20, Vis, **t** 711 350 (*moderate*). An Austro-Hungarian era grandee near the dock. Though snug and modest, rooms boast high ceilings and creaky parquet floors – strike lucky and you'll get one with views over the bay. It also has a good seafront restaurant.

Paula, Petra Hektorovića 2, Vis, **t** 711 362, *www.paula-hotel.htnet.hr* (*moderate*). Modern and friendly, this small family hotel carved from a Kut stone house and with bags of character is the pick of Vis town hotels. Bigger spenders should enquire about a splendid apartment (*expensive*) with a terrace overlooking the bay and vast Jacuzzi.
Biševo, Ribarska 72, Komiža, **t** 713 095 (*moderate*). Simple but comfy rooms, with fridge, from Komiža's only hotel above its beach.

Eating Out

Vis t (021) –

Villa Kaliopa, V Nazora 32, Kut, **t** 271 1755 (*expensive*). Pricey, but the place for a romantic splurge. Fish is consistently excellent on a menu of cuisine that changes with the seasons and the Renaissance-style garden of palms and pines is a delight for al fresco dining. Booking recommended.
Bak, Gundulićeva 1, Komiža, **t** 713 742 (*expensive–moderate*). Move fast to claim a terrace table inches from the sea with the most idyllic views on the island. Catch of the day is on the menu, and for a starter there's octopus cooked in Vis red wine.
Jastožera, Gundulićeva 6, Komiža, **t** 713 859 (*expensive–moderate*). An Austro-Hungarian-era lobster house, where tables are perched on platforms above the holding pen.
Vatrica, Obala Kralja Krešimira IV, Kut, **t** 711 574 (*moderate*). Impossibly popular *konoba* with a harbour-front terrace canopied by vines and a repertoire of fishy delights grilled and cooked under a *peka*.

beside the harbour – locals swear that slabs of the ancient dock loom in the shallows at low tide. Hunt for 19th-century funerary statutory in the **town cemetery** behind – such as a stolid epitaph for Austrian sailors who died *'für Kaiser und Osterreich'* during an 1866 spat with Italy over Vis's ownership, or a saucy 19th-century maiden chiselled by Ivan Redić – before you take the road which cradles the bay then forks right onto a dirt track to the ruins of a British **fortress of St George**, a Union Jack still carved into the portal. Now retired from guard duty over the bay, it has declined into an evocative shell whose gun terrace you'll share only with geckos.

An easy stroll east of the museum, the cosy nest of **Kut** is stuffed with stone mansions which recall days as a summer retreat of Hvar aristocrats. A dirt road from the 16th-century huddle peters out at a headland where a humble **cemetery** salutes

British servicemen who fell defending the island, first from Napoleon's furious ambition in 1812 then from Italian Fascists in the Second World War; their comrades were the only foreigners permitted access to Vis during its years as a Yugoslav navy base. Just behind it is the best **beach** in Vis town.

Ask delicately and **Komiža** locals say their intimate village breeds more compassionate characters; Vis, straggled along a bay, is a cold fish, they sniff. Whatever the truth, the island's enchanting second settlement is a gem. Venetians built creamy 16–17th-century stone houses and stocky fort the **Kaštel** (1585), slightly emasculated by a 19th-century **clock tower**, which huddle around the village harbour. The latter honours traditional local sardine fishing as the **Fishing Museum** (Ribarski muzej; *open May–Sept Mon–Sat 10–12 and 7–10, Sun 7–10 only; adm*), whose prize posession is a reconstructed *falkuša* fishing boat. Stroll around the harbour towards the village's main beach to reach the church of **Our Lady of the Pirates** (Gospa Gusarica), christened after an icon of the Madonna miraculously washed up after its kidnap by pirates, and whose quirky shape emerged as Komiža flanked single-nave churches to a Renaissance progenitor. An octagonal church well outside introduces village protector St Nicholas, also honoured by the fortified Benedictine **monastery of St Nicholas** (Sv. Nikola samostan; *usually locked*) above the town and which gazes over spectacular views of the bay. Marvel at them on 6 December and you'll be joined by the entire village, which puffs uphill to witness a boat-burning sacrifice to the patron saint of fishermen.

Just a speck in the Adriatic perhaps, islet **Biševo** has nevertheless wooed tourists ever since its **Blue Cave** was billed as a Croatian Capri in 1884. Boat trips from Komiža (*70–100Kn depending on season*) pootle out to the cavern for midday, when sunlight spears through a submerged side-entrance, water in the cave fluoresces lapis lazuli, and a crowd of tourists who bob in boats coo in unison. Magic.

Hvar Town

One or two Jadrolinija ferries per day chug year-round to Hvar in 1hr 50mins for 27Kn, and in June–Sept two SEM catamarans a day zip across in 1hr (35Kn). Be aware that cars cannot disembark at Hvar Town; catch a ferry instead to main island port Stari Grad (summer 3–5 per day; winter 3 per day).

Croatians will tell you that the traditional whiff of island Hvar is lavender. Not in its compact capital, however; here it is the expensive perfumes of the rich and beautiful that scent the air of a lovely medieval town which has found a second wind as Croatia's St-Tropez; in cafés which line main square Trg Sveti Stjepana, crisp white Armani shirts show off deep tans and the super-rich aboard super-yachts sip cocktails in the harbour. This is a place to see and be seen, especially in August when the small town fizzes with life despite its guests' studious *sang-froid*. There are showpiece buildings bequeathed by former owners the Venetian Republic, and even a dollop of art and culture, but, for all its Renaissance good looks, Hvar is not one for aesthete pilgrims so much as for idle tourists who want to people-watch with a chilled drink or laze on the beaches of neighbouring islets Pakleni Otoc. *See p.115.*

Touring from Split

Day 1: Hvar: Stari Grad, Jelsa and Vrboska

Morning: If time is on your side, spend an extra day exploring **Brač** (*see* pp.109–11); stay in classy Kaštil (*Frane Radića 1*, **t** *(021) 635 995, www.kastil.hr; moderate*) in Bol then catch a passenger-only catamaran to Jelsa (*see* below). Otherwise, catch one of four daily ferries from Split to **Stari Grad** on island **Hvar**. Start with the Tvrdalj (*open July–Aug daily 10–1 and 5–8, June and Sept 10–1; adm*), residence of humanist Petar Hektorović, in the main square. Explore his 16th-century pile, built to withstand a siege – a fishpond in its courtyard to feed stomachs, walls studded with cerebral *bon mots* to fill minds – then gaze at the aristocrat poet himself as a wizened Joseph of Arimathea on an *Internment of Christ* by Tintoretto, the main treasure of exhibits which tell local history from ancient Illyrian roots in the Dominican monastery museum (*open Mon–Sat 10–12 and 5.30–7.30; adm*).

Lunch: On Hvar, in Stari Grad.

Morning: Go east by bus to **Jelsa**, which spills downhill to a café-filled square and an Austro-Hungarian-era harbour. The lozenge-shaped Renaissance church of St John (Sv. Ivan) is shoehorned into a tiny square of mansions like a set for an Italian operetta. Stroll 4km northwest to fishing village **Vrboska**, strung along an inlet and whose repose is broken only by the bells of fortress-church St Mary's (Crkva-trđava Svete Marija) – the refuge from raiders claims the highest ground in the village. The best beaches for a dip are at the peninsula end, across the harbour bridge.

Dinner and Sleeping: In Jelsa or Stari Grad, *see* below.

Day 1

Lunch in Stari Grad

Ermitaž, Priko, no tel (*moderate*). A gem of a *konoba* on the north side of the inlet whose terrace has the views and interior oozes rustic charm. Choose your fish from the catch of the day presented at your table or try Dalmatian bouillabaisse *brodet*.

Odisej, Trg Tvrdalj, **t** (021) 765 556 (*moderate*). One of several eating options on Stari Grad's smartest square, with a terrace beneath palms and with a wide-ranging menu: try *škampi na buzara* (prawns in a rich tomato sauce) or lobster in cream with green pasta.

Dinner and Sleeping in Stari Grad

Dominko, signed off Braće Batoš, **t** (021) 761 441 (*moderate*). Home cooking and a canopy of vines in a tiny treat with a big welcome hidden in a southern back street (signs uphill from St John's). The chef prepares feasts of *odojak ispod* (suckling pig) or *hobotnica* (octopus) cooked under a *peka* given advance notice.

Napoleon, Mala banda bb, **t** (021) 761 438 (*moderate*). Meats seared on a charcoal grill come with lovely views across the harbour.

Arkhala, Priko, Stari Grad, **t** (021) 756 555 (*moderate*). Best of an uninspiring bunch of package holiday hotels north of the inlet, this early-1980s timewarp has compact but clean and adequate accommodation.

Private accommodation (*inexpensive*): **Mistral**, Grofa Vranjicanija 2 (near bus station).

Dinner and Sleeping in Jelsa

Mina, signed south of centre, **t** (021) 761 244 (*moderate*). A large, uninspiring hotel block that is showing its age.

L'Accento, Mala banda bb, **t** (021) 761 236 (*inexpensive*). Modest but modern rooms above a restaurant, well located just off the harbour.

Private accommodation (*inexpensive*): **Atlas**, Obala bb (on harbour), **t** (021) 672 038.

Day 2: Hvar Town

Morning: While rows of stalls maintain Hvar island's reputation for lavender, the real scent of its eponymous Renaissance capital is expensive perfume – welcome to the Croatian St-Tropez. Begin your tour on Trg svetog Stjepana: **St Stephen's Cathedral** (Katedrala sv. Stjepan) has a poised Baroque façade and a campanile which rises in a crescendo of arches – its treasures are in the adjacent **Bishop's Museum** (Biskupski muzej; *open Mon–Sat 9–12 and 4.30–6.30; adm*). Adjacent to the inner harbour, the Renaissance **loggia** of the former town hall is stamped with the winged lion of Venice patron St Mark; and on the harbourfront is the Italians' 17th-century **arsenal**. Above is Croatia's first **theatre** (*open May–Oct Mon–Sat 10–1 and 3–7, Sun 10–1; Nov–April Mon–Sat 10–1; adm*), which opened doors to prole and aristo alike in 1612, long before London or Paris.

Lunch: In Hvar town, *see* below.

Afternoon: Pause at the tapering windows of the Gothic shell of the **Hektorović Palace** on your ascent to the 1551 Venetian **fortress** (*open daily; adm*); locals were probably little consoled by the excellent views as they watched the Turks rip through their town from its battlements in 1579. South of the main town, there are religious and Roman finds in the Baroque **Franciscan monastery** (Franjevački samostan; *open May–Oct Mon–Sat 10–12 and 5–7; Nov–April through tourist office; adm*). To laze on a beach, visit the islets of **Pakleni Otoci** (*boats from harbour; single 10–20Kn by season*): Jerolim is for nudists; Marinkovac has two pine-fringed bays; and verdant Sv. Klement has a good beach. All have a seasonal restaurant.

Dinner and Sleeping: in Hvar town, *see* below.

....

Day 2

Lunch and Dinner in Hvar Town

Luna, Petra Hektorovića 2, **t** (021) 741 000 (*expensive–moderate*). A stylish and funky restaurant with a top-floor terrace open to – what else? – the moon. Lobster is prepared in a rich sauce of tomato, wine and brandy.

Macondo, Groda bb, **t** (021) 742 850 (*expensive–moderate*). Hvar's finest address, according to many locals, and certainly a charmer, a cosy stone dining room with a superb fish plate and lamb. Don't miss a fiery home-recipe *rakija* for an aperitif.

Kod Kapetana, Fabrika bb, **t** (021) 742 230 (*moderate*). A reliable, usually quieter option on the other side of the harbour with the full Dalmatian menu and views of the Riva.

Junior, Pučkog ustanka 4, **t** (021) 741 069 (*moderate–cheap*). Simple restaurant of a fishing family; there's a three-style squid sampler and a seafood risotto that's one of the best you'll taste.

Pizzaria Leonardo, Riva bb, no tel (*cheap*). The finest pizzas in Hvar on the corner of the buzzy Riva come thin-crust, keenly priced and in diameters to make dieters weep.

Sleeping in Hvar Town

Characterful **private rooms** (*inexpensive*) can be sourced through **Atlas**, Obala bb, **t** (021) 741 911, and **Pelégrini**, Riva bb, **t** (021) 742 743.

Palace, Trg svetog Stjepana bb, **t** (021) 741 966 (*expensive*). An 1800s hotel whose harbour views cost an extra 100Kn. High-ceilinged rooms are spacious though rather dated.

Dalmacija, Obala Ivana Lučića-Lavčevića bb, **t** (021) 741 120 (*moderate*). Modest but comfy accommodation in a quiet seasonal hotel overlooking the Franciscan monastery.

Podstine, Pod Stine, **t** (021) 740 400 (*moderate*). Wake up to sea views in the tasteful rooms, most with a balcony, of this charming family hotel, 20 minutes' walk southwest of the centre and immaculately located before a shingle beach.

Day 3: Korčula Town

Morning: Tear yourself from Hvar and catch a ferry to Korčula (*one passenger cata-maran and ferry per day Hvar–Vela Luka, plus one car ferry per day Stari Grad–Korčula town in peak season*). Hop straight on a bus for Korčula town, a mini-Dubrovnik which rises like a cake above 13th-century walls pierced by the **Land Gate** (1391), with a winged lion of former ruler Venice and a century-older **tower** (*open daily June–Sept 9.30–1.30 and 4–8; adm*) that reminisces over Korčula sword dance the Moreška. Candle of the powerful medieval trader is the spire of Gothic-Renaissance bravura **St Mark's Cathedral** (Katedrala Sv Marka): a *ciborium* by local son Marko Andrijić canopies an altarpiece by Tintoretto, who also dreamed the *Annunciation* in the south aisle near a bristle of pikes left over from Korčula's defence against Turkish forces in 1571. More devotional art plus Tiepolo sketches are in the adjacent **treasury** (*open daily June–Sept 9–1 and 4–8; adm*).

Lunch: In Korčula town, *see* below.

Afternoon: Continue your exploration of the streets of Korčula, planned like a fish skeleton to benefit from balmy breezes from the east in summer but protect against the bitter winter *bura* from the north. A **town museum** opposite the cathedral (Gradski muzej; *open summer Mon–Sat 9.30–2 and 7–9, winter 9.30–2; adm*) relates local history. No Korčula citizen is more famous than Marco Polo, however – even if its claim to be the 1254 birthplace of the brilliant Venetian sea captain is highly dubious, the **House of Marco Polo** in alley Depolo (Kuća Marca Pola; *open daily June–Aug 10–1 and 5–7; adm*) at least affords good views from its tower.

Dinner and Sleeping: In Korčula town, *see* below.

Day 3

Lunch and Dinner in Korčula Town
See 'Day 4' for more eating options.
Kanavelič, Šetalište Petra Kanavelica, **t** (020) 711 800 (*expensive–moderate*). A classy court-yard fish restaurant around the corner from the northern bastion – octopus salad and scampi are delicious, the fish super-fresh.
Morski Konjić, Šetalište Petra Kanavelica, no tel (*expensive–moderate*). Move fast for a table hard against the eastern city walls to enjoy the most atmospheric al fresco dining in Korčula. The stylish 'Sea Horse' prides itself on quality fish – mussels are delicious, fat and in a salty garlic sauce.
Adio Mare, Svetog Roka, **t** (020) 711 253 (*moderate*). Be prepared to queue for a table in this atmospheric medieval house with a taste for tradition and reputation for quality: try a bean-and-noodle soup *juha od graha i tjestenine* and house special *ražnjići* (kebab).

Pizzeria Bistre, Plokata 19 Travnja 1921 bb, **t** (020) 711 004 (*cheap*). Relaxed pizza and pasta eaterie outside the town walls – a good choice for a low-key bite and beer.

Sleeping in Korčula Town
Source **private accommodation** from agencies **Atlas**, Plokata 19, **t** (020) 711 060) and **Marko Polo Tours**, Biline 5, **t** (020) 715 400.
Korčula, Obala Dr Franje Tuđmana, **t** (020) 711 078 (*moderate*). Book ahead for a room in this 1871 old lady; a little dated, fraying at the corners but comfy and with a premier address on the old town esplanade.
Liburna, Obala Hrvatskih Mornara, **t** (020) 726 004 (*moderate*). A resort hotel 1km east of the centre which redeems bland décor with beautiful old town views; demand a balcony.
Badija, Island Badija, **t** (020) 711 115 (*inexpensive*). Cell-like rooms in a former Franciscan monastery on island Badija (taxi boats from harbour) – cheap but beware school groups.

Day 4: Sun, Sea and Sand

Morning: See Korčula's remaining sacred treasures: begin just inside the Land Gate at the Renaissance **St Michael's Church** (Crkva sv. Mihovila), updated into Baroque inside, then pass beneath a bridge on which monks shuffled to church from their adjacent friary to reach the **Icon Museum** (Galerija ikona; *open July–Aug daily 10–12 and 5–7; Sept–June via tourist information; adm*) on Kaporava – a Korčula sea captain swiped its enigmatic Byzantine icons from Cretan churches rather than see them fall to Turks during the Canadia Wars (1645–69). Star turn in adjoining **All Saint's Church** (Crkva svih Svetih) is an 18th-century *Pietà* and, on the other side of the altar, a polyptych by Trogir Renaissance master Blaž Jurjev.

Lunch: In Korčula town, *see* below.

Afternoon: Penance paid, escape to the beach: water taxis from the harbour shuttle to the closest stretches of shingle on island **Badija**, and secluded coves reward those who follow paths from the dock. Hourly ferries also shuttle across to the shingle strips of **Orebić**; the mainland resort opposite Korčula is worth a visit as much for a 1480s Franciscan monastery (Franjevački samostan; *open Mon–Sat 9–12 and 4–7, Sun 4–7; adm*) built on a ridge to venerate a miraculous icon. Make the 20-minute walk uphill and you're rewarded with lovely views. Alternatively, catch a bus 6km southeast of Korčula town to lovely **Lumbarda**, still dozing as it did as the bucolic hideaway of Korčula aristocrats. A sand beach, Pržina, is 2km south from the centre; more private coves can be found east at Bilin Žal. Or hire a scooter and explore west to **Pupnatska Luka** (18km west of Korčula) – you may well have a cove to yourself.

Dinner and Sleeping: In Korčula town (*see* 'Day 3'), Lumbarda or Orebić.

Day 4

Lunch in Korčula Town
See 'Day 3' for more eating options.
Morski Konjić, Šetalište Petra Kanavelica, **t** (020) 711 642 (*moderate*). No relation to the grander 'Sea Horse' and more modest, this snug restaurant at the northern tip of town prepares a small menu of meat and fish. A snug interior is hung with fishing nets.
Planjak, Plokata 19 Travnja 1914 bb, **t** (020) 711 015 (*cheap*). Fine choice for a snack lunch, this informal restaurant in a square behind the port prepares grilled meats and light bites such as *ražnjići* (kebabs).

Dinner and Sleeping in Lumbarda
Pension Lovrić, t (020) 712 052 (*inexpensive*). A friendly welcome and simple, comfy rooms, some with views of the bay, in the *pension* of a fishing family 50yds from the sea. Fresh fish features high on their menu

(*moderate*), accompanied by veggies from the garden and home-made wines.
Zure, t (020) 712 008 (*moderate*). Al fresco dining in a garden and more home cooking rustled up from whatever's fresh – expect catch of the day, seafood stews and pastas – and best washed down with local white Grk.

Dinner and Sleeping in Orebić
Bistro Jadran, Trg Mimbeli II bb, **t** (020) 713 243 (*cheap*). No-nonsense pastas, omelettes and sturdy pork *kotlet* in a seafront snack bar.
Taverna Mlinica, Obala pomoraca bb, **t** (020) 713 886 (*moderate*). A short stroll further along the seafront, this plays up to its old mill heritage with décor of heavy beams and mill wheels. Specials lamb, veal and octopus are slow-cooked under a *peka*.
Orsan, signed north of centre , **t** (0 20) 713 148 (*moderate*). Bland and impersonal three-star package block, the best of a trio before a beach 15 minutes' walk from the centre.

Day 5: Lastovo

Morning and/or Afternoon (depending on ferry times): Trundle by bus back to **Vela Luka** for a catamaran or car ferry (*both daily but not frequent; check times*) to **Ubli**, the port of island **Lastovo**. Immured from foreigners and development until 1989 by a Yugoslav naval base; its proud citizens are self-sufficient in fruit and vegetables and tourism is barely a whisper in pristine bays. Although suffering severe depopulation, **Lastovo town** clings on as the main town (a bus from Ubli meets ferries). Explore lanes which trickle through 15–16th-century houses shoehorned onto a hillside and with unique chimneys like minarets. The Baroque interior of parish church SS Cosmas and Damian (Sv. Kuzme i sv. Damjana) is as much of a pleasant surprise as the pretty 15th-century loggia opposite. French forces crowned its hill Glavica in 1810 with fortress Kašćel – the old cliché about breathtaking views is all too true, but the 360° panorama over Lastovo and the coast is worth the climb. If there's time, take to paths through vineyards and fields scented with wild rosemary and sage to explore the rest of the island. Crumbling fishermen's houses huddle around harbour **Lučica**, a notch in the coast 1km north of Lastovo; **Sv. Mihovil** 500m further on is quieter, with just a quay for yachties and a seasonal bar; and, 3km east of Lastovo, lovely **Zaklopatica** attracts a small fleet to its still bay and excellent *konoba*. South of Lastovo (6km) a road traces sheltered bay **Skrivena Luka**, with its own restaurants and good swimming. The best place for a dip, though, is the sand beach of uninhabited islet **Saplan**, reached on jaunts around the archipelago northeast of Lastovo town (*consult tourist information for times*).

One ferry (4hrs 15mins, two in high season) and one catamaran (3hrs) a day make the return journey to Split, though you may have to stay the night (*see* below).

Day 5

Lunch, Dinner and Sleeping on Lastovo

Bar the hotel below, all Lastovo's beds are in private houses or apartments. Give serious consideration to offers of full-board: the island's *konobe* cluster in bays to serve visiting yachtsmen – fine for those in the bay, but problematic for an evening meal if your room is in Lastovo town. Visit off-season and you should accept gratefully any offer of home cooking, usually washed down with the owner's own wines, because most *konobe* are only open in summer.

The **tourist information**, **t** (020) 801 018, on Lastovo town's central square (opposite the bus stop) holds lists of available **private accommodation** and also hands out useful island maps.

Bačvara, Lastovo Town, **t** (020) 801 057 (*moderate*). Lastovo town's only *konoba* is secreted away in a stone building at the bottom of the village. Catch of the day is served beneath a canopy of fishing nets on the terrace or in a cosy stone dining room.

Triton, Zaklopatica, **t** (020) 801 161 (*expensive–moderate*). By popular acclaim, the island's finest *konoba* and a delight on the quayside of lovely Zaklopatica. Depending on the luck of last night's fishermen, there are all sorts of interesting fish to explore alongside the usual Adriatic favourites, all of it super-fresh and simply but expertly grilled.

Portorus, Skrivena Luka, **t** (020) 801 261 (*moderate*). A favourite with yachtsmen in 'Hidden Bay', this rustic *konoba* is a charming spot for a lazy lunch, with a small menu of seafood and local tipples to tempt.

Solitudo, Pasadur (5km north of Ubli), **t** (020) 802 100 (*moderate*). The island's only hotel, smack on the seafront, has 170 beds in its en suite rooms, all treated to air-conditioning, a balcony and views over the bay. Adventurers can take the plunge on excursions offered by the hotel dive centre; others can hire a mask and flippers. *Booking recommended.*

Croatia: Dubrovnik and Around

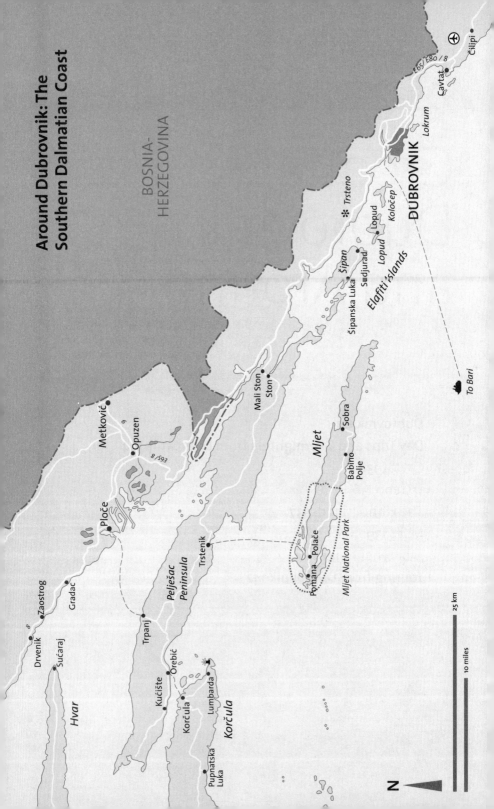

Tourist kunas not mercantile lucre now maintains the looks of Croatia's southern belle, a proud republic until Napoleon scoffed at its watchword of 'Libertas'. Of course, being an internationally fêted beauty does have its drawbacks, especially in peak season when a town besieged by admirers can lose her composure. Fortunately, charming Cavtat is just 22km south and pristine islands among the most dazzling in Croatia's constellation are two hours away by ferry, centuries away in atmosphere.

Dubrovnik

Byron acclaimed it the Pearl of the Adriatic and George Bernard Shaw sighed that 'those who seek paradise on Earth should come to Dubrovnik'. August crowds can make it more purgatory than paradise, but Dubrovnik remains a stunner – a Canaletto cityscape of Baroque mansions and churches painted in cool stone and clear light as if caught in a back-eddy of modernity's riptide. For all the praise lavished on the city inked on to UNESCO 's World Heritage list way back in 1978, the sentiment Croatia's *belle* truly prizes is that on her buses – *Libertas*. It's no accident that St Blaise, the city icon of independence, salutes citizens in every niche, nor that the Dubrovnik Summer Festival arts extravaganza is inaugurated with the Renaissance poetry of local son Ivan Gundulić: 'O you beautiful, o you dear, o you sweet freedom... All the silver, all the gold, all human lives, cannot pay for your pure beauty.'

Dubrovnik has good reason to eulogize. Its status as an independent city-state guaranteed fat profits and high living almost as soon as the trader on Balkan and Mediterranean land and sea routes set up its stall in the 12th century. And, while other towns on Croatia's seaboard laboured under the Venetian yoke, the Ragusan Republic developed as a world power through good sea legs – with one of the world's largest fleets – and a sweet tongue: the canny diplomat maintained relations with Balkan and Ottoman empires when other Christian states let cannonballs do the talking. During a Renaissance golden age, the queen of the Adriatic held court to the region's brightest stars and became a dynamo of literature, art and architecture, and, even if the latter was largely reduced to rubble by a 1667 earthquake which killed around 5,000 people, its Baroque replacement makes up for in elegance what it lacks in Renaissance fizz.

That refined cityscape lures still, huddled tight within iconic city walls that articulate Dubrovnik's defiance better than any words and which have thwarted all invaders bar Napoleon Bonaparte – and even that all-conquering dictator was forced to besiege rather than storm the republic he dissolved in 1808. And it seems only proper that it was the Serbian shelling of this independent city which truly alerted Europe to Croatia's struggle for freedom.

The Pile Gate, City Walls and Lovrijenac Fortress

Enter Dubrovnik's old town (the city sprawls wide to east – Ploče – and west – the Lapad and Babin kuk peninsulas – but this is the city's heart) like the majority of visitors throughout its history, through the western **Pile Gate** (Gradska vrata Pile). From 1537 guards kept a sharp eye on trade passing through the republic's principal

St Blaise, Patron Saint

Four centuries after his AD 316 martyrdom under Roman emperor Diocletian, the Armenian bishop-saint Blaise tipped off a dreaming cathedral priest that a fleet of Venetian galleons anchored off Lokrum (*see* p.134) under the pretence of replenishing water barrels was actually poised to attack. Or so goes the tale to explain the saint's 10th-century adoption as Dubrovnik patron (more prosaically explained by the arrival of his relics) – and a republic never slow to trumpet its freedom after 150 years' rule by arch-rival Venice (until 1358) hailed its hero in sculpture and painting throughout the city.

Nor is such votive salute simply ancient history. In 1991, despairing of half-hearted peace negotiations in The Hague, a band of Dubrovnik refugees invoked the saint as humanitarian aid mission the 'St Blaise Foundation' and attempted to brazen their way through a Yugoslav naval siege of their city on a passenger ferry. Among their number was Croatia president Stipe Mesić, who warmed to his heroics under the protection of global publicity and declaimed, 'You can shoot if you want to, but remember Europe is listening.' It was, too; the Montenegrin army and Yugoslav navy slunk off, embarrassed by the PR disaster of shells casually lobbed into one of the world's most perfectly preserved citadels.

gateway atop a new outer bastion where, framed in a niche, **St Blaise** (*see* box, above) cradles a model of the Renaissance city. During the republican era, the wooden drawbridge to the Pile Gate was hoisted each night with considerable pomp in a ceremony which delivered city keys to the Ragusan rector. Today it spans a dry moat whose garden offers respite from crowds.

Pass through the Pile Gate's original Gothic inner gateway – this St Blaise is by Croat 20th-century giant Ivan Meštrović – to reach one of a trio of access points to the **city walls** (Gradske zidine; *open summer daily 8.30–6.30, winter 9–4; adm*) which offer the finest introduction to Dubrovnik there is (*access also in Svetog Dominika near the Ploče Gate, and by the Aquarium*). Although sections of Dubrovnik's defining feature date back to the 10th century, the stone girdle finally hugged the city tight four centuries later, then was bolstered at lightning pace after shockwaves of panic rippled north from the bombshell of Constantinople's 1453 fall to rampaging Ottomans.

Florentine architectural supremo Michelozzo di Bartolomeo Michelozzi took no chances. Sections of the fortifications power 80ft high and are a no-nonsense 20ft thick on vulnerable inland flanks, protected by the front-guard of a deep moat and scarp wall to thwart siege cannons; seaward walls are a modest 10ft thick. Michelozzi also erected or strengthened fortresses which stand watch at each corner of the city. Cockwise from the Pile Gate entry, they are: the mighty **Minčeta Tower**, whose crenellated battlements and central tower are saluted as an icon of unconquered Dubrovnik; the **Revelin Fortress** adjacent to the southeast Ploče Gate; **St John's Fortress**, a powerful gun emplacement which has kept watch over the port since the 1350s; and the **Bokar Bastion**, which guards sea approaches.

Whatever the defences' warlike conception, the reason to march their 2km circuit today is for peaceful picture-postcard views over belltowers, spires and a terracotta

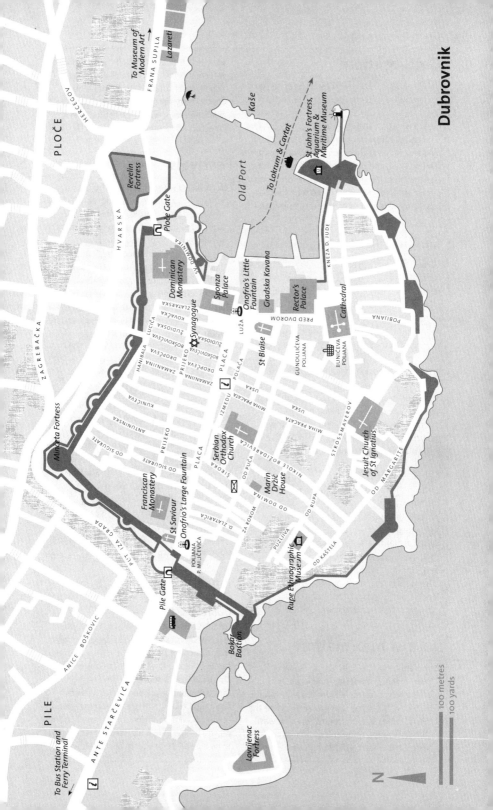

Dubrovnik

PLOČE

To Museum of Modern Art

FRANA SUPILA

Lazareti

HERCEGOVAČKA

Revelin Fortress

Ploče Gate

HVARSKA

UL. DOMINIKA

Dominican Monastery

Sponza Palace

Synagogue

ZLATARSKA

KOVAČKA

ŽUDIOSKA

BOŠKOVIĆEVA

LUCIĆA

PRIJEKO

DROPČEVA

ZAMANJINA

Onofrio's Little Fountain

Luža

Gradska Kavana

Old Port

Kaše

To Lokrum & Cavtat

St John's Fortress, Aquarium & Maritime Museum

KNEZA D. JUDE

Rector's Palace

PRED DVOROM

Cathedral

POBIJANA

GUNDULIĆEVA POLJANA

BUNIĆEVA POLJANA

St Blaise

PLACA

POLJANA

ZAMANJINA

DROPČEVA

HANIBALA LUCIĆA

KUNIĆEVA

ANTUNINSKA

OD SIGURATE

PRIJEKO

Minčeta Fortress

ZAGREBAČKA

Franciscan Monastery

St Saviour

Onofrio's Large Fountain

POLJANA P. MILIČEVIĆA

PLACA

ŠIROKA

D. ZLATARIĆA

ZA ROKOM

OD DOMINA

PUT IZA GRADA

Pile Gate

PILE

To Bus Station and Ferry Terminal

ANTE STARČEVIĆA

ANICE BOŠKOVIĆ

Bokar Bastion

Lovrijenac Fortress

Serbian Orthodox Church

Marin Držić House

OD PUČA

MIHA PRACATA

NIKOLE BOŽIDAREVIĆA

USKA

STROSSMAYEROV

Jesuit Church of St Ignatius

OD MARGARITE

MIHA PRACATA

USKA

PUŽEVA

OD RUPA

OD KAŠTELA

Rupe Ethnographic Museum

IZMEĐU

N

100 metres
100 yards

Getting There

You can reach Dubrovnik by air, or by ferry from Italy, *see* **Getting There**, pp.3–8.

Getting from the Airport

Croatia Airlines **transfer buses** (30Kn) scheduled around its flights drop off passengers at the Pile Gate, and pick them up from the main bus station on Put Republik 2hrs before flight departure. Expect to pay 200Kn for a **taxi**. *See* below for transport from the ferry terminal.

Getting Around

Libertas **buses** 4, 5 and 7 operate circuits from the Pile Gate to hotels on the western peninsulas between 6am and 2am at a fixed price of 10kn – have the exact money ready – or you can buy a 7kn ticket from a Libertas counter at the Pile Gate, newsagents or hotel receptions. Buses 1a, 3 and 7 shuttle between the ferry terminal and the Pile Gate via the principal bus station at Put Republike 7, northwest of the old town.

Taxis wait night and day at a rank outside the Pile Gate or can be called on **t** 970.

Forget **driving**: parking near the old town is near-impossible in summer and expensive year-round. Use a car only for touring.

Car Hire

International players also operate desks at the airport.

Hertz, Frana Supila 9, **t** (020) 425 000, *www.hertz.com*.

Europcar, Kardinala Stepinca 32, **t** (020) 437 179, *www.europcar.com*.

Avis, Vladimira Nazora 9, **t** (020) 422 043, *www.avis.com*.

Mack, Frana Supila 3, **t** (020) 423 747, *www.rentacar-croatia.com*.

Tourist Information

Dubrovnik: Placa, **t** (020) 321 561, *www.tzdubrovnik.hr*, near the Franciscan monastery; *open daily 8am–10pm*; and Ante Starčevića 7, **t** (020) 427 591/426 253, near the Pile Gate bus station; *open 8am–8pm*. Both stock city maps, timetables for Jadrolinija ferries, the usual confetti of brochures and excellent free booklet *Dubrovnik*, a mine of information which contains central and Lapad/Babin kuk peninsula maps, bus routes, ferry timetables, current museum opening times, what's-on listings and a directory of restaurants and services.

Festivals

Feb: **St Blaise's Day** on 3rd fills the old town with religious pomp and is closely followed by three days of **Carnival**, whose good-humoured lunacy of costumed parades and merriment ends on Whit Sunday.

Early July–Aug: Highlight of the Dubrovnik calendar is internationally acclaimed cultural beano the **Summer Festival** (*www.dubrovnik-festival.hr*), a feast of classical music and theatre which takes full advantage of Dubrovnik's stage-set squares, courtyards and castles for its venues.

Shopping

Placa's mansions are stuffed with touristy shops, boutiques, bookshops and smart jewellers, but don't expect any bargains. Nor are there many in parallel **Od Puča**, although it offers a more intriguing mish-mash of leather work, jewellers and galleries. More quirky souvenirs are to be found in **Art Studio I Hajdarhodžić**, Zlatarska 1, which has 15 years' practice of crafting clay fishing boats.

Foodies should peruse the olive oils, wines and liqueurs and good things sold in **Franja**, Od Puča 9, and gallery-delicatessen **Dubrovačka Kuća**, Sv. Dominika 4.

Where to Stay

Dubrovnik **t** (020) –

Bar two exceptions in the old town where reservation is essential and a spanking new Hilton, most of the beds are in pricey hotels 10mins' walk east of the Ploče Gate, or mid-range package offerings 2–4km west on the Lapad and Babin kuk peninsulas. Dubrovnik's fame means bargains are thin on the ground; budget accommodation comes largely from private rooms and in high season you are likely to be met by a crack team of silver-haired touts; triple-check the location of rooms before agreeing.

Pucić Palace, Od Puča 1, Old Town, **t** 326 200, *www.thepucicpalace.com* (*expensive*). Rooms in this five-star boutique hotel carved out of an old town aristocrat's mansion are on the snug side, but benefit from 18th-century high ceilings and quietly flamboyant décor – a mix of modern, antique and opulent fabrics – and the location is unbeatable.

Hilton Imperial Dubrovnik, Marijana Blazica 2, Old Town, **t** 416 553, *www.hilton.com* (*expensive*). A £14m renovation has buffed up two 19th-century palaces to create this 2005 newcomer to Dubrovnik's luxury hotel scene, moments from the Pile Gate and as classy as you'd expect of a five-star member of the international old-hand.

Grand Villa Argentina and **Villa Orsula**, Frana Supila 14, Ploče, **t** 440 555, *www.hoteli-argentina.hr* (*expensive*). Deluxe if rather heavy style meets five-star mod cons and service in a plush traditionalist 10 minutes' walk east from the Ploče Gate; incorporated Villa Orsula retains a whiff of 1930s nostalgia in its rooms of dark woods. Both share a concrete 'beach' and outdoor pool.

Villa Dubrovnik, Vlaha Bukovca 6, Ploče, **t** 422 933, *www.villa-dubrovnik.hr* (*expensive*). Ten minutes further east is this tranquil and friendly retreat wrapped in pines, a bright modernist building flooded with light and arty tastes. Simple rooms are stylish – beg for 101–107 or 222–225 to wake up to glorious views of the old town – and a hotel ferry pootles guests into the centre.

Dubrovnik Palace, Masarykov put 2, Lapad, **t** 430 000, *www.dubrovnikpalace.hr* (*expensive*). Boutique style on a package-hotel scale in a five-star Lapad peninsula newcomer. The decorative tones are delicious – cream, chocolate and *café au lait* – every room has sea views from its balcony and there are all sorts of pools, bars and restaurants to tempt you.

Stari Grad, Od Sigurate 4, Old Town, **t** 321 373, *www.hotelstarigrad.com* (*moderate*). A little pricey considering the adequate but unspectacular furnishings on offer in eight three-star rooms, but the only medium-range hotel within the old town walls, smuggled up a side street off Placa.

Neptun, Kardinala Stepinca 31, Babin kuk, **t** 440 100, *www.hotel-neptun.hr* (*moderate*). Flowery fabrics and blond wood in simple, modern rooms of two blocks set among the unspoilt scrub on the Babin kuk peninsula west of the old town. The sea views are knockout, especially those to the Elafiti islands from rooms 211–14, 311–14 and 411–14. Distance from the peninsula restaurants may be a problem without transport.

Kompas, Šetalište kralja Zvonimira 56, Lapad, **t** 435 777, *www.hotel-kompas.hr* (*moderate*). A little bland in taste, but a comfortable and friendly three-star, well located above the Sumratin beach.

Zagreb, Šetalište kralja Zvonimira 27, Lapad, **t** 436 500 (*inexpensive*). Pleasant small hotel among leafy palms a few minutes' walk from the beach, with 1924 proportions but décor that benefits from a 2005 modernization. Adjacent sister hotel **Sumratin** (same tel, *inexpensive*) offers more of the same if its 22 rooms are full.

Ohran, Od Tabakarije 1, nr Old Town, **t** 414 183 (*inexpensive*). Overlook the fact that the 11 rooms (although spotless and en suite) are basic, and concentrate instead on the location, in a quiet cove beneath the old town Lovrijenac Fortress. A bargain, and one with a good restaurant to boot.

Private Rooms

A little more expensive are private rooms offered by private tourist agencies.

Atlas, Brsalje 17, near the Pile Gate, **t** 442 574/565, *www.atlas-croatia.com*. Friendly.

Globtour, Prijeko 12, Old Town, **t** 321 599.

Generalturist, Frana Supila 9, near the Ploče Gate, **t** 432 974, *www.generalturist.com*.

Dubrovnik Turist, Put Republike 7, by the main bus station, **t** 356 969, *www.dubrovnik turist.hr*.

Eating Out

Dubrovnik **t** (020) –

You'll never be short of a new restaurant in Dubrovnik. Restaurant alley is Prijeko, although it's an uninspiring affair of tourist-orientated offerings. For eats on the go, 24-hour bakery **Tanti Gusti** (Između Polača 11) bakes filled croissants for breakfast and

Buffet Škola (Antuninska bb) rustles up delicious sandwiches prepared with thick home-made bread and local ingredients.

Proto, Široka 1, **t** 323 234 (*expensive*). A semi-smart 1886 old-timer just off Placa, with consistently high-quality cooking: chef's favourite recipes come from grandma's cookbook, but he also prepares a delicate langoustine dish in saffron sauce.

Atlas Club Nautica, Braslje 3, **t** 442 526 (*expensive*). The formal address for visiting dignitaries (the late Pope John Paul II came in 2003), expense-account lunches and evening blow-outs offers views of the city walls and Lovrijenac to accompany exquisite seafood and a house-special lobster.

Rozarij, Prijeko 2 (*moderate*). A little pricey, but by far the most atmospheric restaurant of the glut on Prijeko, with a menu of fresh fish and candlelit tables snuggled against the tiny Church of St Nicholas.

Marco Polo, Lučarica 6, **t** 323 719 (*moderate*). There's a chef's special *riblja plitica* (fish platter) for a two-person blow-out plus reliable fallback appetizers such as *rizoto od morskih plodova* (seafood risotto) and *crni rižot* (squid ink risotto) in a 10-table charmer squirrelled away down a side alley behind St Blaise's church.

Domino, Od Domina 6, **t** 323 103 (*moderate*). Carnivore heaven in a restaurant which prepares speciality steaks in a polyglot of styles and offers a good-value four-course menu. Dining is on the terrace or in a stone house in winter.

Levant, N&M Pucića 15, **t** 435 352 (*moderate*). A romantic gem on the Baban kuk peninsula (on the road to Hotel Neptun) with lovely views across the bay, which are magic at dusk, and friendly service. The inventive menu ranges from traditionals like fish stew *brodet* and an ink-blackened salad of cuttlefish and olives from Elafiti island Šipan, to modern creations such as fish carpaccio and rocket leaves fried with mozzarella.

Lokunda Peskarija, Ribarnica bb (beside the old port), **t** 324 750 (*cheap*). The locals' choice for an early-morning gossip over coffee, or mussels or risottos of seafood or cuttlefish, served in saucepans and washed down with a chirpy local plonk. Unpretentious and excellent – expect to wait for a seat.

Dubrovački kantun, Boškovićeva 5, **t** 331 911 (*cheap*). A taste of tradition in a bistro-café that prepares chunky sandwiches and Dalmatian *tapas*, much of it vegetarian and all using the freshest local ingredients. Anchovies are delicious, there's tangy sheep's cheese from Pag soused in olive oil and smoky *pršut* ham is ever-reliable.

Buffet Kamenice, Gunulićeva poljana 8; no tel (*cheap*). You'll queue for a table in this good-value, brisk favourite of locals and tourists alike in intimate Gunulićeva poljana. Mussels are fat and come piled high; *mala riba pržena* (whitebait) and octopus salad make a tasty light bite.

Cafés and Bars

Buža, Od Margarite. Hunt for a sign which announces 'Cold drinks' to find this locals' secret outside the walls, whose tables shaded by palm leaves gaze out to Lokrum.

Gradska kavana, Luža. Cakes and coffee brought by waiters in black and white in the silver-haired *grande dame* of Dubrovnik cafés located in the former arsenal and with terraces over Luža square and the old port.

Hard Jazz Café Trubadour, Bunićeva Poljana. The best place to sample the buzz of a Dubrovnik summer evening – wicker chairs sprawl across the square and a stylish clientele sip a cocktail to live jazz.

Libertina, Zlatarska. A locals' favourite, cluttered with junky knick-knacks and where service is refreshingly gruff; an antidote to high-season posing.

Entertainment

Monthly booklet *Dubrovnik* (free from tourist information) is a what's-on bible which lists everything from concerts of the Dubrovnik Symphony Orchestra to football matches. Treats are candlelit classical concerts staged in churches, the Dominican Monastery cloisters and the atrium of the Rector's Palace, intimate and atmospheric. More chirpy are the twice-weekly showcases of Croatian traditional song and dance-folk group Linđo stages in the Lazareti (*see* p.133; in 2005, Tues and Fri at 9.30pm).

roofscape like patchwork. Partly because of its UNESCO status, partly due to pride, Dubrovnik was so precious about repairs to a historic kernel two-thirds destroyed by 20th-century Serbian shells – maps at the city gates pinpoint direct hits and minor scars – that it scoured Europe to match the *kupe kanalice* tiles shaped over medieval thighs. Those sourced from French and Slovenian factories are a shock of orange beside the soft tones of the weathered originals, but there's magic in the air when late-afternoon sunshine rakes low and ripens the palette of orange and saffron, ochre and cream, especially from the Minčeta Tower. Early risers may miss a city which seems to hold its breath at dusk, but will get to ponder the views in peace.

For a jaw-dropping perspective of the city huddled like a model, puff uphill to the main road above (shame about the traffic), or, for an alternative view closer to hand, ascend the **Lovrijenac Fortress** (Tvrđava Lovrijenac; *open daily 8.30–6.30; same ticket as city walls*), which hunkers down on a knuckle of rock opposite the Bokar bastion. City fathers demanded walls 40ft thick for the castle to guard western sea approaches – except for those facing inland, whose 2ft wafer provided no protection for disgruntled garrison commanders harbouring dark thoughts of mutiny. Enter the stripped shell of the late 15th-century fortress and you can understand why its fame today is not as a scourge of sea galleons but as the setting for 'Elsinore' during Summer Festival productions of *Hamlet*. Before you enter, look for a piece of indulgent sermonizing on the portal which drummed into guards that 'freedom is not sold for all the goods in the world' (*Non bene pro toto libertas vendit vravo*).

Along Placa

The cameras come out again for **Placa** (aka Stradun) just inside the Pile Gate. So handsome is Dubrovnik's showpiece street that you'd never guess its origins as a swampy channel filled in in the 11th century to unite islet Laus – where the city made its 7th-century debut as Ragusa, founded by Greco-Roman refugees from Epidaurum (*see p.135*) – with the mainland Slavic town christened after holm-oak woods (*dubrava*). The devastating 1667 earthquake which allowed city fathers to rethink their map also allowed them to take in hand Placa's jumble of Gothic palaces and impose a Baroque dress parade. For all the authoritarian bent of its conception, there's no denying Placa's good looks; a handsome stretch of green-shuttered mansions in delicious shades of honey and clotted cream, an occasional touching blush of pink, on a street whose limestone cobbles have been buffed to a sheen by millions of pairs of feet. A 19th-century visitor probably had its width in mind when he noted, 'Dubrovnik is not built in such a way to be admired from a coach. This is a place which leaves a great deal of space for pedestrians.'

The 1667 earthquake which razed Placa also did for **Onofrio's Large Fountain** (Velika Onofrijeva fontana) just inside the Pile Gate; the 16 masks that spout water on a bare dome today barely hint at the heavily ornamented Renaissance beauty of the original, designed in 1438 by architect Onofrio della Cava. The Neopolitan builder's glorified washbasin for new arrivals was one element in a no-expense-spared water-works which piped by aqueduct fresh water from the River Dubrovačka 12km away – no rainwater cisterns like other northern Dalmatian cities for wealthy Dubrovnik.

More recent destruction is visible as shrapnel scars which pock the Renaissance trefoil façade of the diminutive **St Saviour's Church** (Crkva sv. Spasa) opposite, a rum deal for a church which survived the '67 quake in better shape than its sisters and was itself erected as a thank you for the city's survival of a 1520 earthquake. The spartan Gothic interior now serves as a temporary exhibition space and concert venue.

The 1667 earthquake also destroyed a **Franciscan Monastery** (Franjevački samostan) far more ritzy than the present hulk if a surviving late-Gothic portal is any evidence; local sons the Petrović brothers carved its late-Gothic *Pietà* flanked by St Jerome (in a penitent's hairshirt) and St John. Don't linger in the barn-like interior stuffed with so-so Baroque altars, devote your time instead to the delightful late-Romanesque **cloister** (*open daily 9–6; adm*); locate it from a passageway adjacent to tourists trying out the traditional test of balance atop a stone beside the west portal – not as easy as it looks. Craftsmen in 1360 gave free rein to their imaginations on capitals that crown the cloister's double colonnade of pillars with a menagerie of dragons, dogs and griffins; look for a balloon-cheeked self portrait by a sculptor with toothache. It's best appreciated around midday, when the jolly tour groups bustle off for lunch and the garden of fruit trees and palms returns to serenity; then you can explore at leisure the curate's egg of ecclesiastical goodies in the **treasury** (*same ticket and hours*). More charming than its Byzantine icons, votive jewellery and bizarre gold and silver reli-quaries of saints' feet and St Ursula's head are the china jars and painted shelves which once graced Europe's oldest apothecary, still doling out medicines beside the cloister as it has done since 1317.

North of Placa, steep staircases crammed with pot plants clamber uphill and beg you to explore; residential alleys beyond **Prijeko** allow a glimpse behind the scenes of Dubrovnik's stage-set looks. At the east end of Placa's shimmering river of cobbles, **Žudioska** (Jews' Street) was named for the ghetto established by Jews hounded from Spain in 1492 and 1514–15 exiles from southern Italy. With an open mind bred by coastal trade, the republic presented the community with a medieval town house, which explains why Europe's second-oldest **synagogue** (Sinagoga; *open summer daily 10–8; winter Mon–Fri 10–1; adm*), a lovely Baroque nook where brass lamps and cande-labras are suspended from a ceiling framed by Stars of David, is on the second floor rather than in the conventional basement. Not that Dubrovnik embraced its newcomers entirely without reservation – the Ragusan Republic demanded that Jews wash in a separate fountain rather than share those of Christians. A small **museum** chronicles the Jewish community, today 30-strong, in facsimiles of official documents and religious artefacts, including a 13th-century Torah treasured by the first exiles.

Luža Square

Café society idles and tour groups clog the ensemble of attractions in Luža Square, still centre stage of Dubrovnik life as it was during the medieval republic; here the 3 February procession of the Feast of St Blaise climaxes with the full authority of Catholic pomp, and poetry recited here inaugurates the Summer Festival's arts extrav-aganza (*see* 'Festivals', p.124).

Centrepiece of the handsome piazza is **Orlando's Column** (Orlandov stup). The 1418 lectern for public declarations and shaming post for chained miscreants flew the white banner of *Libertas* from its flagpole until Napoleon, never a dictator to recognize such limiting concepts, lowered it after French troops stomped into a city weakened by protracted siege in 1806. The events of 1990 prompted the city council to restore the flag as a morale-booster. The column is named after its Gothic effigy of Orlando (aka Roland). A tall tale claims that the chivalric knight slew a 9th-century Saracen pirate named Spucente near Lokrum to lift a 15-month siege of Dubrovnik – casually overlooking the fact that the nephew of Frankish king Charlemagne and hero of medieval French epic *Chanson de Roland* actually died in AD 778. It is more probable that the favourite of North European cities was imported by Sigismund, 15th-century ruler of Hungary, Bohemia and much of modern Croatia. And whatever the truth, respect was hardly uppermost in the minds of the market traders who measured out 51.2cm standard lengths of cloth on their hero's forearm.

He stands opposite the splendid **Sponza Palace** (Sponza-Povijesni arhiv; 1522; *often open Mon–Fri 9–2 but times vary by exhibition; adm free*), whose Renaissance colonnade and refined Venetian-Gothic windows by architect Paskoje Miličević, frothily ornamented by renowned Korčula sculptor-brothers the Andrijićs, offer a tantalising glimpse of elegant Dubrovnik before the 1667 destruction. The city archives are stored in upper floors where intellectuals once debated and the republic minted its own currency. But downstairs, enter its galleried courtyard, now quiet after years when it rang to the polyglot babble of merchants in the customs house, remembered by a reference to municipal scales above the central arch: 'Our weights do not permit cheating or being cheated: when I measure goods, God measures me'. Here you can hear summer concerts and visit the ground-floor exhibitions – don't miss the moving 'Memorial Room of Dubrovnik Defenders' at the rear, a simple but heartfelt requiem to over 200 local citizens who lost their lives in the 1990s Homeland War.

Local favourite 'green men' clang the hour in the 100ft **bell tower** (Gradski zvonik) at the palace's left shoulder, rebuilt in 1929 to 15th-century plans after its drunken tilt became too woozy to ignore. From here you can sidetrack through an arch to the Dominican Monastery (*see* p.133) or pass the mustachioed guard on the massive Baroque portal of the **House of the Main Guard** to **Onofrio's Little Fountain** (Mala Onofrijeva fontana); pigeons bathe in the light-hearted sister to its big relative at the other end of Placa, and its puffing cherubs are by Milanese sculptor Pietro di Martino.

The backdrop to Luža's ensemble piece is **St Blaise's Church** (Crkva svetog Vlaha); at the peak the city's patron (*see* p.122) waves a cheery salute between Faith and Hope. Small wonder those two Virtues were chosen, because the elegant Baroque church rose over the square in 1715 as a replacement for a Gothic number battered in 1667 then reduced to rubble by a 1706 fire. Inside, upstaged by angels and *putti*, a silver statue of the saint clutches the inevitable city model on the high altar, removed only when it is paraded solemnly on St Blaise's Day as a miraculous survivor of that 18th-century blaze. Whether Dubrovnik will ever revive the custom of freeing minor prisoners for the high day of its religious calendar is doubtful.

The Rector's Palace

Follow the limestone cobbles that flow from Luža past *grande dame* of Dubrovnik cafés **Gradska kavana**, located in the former city arsenal, to the **Rector's Palace** (Knežev dvor), state headquarters of the Ragusan Republic and temporary home of the local son elevated to preside over council meetings for a month. For all the high talk of republican egalitarianism, the ruling aristocracy kept a firm grip on power and the incumbent was little more than a ceremonial puppet – during his tenure, the symbol of sovereignty, aged 50-plus, lived apart from his family and was only permitted to leave his glorified prison on state business.

But what a prison. Gunpowder explosions (the palace originally led a double life as an arsenal), fire and earthquake, which necessitated over 230 years of home improvements, have fashioned a stylistic encyclopaedia of Gothic and Renaissance from the drawing boards of a *Who's Who* of Adriatic architects: Naples' Onofrio; Michelozzi, putting fortifications work on hold; and Korčula's Petar Andrijić. If the city fathers hoped for public showiness, they must have been delighted with Michelozzi's Renaissance *loggia*, even if the conservative custodians frowned at most of his plans as too racy and the architect harrumphed back to Florence. Do hunt among his frothy capitals for Asclepius in his pharmacy – a vainglorious attempt to appropriate the classical authority of a Greek demigod physician linked with Epidaurum (today's Cavtat, *see* p.135) – before you enter its elegant Renaissance atrium, prize venue for classical music concerts. For want of an heir, powerful ship owner and merchant Miho Pracat bequeathed his fortune to the city and is honoured in a 1638 bust at the rear of the courtyard. It must have been some fortune – the Lopud (*see* p.138) resident was the only commoner so honoured in the republic's history.

Musty displays of coins, official seals, documents and weaponry are in the ground-floor former courtroom and prison cells, then the **city museum** (Gradski muzej; *open summer daily 9–6; winter daily 9–2; adm*) perks up in first-floor state rooms, reached via a Baroque staircase that sweeps up to the assembly hall whose portal exhorts councillors to 'Forget private concerns, focus on public affairs'. Councillor nobles pout shamelessly on the walls of period rooms whose *objets d'art* and costumes such as the rector's red damask toga fast-forward through decorative styles and hint at Ragusan glory snuffed out by Napoleonic dissolution. Informative the rooms are not, however; a museum guide is a must if you want to do anything but skim.

The Cathedral and St John's Fortress

Making an emphatic full-stop to **Pred Dvorom** is the powerful **cathedral** (Katedrala), crowned by a surprisingly dainty cupola. An ex-pat intellectual, enthused by the churches of his Eternal City adopted home, recommended Andrea Buffalini of Urbino to draw its Roman Baroque, which rose over the ruins of a Romanesque church destroyed in 1667. Fiction – or at least local legend – claims the progenitor was funded by Richard the Lionheart in thanks for his life after shipwreck near Lokrum after an 1192 Crusade. Fact – or at least early foundations – retorts that a church has existed at the location on former islet Laus since the 7th century.

The star artwork in a bleached but stately interior is a gloomy *Assumption of the Virgin* polyptych above the altar, attributed to Venetian master Titian. Inevitably, St Blaise and his model put in an appearance on the left-hand panel, although this time with good reason because bits of the saint are venerated in the **treasury** (Riznica; *open Mon–Sat 8–5.30, Sun 11–5.30; adm*), a wonder of the Adriatic before the 1667 earthquake, which the republic safeguarded by entrusting its different keys to the archbishop, cathedral rector and state secretary. Among body parts crammed into Byzantine gold reliquaries and displayed on gloriously cluttered shelves like a holy junk shop are the saint's right and left hands, the latter reputedly picked up in 1346 by a keen-eyed Dubrovnik merchant trading in the East; his throat, in a bizarre 11th-century monstrance like a foot; and, the treasury's prize, his head, encased in a jewel-encrusted Byzantine crown whose *cloisonné* enamel depicts cartoony saints amid floral tendrils. Overlooked among such star pieces is a modest 16th-century silver casket – apparently crafted to treasure baby Jesus's nappies.

Narrow **Kneza Damjana Jude** opposite the cathedral's main portal burrows past tatty side-streets stuffed with once-splendid Renaissance nobles' mansions now living in reduced circumstances, towards stolid port guardian the **St John's Fortress** (Tvrđava sv. Ivana). Its refurbished ground floor houses a 27-tank **Aquarium** (Akvarij; *open summer daily 9–8; winter Mon–Sat 9–1; adm*) where small sharks and rays steal all the attention from more prosaic Adriatic sea life such as octopus. Also in the fortress, rooms where cannons once thundered above now salute the maritime prowess which elevated Dubrovnik to world power-player as the **Maritime Museum** (Pomorski muzej; *open summer daily 9–6; winter Tues–Sun 9–1; adm*); thanks to a diplomacy of neutrality which ensured control of Balkan gold and silver, late-1700s Dubrovnik maintained consulates in over 80 cities and expanded the English vocabulary with the word 'argosy', derived from Ragusan boats. Exquisite models of tubby traders and an intriguing snapshot of everyday life afforded by cargo salvaged from a 1600s trader are a highlight of the museum's bosun's locker of nautical knick-knacks, sailors' uniforms and chests, and fiddly 16th-century charts.

Around Gundulićeva Poljana

For all her wardrobe of architectural ballgowns, Dubrovnik is just as charming in her everyday dress, worn in Gundulićeva poljana, home to a morning market (*Mon–Sat*) whose stallholders also hawk Hvar lavender, fat cheeses and, decanted into old water bottles, home-made wines and *rakija*, a spirit laced with herbs which locals swear is medicinal. The drama queen who poses in the centre is Ivan Gundulić (1589–1638). Such is the acclaim afforded the Ragusan poet's epic *Osman* – a eulogy to Polish routs of the Turks saluted in relief beneath Ivan Rendić's 1892 statue – that he is afforded a place on the 50Kn note. Such veneration came late, however – Gundulić's *magnum opus* didn't even make it into print until 1826 and even then thanks only to the Croatian Illyrian movement, which hailed his work as exemplary stuff during a campaign to reassert Croatian over German as the official language.

Climb a 1738 staircase that alludes to Rome's Spanish Steps off the square's south side to stand before the **Jesuit Church of St Ignatius** (Jezuitska crkva i samostan), quiet above the market's chatter and modelled on Rome's imposing Il Gesù. As if to compensate for the restraint shown in other churches, Dubrovnik's 1729 prize of Baroque lets rip the razzmatazz; the roof is a frothy gush of pinks, side-chapels whirl with *trompe l'œil* knobbles and drapes painted in rich hues, and in a richly frescoed sanctuary Jesuit founder St Ignatius proffers his religious credo before a quartet of comely *belles*, the four continents on which the order spread the word. Less cultural but just as enjoyable is a Lourdes grotto by the entrance, whose glorious dollop of kitsch has filled a north aisle chapel since 1885.

Away from public grand airs, Dubrovnik relaxes into easygoing mode. The crowds disappear among cobbled streets south and north of the church in a residential district perfect for a happy-go-lucky amble; time has held its breath in the mazy string of alleys and staircases that knot into small squares or tease with a dead end.

Od Puča and Around

Halfway along Od puča, the street parallel to Placa which is crammed with interesting jewellery boutiques and galleries, is the **Serbian Orthodox Church** (Srpska pravoslavna crkva), spacious and dignified with a painted panelled ceiling, and a few doors away at Od puča 8 is the **Orthodox Church Museum** (Muzej pravoslavne crkve; *open Mon–Sat 9–2; adm*) of religious icons. Treasures among a four-century *œuvre* of oval-faced Madonnas and serious saints, mostly from nearby Kotor in Montenegro, Crete and Greece, are a sumptuous 16th-century image of resurrected Christ appearing to Mary Magdalene in Room One and an 18th-century Russian calendar.

More culture is five minutes' walk away at Široka 7. Croatia's Shakespeare, Marin Držić (1508–67), would probably have knocked over his inkpot in shock were he to see the interior of his former home. Gutted as **Marin Držić House** (Kuča Marina Držica; *open summer daily 9–6; winter Mon–Sat 9–2; adm*), the museum displays meagre everyday relics from Držić's era and a mock-up of his cell-like bedroom. Far better is its 40-minute audiovisual presentation (*available in English*) which explores the Ragusan society he lampooned in comedies such as Croat favourite *Dundo Maroje* (*Uncle Dundo*). On Od Rupe the **Rupe Ethnographic Museum** (Etnografski muzej Rupe; *open daily 9–6; adm*) houses three floors of homespun tradition – costumes, from simple smocks to embroidered Sunday best and rural handicrafts – let down by dull displays and a lack of labels; ask friendly staff to explain quirks such as horses' skulls placed on beehives to scare off evil spirits intent on souring the honey. As much of an exhibit is the museum's Renaissance building itself; storage bins dug from the rock bed visible through holes (*rupe*) in the ground floor confess its origins as the granary of a city twitchy about sieges and wholly reliant on imported grain.

The Old Port and Dominican Monastery

Suddenly intimate after the grand airs of Placa, **Sv. Dominika** east of the Sponza Palace twists past the **old port**, where fishing boats not traders' barques nod at moorings, ferries thrum to Lokrum (*see p.134*) and Cavtat (*see pp.134–5*), and tourist boat captains tout sprees to admire the city walls as merchant sailors knew them. Coffee-drinkers in café **Gradska kavana** now laze before the three arches through which

state-owned galleons were hauled from the port to be refitted in the city arsenal;
not a city to take chances, Dubrovnik bricked them up while new ships were in build.

Beyond on Sv. Dominika, the **Dominican Monastery** (Dominikanski samostan;
open as museum, see below) presses hard against the city walls following its conception as a fortress to protect a chink in Dubrovnik's stone armour. Chipping in funds,
the Ragusan government exhorted citizens to put other projects on hold until the
14th-century edifice stood for 'the preservation, protection and safety of the city of
Dubrovnik' and, fearing for this city on the outer ramparts of Christendom, Pope
Benedict XI issued a 1304 papal bull 'inviting' church members to dig deep into
their coffers. Ascend a **staircase** whose classy balustrade is marred by concrete filler –
the vandalism of monks desperate to spare brothers the temptation of churchgoing
ladies' shapely ankles – to reach a beautiful **cloister** whose restrained Gothic and
Renaissance triforas beat time around a garden of palms and orange trees. Its hushed
haven, a world away from Dubrovnik's summer hubbub, comes from the drawing
board of Rector's Palace architect Michelozzi and is a cerebral overture to a hoard of
devotional art treasures stored in the city's richest **museum** (*open summer daily 9–6;
winter daily 9–5; adm*). A trio of Renaissance works by Nikola Božidarević, finest artist
of the city's golden age, steals the show: his humanist *Virgin and Child* altarpiece
seems wafted from the other side of the Adriatic; a lower panel of an *Annunciation*
played out to a rapt audience of cherubs features the anchored vessel of the Lopud
captain who commissioned it; and, in a lovely *Madonna and Child* steeped in
Byzantine mystery, St Blaise holds out for inspection a model of 16th-century pre-
'quake Dubrovnik. In the same room is a polyptych by Lovro Dobričević: first
Dominican Order martyr St Peter suffers the cutlass and sword of pirates to witness
the baptism of Christ. Star piece among works by Baroque foreigners is a Titian altarpiece of *Mary Magdalene and St Blaise* in an adjacent room.

The **church** itself is a let-down after such magnificence, worth a look only for a
Miracle of St Dominic altarpiece by late-19th-century Cavtat artist Vlaho Bukovac.

Through the Ploče Gate

As eastern counterpart to the the Pile Gate, the 15th-century **Ploče Gate** signs off
the old town with its own drawbridge and statuette of Dubrovnik's bearded patron,
and beyond is the 1540s **Revelin Fortress**; all building work paused while Dubrovnik
beefed up a century-old fortress at the vulnerable landward gate because of Venetian
sabre-rattling. Beyond the walls, modernity returns with a jolt, broken only by the
Lazareti 200m away – artists' studios and the performance space of folk group Linđo
now occupy the 16th-century brick sheds on the Turkey trade route where all foreign
travellers sat out 40 days' quarantine. If you can find towel space in summer, shingle
beach **Banje**, backed by cafés, is an enticing spot for a dip, otherwise continue uphill
for a shot of cultural adrenaline in the **Museum of Modern Art** (Umjetnička galerija;
open Tues–Sun 10–7; adm). Vlaho Bukovac's formal portraiture, which dabbles with
Impressionism, wins plaudits among the gallery of 20th-century Croatian artists;
more enjoyable are colourful local landscapes by Marko Rešica or *Lapad*, a dainty but
delectable work by Antun Masle. The ground floor hosts temporary exhibitions.

Lokrum

Ferries every 30mins from old port, summer daily 9–6; 15mins, 35Kn return.

Covered in a thick fuzz of pine tantalizingly close offshore, Lokrum is the perfect escape when Dubrovnik's summer crowds induce claustrophobia. 'Only the imagination of a skilled writer could have placed an island like Lokrum off a city like Dubrovnik,' sighed 20th-century dramatist, author and local son Luka Paljetak. 'When you set foot upon Lokrum, you encroach upon a mystery... it is under a spell that you cannot hope to undo.' Believe the local tales, and spells are the *leitmotif* of a 72-hectare (180-acre) idyll unofficially dubbed 'Magic Island'.

It may have been the whiff of the otherworldly that lured Benedictine monks to found an abbey and monastery here in 1023, and legend claims they would have got a church, too, had Richard the Lionheart fulfilled an 1192 pledge to erect one where he reputedly staggered ashore after being wrecked en route home from a Crusade. Their order dissolved by Napoleon, the monks are said to have laid a curse on anyone who claimed their sanctuary for anything so frivolous as pleasure, and superstitious locals swear it cursed Archduke Maximilian Ferdinand von Habsburg: he purchased Lokrum as an idyllic retreat in 1859 only to be executed as emperor of Mexico by soldiers in 1867. The battalion of sorrows – bankruptcy, drownings, suicide pacts by thwarted lovers – which befell future owners have only helped sustain the legend.

In the three halcyon years before Maximilian travelled to Mexico to accept his poisoned chalice, he rethought the monastery as a pleasure palace, imported peacocks and dug a **botanic garden** in which to ponder verses of poet Heinrich Heine while his wife Charlotte toiled over her silk embroidery. Only his garden remains open to the public, somewhat neglected at the side of his mansion; Australian and South American species spread leafy canopies alongside the archduke's cacti. More enticing is the monks' semi-ruined **cloister**, going nicely to seed with agave, palms and cacti. You'll probably have it to yourself, because most visitors head straight for the excellent swimming off flat rocks a five-minute stroll southwest of the monastery or wallow in the warmer shallows of an adjacent saltwater lake enclosed by low cliffs; more secluded coves, including a nudist 'beach', are on the island's south tip.

Explore Maximilian's paths, which idle around a drowsy island cocooned in hush, and you'll discover **Fort Royal**. Built by Napoleon as an 1806 stronghold, the star-shaped gun battery broods among the pines at Lokrum's highest point.

Day Trips and Overnighters from Dubrovnik

Cavtat

After heady days as medieval sidekick to the Dubrovnik republic, charming Cavtat spends her dotage as a gentle lady of leisure. Yes, there's a whiff of aristocracy on a seafront promenade of Baroque stone mansions – Dubrovnik's Placa in miniature – but the real seduction of this village snuggled in a pine-fringed harbour is as the lazy resort which lured in-the-know Austro-Hungarians in the early 1900s.

Getting There

Hourly **bus 10** from Dubrovnik takes 40mins to trundle 22km south to Cavtat and costs 12Kn. Alternatively, private companies operate summer-only **ferries** (45mins, 40Kn single, 60Kn return) from the old port (Gradska luka), and there's a Nova International ferry (25min, 50Kn single) also from the old port.

Tourist Information

Cavtat: Tiha 3 (200yds from the bus station), **t** (020) 479 025, *www.tzcavtat-konavle.hr. Open April–Aug daily 8–8; Sept–Nov Mon–Sat 8–4, Sun 8–12; Dec–Mar Mon–Fri 8–3.*

Eating Out

Leut, Trumbićev Put 11, **t** (020) 479 050 (*moderate*). Passing celebrities salute the privacy of its terrace beneath pine trees, but the main reason to visit this family restaurant near the Rector's Palace is for the catch of the day or a house special cold platter of *pršut* ham, cheese, octopus salad and mussels.

Galija, Vuličevićeva 1, **t** (020) 478 566 (*moderate*). The locals' choice for a slap-up near the monastery church serves consistently excellent fresh fish, perfectly grilled or in rich olive sauces, plus exotic delights such as sea urchin caviar for culinary adventurers.

Ironically, it's Dubrovnik which owes Cavtat a debt. Slavic and Avar tribes ripped through 7th-century **Epidaurum**, founded by Greeks from Vis (*see* pp.111–13) then Romanized as Civitas Vetus in 228 BC, and evacuees fled north to start afresh on the town that became Dubrovnik. Only the ruins in the bay (consult the tourist board for diving trips) and foundation walls on the tip of a pine-covered peninsula recall that progenitor settlement, and, after Dubrovnik looked inward during a collective tightening of belts in the 1700s, Cavtat shrugged and turned to fishing instead.

During its halcyon years, a Dubrovnik-appointed governor lorded it over Cavtat from the Renaissance **Rector's Palace**, a grand opening statement to the old town and host to its finest museum, the **Baltazar Bogišic Collection** (Zbirka Baltazara Bogišića; *open Mon–Sat 9.30–1; adm*). Treasured books and early European prints of the Cavtat-born promoter of Slavic culture claim most space, although the 19th-century lawyer reveals his cultured mind and jackdaw enthusiasms in collections of Ragusan Republic coins, folksy embroidery and *objets d'art* cherry-picked from France and Italy. His personal treasures are upstaged by the vivacious *Carnival in Cavtat*, whose depiction of the town's finest – Bogišic included – kicking up their heels in fancy dress is by local son Vlaho Bukovac. Three more Bukovacs plus a gallery of glitzy Italian devotional works hang in the **Pinakoteka-Galerija** (*open summer Mon–Sat 10–1; winter by appointment, tel on door; adm*) of parish church **St Nicholas**, at the shoulder of the Rector's Palace, but far better is the career-spanning *œuvre* of the 19th-century father of Croatian art on show in his restored **birthplace** (Kuća Bukovan; *open May–Nov Tues–Sat 9–1 and 4–8, Sun 4–8; Dec–April Tues–Sun 10–5; closed Mon; adm*) located in sidestreet Bukovčeva. Student works to impress Paris Academy examiners are an exercise in stuffy realism compared with later dabbles in Art Nouveau and the Impressionism of lively Cavtat crowd scene *Procession in Tiha* (1902), although the house is worth a visit as much for rooms frescoed with exotic birds and animals by a 16-year-old Bukovac.

Bukovac also painted the Cavtat harbour scene that spans the chancel in the Franciscan monastery church of **Our Lady of the Snow** (Samostan snježne gospe) which signs off the seafront promenade. Do take time to hunt out a pair of sumptuous Renaissance altarpieces – applauded by sinners and admired by saints Nicholas and John, archangel St Michael smites a demon in a rear chapel, the vision of Vicko Lovrin; and a tender *Madonna and Child* is lost in the gloom as a main altar – before you allow a path around the peninsula to lead you into temptation of Cavtat's most enticing coves for a dip. Pebble **beaches** are a 10-minute stroll around the bay before package hotels – so don't expect them to yourself.

Crowning glory of the town **cemetery** at the peak of the hill above is the **Račić mausoleum** (*open daily 10–12, summer also Mon–Sat 5–7; adm*), a dream of creamy white stone from Brač (*see* p.109), beautifully sited over the coastline. Croatia's finest modern sculptor Ivan Meštrović designed the Cavtat shipowners' 1912 tomb to honour a parting request of rumoured sweetheart Maria Račić. Not that he succumbed to lyricism in its stern historicist synthesis of Byzantine, Assyrian and ancient Greek imagery, drawn with his eye for pure lines and softened by a whiff of Art Nouveau. Or at least not on the outside. Inside, above allegories of birth, life and death, hidden amid fluttering angels on the cupola, Meštrović engraved the bell with a heart-felt adieu to Maria: 'Understand the secret of love and you will solve the secret of death and believe life is eternal.'

Trsteno

Gazing over his clifftop estate in 1494, Dubrovnik nobleman Ivan Marinov Gučetić-Gozze realized the site's potential for a fashionable summer retreat and seeded one of the finest landscaped parks in Croatia. Visit in spring and his relic of Renaissance sophistication, lovingly tended and expanded by future generations of the aristocratic dynasty until seized by a nation enthused by Communism and presented to the public in 1948 as the **Trsteno Arboretum** (*open daily May–Oct 7–7; Nov–April 8–3; adm*), explodes with colour and promise. Idle among its 63 acres of aromatic greenery or gaze out to the Elafiti islands in summer and you'll wonder how 16th-century humanist Nioklai Vitov Gučetić ever roused himself sufficiently to jot down his philosophical musings.

At the heart of the complex, reached by a path beyond two epic plane trees at the bus stop, is the **summer villa** rebuilt after the 1667 earthquake which shook Dubrovnik and today a missed opportunity, empty and closed to the public. Fortunately, you are free to explore Gučetić's lovely gardens before it, structured in Dubrovnik style with an axial walkway and pergola which once supported vines, dividing stone walls and, as a casual nod to the Age of Reason, orderly triangles of box hedge planted with rosemary, lavender and cyclamen. Sweet jasmine and passion flower picked up as holiday souvenirs by Dubrovnik merchants complement the indigenous species in a horticultural world tour, which explored further afield in the 19th century and introduced exotica: Chinese bamboos, Japanese pines and exuberant Mexican palms. A clifftop **pavilion** offers idyllic views over the Elafitis, and hidden in the gloom of nearby outbuildings is an ancient olive press.

Getting There

Tell the driver in advance and any **bus** travelling north – the 12 to Brsečinem, 15 to Ston, 21 to Orebić and those to Split – will stop in Trsteno. Average journey time is 45mins, the cost 12Kn each way.

Eating Out

Cannosa, opposite bus stop (*moderate*). The only restaurant in Trsteno, its terrace sheltered from traffic on the main road by a hedge. The full range of southern Dalmatian delights is on the menu, from seafood risottos for a snack to fresh seafood and chunky steaks.

The restaurants of the summer-only guest-houses offer other options for lunch and a seasonal campsite café near the garden entrance rustles up light bites.

Beyond a family **chapel** dedicated to St Jerome at the rear of the villa (and invariably locked), the gardens live up to the arboretum of their name in a **woodland** of carefully labelled specimen trees which is a joy to explore, threaded by casual paths and dappled by gold coins of sunlight. Amble deep into its centre, beyond a clearing where Dubrovnik's Ragusan Council deliberated matters of state, and Neptune strikes a noble pose with dogged professionalism among bit-part nymphs and dolphins who steal the scene with hammy amateur dramatics, spouting water into a fishpond of a **Baroque grotto** created in 1736 and fed by a 230ft aqueduct.

A garden of southern Adriatic cypresses and pines appears somewhat shabby at the side of its sophisticated sister, its ruined sundial and grasses the product of late-19th-century neo-romantics rather than Yugoslav Army shells lobbed in October 1991 to set ablaze much of the arboretum; some trees still bear the scars. Stone steps descend to the sea in faux Renaissance grandeur; a footpath on the other side of the arboretum leads to Trsteno's quaint harbour, perfect for a refreshing dip.

The Elafiti Islands

'Those islets lovelier than gardens,' sighed 16th-century Dubrovnik bishop Lodovico Beccadelli of the enchanting Elafiti islands just off the coast of Dubrovnik to the northwest. His comment echoes through the centuries because the three inhabited 'deer islands' – a corruption of the Greek *elafos* – are minor paradises where tourism is acknowledged only with a casual shrug and cars are outlawed. Wander the footpaths through interiors of pine and aromatic shrubs and you understand why the eyes of Dubrovnik Renaissance aristocrats turned to the Elafitis for a summer retreat; many of their mansions remain, bolstered with defence towers after Ottoman raids in the mid-16th century.

Koločep

Just 3km from Dubrovnik, little Koločep is a speck just 2.35km² that gathers its 150 residents in drowsy hamlets **Donje Čelo**, the port on the northwest coast, and **Gornje Čelo** in the southeast. Little more than clusters of stone houses and a parish church huddled in verdant bays (the best beach is at Donje Čelo), the pair are linked by a

Getting There

From Dubrovnik port, Jadrolinija **ferries** skip along the islands year-round: ferries to Koločep take 25mins (22Kn single); to Lopud 50mins (22Kn single); and to Šipanska Luka on Šipan 1hr 15mins (28Kn single). Marginally faster are the summer-only Nova International ferries which fill holes in the Jadrolinija timetable and cost 40Kn. For those in a hurry, Dubrovnik tourist agencies such as Atlas organize rushed one-day trips around the trio: expect to pay 200Kn per person.

Tourist Information

Lopud: t (020) 759 086. *Open June–Sept Mon–Fri 8–1 und 5–7, Sun 9–12.*
Šipanska Luka: t (020) 758 084. *Open June–Sept Mon–Fri 8–1 and 6–8, Sat–Sun 9–12.*

Eating Out

Elafiti Islands t (020) –
Obala, Obal I Kuljevan 18, Lopud, t 759 108 (*moderate*). Surprisingly stylish dining on the seafront, with waiters in black-and-whites and jazzy Muzak to form a soundtrack to a lunch of catch of the day or excellent salads.
Barbara, Od Šunja 2, Lopud, t 759 087 (*moderate*). On the footpath to Šunj from Lopud, this has a vine-covered terrace and light snacks, such as grilled squid and *pršut* and cheese.
Domaca Prirodna Hrana, Od Šunja 19, Lopud; no tel (*moderate*). An evening-only treat just uphill from the Barbara, this family home offers mother's cooking and a changing menu prepared from the freshest home-grown ingredients.

footpath which idles through pines. Not that a trip between them is ever direct, however – paths entice you to wander through olive groves to ruined Romanesque churches, some carved with the plait motifs of Croatia's early medieval stylebooks.

Lopud

Home to 76 families, middle island Lopud has hosted tourists for nearly a century, but then it was always the most outgoing of the trio. In 1457 the 2km by 4.5km island was elevated to regional headquarters, a nod of gratitude perhaps for its tradition of local seamen who drip-fed wealth into the Ragusan Republic as prosperous merchants and commanded Dubrovnik fleets as admirals. An 80-strong fleet which called Lopud its home port also swelled the coffers of ship-owners, who erected the stone mansions which crumble on the bay of its eponymous village-port.

As you enter the bay, keep an eye open for a trio of **Gothic windows** which recall the Rector's Palace of Lopud's golden age, then start your tour at the 15th-century parish **church of the Franciscan monastery**; the guardian of the harbour's northern entrance was fortified into a refuge from Turks a century after it was built in 1483. Despite decades of talk about renovation into a hotel, the monastery remains a shell, but the church (*if open; consult tourist office for times*) contains ritzy Renaissance altars.

Crests on the lintels of harbourfront mansions salute the merchant owners, none more successful than Miho Pracat (1522–1607). A nook-like **chapel** just beyond the tourist office is that of the shipping magnate celebrated in bronze in Dubrovnik's Rector's Palace (*see* p.130); the jury is still out on whether the adjacent stone mansion living in reduced circumstances as a barn is his.

Past a small **museum of local history and traditional skills** (*adm*) which opens according to whim on the central square, a signposted path ascends inland past the shell of **St John the Baptist's Church** (Sv. Ivan Kristitelj) to the ruins of **Fort Kaštio** (Trđava Kaštio), whose battlements command the sweeping views over neighbouring islands and sea approaches which made it a prize fortification during Lopud's merchant heyday. Energetic strollers can continue on a 12km circuit of the island via the signposted **Pjšačka staza** (trekking way); everyone else should wind downhill past the tiny Romanesque chapel of **St Nicholas the Greek** (Sv. Nikola grčki), almost lost among olive groves, to **Šunj**, a pine-fringed notch in the coast whose sand beach backed by a beach restaurant and snack bar is the stuff escapist dreams are made of.

Šipan

Šipan may be the largest of the Elafitis, but it's by far the least developed – come here to enter a timewarp. Ferries thrum into principal settlement **Šipanska Luka**, a palm-fringed bay at the end of a deep inlet where the occasional summer manor of a 15th-century aristocratic family hints at former glories; Dubrovnik dynasty the Sorkočevićs fronted theirs with a leonine balcony. A scrap of sandy **beach** is a short walk from the centre. Smaller Renaissance villas huddle in enjoyably tatty fishing village **Suđurad**, at the opposite end of Šipan and in awe of a pair of 16th-century towers which stood guard over the palace of an Dubrovnik noble and, nearby, the **Church-fort of the Holy Spirit** (Crkva sveti duh), village refuge during Turkish raids. Between the two villages is **Šipansko Polje**, a lovely valley of olive groves and vine-yards where the eulogy of Beccadelli, who knew Šipan well, rings true. Maps point out that the pair are just 5km apart, but you could lose a happy day pootling on hiking paths to discover Baroque chapels and medieval summer palaces.

Mljet

Timetables may swear the island of Mljet is just 1½hrs from Dubrovnik, but the distance in atmosphere to the Adriatic's greenest island is centuries. Explore this 32km sliver of an island clad in Aleppo pines and vineyards and you'll discover a Mediterranean idyll where tourism is a sideshow to traditional obsessions of fishing, wine and olive oil. Get truly off the beaten track among dozy eastern villages and it doesn't stretch the imagination too far to believe this is indeed Homer's Ogyia, the 'wave-washed island' of 'wood in abundant growth – alder and aspen and fragrant cypress' where the love-sick Calypso, nurturing dreams of marriage, held Odysseus captive for seven years. Hotel Odisej in the resort town of Pomena organizes summer sprees to south coast cove Uvala Jama, supposedly the 'arching caverns' where she whispered sweet nothings into the Greek hero's ear. You can't fault the nymph's savvy – few Croatian islands are more romantic for those who let Mljet's yesteryear pace get under the skin.

Homer probably knew the island as storm refuge and freshwater source Melita (derived from the Greek *melite*, honey), peopled by Illyrians until they plundered one galleon too many and felt the wrath of Emperor Augustus, who founded **Polače** in 35 BC. Buses squeeze through an arch of the 4th-century palace (*palača*) which

Getting There and Around

Year-round Jadrolinija **car ferries** chug to Mljet port Sobra in 1h 50mins, where a connecting bus travels to Polače and Pomena. However, its afternoon departure necessitates an overnight stay. In summer only, day trippers can catch Nova International's high-speed morning catamaran to Polače (*daily May–Sept; 1hr 30mins; 90Kn return*); in 2004 outgoing ferries departed Dubrovnik at 9am.

A limited **bus** service prevents true exploration: better is to hire one of the handful of **cars** or a **scooter** or **mountain bike** from agencies in Polače and Pomena.

Tourist Information

Polače (opposite ferry dock): **t** (020) 744 086. *Open mid-June–mid-Sept Mon–Sat 8–12 and 4–7; mid-Sept–mid-June Mon–Fri 8–1.*
Babino Polje: t (020) 745 125. *Open as above.*

Where to Stay

Mljet t (020) –
Hotel Odisej, Pomena, **t** 744 062, *www. hotelodisej.hr* (*moderate*). Just the wrong side of inexpensive, Mljet's only hotel features 150 simple but spotless three-star rooms which make up for bland décor with air-conditioning and a minibar; sea views cost an extra €20. *Closed Nov to mid-April.*

Pension Pomena, Pomena 14, **t** 744 075 (*inexpensive*). If that's full (or the budget's tight) try this cheap and cheerful restaurant-pension next-door, which offers 10 rooms and a couple of apartments.

The pick of the **private rooms** (*sobe*) are those in sleepy lake-side hamlet Babine Kuće. Alternatively, restaurants in Pomena offer accommodation and the tourist offices hold lists of private accommodation.

Eating Out

Mljet t (020) –
Galija, Pomena bb, **t** 744 029 (*expensive–moderate*). Smartest of the harbour-front *pension*-restaurants opposite Hotel Odisej. Seafood is super-fresh, or you could try a beautifully presented cold platter of *pršut* ham, octopus salad and olives; though listed as a starter, the chef's special is a meal in itself.
Mali raj, Babine Kuće 3, **t** 744 067 (*moderate*). House special lobster comes super-fresh from the tank, and kid goat cooked in a *peka* is washed down with local wines and brandy in this laid-back lakeside *konoba* – a 'little paradise' indeed.
Melita, St Mary's Islet, **t** 744 145 (*moderate*). Frequently busy, but bag a terrace table overlooking the lake and the Benedictine monastery restaurant is a lovely spot for a lazy lunch of seafood or steaks.

christened the village – locals saw no sense in diverting the coast road inland for the sake of a few old walls. Overlooked nearby is the shell of a century-older Christian **basilica** inspired perhaps by St Paul, who is said to have preached in Mljet after a shipwreck enforced a three-month pause in his Adriatic voyage.

Officially, the hamlet strung out along a perfect natural harbour is within the **Mljet National Park** (*adm mid-June–mid-Sept 65Kn, mid-Sept–mid-June 45Kn; tickets from kiosks at Pomena and Polače*), but the main draws of the protected area on Mljet's western third are little and large lakes **Mala jezero** and **Veliko jezero**, reached via a well-signed path (*approx 1hr*). Even summer tour groups cannot mar idyllic tidal lakes fringed by aromatic pines and knitted together by the **Mali most** (Little Bridge), where you can hire bicycles, canoes and rowing boats (*20Kn/hour, 100Kn/day*) or laze on a scrap of 'beach'. Explorers will find more secluded niches on a forest path which loops around the lakes (a channel which links Veliko jezero to the sea prevents a full circuit) or can truly escape the crowds by climbing island peak **Montokuc** southeast of Veliko jezero – as you puff up the steep path, keep in mind the anticipated lovely views to Korčula and over the Mljetski kanal to the Pelješac Peninsula.

The island high point for most tourists, however, is a jaunt on hourly ferries from Mali most and Pristanište (*price included in park ticket*) to romantic **St Mary's Islet** (Otočić svete Marije). The final indignity for the Benedictine monastery which was built on the island gifted to the Italian order of St Margano in 1151 was its reinvention as a hotel under Tito (*now closed*) – Napoleon, never an emperor to smile on rival powers, instigated its fall from grace when he dissolved the order in 1809. Circle the **monastery** whose 12th-century core is rebuilt in Renaissance, then peer into the gloom of its **church**; turquoise pillars and ruby scrolls of Renaissance and Baroque altars give the shabby interior an unexpected shot of pizzazz.

Montenegro

Tantalisingly close to the south of Croatia, Montenegro feels like undiscovered country. The rugged Balkan neighbour, finally reopened to tourism after the turbulence of the 1990s Homelands War, boasts its own answer to the Croatian southern belle 54km over the border. Like Dubrovnik, UNESCO-listed **Kotor** is huddled tight within defence walls sketched by Illyrians then bolstered by 18th-century engineers into a 4.5km girdle 20m high and 15m thick and pierced by three Renaissance town gates; like the Croatian former republic, Balkan trade from Asia funded one of the Adriatic's best-preserved Romanesque churches, the **Cathedral of St Tiphun** (1166) with 14th-century frescoes and a glittering treasury (*adm*), and paid for the Gothic-Renaissance and Baroque palaces of Montenegro's medieval gem; and, like a mini-Dubrovnik, its triangle of showpiece streets is stuffed with cafés in which to idle. What it lacks is the crowds – for now. The town which still feels like a secret also has a jaw-dropping location at the head of a fjord-like valley snaking 28km inland from the Adriatic. Picture-postcard views are available from the **Fortress of St John** (Sv. Ivan) which crumbles on its perch 260m above Kotor.

Coast road B2 follows the bay then cuts inland as it travels 40km further south to **Budva**. Whatever the truth of a Greek legend that Cadmo, son of Phoenician king

Getting There

Dubrovnik tourist agencies offer whistle-stop **day trips** to Kotor, Budva and Sveti Stefan, but those who prefer relaxed touring should hire a **car** over two or three days; EU, US and Canadian passport-holders do not require a visa, and the Montenegro currency is the euro.

Where to Stay

Marija, Stari Grad 449, Kotor, **t** +381 (082) 325 062 (*moderate*). Book ahead to claim one of the 17 rooms in Kotor's finest hotel, carved from a Baroque mansion in the old town and whose elegant wood-panelled interior oozes 19th-century nostalgia.

Sveti Stefan, t +381 (086) 468 090/468 118; (*expensive–moderate*). The décor in the unrenovated cottage-hotels is frayed at the edges and admits the 1960s vintage of Montenegro's yesteryear glitterati hideaway, but this remains the country's most exclusive hamlet-hotel (*see* main text). And, oh, the escapism of its islet idyll – reservation is essential.

Agenon, tired of his wanderings after he was expelled from Thebes to found one of the Balkans' oldest settlements, the small town at the end of a peninsula is a delight to explore; its cosy nest of narrow alleys and tiny squares behind an old-town water-front barely shows the joins of restoration after a 1979 earthquake. Royal among Montenegro destinations, however, is **Sveti Stefan** 5km south. Under Yugoslavian president Josep Broz Tito, the virtually abandoned fishermen's settlement on a rocky islet was reinvented as an escapist hamlet-hotel for the 1960s jet-set; Richard Burton and Kirk Douglas ambled its lanes in flip-flops, Doris Day lazed beside the pool of a refurbished cottage-hotel beyond the wildest dreams of its original owner, and Sophia Loren swooned at 'a town from the most beautiful fairytale of my childhood'. Not that Montenegro's tourism icon relies on nostalgia – in 2002 English actor Jeremy Irons relaxed during filming (and notched up a £65,000 bill for extras) in a snug hamlet draped with honeysuckle and open to non-residents (*adm*) for short trips.

Touring from Dubrovnik

Island-hopping is the lure of a three- or five-day tour from Dubrovnik, and is possible with or without a car. You could spend day one on idyllic **Mljet** (*see* pp.139–41): paddling a canoe on the lakes and exploring pine-shaded footpaths of the national park, then embark from Pomena for a spree to the cave where Homeric hero Odysseus was reputedly held captive by goddess Calypso. The next day, catch a ferry from Polače to charming port **Trstenik** on the mainland and, if you have a car, drive north to **Orebić**, an easygoing beach resort with a lovely pilgrimage church linked by hourly ferries to medieval **Korčula**, a mini-Dubrovnik known for its sea captains, none more famous than local son Marco Polo (*see* p.116). If travelling on public transport, be aware that only two buses a day trundle between Trstenik and Orebić; turn on the charm and you may hitch a ride aboard returning Korčula tour boats from Mljet resort Pomena. From Korčula, you can join the tour from Split (*see* pp.114–18) to island idyll **Lastovo**, just waking up to tourism after years off-limits as a navy base.

Otherwise return to Dubrovnik by car ferry (*4hrs, four a week, peak season*) or if you have a car via the rugged **Pelješac Peninsula**, famed for vineyards that produce Croatia's finest reds, Dingač and Postup, and whose stem is guarded by small-town gem **Ston**. So highly did medieval Dubrovnik prize the salt-pans of its second city, it fortified the town on the ramparts of its northern frontier with what were Europe's longest city walls. Enjoy guard's-eye views over Ston's neat medieval grid of streets from the 3km that remain of those original 5.5km, then follow their march over the hill to sister village **Mali Ston**, treasured by Croatian gourmets for its shellfish. Here you can sample famous oysters and treats such as Grandpa's octopus salad at family-run restaurant **Kapetnova Kuća** (**t** (020) 754 264; *expensive–moderate*) and bed down at the nine-room **Hotel Ostea** (**t** (020) 754 556, *www.ostrea.hr; moderate*), tasteful throughout and furnished with antiques in a beautiful apartment (*expensive*), or at **Vila Koruna** (**t** (020) 754 359, *www.vila-koruna.hr; cheap*), an old-fashioned but good-value, friendly *pension* with a decent restaurant. Three buses a day make the return trip to Dubrovnik in 1hr 40mins.

Slovenia:
Travel, Practical A–Z and Language

Travel

Entry Formalities

Passports and Visas

Slovenia became a member of the European Union on 1 May 2004. Holders of full, valid EU, US, Canadian, Australian and New Zealand passports do not need a visa to enter Slovenia for stays of up to 90 days. In theory, EU nationals need only a back-up pass (an international driving licence, for example) to enter if they can produce a valid passport that has expired within the last five years; whether Customs officials have been informed of this is another matter. All other visitors will have to obtain a Slovenian **visa**.

Customs

EU nationals over 17 can now import a limitless amount of goods, with the proviso that they are for personal use. Reasonable limits are 3,200 cigarettes/400 cigarillos/200 cigars/3kg of tobacco; plus 10 litres of spirits, 90 litres of wine and 110 litres of beer. Bear in mind that UK Customs & Excise only permits 200 cigarettes to be imported into the UK from Slovenia.

Non-EU arrivals have to pass through Customs inspections at Brnik airport or at land crossings, which are cursory to the point of non-existence but are subject to the following cap on imports: 200 cigarettes or 50 cigars or 250g of tobacco; 1 litre of spirits, 2 litres of wine; 50ml perfume, 240ml *eau de toilette*. All cash and securities in excess of 3,000,000 SIT must be declared to border Customs authorities on arrival or departure.

On leaving the country, non-EU travellers are rewarded with a refund on Slovenian VAT (DDV) if they can prove a one-day, single-retailer spend of over 15,000 SIT; *see* 'Money and Banks', p.150.

Getting Around

By Train

Perhaps because it was pioneered by thorough Austrians, **Slovenske železnice** is a paragon of efficiency compared with the national rail operators of former Yugoslav republic sisters. Its 1,229km of track snake out from transport hub Ljubljana into most corners of the country, carriages are invariably clean and your *tolars* buy more kilometres on a train than on a bus.

Prices are dictated by the hierarchy of train. Royals of the service are express Inter-City Slovenia (ICS) trains, which journey to international neighbours such as Italy, Croatia, Austria and Germany and lean into the corners to reach major transport nodes in double-quick time; fastest time between Ljubljana and Maribor is 1hr 47mins. First-class passengers are treated to a free snack and non-alcoholic drink in the ticket price – second-class travellers must make do with a restaurant carriage which provides drinks and light bites – and, whatever the ticket, all carriages are air-conditioned and comfortable. Such class costs extra, of course; a second-class Ljubljana–Maribor ticket costs 2,790 SIT. Second-tier of the service are InterCity (IC) or EuroCity (EC) trains, which pause at fewer stations than regional trains (*regionalni vlaki*, RG). These are marginally faster than local trains (*potniški vlaki*, LP), which pootle through the countryside and pause at every hamlet on the way. Prices are calculated by distance covered – 890 SIT for 50km or 1,250 SIT for 100km (300 SIT supplement on IC trains) – and a return ticket (*povratna vozovnica*) costs double that of a single (*enosmerna vozovnica*). Treat yourself to first class and you'll pay around 50% extra. With the exception of ICS trains, all permit bicycles for an extra 630 SIT.

Tickets can be bought from the train station (*železniška postaja*), where yellow timetables list departures (*odhodi*) and white timetables list arrivals (*prihodi*); trains marked with an R permit free seat reservations (*rezervacije*); those with a boxed R demand one (ICS and international services) and are best purchased in advance. Credit cards are making inroads for payment, but don't bank on them except in major stations – cash is the norm nationwide. **Timetables** will also list the correct platform (*peron*) for your train. If you run late and purchase a ticket from the inspector, you'll incur a 440 SIT charge.

Slovenia doesn't believe in **rail passes**, but the Tourist Weekend (*Turist vikend*) ticket concedes 30% discounts to passengers who make return journeys on Saturdays, Sundays and holidays; extend your stay and return on a working day and you must pay the difference between the full price of a one-way ticket.

Major stations have facilities to store **left luggage** for up to 72hrs in automatic lockers, paid for in tokens (400 SIT/24hrs) or euros (€2/24hrs). Rail information is available in Slovenia on **t** (01) 291 33 32 (*5am–10pm*). Slovenske železnice's website, *www. slo-zeleznice.si* (available in English), lists timetables and tourist agencies which sell advance rail tickets, and updates rail delay information every 7mins.

By Bus

Slovenia's love affair with car culture has been a double-edged sword for a bus network operated by local companies. While the country's clean and generally comfortable buses now boast more free seats (except during commuter rush-hour in larger towns), the number of departures has been slashed, especially at weekends – skeleton services are the norm on Sundays and in remote areas they take the day of rest literally. Explore into the rural east and you can expect problems. These may also occur if you roll up without a ticket expecting a jaunt to coastal or mountain destinations on Fridays or public holidays from Ljubljana – advance purchase from computerized booking terminals is recommended.

Otherwise, **tickets** can be bought directly before travelling from the bus station (*avtobusna postaja*) or from the driver on boarding. Fares are calculated by distance on a strict sliding scale regardless of the bus company; expect around 1,300 SIT for 50km, 2300 SIT for 100km. Luggage stored in the hold will cost about 280 SIT extra.

Baffling multicoloured **timetables** with a colour-coordinated system of departures (*odhodi*) and arrivals (*prihodi*) abbreviate days to initial letters – Po for *ponedeljek* (Monday), So for *sobota* (Saturday) and throw in occasional curveballs such as SN (*sobota, nedelja* (Saturday, Sunday). It's actually far easier to ask at the ticket booth.

By Car

All the day trips we propose are cherry-picked to be easily accessible by public transport, but for the touring itinerary a car is essential.

In general, driving in Slovenia is a joy; distances are short, the scenery, especially in the Julian Alps northwest, magnificent and roads are well maintained. The only blight on this sunny picture is that high car-ownership means congestion is a problem on major routes at weekends and rush hours, especially in summer when entire cities seem to flee to the coast or country. Similarly, small roads struggle with high-season crowds in popular districts such as Lake Bled.

Slovenia has dug deep into its coffers to upgrade its roads, which are generally excellent and come in two categories. The nation's A1 and A2 three-lane **motorways** (*avtocesta*) centred on Ljubljana are indicated with blue signs (green and E for international routes), as is the H4, inching east from Nova Gorica towards Postojna. All charge **tolls** for their use, payable on exit in *tolars*, euros, Croatian *kunas* and, in theory, American dollars; whether booth cashiers are *au fait* with the latter is doubtful. As an idea of prices, Ljubljana–Postojna costs 490 SIT, Ljubljana–Maribor 1,160 SIT. For your money you get to blast largely without interruption at up to 130kph. Sections of the northeast–southwest and northwest–southeast cross remain incomplete, which is when you'll be forced onto secondary or tertiary roads.

Petrol stations (*benicinska črpalka*) dispense unleaded (*neosvinčen bencin*) fuel and diesel between 7am and 8pm, although those on motorways will open longer and the outskirts of major towns and resorts may even boast a 24hr garage. Either way, fuel comes at bargain prices, typically 200 SIT (€0.83) per litre, and can be paid for using standard credit cards.

Most Ljubljana hotels have dedicated **parking**, but elsewhere spaces in cities are limited. Car parks are generally on the periphery of pedestrianized areas – as ever, follow the blue P – and charge around 250 SIT/hr. Street parking is on white lines, which cost 100 SIT/hr payable at ticket machines or news stands – write the parking time on the ticket and display it on the windscreen – or in blue zones, free for up to 30mins.

Emergency roadside assistance is provided by national auto association the **Avto-Moto zveza Slovenije** (AMZS) by calling t 19 87. It also proffers advice on routes and road conditions on t (01) 530 53 00 (5.30am–8pm) or at its Ljubljana office (Dunajska 128; Mon–Fri 9–5). Even though its website (*www.amzs.si*) is in Slovenian only, English-speakers can still comprehend traffic information plus links to affiliate offices countrywide. In the event of any accident, call the police on t 113.

Rules and Regulations

All drivers are expected to have to hand a full national driving licence, and those driving their own cars will be required to present on demand a vehicle registration document and a valid certificate of third-party insurance. Driving is on the right, overtaking on the left and seatbelts are compulsory for all passengers. Drivers are forbidden from using mobile phones at the wheel and dipped headlights are required during the day. Carrying a reflective breakdown warning triangle is mandatory and it should be set up a sensible 100m behind the vehicle if you pull over for anything other than the briefest halt.

Secondary or tertiary roads have **speed limits** of 100kph and are indicated by two or three numbers. The speed limit in towns and villages is 50kph.

Fair but determined traffic police, who often linger at town fringes to snare speeding motorists, issue on-the-spot fines for all driving infringements, which start at 5,000 SIT and rise to 45,000 SIT. The maximum blood alcohol limit is currently 0.05mg/100ml blood. Penalties for those over (or even on) the limit are severe, with fines of up to 100,000 SIT, and licences are removed from offenders.

Hiring a Car

Car hire is a simple business in Slovenia – drivers generally must be over 21 (although some firms insist they must be over 25) and must have held an EU or international driving licence for (usually) one year. Cheap it is not, however. Although quotes from international players fluctuate between firms and according to the season, you can expect to pay

11,400 SIT (€47) per day for a modest two-door runaround (Renault Clio 1.2 or Fiat Punto) and 28,300 SIT (€120) for a Mercedes. Longer-term hirers are rewarded with more favourable day rates, but unlimited mileage clauses can sting. On the bright side, prices include tax, personal accident insurance and collision damage waiver (CDW); be warned, the latter doesn't usually extend to tyres, wheels, the underside and the interior.

Shopping around with major firms (all of which operate bureaux at the airport) before you travel will turn up special deals; local outlets are usually cheaper if you are not overly concerned with as-new cosmetics. All hire companies require drivers to present on collection of the car a passport, driving licence and credit card (sometimes two) as deposit. Triple-check whether they impose restrictions on crossing international borders.

Practical A–Z
Climate and When to Go

A location at the crossroads of Europe means that Slovenian weather presenters need to stock the full range of chart symbols. When the Mediterranean southwest of hot summers and mild winters basks in spring sunshine, villages of the alpine northwest can vanish beneath a blanket of fresh snow, and the country's continental south and east may just be emerging from a bitter winter and looking forward to a dry, hot summer. The watchword is diverse: July jumpers, *de rigueur* in the Alps, are only fashion accessories on the coast.

Summers which are warm without being overpowering in the northeast highlands come on hot and dry on the Adriatic coast and can leave you gasping for breath in the continental east. The tourist season opens for business in June and the excesses which are rampant by mid-July get worse in August, when holiday resorts are at their busiest. Vacationing Italians nip over the border to colonize coastal towns such as Piran; arterial roads around Lake Bled and Lake Bohinj clog with coach tours; and hotel prices soar – reservations are a must. Even Ljubljana can suffer from peak-season claustrophobia,

Average temperatures °C											
	Jan	Feb	Mar	April	May	June	July	Aug	Sept	Oct	Nov	Dec
Ljubljana	−1	1	6	11	16	19	21	21	16	11	5	1
Murska Sobota	−2	1	5	11	16	19	22	20	15	9	4	−1
Kranjska Gora	−3	−2	3	6	11	15	17	17	12	7	2	−3
Koper	5	6	9	12	17	20	24	24	21	16	10	7

although the sociable city is now at its effervescent best in streets and cafés – if you can secure a seat. This is also a time when Slovenian festivals get into full swing.

Spring and autumn are the loveliest times to visit – crowds thin, prices fall. Spring is a joy in a countryside which bursts with the sort of promise only seen in vintage technicolour musicals. Snow thaws allow alpine walkers to enjoy waterfalls at their most impressive in a region where peaks are still dusted with snow and meadows are speckled by an infinity of May flowers. Coastal towns dip a toe into the Adriatic and Ljubljana scents the first whiff of spring and moves on to its terraces. Don't bid farewell to torrential downpours in the centre and north just yet, though. Nor should you in autumn, luxurious and fruitful, with vineyards in the northeast and southeast, and gorgeous colours everywhere. Better still, the crowds evaporate after schools return in early September, and the lakes are still warm for swimming.

Many museums close their doors for **winter** in November, which is the wettest month of the year, especially in the Alps. By its end, ski resorts such as Kranjska Gora gear up for a season which runs until mid-March. Winters, which are at their mildest on the coast, bite hard in the east, compensated by the lowest precipitation in the country. Ljubljana is wetter but is at its fairytale best on crisp, clear days when the Baroque beauty wears a foundation of hoarfrost and icicle jewels.

Crime and the Police

Police **t** *113*

Maybe thanks to the fact that its 2 million population either lives in or retains strong ties to pastoral communities, Slovenia is safe to the point of complacency. Even in small-town capital Ljubljana, with a population of just 300,000, your closest brush with big-city deprivation is likely to be a rare beggar or the occasional boozy scruff, both harmless. Instead, all tourists need worry about in a country with one of the lowest crime rates in Europe, and where violent crime is the exception, is petty theft in cities such as Ljubljana and Maribor, although even this is rare. All the usual precautions apply: leaving valuables unattended in public places is asking for trouble, and cars should be locked and cameras or bags hidden from view. Similarly, although street pickpockets are rare, keep your wits about you at train and bus stations. Theft from hotel rooms is unheard of.

In the unlikely event that anything is stolen, police (*policija*) are generally good-natured and courteous. Better still, they can usually rustle up someone with a smattering of English – you will need to report crimes to receive an insurance claim number.

Disabled Travellers

Not Slovenia's strong point. Although pedestrian crossings beep as the green man flashes and awareness of disabled needs is improving, steps rather than ramps are the norm in museums and on public transport, with the exceptions of international and the most modern national trains. Ask at the ticket office; larger train stations will have ramps for boarding. Similarly, only top-end hotels offer wheelchair-friendly facilities, although nearly all larger hotels provide lifts.

Your most comprehensive source of information for advice is the **Paraplegics Association of Slovenia** (Zveza Paraplegikov Republike Slovenija; Štihova 14, Ljubljana, **t** (01) 432 71 38, *www.zveza-paraplegikov.si*).

Electricity

Mains voltage is 220V, 50Hz. British and Irish appliances require a standard two-prong, round-pin adaptor. North American appliances require a transformer.

Embassies and Consulates

Slovenian Embassies Abroad

UK: 10 Little College Street, London SW1 P3SJ, **t** (020) 7222 5400.

USA: 1525 New Hampshire Ave NW, Washington DC 20036, **t** (202) 667 53 63.

Canada: 150 Metcalfe Street, Suite 2101, Ottawa, Ontario K2P 1P1, **t** (613) 565 57 81/2.

Foreign Embassies in Ljubljana

UK: 4th Floor, Trg Republike 3, **t** (01) 200 39 10, *www.british-embassy.si.*

USA: Prešernova cesta 31, **t** (01) 200 55 00, *www.usembassy.si.*

Canada (consulate): Miklošičeva 19, **t** (01) 430 35 75.

Festivals and Events

Slovenia shakes off winter blues and celebrates the arrival of spring in pre-Lent carnival the **Pust**, at its most ebullient in Ptuj. Masked *kurenti*, like walking haystacks in head-to-foot sheepskins, chase out evil spirits from houses in 10-day extravaganza the **Kurentovanje**, which culminates on the Sunday before Shrove Tuesday and whose pagan roots are just a whisper away – not one for nervous children. More modest events are staged in Cerkno and Cerknica. Also in mid-March is the **world ski jump championships** in Planica (near Kranjska Gora), a three-day weekend event fuelled by an orgy of beer, food and music.

April quietens in preparation for summer festivals when Slovenia rushes out of doors. In late June Škofja Loka stages medieval pageant **Vererira pot** against its historic backdrop and Maribor draws together folksy whimsy with popular music and high-brow culture during the riverside **Festival Lent**. Now, too, Ljubljana's streets are reinvented as impromptu stages for the **Ana Desetnica International Festival of Street Theatre**, although this is merely a warm-up act for a two-month cultural beano of classical music, theatre and dance during the **International Summer Festival**. Though not as prestigious as the nation's showpiece festival, most large towns host some form of cultural jamboree over July/August; second billing goes to the summer festival of Primorska. The September highlight is the marvellous **Cow's Ball** in Lake Bohinj, an unashamedly bacchanalian weekend of folk music and dance, wine and food, which celebrates the return of cows from mountain meadows in the country's lushest dairy region. Wine is drunk on 11 November for **St Martin's Day**, the official date when lowly grape juice becomes wine – Metilka wine village Drašiči spins out the booze-up for a week. During December Slovenia succumbs to nostalgic homespun sentimentality during Christmas celebrations inaugurated with **St Nicholas Day** (6 December) gift-giving and rounded off with concerts.

Health and Insurance

Ambulance and fire **t** 112

EU citizens with a stamped E111 form (available from post offices) receive free emergency medical treatment; an accompanying booklet explains whats and wherefores, but be aware that the reciprocal agreement does not cover medical repatriation, private care or dental treatment. If you have to pay for any treatment, obtain a receipt to guarantee reimbursement later. Non-EU residents can also receive medical assistance, but it comes at a price. Therefore private medical insurance is a sensible precaution to cover costs of treatment and return home. As ever, skiers will have to pay a 'dangerous sports' supplement, as will those who intend to go white-water rafting on the Soča river; check the small print to determine whether less adrenaline-fuelled equivalents such as kayaking are covered.

Highly trained staff at the town or village **pharmacy** (*lekarna*) proffer over-the-counter advice, usually in English, and can provide basic medicines for the usual upset stomachs or bad colds plus antibiotics. For more serious medicines, bring a signed letter from your GP stating generic medicine names. Pharmacy hours are 7am–8pm and one pharmacy in town works the night-shift and Sunday organized by rota; a notice of the current incumbent is posted on all pharmacy windows. Tourist information and hotel concierges are the best sources of local knowledge for the nearest **doctor**. Again, the standard of English is excellent, but for intricate discussion contact embassies, which hold lists of fluent English-speaking doctors. These are your first port of call for sickness – a **hospital** (*bolnica*) is only for a genuine emergency or in case of referral.

Slovene health standards are high and, accidents aside, your only problems are likely to be climatic: hypothermia for those caught out by inclement weather in high alpine peaks, or heatstroke and sunburn just about anywhere in summer. Having said that, British and US embassies recommend that those who tramp deep into Slovenian forests in summer are vaccinated for tick-borne encephalitis. Less dangerous perhaps but still infuriating are the mosquitoes near lakes and ponds in summer. Tap water is drinkable everywhere.

While crime in Slovenia is low, travel insurance remains a worthwhile precaution. Some high-end credit card policies offer rudimentary insurance free of charge (consult your supplier) and most credit systems offer insurance on their purchases within a specified time period and on production of a receipt; again, check with your card supplier. If you take out dedicated travel insurance be sure to confirm whether it covers cancelled flights and extra expenses if you get caught due to rail or air strikes, admittedly not very likely in hard-working stolid Slovenia. And ensure the policy limit per article covers the most expensive items such as high-end cameras – obvious, perhaps, but easily overlooked.

Internet

The cyber revolution has yet to seize imaginations in a largely rural nation. Internet cafés (500–700 SIT/hr) are few and far between, even in Ljubljana. Some city tourist information centres have a lone terminal for short-term use, or try public libraries, which shut at weekends. Don't expect whizzy broadband speeds in either. Inveterate e-mail addicts with fat wallets will be relieved that top-end hotels boast ISDN connections. For laptops, the phone socket connection is US RJ-11.

Maps

Town maps are provided by tourist information offices either for a nominal fee or free of charge depending on whether you're getting glossy printed sheets or a photocopied black-and-white sketch. Commercially produced country maps, whether of official Ordnance Survey body Geodetski zavod Slovenije or private German outfit Freytag & Berndt, are best sourced in Ljubljana. Excellent sources are Kod & Kam (Trg Francoske revolucije 7, **t** (01) 200 27 32), and Geonavtik (Kongresni trg 1, **t** (01) 252 70 27), which also stocks hiking maps of the Alpine Association of Slovenia (Planinska zvaza Slovenije), generally at 1:50,000 scale but sometimes at 1:25,000.

Money and Banks

The official unit of currency is the Slovenian *tolar*, which divides into 100 *stolni*. Wonderfully colourful notes which depict Slovenian cultural and intellectual heroes come in denominations of 10,000, 5,000, 1,000, 500, 200, 100, 50, 20 and 10, and brass coins are available in sums of 50, 20, 10, 5, 2 and 1. Approximate **exchange rates** (March 2005) are: £1 = 345 SIT; €1 = 240 SIT; $1 = 180 SIT. However, Slovenia plans to join the euro in 2007, a currency already accepted in motorway toll booths and many hotels, which often list prices in euros.

While it's a good idea to arrive with a fistful of notes (euros will suffice) to safeguard against delays, bus strikes or failed ATM machines, carrying pocketfuls of cash is not the most prudent choice even in safe Slovenia. **Travellers' cheques** remain the most secure means of transporting money; bank clerks are happiest to accommodate those issued by American Express. Like cash, these can be exchanged at banks (*banka*) for a commission of 1% or at money exchanges (*menjalnica*) in post offices, tourist information centres and private agencies, and hotels, which typically levy 3% commission.

The downside is that travellers' cheques tie you to opening hours (*see below*). More convenient for weekend visits is to withdraw cash directly from **ATM cash dispensers** (*bančni avtomat*) which are ubiquitous throughout Slovenia, from city to village and usually motorway petrol stations; all have an English-language option. ATMs readily accept credit cards, usually Visa/MasterCard/ EuroCard and American Express, and occasionally Diner's Club, with a PIN (personal identification number). However, remember that interest accrues as soon as those crisp notes emerge from the slot. Cheaper are debit cards affiliated to credit operators such as Visa or recognized credit systems such as Plus, Cirrus and Maestro, which are liable to a one-off fee either at a set rate or calculated as a percentage of the sum withdrawn; consult your bank before departure.

The major **credit cards** are widely accepted in towns and major tourist centres but smaller *gostišče* (inns, guesthouses), pensions and *gostilna* (inns) may just shrug and demand cash – as ever, double-check, preferably before you finish coffee.

Value added tax (DDV), charged at 20% on most goods and at 8.5% reduced rate for food, books and accommodation, can be reclaimed by non-EU residents (except on alcohol and tobacco) if their receipt/s on one day from the same retailer exceed 15,000 SIT. Ask sales assistants to complete a DDV-VP form or equivalent when you get the receipt, which is stamped as you leave the country, to collect refunds at Kompas offices at the border.

Opening Hours

Banks: open weekdays 8.30–12.30 and 2–5, Saturday 8.30–11/12, closed Sun.

Post offices: official hours are weekdays 8–7, Sat 8–1. The main office in larger towns may operate longer hours – the Trg Osvobodilne fronte 5 office in Ljubljana opens a staggering schedule of weekdays (7am–midnight, Sat 7–6 and Sun 9–12, for example).

Shops: business hours are generally weekdays 8–7, Sat 8–1, closed Sun. However, some stores and chain supermarkets may pull up shutters on Sun morning 9–1 and in cities can extend opening hours until 5.

Tourist information: hours vary hugely depending upon the location and season. Ljubljana opens up to 13 hours daily, but smaller towns tend to operate office hours in

National Holidays

1–2 Jan New Year
8 Feb Slovenian Culture Day (Prešeren Day)
Mar/April Easter Monday
27 April National Resistance Day
1–2 May International Labour Day
25 June Slovene Statehood Day
15 Aug Assumption Day
31 Oct Reformation Day
1 Nov All Saints' Day
25 Dec Christmas
26 Dec Independence Day

summer, then reduce to weekdays only in winter. As a rule of thumb, you can expect those in tourist centres to operate daily 9–7 in peak season.

Museums and galleries: most treat themselves to Monday off and open Tues–Sun 10–6, often with a pause for lunch between 12 and 2. In addition, those that do not close for winter months reward themselves after a hectic summer with a month or two's break, often in November, or open at weekends only. Specific information is provided in the text.

Churches: access is generally excellent all day, although do respect services in such a devout Roman Catholic country.

Post

Look for canary-yellow signs emblazoned with a curled bugle when locating offices of the **Pošta Slovenije**, which are rarely crowded and a model of queuing etiquette. Here you can buy stamps and telephone cards (*see* below), send faxes and exchange money; stamps (*znamike*) are also sold over the counter at newsagents. Postage prices (2005) are: 49 SIT for internal mail letters (*pismo*) under 20g; 83 SIT for postcards to foreign destinations; 95 SIT for international mail letters under 20g; 3,930 SIT for parcels (*paket*) within the EU under 2kg; 9,179 SIT for parcels to the USA and Canada under 2kg.

Price Categories

The hotels and restaurants listed in this guide have been assigned categories reflecting a range of prices, as follows:

Hotels

Hotel prices quoted are for a double room with WC and bath or shower in peak season – July–Aug in most cases, but December–March in ski resorts. Not factored in is a 'tourist tax' of 200–350 SIT levied per person per night.

expensive above 33,000 SIT / €140
moderate 16,000–33,000 SIT / €65–140
inexpensive under 16,000 SIT / €65

Restaurants

Restaurant prices cover the cost of a meal for one people, with an average-priced main course and a shared bottle of house wine.

expensive over 4,250 SIT / €18
moderate 2,500–4,250 SIT / €10–18
cheap under 2,500 SIT / €10

Telephones

Telephone boxes only accept magnetic-strip telephone cards (*telekartica*) which are available from post offices and newsagent kiosks and come in denominations of 700 SIT, 1,000 SIT, 1,700 SIT and 3,500 SIT. Credits fall at a skydiver's pace during peak rates between 7am and 7pm, when a three-minute call to the UK, USA or Canada will cost around 214 SIT. After these times, rates drop by 20%. Slovenian telephone boxes do not display telephone numbers, so it's not possible for the other party to phone you back. For longer international calls, head for the phone booths in post offices; be warned, the bill for a leisurely chat on hotel telephones can add up.

Slovenia employs GSM 900/1800 standard for mobile phone network, compatible with the rest of the Europe and US tri-band phones, but not with the North American GSM 1900/900. Coverage, which extends across 98% of the country, is excellent if phones are set to roam operators automatically to source the strongest signal. Service providers switch on international access on request free or for a nominal charge. And no wonder – phone bills when you return home can asphyxiate; home operators charge vastly inflated prices for the privilege of tapping into affiliated networks and usually charge you for incoming calls, too.

To **call Slovenia from abroad**, dial the country code 386, omit the first zero of the area code then dial the number.

To **call abroad from Slovenia**, dial oo then the country code (UK 44; Ireland 353; USA and Canada 1; Australia 61; New Zealand 64), then dial the number, again omitting the first zero of the area code.

Time

Slovenia operates within the Central European Time zone, one hour ahead of GMT, six hours ahead of Eastern Standard Time and nine ahead of Western Standard Time. Clocks go forward one hour in the wee hours on the last Sunday in March, back one hour on the last Sunday in October.

Tipping

Although not the Communist anathema of old, tipping in Slovenia is a matter of etiquette. Because service is not usually included in the bill, as a rule of thumb round up to the nearest decimal figure in cafés and leave 10% in restaurants.

Toilets

By and large clean and hygienic – if you can find one. While most large shopping malls will have a public toilet (*javno stranišče*), more reliable than pacing streets in increasing desperation is to head for the train station, where you will be charged 30–50 SIT. Men should enter *Monški*, women *Ženske*, hence occasionally M and Z, but more commonly a picture on the door. If your expression is sufficiently pained, bar and café owners will usually let you use their facilities for free.

Tourist Information

Smiles may sag at the corners in peak season, but the staff in Slovenia's 45 official tourist information offices are generally enthusiastic and speak excellent English. In towns where there is no official bureau, dig for information in a private tourist agency (often around the train station). National tourism coordinator the **Slovenia National Tourist Office** is superb – make its Ljubljana office (Krekov trg 10, **t** (01) 306 45 75/76; *open June–Sept*

8am–9pm, Oct–May 8–7) bursting with Slovenia-wide information a last port of call before you explore elsewhere. It also operates a first-rate website, *www.slovenia-tourism.si*.

Most large towns in Slovenia have a web presence, usually with a searchable database of entertainment and festivities, accommodation listings and details of tourist sights. Addresses are provided in the text among tourist information where relevant, and websites of tourist favourites such as Ljubljana, Lake Bled and Škofja Loka are available in English, as are sites of government departments or official organizations such as the Slovenia post or the police. When searching for addresses, be aware that Slovenes, with characteristic pragmatism, dispense with all accents. Informative official websites include the Slovenia tourist board's excellent nationwide window, *www.slovenia-tourism.si*; the state portal of the Republic of Slovenia, *www.e-uprava.gov.si/e-uprava/en/portal.euprava*; and government PR portal, *www.uvi.si*, with an excellent country overview and links aplenty; even more impressive is the network of Slovenian connections on *www.matkurja.com/en*.

Slovenia Tourist Offices Abroad

UK: The Barns, Woodlands End, Mells, Frome, Somerset BA11 3QD, **t** (01373) 814 233, *info@slovenian-tourism.co.uk*.

USA: Slovenian Tourist Office, 2929 East Commercial Boulevard, Suite 201, Fort Lauderdale, FL 33308, **t** 0954 491 01 12, *slotouristboard@kompas.net*.

Where to Stay

City hotels tend to woo expense accounts, while those in popular resorts such as Lake Bled are geared up to the package tourist *tolar*. Consequently, bar a few treats such as Vila Bled, Lake Bled, or beautiful manor-castles at Mokrice and Otočec, few burst with character or will make stylists swoon. Expect comfortable but bland or dated décor, usually with en-suite facilities and a TV, and you will not be disappointed. Grading is by the usual five-star system which can and does spring surprises, especially at three-star level – cross your fingers; they may be good as well as bad

– and most include breakfast in the price. Prices in Ljubljana and major resorts are the highest in the country and peak in high season (except in the capital, where rates are consistently expensive; booking Is advisable), and are moderate in shoulder months; visit off-peak and there are bargains to be snatched in hotels which do not close for the season. *See* 'Price Categories', p.151.

Open all year and usually with more character, if sometimes a little worn, are family-run *pensions* or accommodation in a *gostišče*, the equivalent of a British inn. Cheaper still are the *sobe* (rooms) and apartments (*apartmaji*) advertised by private houses, especially plentiful on the coast and in the Julian Alps and which are catagorized from one to three stars: a one-star shares facilities but provides a basin; two-star rooms are en suite; as are plusher three-stars. Expect to pay 4,000–6,500 SIT per night for rooms, although a 30% surcharge is levied for stays of under three days. Roughly the same price, and definitely more escapist, are tourist farm retreats (*turističnih krnetji*), which often offer a cupboard of home-made goodies and country pursuits such as horse-riding.

Regardless of accommodation type, a 'tourist tax' (*turistična taksa*) of 200–350 SIT is levied every night.

An excellent source of accommodation information is the Slovenia National Tourism website, *www.slovenia-tourism.si*.

Language

The south Slavonic tongue of Slovene is one of the few Indo-European languages to retain the dual form, slipped in between singular and plural (three or more) to present scholars with another noun ending to learn. Include on the curriculum three genders and six cases for pronouns and it's no surprise even assured European linguists pause before signing up for lessons. And that's before they consider a polyglot of over 40 dialects.

Fortunately most Slovenes speak a second language – top-notch English among young Slovenes and those in the tourist trade, German among the older generation, and Italian in border region Primorska – but that shouldn't stop you tasting their delicious rolled Rs or mouth-filler phonetics; locals will appreciate all efforts. Food vocabulary is on pp.157–8.

Pronunciation

The good news for budding linguists is that all 25 letters in Slovenian are pronounced, the bad that stress roams freely and simply has to be learned. Modified Roman consonants with a caron (ˇ) indicate 'sh', 'ch' and 'zh' phonetics, otherwise pronunciation of consonants is largely the same as English.

Consonants

C is pronounced as 'ts' as in 'cats' while č is softer, spoken as the 'ch' in 'change'. D is hard unless combined as dž, as in 'j' of 'jane', and g is consistently hard as in 'gain'. J is spoken as 'y' as in 'yellow' and is far easier than it appears when combined with other consonants: nj is 'ny' as in 'canyon' or the Spanish ñ; lj is spoken as the 'li' of 'million'. R is enjoyable, trilled deliciously on the tongue. Š is pronounced as 'sh' as in 'sheet', just a mite more high-pitched than ž, which is spoken as 's' of 'leisure'. V and l are as English unless they appear at the end of a word or before another consonant, when they become the soft 'w' of 'know'; e.g. pol (half) is pronounced 'poe'.

Vowels

Because phonetics change with the length of the sound, Slovenian vowels are a challenge. A and e are short as in 'pat' and 'pet' or long when unstressed as in 'father' and 'pear'. I is pronounced either as the short 'i' of 'pit' or a longer 'ee', while o comes as the short 'o' of 'on' and the long 'or' of 'horn'. U is pronounced as 'oo' as in 'frugal'.

Useful Vocabulary

Greetings and Courtesies
hello *dober dan*
goodbye *nasvidenje*
hi/bye! *zdravo* or *živijo!* (also *adijo*, see you later!)
good morning *dobro jutro*
good evening *dober večer*
goodnight *lakho noč*

please *prosim*
thank you (very much) *hvala (lepa)*
how are you? (formal) *kako se imate?*
how are you? (informal) *kako se imaš?*
fine, thanks *dobra, hvala*
I am from England/US *sem iz Engleske/ Amerike*
pleased to meet you *me veseli*
sorry (excuse me and apology) *oprostite*

Basic Words and Phrases
yes/no *ja/ne*
do you speak English? *govorite angleško*
I (don't) understand *(ne) razumijem*
I don't speak Slovenian *ne govorim slovenščina*
I'd like (m/f)... *rad/rada bi...*
how much does this cost? *koliko stane?*
cheap/expensive *poceni/drag*
do you take credit cards? *ali vzamete kreditne kartice?*
big/larger *velik/večji*
small/smaller *malo/manjše*
hot/cold *topla/mrzla*
why? *zakay?*
when? *kdaj?*
where? *kje?*
I'd like to book a (m/f)... *rad/rada bi rezerviral...*
do you have... *ali imate...*
single/double room *enpostelnja/dvopostelnja sobu*
rooms (for rent) *sobe*
can I see the room? *ali lahko vidim sobu?*
do you have anything less expensive? *ali imate kaj cenejšega?*
Key/shower/clean sheets/blanket/towel *ključ/tuš/svežo/posteljnino/odejo/brisačo*
I am ill (m/f) *bolan/bolana sem*
ache/pain *bol*
headache/diarrhoea *glavobol/driska*
doctor/dentist *zdravnik/zobar*

Around Town
open/closed *odprto/zaprto*
entrance/exit *vhod/izod*
where is/are... *kje je/so*
toilet *stranišče*, WC (pronounced 'vay-tsay')
ladies/gents *ženske/moški*
bank *banka*
bureau de change *mjenalnica*
police *policija*
embassy *ambasada*
hospital *bolnica*

pharmacy *lekarna*
post office *pošta*
airport *letališče*
railway station *železniška postaja*
bus station *avtobusni postaja*
market *tržnica*
tourist office *turistički urad*
museum *muzej*
cinema *kino*
church *cerkev*
monastery *samostan*
old town *staro mesto*
street/road/square *ulica/cesta/trg*

Getting Around and Driving

when is the next train/bus/ferry to... *kdaj je
  naslednji vlak/avtobus/trajekt za...*
a single/return ticket to... please *enosmerno/
  povratno vozovnico za... prosim*
arrivals/departures *prihodi/odhodi*
excuse me, is this the train/bus for... *oprostite, je
  to vlak/avtobus za...*
is this the road to... *je to cesta za...*
I am lost (m/f) *izgubil/izgubila sem se*
left/right/straight on *levi/desni/naravnost*
driver's licence *vozniško dovoljenje*
car registration *prometno dovoljenje*
petrol station *bencinska črpalka*
petrol/diesel/oil/air *benzin/dizel/olje/zrak*
I have had an accident (m/f) *imel/imela sem
  nesrečo*
the car has broken down at... *avto imam
  pokvarjen pri...*
car mechanic *avtomehanika*
can I park here? *lahko tukaj parkiram?*
no parking *prepovedano parkiranje*
one way/detour *ena smer/obvoz*

Days, Months and Time

Monday *ponedeljek*
Tuesday *torek*
Wednesday *sreda*
Thursday *četrtek*
Friday *petek*
Saturday *sobota*
Sunday *nedelja*

January *januar*
February *februar*
March *marec*
April *april*
May *maj*

June *junij*
July *julij*
August *avgust*
September *september*
October *oktober*
November *november*
December *december*

what time is it? *koliko je sati?*
in the morning *zjutraj*
in the afternoon *dopoldan*
day/week/month *dan/teden/mesec*
today/yesterday/tomorrow *danes/včeraj/jutri*

Numbers

1 *ena*
2 *dva*
3 *tri*
4 *štiri*
5 *pet*
6 *šest*
7 *sedem*
8 *osem*
9 *devet*
10 *deset*
11 *enajst*
12 *dvanajst*
13 *trinajst*
14 *štirinajst*
15 *petnajst*
16 *šestnajst*
17 *sedemnajst*
18 *osemnajst*
19 *devetnajst*
20 *dvajset*
30 *trideset*
40 *štirideset*
50 *petdeset*
100 *sto*
101 *stoena*
150 *stopetdeset*
200 *dvesto*
300 *tristo*
1,000 *tisoč*

Slovenia: Food and Drink

10

Capital Ljubljana is refining its international palate, but Slovenes are happiest with a meal of robust fare from grandma's kitchen, even when they dip into the cookbooks of neighbours Italy, Austria and Hungary to prepare dishes such as *žlikrofi* (ravioli), *rižota* (risotto), *zavitek* (strudel) and sturdy *golaž* (goulash). This is a country which likes its hearty platters unpretentious, meaty and in country portions – fortunately for vegetarians, it also has a taste for salads.

Eating Out

Although hotels cater to foreigners' baffling tastes by laying on a spread of bread, jam and sometimes cheese, or cereal and a cooked breakfast in smarter establishments, **breakfast** (*zajtrk*) for most Slovenes is simply a wake-up call of caffeine. Food comes either as late-morning or noon nibble *malica*, a two- or three-course light meal, or, in country heartlands with no office clocks to watch, a proper **lunch** (*kosilo*), the main meal of the day. **Dinner** (*večerja*) at 7–8pm is a light snack by comparison, with the exception of cosmopolitan Ljubljana, which has adopted international customs, and resort restaurants, which indulge tourists' quirk for evening meals.

Although the catch-all eaterie is a *restavaracija* (restaurant), for traditional lunching, especially at weekends, do as Slovenes do and flee to town fringes or into the country to ease top trouser buttons among the folksy furnishings of a *gostilna*, equivalent to a British inn, whose menus of traditional home cooking are worth investigating.

Regional Specialities

Wherever you are, menus vary little. Standard **starter** (*predjedi* or *začetne*) is soup (*juha*) often thickened with noodles (*kokošja*) or in east Slovenia offered as beans-spuds-and-sauerkraut broth *jota*. Keep an eye out, too, for: *pršut*, slivers of Karst ham like Italian prosciutto cured in the dry *bora* wind; doughy dumplings *štruklji*, available in over 70 guises, usually cheese-filled, and sometimes as dessert; and peasants' filler *žganci*, a thick buckwheat porridge after which second courses are optional. Slovenes who huff if a main has no **meat** (*meso*) like pork (*svinjina*), which comes in a baffling variety of cuts, and are partial to veal (*teletina*), beef (*govedina*) and horse (*žrebe*). Turkey (*puran*) replaces chicken (*pičanec*) as poultry of choice; lamb (*janjetina*) is a rarity. Smarter menus list rich dishes of **game** such as pheasant (*fazan*), rabbit (*zajec*) and venison (*srna*), and coastal restaurants expertly grill a net of **Adriatic fish and seafood**, while trout (*postrvi*) reeled in from the Soča River sends the nation's gourmets into ecstasies. Traditional **desserts** fill the corners: *zavitek* (strudel); nut, raisin and honey roll potica; or *gibanica*, a multi-layered pastry of walnuts, apple and poppy seeds with generous dollops of cream to make dieters give up.

Drinks

Romans seeded Slovenia's first vineyards and developed a taste for national **wines** (*vino*), best drunk young and which are not nearly as well known internationally as

Slovenian Menu Reader

dober tek! bon appetit!
jedilni list menu
kosilo lunch
kozarec glass
krožnik plate
malika brunch
natakar/natakarica waiter/waitress
na zdravje! cheers!
nož knife
račun, prosim bill, please
večerja dinner
vegetarijanec vegetarian
vilica fork
zajtrk breakfast
žlica spoon

Cooking Terms
domača home-made
gnjat smoked
na buzaru flash-fried with white wine, garlic and parsley
na žaru grilled
ocvrto fried
pečeno baked
praženo roasted
šunka/kuhano boiled

Juhe Soups
fižola juha bean soup
goveja juhe beef soup
jota sauerkraut, beans and potato broth/stew
paradižnikova (kremna) juha (cream of) tomato soup
prežganka toasted flour soup made with water or cream
zelenjavna juhe vegetable soup

Predjedi/Začetne Starters
narezek platter of cold meats
pršut air-cured ham

salama salami
štruklji baked or boiled dumplings filled with cheese
šunka ham
žganci buckwheat porridge
žlikrofi Slovenian ravioli stuffed with cheese and bacon

Meso Meat
čevapčiči spicy meat rissoles
dunajski zrezek Wiener schnitzel
fazan pheasant
govedina beef
golaž goulash
gos goose
goveji zrezek rump steak
hrenovka hotdog
kranjska klobasa fat, spicy sausages
(mesano) meso mixed grill
na žaru
piščanec chicken
polnjene paprike peppers stuffed with meat
puran turkey
raca duck
ražnjiči shish kebab
sarma cabbage leaves stuffed with meat and rice
srna venison
svinjina pork
svinjska pečenka roast pork
svinkski kotlet pork chop
svinjska krača pork shin
teletina veal
zajec rabbit
zrezek steak (e.g. *zrezek puran*, turkey steak)
žrebickov zrezek horse steak

Riba Fish
brancin sea bass
lignji/kalamari squid
losos salmon
morski list sole

they deserve. Finest whites (*belo*) come from the hills of the northeast region, the Podravje – a noble Renski Rizling (Riesling) with a hint of acidity; Traminec, spicy and smooth; Šipon and Sauvignon; and a rich Beli Pinot – although medium or semi-dry Malvazija, produced from over-ripe grapes, is tailor-made for its region's coastal fish. Connoisseur's choice reds (*črno*) come from Primorska, the most famous being Karst tipple Teran, ruby-red with a crackle of pepper. Austro-Hungarian rulers bequeathed a taste for Pils-style **beer** (*pivo*), the best being ubiquitous national brews Laško and

orada sea bream
oslič cod
postrvi trout
ribja plošča mixed fish platter
škampi shrimps
skuša mackerel

Zelenjava Vegetables
fižolova solata bean salad
grah peas
korenje carrot
krompir boiled potato
krompirjeva solata potato salad
kruhovi cmoki bread dumplings
kumara cucumber
njoki gnocchi
pomfrit chips
prardižnik tomato
paradižnikova solata tomato salad
riža rice
rižot risotto
solata (zelena/mešana) salad (green/mixed)
šparglji asparagus
špinat spinach
zelje cabbage

Sladice Dessert
baklava syrupy Turkish pastry with walnuts
gibanica pastry layered with fruit, nuts, sprin-
    kled with poppy seeds and dolloped with
    cream
palačinke (z čokolado/marmelado/orahi)
    pancakes (with chocolate/jam/nuts)
potica nut roll
sladoled ice cream
torta gâteau
zavitek strudel

Sadje/Orah Fruit/Nuts
breskev peach
češnje cherries
figa fig
grozdje grapes

hruška pear
jabolko apple
jagode strawberry
lešnik hazelnut
limona lemon
mandelj almond
marelica apricot
melona melon
oreh walnut
pomaranča orange
ribez raisin

Miscellaneous
češen garlic
čokolada chocolate
jajce egg
kis vinegar
kruh bread
marmelado jam
maslo butter
mleko milk
omaka sauce
poper pepper
sendvič sandwich
sladkor sugar
sir cheese
smetana cream
sol salt

Drinks
čaj tea
kava (z mleko/smetana) coffee (with
    milk/cream)
pivo beer
pomarančni sok orange juice
sok juice
špricar wine spritzer
vino (črno/belo/domače) wine (red/white/
    house)
voda (mineralna/negazirana) water
    (sparkling/still)
zeliščni čaj herbal tea

Zlatorog, supped by draught in little (*malo*) and large (*veliko*) measures of 0.3cl and 0.5cl. An exception to easy-sipping chilled beers is stout *temno pivo* (literally dark beer). *Špička* (schnapps) is tossed down as an aperitif and digestif. More interesting is Slovenia's drinks cabinet of **brandies**: potent plum spirit *slivovica* aged in oak barrels; juniper brandy *brinjovec* like dry gin; and *sadjevec*, fermented from mixed fruits. *Kava* (**coffee**) is served black in *kavarna* (cafés) unless you request milk (*mleko*), and traditional Brits will sigh in resignation at Slovenia's weak *čaj* (**tea**).

Slovenia: Ljubljana

Slovenia: Around Ljubljana

AUSTRIA

Kranjska Gora

Jesenice

Vršič Pass

✳ Alpinum Juliana

Trenta

Lake Bled

Bled

Radovljica

Soča

Srednja Vas

Dom Savica

Stara Fužina

Kropa

Podnart

Ukanc

Lake Bohinj

Ribčev Laz

Bohinjska Bistrica

Kobarid

Zatolmin

Tolmin

ITALY

Škofja Loka

Zelin

LJUBLJANA

Spodnja Idrija

Idrija

Vrhnika

Nova Gorica

Gorizia

Ajdovščina

Postojna

Divača

Skocjan

TRIESTE

N

Koper

Piran

25 km

10 miles

Although a population of 300,000 elevates lovely Ljubljana to metropolis status in Slovenia, the national touchstone still reflects its nation's bucolic charm. This is a capital city, certainly, but one that's provincial in scale, easygoing in attitude. Gaze from its castle belvedere northwest on gin-clear days and you glimpse the mighty Julian Alps, an ever-powerful presence on our tour of the most spectacular scenery in Slovenia's front garden.

Ljubljana

Twelfth-century Slavs had no thoughts of poetry when they inked 'Luwigana' on to 1146 maps, but a quirk of linguistics today allows Slovenes to sigh 'Ljubljana is *ljubljene*' (beloved). It seems entirely appropriate, because the compact city makes a strong case to be crowned Europe's most convivial capital. Grand old metropolises can boast all they want about cultured minds and racy lifestyles; the continent's easy-going younger sister has charm in abundance, whether in a Baroque old town which begs for a vintage Technicolor musical or among cafés on the willow-fringed banks of arterial river Ljubljanica.

Legend has it that Jason and his Argonauts paddled up that central waterway to found the Slovenian capital, a yarn illustrated on the coat of arms (which should know better) of a local dragon the mythic hero is said to have slain. Prosaic archae-ology hails the first settlement of note as Emona in 50 BC, where 6,000 Romans trod a neat grid between today's Mirje and Trg Republike until blasted by Attila in AD 450. However, it was Habsburgs, not Huns, who did most to shape Ljubljana's future. The Austrians eased themselves on to the throne in 1335 and found it so comfortable that they stayed there until 1918, bar a five-year Napoleonic hiccup (1809–13). After a 1511 earthquake reduced medieval Ljubljana to rubble, the rulers looked across the Adriatic to Italy and copied its elegant Baroque styles, a rethink replayed in Viennese Secession and Art Nouveau after an 1895 'quake; and it was the Vienna and Trieste rail links that filled Ljubljana's late-1800s coffers and nurtured its development as the nerve centre of a Slovene nation finding its voice.

Although the upstanding Austrians also founded a clutch of galleries and museums, Ljubljana's joys are far more human. Provincial in scale, positive in attitude as the heart of an optimistic European newcomer, lovely Ljubljana offers the city-break *par excellence*: lazy, sociable and with no must-sees of high-culture to nag the conscience. Better still, it is one that retains the feel of a secret – discover it while you can.

Prešernov Trg

There is no finer introduction to Ljubljana's engaging character than its geograph-ical heart Prešernov trg, sociable, intimate, and with a ragbag of buskers tooting and touting before al fresco cafés. Centre stage of the former crossroads to which medieval traders trundled from the city gate is Romantic poet France Prešeren, whose musings on love and freedom found a special place in Slovenian hearts after the elevation of his tub-thumping ballad *Zdravljica* ('A Toast') to national anthem. 'God save our land and nation/And all Slovenes where'er they live... Let thunder out of heaven/Strike down and smite our wanton foe!' he thunders, then sighs, 'Our girls! Your beauty, charm and grace!/Here surely is no treasure/To equal maidens of such race.' Slovenia's Shakespeare may well have had in mind local beauty Julija Primic when he penned the latter lines, because his heart never recovered from rejection by the minor aristocrat's daughter; he dedicated the tear-soaked 15-verse *Sonetni venec* ('Wreath of Sonnets') to 'the Master Theme of my whole life/Which will be heard when I have ceased my strife' as 'a record of my pain and of your praise'.

Ljubljana

↑ To Museum of Modern History

Tivoli Park

Swimming Pool

Railway Station ℹ️

TRG OSVOBODILNE FRONTE

Bus Station

TIVOLSKA CESTA

DVOŘAKOVA ULICA

KOLODVORSKA ULICA

PRAŽAKOVA ULICA

VOŠNJAKOVA ULICA

GOSPOSVETSKA CESTA

SLOVENSKA CESTA

TRDINOVA ULICA

MIKLOŠIČEVA CESTA

CUFARIEVA ULICA

RESLIEVA CESTA

PUHARJEVA

ŽUPANČIČEVA ULICA

ŠTEFANOVA ULICA

CANKARJEVA CESTA

TAVČARIEVA ULICA

DALMATINOVA ULICA

KOMENSKEGA ULICA

National Gallery

PREŽIHOVA ULICA

PREŠERNOVA CESTA

Nebotičnik Skyscraper

Miklošičev Park

MAIA ULICA

SLOVENSKA CESTA

MIKLOŠIČEVA CESTA

Modern Gallery

Opera House

Hotel Union

Church of the Annunciation

TRUBARIEVA CESTA

TOMŠIČEVA ULICA

BEETHOVNOVA ULICA

NAZORIEVA ULICA

ČOPOVA ULICA

Slovenian Museum of Natural History / National Museum

Parliament

ŠUBIČEVA ULICA

PLEČNIKOV TRG

PREŠERNOV TRG

VELASOVJEVA UL

VESELOVA ULICA

TRG REPUBLIKE

St Nicholas' Cathedral

VODNIKOV TRG

PETKOVŠKOVO NABREŽJE

Ljubljanica

ADAMIČ-LUNDROVO NABREŽJE

KOPITARIEVA UL

TRIPLE BR.

ŠTRITARIEVA UL

Ursuline Church of the Holy Trinity

WOLFOVA ULICA

MAČKOVA

CIRIL METODOV TRG

KREKOV TRG

Park Zvezda

KONGRESNI TRG

ERJAVČEVA CESTA

Slovene Philharmonic Hall

HRIBARJEVO NABREŽJE

CANKARJEVO NABREŽJE

RIBJI TRG

MESTNI TRG

Town Hall

ZA OGRAJAMI

OLD TOWN

Ljubljana Castle

PREŠERNA STEZA

Slovenian National Theatre

University of Ljubljana

DVORNI TRG

GREGORČIČEVA ULICA

IGRIŠKA ULICA

SLOVENSKA CESTA

COBBLER'S BRIDGE

MAČJA STEZA

OSOJNA STEZA

GRAJSKI DREVORED

PREDOR POD GRADOM

RIMSKA CESTA

VEGOVA ULICA

TURIAŠKA ULICA

NOVI TRG

Slovenian Academy of Arts

National and University Library

GALLUSOVO NABREŽJE

ULICA NA GRAD

SODARSKA STEZA

OSOJNA POT

AŠKERČEVA CESTA

EMONSKA CESTA

RIMSKA CESTA

KRIŽEVNIŠKA UL

TRG FRANCOSKE REVOLUCIJE

SALENDROVA

City Museum

BREG

STIŠKA

GORNJI TRG

Church of St James

ROŽNA ULICA

St Florian's Church

KARLOVŠKA CESTA

Križanke Theatre

ZOISOVA CESTA

LEVSTIKOV TRG

KRAKOVSKI NASIP

MIRJE

MIRJE

KRAKOVO

EMONSKA CESTA

KRAKOVSKA ULICA

KLADEŽNA ULICA

Gruber Palace

ROŽNA ULICA

Ljubljanica

N

GRADAŠKA

↓ To Trnovo

200 metres
20 o yards

Getting There

EasyJet flies from London Stansted, and Adria Airways flies from London Gatwick in 2hrs 5mins. *See* **Getting There**, pp.3–8.

Getting from the Airport

Brnik airport is 23km north of the city, linked by public **buses** which take 50mins and cost 850 SIT to shuttle to the bus station. Return to the airport is from Bay 28, Mon–Fri 5.20am–8.10pm; Sat–Sun 6.10am, then every odd hour from 9.10am to 7.10pm.

Private bus company Avtobusni prevozi Markun, **t** 041 670 528, takes 25mins, costs 1,000 SIT and shuttles to the bus station around every 90mins, 7.30am–midnight. Its return service operates in the same intervals between 5.20am and 10.30pm, or big spenders can request an Orbita **airport minibus** 24 hours a day, **t** 040 887 766, which runs door to door and costs 4,100 SIT per person.

Expect to pay 8,000 SIT for a **taxi** to the bus station.

Getting Around

Public **buses** rumble along a baffling network of routes from the bus station on Trg Osvobodilne fronte (aka Trg OF) north of the centre between 5 and 10.30pm and cost a flat-rate 300 SIT from the driver or 200 SIT for **tokens** (*žetoni*) bought from newsagents and post offices; a **daily ticket** (*dnevena karta*) costs 900 SIT and the **Ljubljana Card** (*see* 'Tourist information') buys free transport for its 72hr duration.

In truth, you'll rarely need a bus, nor strong shoe leather, because Ljubljana's city centre is a delight to stroll: compact, largely pedestrianized and crammed with cafés for refreshments. The lazy can ascend to the castle from Prešernov trg on a **tourist train** (*on the hour, June–Sept 9–9; Oct 9–7; Nov–Mar 11–3; April–May 9–6; 400 SIT*).

More useful than public transport is the tourist board's laudable **Ljubljana Bike Project** (*May–Nov*): bikes with a basket, available from central Prešernov trg, Plečnikov trg (near Trg Republike) and in front of the railway station

on Trg Osvobodilne fronte, and free for tourists for the first 2hrs (1,000 SIT deposit), then 200 SIT for every extra hour. Be warned, they're popular. If they're all taken, **Tir Bar** (in train station) hires bikes for 2,500 SIT/day.

Taxis congregate at the station and on Prešernov trg, or can be hired in advance on **t** 9700 to 9709.

Car Hire

All international players operate second bureaux at the airport.

Avis, Čufarjeva 2, **t** (01) 430 80 10; or Hotel Lev (*see* p.164), **t** (01) 438 32 50.

Budget, Miklošičeva 3 (Grand Hotel Union), **t** (01) 421 73 40.

Hertz, Dunajska 122, **t** (01) 530 54 38.

Ines, Mestni trg 9, **t** (01) 422 29 60.

Tourist Information

Ljubljana: Stritarjeva, before the Triple Bridge, **t** (01) 306 12 15, *www.ljubljana-tourism.si. Open daily June–Sept 8am–9pm; Oct–May 8–7.* The excellent main office is supplemented by a smaller office at the railway station (*Trg OF 6*, **t** *(01) 433 94 75; open daily June–Sept 8am–10pm; Oct–May 8–7*). Both proffer advice on accommodation (hotel and private) and stock detailed city maps, informative free city guide booklets and the what's-on guide *Where to?*, plus the usual confetti of leaflets. The equally helpful **Slovenian Tourist Information Centre** (*Krekov trg 10*, **t** *(01) 306 45 75/76; www.slovenia-tourism.si; open June–Sept 8am–9pm, Oct–May 8–7*) near the market tackles national tourism, sells tickets for city entertainments and a handful of souvenirs, and operates eight computer terminals for inveterate e-mail addicts (first 15mins free); the main tourist office also has one terminal.

Ljubljana Card

All offices stock the **Ljubljana Card**: stump up 3,000 SIT and you won't fork out for public transport or museum and gallery entry for 72hrs and will be treated to discounts in selected hotels, restaurants and car hire outfits.

Festivals

Late June: The Križanke theatre and castle swings to hot sounds of the superb **International Jazz Festival** and rings to world and alternative music early in the month for the **Druga Godba**.

Mid-June–Sept: Cutting-edge trends of graphic art are celebrated every odd year during the prestigious **International Biennial of Graphic Arts** in the International Centre of Graphic Art and Museum of Modern Art.

End June–early July: You can expect to stumble upon wacky street theatre during the **Ana Dsetnica** festival.

July–Aug: Ljubljana parties in summer. Best frocks and big hats come out for the star concerts of the **International Summer Festival** (*www.festival-lj.si*), over 50 years young and still the highlight of Ljubljana's calendar thanks to a roster of national and international stars who stage a feast of music, theatre and dance in the Križanke (among other venues).

Dec: Christmas **street fairs and events** sprawl on the river banks and fill squares before New Year's Eve grand finale fireworks.

Shopping

High street chain stores line Čopova ulica, but more enticing (if targeted at the tourist *tolar*) is the mish-mash of small shops in Mestni trg or **independent boutiques** of neighbours Stari trg and especially Gornji trg; Rustika (Ljubljana castle) and Dom (Ciril Metodov trg 5 and Mestni trg 24) cast their net Slovenia-wide for rather kitsch **souvenirs**; tiny Galerija Idrijske čipke (Gornji trg 23) dedicates itself to delicate lacework from Idrija. An excellent range of **handicrafts** – Idrija lace, pottery, twee painted chests – is also available from Skrina (Breg 8), and Atelje Rebeka Galerija (Cankarjevo nabrežje 9) has home-made patchwork covers and quilts.

Best of all is the **flea market** which claims riverbank Cankarjevo nabrežje on Sunday mornings (*8–1*); expect the occasional antique and Communist-era relics among stalls of good old-fashioned junk. A rummage through the Pogačarjev trg section of the **daily market** on Vodnikov trg (*Mon–Fri summer 6–6, winter 6–4*) will turn up a few handicrafts stalls plus home-made olive oils and honey.

Foodies can also marvel at a cellar of around 500 Slovenian **wines** in Vinoteka Bradeško, 500yds north of the railway station (Fairgrounds, Pavilion Jurček, Dunajska 18), or taste and buy tipples in the central Vinoteka Movia (Mestni trg 1).

Where to Stay

Ljubljana t (01) –

Bar a few noteworthy exceptions, Ljubljana hotels are neither characterful nor cheap; most woo expense accounts and prices can rise by 20% in summer, then rise further to extortionate amounts when trade fairs and congresses roll into town.

Grand Hotel Union Executive, Miklošičeva 1, t 308 12 70, *www.gh-union.si* (*expensive*). You can almost smell the moustache wax in the *grande dame* of Ljubljana's hotels; beg for a room on floors 1–3, the best with balconies, to wallow in Secessionist-era proportions. The most sumptuous décor in town elegantly updates Art Nouveau. Facilities are four-star, and there's a rooftop pool. Adjacent sister hotel **Grand Hotel Union Business,** t 308 11 70, is a second-best, just €10 cheaper, although the location moments from Prešernov trg is still excellent.

Lev, Vošnjakova 1, t 433 21 55, *www.hotel-lev.si* (*expensive*). Modern luxury near Tivoli Park from Ljubljana's only five-star hotel, where executive expense accounts pay for tasteful rooms of repro-antique furnishings and marble bathrooms.

Slon, Slovenska 34, t 470 11 00, *www.hotelslon. com* (*expensive*). Apparently, Austrian Archduke Maximilian and his elephant (*slon*) lodged in an inn here to christen this four-star member of the Best Western chain. Parquet floors, homely fabrics and rugs are pleasantly old-fashioned in rooms that have more character than newer rivals; large room upgrades are worth the extra *tolars*.

Grand Hotel Union Garni, Miklošičeva 9, t 308 43 00 (*moderate*). The latest member of the GHU family is priced just the right side of expensive – for now. Colourful bedspreads add character in refurbished modern rooms.

City Hotel Turist, Dalmatinova 5, t 234 91 30, *www.hotelturist.si* (*moderate*). Compact but cheerful rooms in a friendly central three-star, just east of Miklošičev Park.

Pri Mraku, Rimska 4, t 421 96 00, *www. daj-dam.si* (*moderate*). Comfy and modern-traditional décor in a guesthouse with a good Slovenian restaurant near Trg Francoske revolucije.

Emonec, Wolfova 12, t 200 15 20, *www.hotel-emonec.com* (*inexpensive*). Not just the best cheapie – a friendly two-star newcomer (2004) with simple but stylish en suites – but a hotel with one of the best locations in Ljubljana, moments from the action on Prešernov trg. The best bargain in town.

Celica, Metelkova 8, t 430 18 90, *www. souhostel.si* (*inexpensive*). Bars on the windows are the only clues that this quirky and original backpacker haven began life as a barracks' prison; reservation is essential to claim a single or two-bed room. Non-residents can tour former cells whose individual décor was dreamed up by artists (*daily, 2pm; adm*).

Park, Tabor 9, t 433 13 06, *www.hotelpark.si* (*inexpensive*). Refuse cell-like one-star rooms and demand instead a two-star in this apartment block northeast of the Dragon Bridge. Still fairly basic, but en suite and with satellite TV.

Eating Out

Ljubljana t (01) –

In addition to our selection, ex-pat quarterly *Ljubljana Life*, free from hotels and tourist information offices, lists more choices for eating (and drinking) out.

Chez Eric, Mestni trg 3, t 251 28 39 (*expensive*). Smart dining and the sort of gourmet French cuisine where smoked goose is served with chestnut purée and hints of honey and the aubergine mousse has a whiff of lavender flower sauce. Chef Eric is especially proud of his *crème brûlée* trio. *Closed Sun*.

Gostilna As, Čopova 5 (entrance on Knafljev prehod off Wolfova ulica), t 425 88 22 (*expensive*). An enjoyably stuffy upmarket traditionalist which prepares the finest Slovenian dishes you will eat plus superb seafood, and stocks an excellent cellar. Reservations essential to join Ljubljana's élite for Sunday lunch.

Pri Vitezu, Breg 18–20, t 426 60 58 (*expensive*). Slovenian fare such as horse fillets and a chef's-special veal is beautifully presented in a relaxed aristocrat among Ljubljana restaurants with a connoisseur's eye for antiques. *Closed Sun*.

Špajza, Gornji trg 28, t (*expensive–moderate*). Snug dining rooms furnished with homely charm, a talented chef who prepares superb Slovenian-international crossover cuisine (try venison in wild berries or acclaimed seafood dishes such as monkfish with truffles) and a superb wine list of national tipples – make this first choice for an intimate, romantic dinner.

Zlata ribica, Cankarjevo nabrežje 5–7, t 426 94 90 (*moderate*). Ljubljana's first riverside bar is now its best brasserie, laid-back but stylish, with the finest terrace in town for an al fresco lunch. Dishes such as grilled lamb or game in fruits-of-the-forest sauce and cheese *štrukji* plus the fish of its name (*ribica*) star on a menu which includes cheaper pastas.

Gostilna Sokol, Ciril Metodov trg 18, t 439 68 55 (*moderate*). An unassuming exterior hides a marvellous rustic-style inn which rambles over two levels and hides plenty of snug nooks. No surprise the cuisine is a taste of tradition – game goulashes, venison, wild boar and thick sausages with dumplings – served in country portions.

Julija, Stari trg 9, t 426 64 63 (*cheap*). Pork with feta and roast tomatoes or chicken in a basil sauce is typical of Mediterranean-influenced cooking in an old-town café-restaurant of neo-Baroque Italian mirrors and repro *fin-de-siècle* posters. Charming for a low-key candlelit dinner or a lunch of toasted ciabatta or pasta.

Šestica, Slovenska 38, **t** 242 08 50 (*cheap*). This 1776 vintage inn has been modernized, but the gruff service is a taste of yesteryear and the menu of sturdy veal ragoûts, beef goulashes with dumplings and grilled sausages comes from grandma's kitchen. A robust set lunch menu is a bargain. *Closed Sun.*

Pri Skofu, Rečna ulica 5, **t** 426 45 08 (*cheap*). A cheerful Krakovo local whose Slovenian home cooking presented bistro-style has earned it a city-wide reputation; a daily three or four-dish menu is decided by the chef's whim and the season.

Cafés

Sociable Ljubljana excels at café society: for drinks al fresco, snaffle a seat on Cankarjevo nabrežje; for old world atmosphere, take your pick on parallel Stari trg.

Planet Pločnik, Prešernov trg 1. A touch pricey, but an unbeatable location for people-watching and enjoying the buskers on Ljubljana's main square.

Le Petit Café, Trg Francoske revolucije 4. A charmer, hugely popular with students from the nearby university library (expect to wait for a terrace seat beneath willow trees), who sup large mugs of coffee and tuck into excellent breakfasts.

Zvezda, Wolfova 14. The décor is stylish, but the true draws to this Kongresni trg café are decadent home-made gâteaux and ice creams to make dieters give up – an after-noon treat.

Čajanna Hiša, Stari trg 3. A chatty and friendly teahouse with a baffling assortment of black, green and herbal infusions.

Maček, Krojaška 5. Visit – respectably late, of course – on Sunday morning to pose among the movers and shakers in a see-and-be-seen right-bank café. If you can find a seat.

Entertainment and Nightlife

The free English language booklet, *Where to?*, available from the tourist office, provides a monthly what's-on guide of concerts and exhibitions. Bang-up-to-date listings can be found in the Kažipot section of daily newspaper *Delo*.

Cankarjev dom, Prešernova 10, **t** 241 71 00, *www.cd-cc.si*. An arts and convention centre south of Trg Republike that's the nerve centre of Ljubljana cultural life; expect classical and pop concerts, dance, and art and photography exhibitions in its 13 performance spaces.

Philharmonic Hall (Slovenska filharmonija), Kongresni trg, **t** 241 08 00. Concerts by the Slovenian Philharmonic Orchestra and Slovenian Chamber Choir in the restored spiritual home of one of Europe's élite musical societies.

Slovenian National Opera and Ballet Theatre (SNG Opera in balet), Cankarjeva 11, **t** 241 17 40. Premier-league productions of opera and ballet are staged by Slovenia's finest in what is a suitably grand neo-Renaissance hall.

Slovenian National Theatre (SNG Drama), Erjavčeva cesta 1, **t** 252 14 62. Little and large stages host standards as well as challenging new works in the Austrians' Secessionist theatre.

Jazz Club Gajo, Beethovnova 8, **t** 425 32 06. An intimate and late-night bar which swings to trad jazz sounds: domestic and foreign acts perform on Wed and Thurs; Monday night is an open-to-all jam session.

Orto Bar, Grablovičeva 1, **t** 232 16 74. Raucous rock and blues in a smoky room upstairs and a louche red velvet lounge of DJs and drinkers east of the station – marvellous.

K4, Kersnikova 4, **t** 431 70 10. Expect everything from hip-hop to house via techno and dub in this bastion of alternative Ljubljana, which hosts occasional live gigs.

Sax Pub, Eipprova 7. A funky Trnovo bar off the tourist trail, which spills out beside the Gradaščica with the first whiff of spring and swings to live jazz sounds (*usually Thurs*).

Vinoteka Movia, Mestni trg 1. Sample (and buy) from a wide-ranging cellar of Slovenian wines in a romantic candlelit wine bar.

The 1905 bronze of the lovesick poet, who confessed 'How often through the town with watchful eyes/I wander, praying for a fate more kind/Yet catch no glimpse of that elusive prize', now has eyes forever fixed on his sweetheart, depicted in relief at Wolfova ulica 4, and blanks a saucy muse above, whose nudity in front of the Franciscan church outraged Ljubljana's contemporary moral guardians. While on the west side of the square, have a look at the showy Art Nouveau **Hauptmann House** – its bright aqua, jade and terracotta tiles arranged in *à la mode* 1904 patterns was the whim of a paint merchant.

Once isolated in a suburb, the Franciscan order's stately 1650s **Church of the Annunciation** (Cerkev Marijinega oznanenja; *open daily 8–12.30 and 3–8*) blushes on the north side of Prešernov trg as if embarrassed by being thrust into the heart of Ljubljana life. A gloomy interior is a disappointment after one of the town's grandest façades, worth a look only for its swaggering high altar (1760) by Venetian sculptor Francesco Robba. This vision of the luminary of Ljubljana Baroque steals all the attention from the relics of St Deodatus; 1758 Franciscan brothers purchased the ghoulish remains of the French bishop-hermit displayed in a glass case left of the main event.

Warm your chilled blood with the Seccessionist exterior of the **Urbanc Store** (aka Centromerkur) east of the church. If Felix Urbanc wanted first impressions to count he must have been delighted with the doorway of Ljubljana's first department store, a 1903 beauty which aspires to the traditional retail heights of Paris, Vienna and Budapest in wrought iron, glass like flower petals and crowning glory a neo-Baroque Mercury, god of trade, while in the Art Nouveau interior a staircase swoops up to the gallery beneath a personification of Craft.

Miklošičeva Cesta

The store is an overture for Miklošičeva cesta's Secessionist stylebook, drawn after an 1895 earthquake wiped the slate clean for experiments in a cutting-edge style. First on the street which arrows northeast off Prešernov trg is the **Hotel Union**, still as it was when 1905 guests first gawped at the grandest dining hall in the Balkans. Small wonder military top brass commandeered it as staff headquarters to master-mind the 1915–17 Soča Front trench campaign against Italy. Two years after its doors opened, architect Josip Vancaš turned his attention to the vacant plot opposite and created a swoopy façade for the **People's Loan Bank**, at whose peak buxom belles brandish a purse and beehive, emblems of thrift and diligence. Have a peek at the contemporary stained glass inside like frozen rosewater, before you reel at the blast of colour on Ljubljana Art Nouveau showpiece the **Co-operative Bank** (1921). Enthused by studies of national architecture, architect Ivan Vurnik drafted in his Viennese wife Helena to paint the traditional geometrics which bud around its windows in Slovene tricolour red, white and blue, though these are modest compared with a jaw-dropping interior which casts a jackdaw-eye around Slovenia for its stylized motifs of wheat fields, pine forests and vineyards.

Envious of the parks in Prague, city father Ivan Hribar seized upon the 1895 earth-quake to create **Miklošičev Park** 100 yards further along. Maks Fabiani's Art Nouveau flowerbeds have been lost to an uninspired X of paths, but the flanking Secessionist buildings remain as the Otto Wagner student intended. As if to celebrate the park's completion, Fabiani's first creation is his quirkiest; stylized squiggles and ceramic tile 'flowerheads' draw floral doodles on the façade of **Krisper House** (Miklošičev 20), whose balcony is capped with an iron bell.

Architectural explorers should also seek out the **Nebotičnik 'Skyscraper'**, an Art Nouveau landmark on the corner of Slovenska cesta and Štefanova ulica, which peered over every building in Central Europe when the last brick was laid in 1933. Not that everyone was enthused by the Pension Insurance Fund's whimsical take on Americana erected during the economic boom – contemporary critics fumed that it was 'a punch in the eye for Baroque Ljubljana'.

Across the River Ljubljanica: the Triple Bridge, Market and Cathedral

He dotted Vienna with creations under teacher and mentor Otto Wagner and reno-vated Prague Castle as chief city architect, but so ubiquitous is the stamp that Jože Plečnik (1872–1957) left on his home town, tourist board authorities allude without hyperbole to 'Plečnik's Ljubljana'. Other showpieces penned to dignify the burgeoning capital of Slovenia may boast more architectural authority, but none of the local son's creations charm like the **Triple Bridge** (1931), which links Prešernov trg to the Old Town. Plečnik created a picture-postcard favourite when he rethought an existing stone bridge and added flanking footbridges angled to direct eyes to Ljubljana's Baroque beauties; the bridge's descending neo-Renaissance balustrades allude to Venice. Banisters like massed ranks of *Alice in Wonderland* pawns play strobing optical tricks, and there's magic in the air when the lamps bathe evening strollers in a soft glow.

Abutting Plečnik's most enchanting creation is his open **Market Colonnade** (1944), a dignified sweep alongside the river, certainly, but the main lure is its food stalls. Drag yourself past bakeries and delicatessens piled with fresh cakes and pastries – look out for patterned *Medeni kruhek* (honey bread), a traditional festive treat shaped into hearts or rings – and you'll discover an effervescent market (*Mon–Sat*) which sprawls across Vodnikov trg and is especially boisterous on Saturday mornings; this is the spot to piece together a Tivoli Park picnic (*see* p.175). At its shoulder, the **Dragon Bridge** bookends the riverfront colonnade with a swooping Secessionist span across the river; locals were so fond of Wagner pupil Jurij Zaininovich's cartoony lizards which guard-ed the 1901 newcomer that city councillors grudgingly adopted their nickname for a bridge intended to celebrate Emperor Franz Josef I's 40 years on the Austrian throne. Local wags claim the city icons twitch their tails when a virgin crosses the bridge.

Dedicated architectural aficionados should sidetrack west to Plečnik's **Iron Building** (1934), a wedge-like solution to a tricky corner plot on Poljanska cesta and Kapiteljska ulica; everyone else can marvel at **St Nicholas' Cathedral** (Stolna cerkev sv. Nikolaja). Its mighty Baroque spires and dome blossomed above Ljubljana's roofscape in 1706 thanks to the passion for Italian Baroque espoused by the Academia Operosorum Labacensis. The intellectual think tank which exhorted architects to dress the city in the latest fashions must have thrilled at the Rome supremo Andrea Pozzo's plan to recreate the Eternal City's Il Gesù in Ljubljana, a far cry from the first Romanesque basilica built on the riverbank to honour the patron saint of fishermen. Hunt on the south façade for a *Pietà* saved from the Gothic church which emerged from that 13th-century progenitor, then pass through cast iron doors which relate 1,250 years of Slovenian Christianity and marvel at an exuberant interior that lets rip with full Catholic razzmatazz. Even its riot of pink and cream marble trimmed with gilt pales beside fabulously frothy frescoes. Vienna commitments forced Pozzo to abandon his creation and he handed painting duties to Giulio Quaglio; the north Italian artist who nodded to Carracci and Correggio does not disappoint. His illusionist frescoes are Baroque at its flashiest, lifting the church's lid to stage a theatrical vision of Heaven where St Nicholas undergoes his transfiguration before a rapt audience of apostles, saints and cardinal Virtues while Christians meet a grisly end under Roman emperors Nero and Diocletian in the wings. Quaglio couldn't resist signing his masterpiece in the chancel: the artist is conspicuous by his wig among devotees who receive bread from St Nicholas. Look, too, for a ritzy Baroque pulpit and choir stalls and the swooning angels shaped by Francesco Robba's impeccable chisel on a north transept altar.

More Quaglio frescoes grace a **public library** in the seminary opposite the cathedral; Pozzo's lumpen Atlantes in lion-skins have shouldered its portal pillars since 1714 (and look thoroughly cheesed off about it). Consult the tourist board about the erratic opening times to wallow in one of Slovenia's most exquisite Baroque spaces, its shelves crammed with sensuous leather spines and where ecclesiastical fathers gaze idly from puffy clouds on Quaglio's roof.

Around Mestni Trg

A cosy cat's-cradle of streets between the river and the castle, the pedestrianized **Old Town** is Ljubljana's treat, crammed with cafés and interesting boutiques which untie purse strings as if by magic – there are few finer places to lose track of time. Begin your exploration of it on handsome Mestni trg beyond the Triple Bridge. Allegories of the Slovenian rivers Sava, Ljubljanica and Krka can be seen on Robba's **Fountain of the Three Carniola Rivers** (1751); its none-too-subtle allusions to Bernini's Piazza Navona water-feature Fontana dei Fiumi confirms the Academia Operosorum Labacensis's aspirations to create a Rome of the North. No such whimsy for the stentorian **town hall** behind, which imposes itself among Baroque townhouses after its Gothic core was beefed up during a 1719 rebuild. For all its outward bluster, however, the municipal power base is so relaxed in its lovely galleried courtyard (*open Mon–Fri 9–7*) – which led a double life as a theatre – that it even cracks jokes in *sgraffito*. Here, too, you'll find a Baroque *Hercules*, retired after nearly 300 years atop a Stari trg fountain, and Robba's *Narcissus* absorbed by his reflection.

Take a look at an elaborate Baroque mansion opposite the town hall at Mestni trg 2 – mayor Janez Krstnik's treat to himself, handily placed for the office – before you follow a gentle curve of Baroque houses painted in smart pastel shades. Don't go far, however: a side-passage nips off to **Ribji trg**, an intimate charmer named for the daily catch hawked by 1500s fishermen and home to the city's 1521 great-grandfather enjoying a second wind as a café (Ribji trg 2). An adjacent pier is the embarkation point for sprees on the Ljubljanica by tourist boat (*May–Sept Mon–Fri 5.30, Sat–Sun 10.30 and 5.30; adm*).

Few streets unite Ljubljana's charms better than adjacent riverbank promenade **Cankarjevo nabrežje**, shaded by willows and crammed with cafés. On Sunday mornings (*8–1*) a good-natured flea market sprawls along it. Potter south and you reach **Cobbler's Bridge** (Čevljarski most), another Plečnik vision (1931) which swept away a bridge where 16 shoemakers hammered nails in huts as on Florence's Ponte Vecchio. City bailiffs used to punish the dishonesty of the town's bakers with a dunking from the bridge into the sewage-filled river.

Stari Trg and Levstikov Trg

Stari trg ('Old Square', though not really a square), appears every bit the medieval street of its origins. Keen eyes will spot quirky details and enticing window displays as you walk west to the rococo ruffles of **Schweiger Haus** at Stari trg 13 (not numbered), one of Ljubljana's grandest secular houses, created for one Herr Schweiger. His surname's English translation as 'silent one' explains the stone figure who hushes pedestrians above the portal, not a fate suffered by later resident poet Lily Nova, judging by her bust left of the door.

Stari trg opens at its southern end as Levstikov trg, punctuated by a replica of the Hercules Fountain erected in 1991 after Ljubljana hankered after the Baroque original. Students of the Academy of Music now practise tricky passages in the solid **Stična Manor**, which abbots treated themselves to on the square's west side,. Beyond, the Jesuits' 1650 church of **St James** (Cerkev sv. Jakoba) springs a surprise with a zingy acid-yellow paint-job on its Baroque façade. Time a visit to coincide with Mass (*6.30pm*) to rummage through side chapels stuffed with playful Venetian altars and a modest but lovely high altar by Francesco Robba, a commission Ljubljana's Baroque supremo must have enjoyed because he lived on the square. All the church's chapels pale beside that of the St Francis Xavier Chapel, a charming octagonal nook iced with stucco on whose altar the 'Black King' and 'White Queen' of Africa and Europe acclaim voyages of the Jesuit order founder to preach his doctrine.

At the church's shoulder, the **Shrine to Mary** was erected in 1682 as votive thanks that Turkish forces passed Slovenia by during their blast across the Balkans. Across busy Karlovška cesta is the creamy yellow **Gruber Palace**, where Ministry of Culture officials file national archives in the Zopf-style manor (a dither between late-Baroque and early neoclassicism) which Jesuit Gabriel Gruber intended as a school of hydraulics and mechanics. Security officials will allow you to ascend one of the finest Baroque staircases you'll see, which spirals through stucco flower braids like fairy buntings to a dome with an allegorical fresco of trades, crafts and technology. Ask politely and they'll escort you to a second-floor chapel painted by Austrian artist Johann Kremser Schmidt; if not, ask at tourist information about an official visit.

Gornji Trg to Ljubljana Castle

Gornji trg is a snapshot of Ljubljana's days before she matured into Baroque: lined with cosy medieval dwellings crowned by a single gable and separated by narrow passages for waste – household and bodily. More enticing than the architecture, perhaps, are the designers and galleries that have set up shop here. After the grand airs of the Baroque lower town, 'Upper Square' relaxes as it funnels uphill to a lovely, villagey corner of the city in awe of **St Florian's Church** (Cerkev sv. Florijana). Local residents who prayed for protection while a blaze reduced to ashes much of the lower town fulfilled a vow in 1672 when they erected this homage to the protector against fire. It's invariably locked, but luckily its interest is external: a Robba relief of Prague prelate St John of Nepomuk being tossed into the river on the orders of Bohemian king Wenceslas IV; and a doleful portrait of an Emona Roman beside the portal.

And so up, up, via Ulica na Grad, which ascends beside the church, then along paths to **Ljubljana Castle** (Ljubljanski grad; *open daily May–Sept 9am–10pm; Oct–April 10–9*), which lords it over the city from its hilltop perch; an alternative path climbs off Ciril Metodov trg opposite the market, or tourist trains pootle up from Prešernov trg (*on the hour June–Sept 9–9; Oct 9–7; Nov–Mar 11–3; April–May 9–6*). The Celts, Illyrians and Romans took advantage of its defensive perch; the 1144 Spanheim Carinthian dukes erected the first stone fortress to maintain a strict eye on citizens and mint coinage; and a castle largely rebuilt after a 1511 earthquake suffered an ignominious demotion through the ranks from palace of Austrian-appointed rulers to garrison after the mid-1600s, then hit rock-bottom in the 20th century as a prison and shabby almshouse. You'd never know. Despite the authoritarian, glowering looks which keep up appearances to the Old Town beneath, post-1960 renovation has modified the fortification into a cultural centre where newlyweds beam and orchestras let rip in the courtyard during concerts of the Summer Festival. Plečnik would have harrumphed at the bland reinvention of a monument he longed to mould into a Slovene Acropolis.

For academic minds, the fast-forward of the **Virtual Museum** (Virtualni muzej; *open daily May–Sept 9–9; Oct–April 10–6; adm*) through Ljubljana's urban and architectural development is an instructive (if humourless) reason for a visit. And even loafers should brave the didactic narrative pepped up with 3-D specs because the same ticket buys you a climb to the top of a pompous little neo-Gothic clock tower, grafted on in 1858, which provides the best views over Ljubljana that exist – a glorious 360° panorama which sweeps over a jumbled Baroque roofscape and city landmarks such as the cathedral and Franciscan church to Alps which sawtooth the horizon on clear days. In your hurry to climb up, don't overlook the Gothic **Chapel of St George**, emblazoned with cartoony heraldic crests of Carniolan governors like a child's history book. Join one of the castle tours (*June–Sept daily 10 and 4; adm*) from the drawbridge and you can also explore halls and dungeons that are otherwise off-limits.

Kongresni Trg

Taking its duties as host seriously, Ljubljana razed a Capuchin monastery to lay Kongresni trg (Congress Square) in honour of the 1821 Congress of the Holy Alliance and inadvertently created a rallying point: Slovenia celebrated the 1918 establishment of the Kingdom of Serbs, Croats and Slovenians in the park that was seeded after years as a parade ground; on 9 May 1945 locals gathered to cheer their liberation from the barbed wire ring with which German forces had isolated the city; and in 1999 US president Bill Clinton addressed the Slovenian people in a park dubbed 'Zvezda' for its 'star' of paths. The most charming of its flanking buildings is the neoclassical **Slovene**

Philharmonic Hall (1891), prim, neat and slightly withdrawn at the southeast corner in a display of manners as immaculate as you'd hope from the home of a royal among European orchestras – the 1701 Academia Philharmonicorum casually lists Haydn, Beethoven and Brahms among its roll call of honorary members and came under Mahler's baton in 1881–2. No such modesty for the neo-Renaissance braggart at its shoulder – the city governor might have spluttered into his claret if he knew that **University of Ljubljana** students would one day attend lectures in his 1902 palace.

To the west, the idiosyncratic **Ursuline Church of the Holy Trinity** (Uršulinska cerkev) is a defiantly individual member of Ljubljana's Baroque family which nods to Palladian role models on a graceful façade of stolid pillars, Gothic arches and an undulating Borromini canopy like an arrow directing eyes to heaven. An interior that's a plain Jane compared to her showy sisters in their lavish make-up only boosts the impact of the ace up the church's sleeve – a gloriously over-the-top high altar by Baroque genius Francesco Robba. Carrara marble allegories of Faith, Hope and Charity pose and pout on its grand stage, 55ft high and crafted of African marble. Make your pilgrimage via an underpass from the park and you'll spot a replica 2nd-century Roman noble (original in the National Museum) and real McCoy sarcophagus, both unearthed in the Emona necropolis that was located outside the ancient Italians' city walls on the main north road, which still marches as Slovenska cesta.

Novi Trg to Trg Francoske Revolucije

When the spending power of 16th-century aristocratic families forced out fisher-men from a ramparted Middle Ages settlement, 'New Square' on the left bank of the Ljubljanica blossomed into the most prestigious address in the city. The **Slovenian Academy of Arts and Sciences** has claimed the best building in the square, the 1790 Lontovž (Novi trg 3), where Habsburg rulers hammered out policy during Carniola province Diets (parliaments) – peek into a lovely courtyard if it's open. North, **Zidovska ulica** (Jewish Street) and **Zidovska steza** (Jewish Lane) recall a former ghetto in narrow medieval alleys where the Middle Ages seem just a whisper away, and south is **Breg**, now quiet after days when it rang to a polyglot of Mediterranean sailors as the city's main port until silt clotted the trade artery in the 1700s.

The brick pile studded with rough stone at the junction of Gosposka ulica and Turjaška ulica is Plečnik's most audacious work, stolid and upstanding as the **National and University Library** (Narodna in Univerzitetna Knjižnica; *open Mon–Fri 9–8, Sat 9–1*). Seize the Pegasus door handle and his conceptual approach continues in an interior whose staircase of charcoal-grey marble ascends to an upper atrium flooded with light as a metaphor for its students' transition from the 'twilight of ignorance to the light of knowledge and enlightenment'. Collar a scholar (or ask at reception) and you may be able to glimpse his reading room, with bizarre brass lamps like alien flora.

A block south, stretched square **Trg Francoske revolucije** is punctuated by the exclamation mark of Plečnik's austere **Illyrian Monument**, a 1929 salute to Napoleon, who elevated Ljubljana to capital of his Illyrian Provinces (1809–1814). Slovenia has good reason to cheer, too – the dictator, not known for pandering to nationalist senti-ment, for once relented and Slovene schools switched from German to their mother tongue. While the sour-faced emperor pouts, fresh-faced beauty Illyria smiles coyly beneath the crescent and stars of the region fashioned from Carniola, western Carinthia, Görz (modern Gorizia), Istria (now in Croatia) and chunks of Croatia. An 80-year-old Plečnik returned to the square in 1952, called out of retirement by city fathers to rethink a deserted monastery complex of Teutonic Order Knights of the Cross. His parting gift to his home town created the **Križanke Theatre** just east of the monument, 1,400-seater main stage of the International Summer Festival, with *sgraffito* scrawls on faux Renaissance arcades in a courtyard lit by odd lamps like Triffids. Plečnik's extraordinary vision also blobbed courtyard Hell's Yard (Peklensko dvorišče) beyond the restaurant with its pod-like lights.

The architectural supremo's transformation was just the latest rethink of the knights' complex, however. Until their St Mary's Church received its 1715 Baroque makeover, it was a Gothic church, on display as a model in the **City Museum** (Mestni muzej; *open Tues–Sun 10–6; adm*), the aristocratic palace of Auersperg counts which closes the square at the east end. In 2006, exhibits organized by theme will narrate Ljubljana's tale from prehistory to the present, following painstaking renovation.

Krakovo and Trnovo

Away from her public grand airs, Ljubljana relaxes into easygoing pace in spacious suburbs south of Zoisova cesta. Such was the concentration of artists wooed to its rustic whimsy, charming **Krakovo** was dubbed Ljubljana's Montmartre. Paris it is not, however. Instead, while not quite a timewarp, this cosy corner drops heavy hints of its roots as a village of medieval fishermen in streets Krakovska ul. and Klaoezna ul., lined with squat single-gable houses which overlook tidy allotments nurtured by the green fingers of pensioners who continue a centuries-old tradition as market gardeners.

Slovene artist Rihard Jakopič sought inspiration for his Impressionist canvases at Karakovska 11, although his office was a short stroll west at Mirje 4. The **Jakopič Garden** where he daubed bold Impressionist works in a summerhouse is more famous for Roman ruins which sketch the floorplan of a house still with heating and sewage pipes and floors laid in mosaics (*viewing by appointment through City Museum Cultural Information Centre, Trg Francoske revolucije 7, **t** (01) 251 40 25; open Mon–Fri 10–6, Sat 10–1*). The wealthy citizen's residence was just outside the AD 14–15 city walls which protected Emona's south flank – they march alongside Mirje after a rebuild by Plečnik, who couldn't resist signing his work with a misplaced pyramid and entrance arches which would have scandalized Roman defence engineers.

Plečnik also penned the Trnovo Bridge (and, again, spiked it with pyramids) that crosses the Gradaščica canal. The waterway slips past a huddle of bars and inns perfect for lazy evenings and also demarcates the suburb of **Trnovo**, seemingly far too leafy and laid-back to be the home of Slovenia's biggest rap star, Klemen Klemen. Its landmark is the late-19th-century **Church of St John the Baptist** (Cerkev sv. Janeza Krstnika), where poet France Prešeren stood dumbstruck in 1833 after the thunderbolt of spying love of his life Julija Primic. 'Trnovo, a place of miserable name!' he spat later, embittered that she spurned his advances, much to the relief of her parents, who were wary of Prešeren's reputation as a boozy troublemaker.

South of the church at Karunova 4, the house from which Ljubljana's 20th-century urban artist shaped his home town is preserved as the **Plečnik Collection** (*open Tues and Thurs 10–2; adm; tour groups max 7, reservation recommended, **t** (01) 280 16 00*). In the homey rooms of his first creation in the capital, where architectural models clutter the study and the kettle is still on the stove, Plečnik shelves the public displays of his occasionally overbearing architecture and reveals himself as an almost ascetically modest man, surprisingly blessed by humility.

The Museum Quarter

Ljubljana helpfully gathers its dollop of high culture around the neo-Renaissance **Opera House** (1892), northwest of Prešernov trg. Cultural highbrow of the trio of galleries and museums is the **National Gallery** on Prešernova cesta (Narodna galerija; *open Tues–Sun 10–6; adm*), where premier-league Slovenian artists are treated to a palatial Habsburg-era palace and second-division Europeans are exiled to a modern extension. To tour the Slovenians chronologically, cross the central grand hall to Gothic devotional sculptures whose chubby yokels and dour saints hide two star pieces: a *Standing Madonna* like a coquettish figure of Meissen china, and a lovely 15th-century *Enthroned Madonna* whose skirts billow in the breeze. Devotional artist Valentin Metzinger, who created altar paintings in St Ursula's Church, adds Baroque works in the hall whose prize is Almanach's boozy *Cardplayers I* – the gallery dubiously claims the Flemish artist for Slovenia under the ruse he was active in Carniola during the latter years of the 17th century. Slip past fat-lipped nobles and so-so Realists in an adjoining corridor to linger at *Before The Hunt* by Juri Šubic, the first Slovene in Paris to embrace his adopted home's bright colours and light touch with a brush; and Ivana Koblica, Slovenia's foremost female painter, who proves her social critique is as sharp as her technique with the idyllic *Summer*, characterful *Woman Drinking Coffee* and unflinchingly realistic *Woman Selling Vegetables*.

The gallery's pride and joy is its hoard of Impressionists – Ivan Grohar's speckled white-out *Škofja Loka in a Snowstorm*, Krakovo local Rihard Jakopič, teetering on Expressionism, and Matija Jama, indebted to lighter French schools. However, don't miss superb sculpture by Franz Bernecker and Ivan Kajec before you potter through Europeans in the north wing: Almanach's gamblers are much the worse for wear in *Cardplayers II* and Expressionist Alexej von Jawlensky injects cultural adrenaline beyond Baroque Venetians.

More modern tastes are catered for in the **Modern Gallery**, 100 yards south on Prešernova cesta (Moderna galerija; *open Tues–Sun 10–6; adm*). Here, a 1950–2000 round-up of Slovenian artists shifts from canvases indebted to modern art giants such as Picasso, Dalí and Bacon to playful installations of retro-kitsch by *enfants terribles* of the NSK (Neue Slowenische Kunst; New Slovenian Art).

There is no such challenging fare in the 1880s palace opposite. Stuffed mammals and birds, a 210 million-year-old fossilized fish and the vast mineral collection of 19th-century geologist Žiga Zois entice enthusiasts to the **Slovenian Museum of Natural History** (Prirodoslovni muzej Slovenije; *open Tues, Wed and Fri–Sun 10–6, Thurs 10–8; closed Mon; adm*). In 2007, the collection will shift to a new home near the city zoo (*open April–Oct Tues–Sun 9–7, Nov–Mar Tues–Sun 9–4; closed Mon; adm*) beneath northwest hill Rožnik (*see* below) and the nation's largest hoard of archaeological finds and *objets d'art* will claim the whole space as the **National Museum** (*same hours; adm*). Until 2006, temporary themed exhibitions tantalize with a glimpse of the treasures stored in packing crates. Console yourself with a lovely foyer, ennobled by neo-Baroque frescoes and where porcelain girls whizz down the banisters.

Other museum options for a rainy day, further outside the centre, include: the **Slovenian Ethnographic Museum**'s displays of folksy handicrafts and culture (Slovenski etnografski muzej; *Metelkova ulica 2; open Tues–Sun 10–6; adm free*); immaculate steam engines and rolling stock in the **Railway Museum** (Železniški muzej; *Parmova ulica 35 and* Kurilniška *ulica 3; both open Mon–Thurs 9–1; adm*); and tours of the Union Brewery on the first Tuesday of the month as the **Brewery Museum** (Pivovarski muzej; *also by appointment,* **t** *(01) 471 73 40*).

Tivoli Park

Ljubljana locals can thank the Austrian-appointed rulers of 1812 for Tivoli Park, their city playground to gossip in after or jog off Sunday lunch; its paths relax after initial formality to idle through mature trees and criss-cross lawns. Beyond an underpass at the end of Cankarjeva cesta, Plečnik's Jakopič Promenade hurries straight to temporary exhibitions at the **International Centre of Graphic Arts** (*open Wed–Sun 10–6; adm*) staged in the Baroque **Tivoli Castle** (Tivolski grad); visit between mid-June and September on an odd-numbered year and you're treated to the world's oldest graphic-arts beano, the International Biennial of Graphic Art.

Perhaps inspired by the Jesuits' 1713 manor, Count Leopold von Lamburger demanded his own mansion in 1720, located northwest and today the **Museum of Modern History** (Muzej novejše zgodovine; *open Tues–Sun 10–6; adm*). Its narration of Slovenia's painful birth and troubled adolescence skimps on hard details, but the contemporary artefacts and personal mementoes are intriguing: a stage-set trench on the Soča Front; uniforms, cartoons and posters which chronicle teething troubles of the Kingdom of Yugoslavia; the seething resentments of the Second World War (look for a chess set crafted from bread and spit by a Venetian POW); 46 years of Communism which collapses in an explosion of consumerism; and the wreckage of a helicopter downed during Slovenia's 1991 Ten Days' War.

For longer strolls, paths ascend through woods which carpet a cluster of hills behind the Tivoli Park's lawns. An inn at the peak of **Rožnik** (394m/1,293ft), where Slovenian poet Ivan Cankar wrote his works, offers a beer and a bite before the return.

Day Trips and Overnighters from Ljubljana

The Škocjan Caves

In a country blessed with more than its fair share of natural splendours, the Škocjan Caves remain perhaps the most impressive. So awesome is the queen of the Karst, the Slovenian limestone region that named a genre of geography, UNESCO added it to its list of World Heritage sites in 1986. And no wonder; no matter how many cave systems you have explored, its 5.8km wonderland of natural bridges, subterranean waterfalls, arching caverns, lakes and gorges will not disappoint.

Second-century BC Roman scholar Poseidonius of Apamea noted that 'the river Timavus springs in the mountain, flows into an abyss, reappears after the distance of 130 stadia and flows into the sea', and 16th- and 17th-century cartographers – notably Slovene polymath Janez Vajkard Valvasor in his rigorous 1689 topographia *The Glory of the Duchy of Carniola* – pondered the Reka river's disappearance into a gorge near the village of Škocjan before its re-emergence 40km northwest as the Timavo spring near Trieste. True exploration of the system came late, however. Following in the footsteps of 1840 pioneer Ivan Svetina, and a decade later Adolf Schmidl, who employed the expertise of Idrija miners to clamber 1,650ft, a determined triumvirate from the German-Austrian Mountaineering Society secured a lease on the system in an effort to conquer a tricky sixth waterfall. In 1887 they reached a 14th waterfall in the Hanke Canal (*see* p.177).

The tours (*1½hrs, daily June–Sept on the hour 10–5; April, May and Oct 10, 1 and 3.30; Nov–Mar 10 and 1 plus Sun 3; adm; in English*), which congregate at picnic benches outside the park ticket office and explore 2.3km, are infinitely more gentle, though underground temperatures of 12°C and slippy paths necessitate sweaters and sturdy footwear. A sensitive eye for lighting retains the atmosphere in the stalagmite- and stalactite-decorated Silent Cave, first cavern of a system carved by the Reka over 2 million years and enlarged by the occasional shrug of a tectonic plate. More impressive, beyond the dripstones of lovely Paradise Cavern, is the Great Hall, an understatement for the 120- by 30-yard cave blotched by red iron stains and furnished with a 250,000-year-old, 50ft-high stalactite tower, the Giant, together with the Organ, named for its stalactite pipes which thonk in pitch when rapped.

The sound of the Reka as it tumbles through rapids introduces a Slovenian highlight, the Murmuring Cave. For once all the clichés about jaw-dropping ring true in

Getting There

Trains every 1hr–1½hrs travel from Ljubljana direct to Divača; local trains take 1hr 40mins and cost 1,340 SIT (single); 1½hr InterCity trains cost 1,660 SIT. From here a 3km **footpath** leads via Dolnje Ležeče to the Park Škocjanske Jamevia in the village of Matavun; if in doubt, ticket office officials will confirm directions.

Tourist Information

Škocjan Caves: The cave ticket office, **t** (05) 763 28 40, sells 1:5,000 cave maps and 1:6,000 regional park map *Regijski park Škocjanske jame*. The Škocjan Caves Park website is *www.park-skocjanske-jame.si*.

Eating Out

Café-restaurant **Pri Jami** at the park centre rustles up basic meals and snacks; otherwise food is available in Divača.

Malovec, Kraška cesta 30a, Divača, **t** (05) 763 02 00 (*cheap*). There's *telečja krača* and *svinjska krača* (roast shin of veal and pork) for a post-walk filler, plus veal and beef steaks in mushroom and truffle sauces, in a *gostilna* whose dining room has a whiff of old-fashioned formality.

Risnik, Kraška cesta 25, Divača. **t** (05) 763 00 08 (*cheap*). More basic fare is prepared in this no-nonsense locals' choice for a cheap feed; expect to find a menu of sturdy pork chops and goulashes.

Europe's largest gorge; like a show-stopping set from *Lord of the Rings*, lights of a footpath twinkle into the distance in a cavern over 300yds long and 110yds high. It is, without hyperbole, astounding, nowhere more so than when seen from a vertiginous bridge which hangs 150ft above a torrent that thunders along the Hanke Canal before it wriggles through 5km of caverns (off-limits to the public) to the Dead Lake, where the German-Austrian triumvirate decided to call it a day. Walk through the mighty cavern, now 900ft below the surface at the deepest point, to the Bowls Hall, with bizarre limestone 'rice paddies' caused by swirling waters.

Its vaulting neighbour, Schimdl Hall, was home to Bronze Age and Iron Age settlers, who clambered down through collapsed cavern Velika Dolina (literally, big valley), from where a funicular now rises to a path towards reception or a 2km nature trail around the valley and sidekick Mala Dolina. Follow it and you'll be rewarded with excellent views over the little and large duo. In the hamlet of **Škocjan**, renovated Jurjev and J'kopin stone barns narrate respectively an intriguing chronicle of cave exploration and local ethnology (*adm free with cave ticket*).

Škofja Loka

Škofja Loka was the benevolent gift of German emperor Otto II to Freising bishops of Bavaria in AD 973. They must have been pleased, because Slovenian granddaddy 'Bishop's Meadow' is now one of the nation's charmers: light-hearted and colourful, with a dollop of culture to sate cultural appetites and a couple of joyfully frescoed churches within striking distance. Its cosy kernel at the confluence of rivers Poljane Sora and Selca Sora blossomed beneath the skirts of the bishops' '*castrum firmissimum*' of 1215, on the opposite bank from progenitor settlement Loka (today's suburb Stara Loka), and fattened up thanks to a merchant's eye for a bargain of wool, linen and leather. 14th-century traders would still recognize the single-arch **Capuchin Bridge**. Local lore relates that Bishop Leopold got in such a lather when asked to stump up the toll to cross his creation in 1381 that his horse bolted and plunged the pair into the drink; perhaps that's why the Austrians who wrested control from the bishops in 1803 added a balustrade to one of Europe's oldest bridges during 1888 renovations. The tale may also explain its statue of St John of Nepomuk, the Prague prelate tossed off the Charles Bridge by Bohemian king Wenceslas IV in 1393. The narrow stone span is christened after the Capuchin monks who pondered scripture in the 17th-century church and monastery 100yds west of the bus station; their library (*open by appointment through tourist board*) has medieval manuscripts and the *Škofja Lokia Passion* (1721), the first dramatic text (actually more an enacted procession) penned in Slovene which was premiered by a cast of 600 in 1999; the tourist board hopes to stage another performance in 2006.

Once safely across the Charles Bridge and through the Selca Gateway, one of five bastions which regulated entry to a town encircled by defence walls (1315), turn left through alleys faithful to a medieval street plan (despite the town's being reduced to ashes by Celje counts and warlike Turks in the mid-1400s) to reach the late-Gothic hall church of **St Jacob** (Šentjakobska cerkev). Its drab grey hulk hides a lovely three-

Getting There and Around

Hourly **buses** from Ljubljana take 40mins to reach Škofja Loka and cost 670 SIT single. Velosport (Poljanska 4, **t** (04) 512 32 00) and the tourist office hire **bikes** for jaunts to Crngob and Suha.

Tourist information

Škofja Loka: Mestni trg 7, **t** (04) 512 02 68, *www.skofjaloka.si*. *Open Mon–Fri 8.30–7, Sat–Sun 8.30–12.30 and 5–7.30; Oct–May Mon–Sat 8.30–7, Sun 8.30–12.30.*

Festivals

Last weekend June: the *Vererira pot* stages a medieval pageant of stalls, food and music.

July–Aug: Friday evening concerts (8 and 10pm) outside Homan House on Mestni trg.

Eating Out

Škofja Loka **t** (04) –
Kašca, Spodnji trg 1, **t** 512 43 00 (*moderate*). Hearty fillers in an unpretentious pub-cum-wine bar in Škofja Loka bishops' granary. *Closed Sun.*
Homan, Mestni trg, **t** 512 30 47 (*cheap*). The café in Škofja Loka's grandest old-timer; pizzas and pastas, plus cheesecake and gâteaux on the best terrace in town.
Pr' Starmen, Stara Loka 22, **t** 512 64 90 (*cheap*). All sorts of strange pork dishes plus veal and game are prepared in this *gostilna*. Find it by homing in on the spire of St George's,a 15-minute walk north of the bus station.

---

nave interior whose stellar vaulting billows atop columns like some exotic tent; peer into the gloom to pick out anvils, keys or shears frescoed on bosses, various guilds' shameless boasts of their donations to construction coffers. The arm of Ljubljana's Jože Plečnik reached as far as Škofja Loka – he created the chandeliers and baptismal font – but it's the Renaissance black marble altars which flank the choir that go straight to the head.

South is medieval square **Mestni trg**, relaxed and handsome focus of the smart upper town, whose three-storey, 16th-century houses boast of wealth and whose mosaic of colours has nicknamed the town 'Colourful Loka'. Square grandee is **Homan House** at the west end, a united trio of Gothic and Renaissance burgher houses daubed on the south wall with a soldier and St Christopher's legs among fishes and mermaids. Its bulk outshines the claret-red former **town hall** (Mestni trg 35), with faded Baroque frescoes, whose stolid Gothic portal leads to a Renaissance courtyard, opposite which Mary and Christ casually spear a serpent atop a Baroque pillar erected in thanks for a 1751 clean bill of health after plague. **Martin House** closes the square and once peered over the ramparts of town fortifications, here at their most extant.

That a passageway at Mestni trg 11–13 which descends to lower square **Spodnji trg** is christened 'Hell' speaks volumes about the parallel district once populated by poorer burghers. On a tatty square now blighted by traffic, shabby houses are reduced to two storeys, too great an extravagance for the old and crippled in the Špital almshouse (now flats) tacked behind the humble Baroque Špital church. Škofja Loka took more care over the Renaissance **granary** at its northern end – so valuable was its stock of grain collected as taxes that only the bishops' number one held door keys. Those ecclesiastical fathers stamped their plaque on a stone barn which now contains a restaurant (*see* 'Eating Out', above) and a **gallery** of nightmarish canvases by 20th-century artist France Mihelič (*open Tues–Sun 12–5; adm*).

The 1511 earthquake which shook Ljubljana also necessitated a rebuild of the **bishops' castle** (Loški grad), stolid and overbearing on a hilltop. Its town history museum, the **Loka Museum** (Loški muzej; *open April–Oct Tues–Sun 9–6; Nov–Mar Sat–Sun 9–5; adm*) perks up on a second floor crammed with folksy handicrafts and costume. More authentic still is 1755 **Nace's House** (Nacetova Hiša; *open Sat plus first Sun in month 10–6 or contact Tone Polenec, **t** (04) 029 59 16; adm*), where you can step into the pastoral time-capsule of one of Slovenia's most treasured remnants of rural architecture. Find it in the villagey suburb of Pustal; continue south of Spodnji trg and over the wooden Devil's Footbridge.

Modernity seems almost as remote in the hamlet of **Crngob**, 4km north of Škofja Loka (map from tourist office), renowned country-wide for a rather faded 47-part sermon of Holy Sunday dos and don'ts frescoed in 1460 on the pilgrimage **Church of the Annunciation** (Cerkev Marijinega Ozananenja). Ask for the key from the adjacent house (No.10) and you can also gawp at the razzmatazz of Slovenia's largest golden altar, a Baroque blur of nearly 100 statuettes, in an interior of painted stellar-vault cobwebs.

Such is the fame of one of Slovenia's most important frescoes that it's possible to overlook those in the diminutive Gothic church of **St John the Baptist** (Cerkev sv. Janez Krstnik) in the village of **Suha**, 2.5km east of Škofja Loka. Don't miss it – its presbytery (No.32 holds the church key) narrates colourful 16th-century bible stories and spares no detail in its *Last Judgement*.

Lake Bled

Were Walt Disney asked to mock-up a fairytale landscape, the result wouldn't be far off Lake Bled. In its absurdly picturesque locale, a Baroque church perches romantically on the islet of a lake sculled by gondolas and a picture-book medieval castle glowers on a cliff against a backcloth of alpine peaks. Small wonder that 19th-century English naturalist Sir Humphrey Davy reported that Bled was 'the most beautiful place I have seen in Europe'.

High-season crowds to Slovenia's most popular tourist destination can clot those showpieces – blame Swiss doctor Arnold Rikli, whose 1855 health spa opened the floodgates for a volume of tourists which would have spun the heads of founding 11th-century bishops – and the small modern town is very far from beautiful. But neither detract from Bled's scenic majesty. Whether by bike or boat, escape from the jolly coach groups is easy and there are wonderful walks within striking distance. *See* 'Touring from Ljubljana', pp.180–81, for more details.

Getting There

Buses which depart each hour (reduced service Sun) go north to Lake Bled in 1hr 20mins and cost 1,400 SIT single.

See pp.180 and 181 for accommodation and eating out suggestions.

Tourist Information

Bled: Cesta Svobode 11, **t** (04) 574 11 22. *Open July–Aug Mon–Sat 8am–10pm, Sun 10–10; June and Sept Mon–Sat 8–8, Sun 10–6; Mar–May and Oct Mon–Sat 8–7, Sun 9–5; Nov–Feb Mon–Sat 9–5, Sun 9–2)*. Advice on activities, from fishing to panoramic flights.

Touring from Ljubljana

Day 1: Blacksmiths and Beekeepers

Morning: Off the A2 northbound, take the A101 exit, turn off for Podbrezje, then follow signposts towards Podnart to reach **Kropa**, tucked into a valley, a village renowned in Slovenia for its blacksmith skills. Admire master-forger Joža Bertoncelj's chandeliers and wrought gratings in a museum (Kovaški muzej; *open May–Oct Tues–Fri 10–1 and 3–6; Mar–April and Nov–Dec Wed, Sat, Sun 10–12 and 3–5; adm*), which traces the beginning of a trade honed after the 15th-century discovery of nearby iron ore; you can pick up the work of modern artisans in the UKO workshop (*open Mon–Fri 7–3 (July–Aug 7–7), Sat 9–12*) opposite. Then hunt out iron headstones (including Bertoncelj's) in the churchyard of Gothic church of St Leonard (Cerkev sv. Lenarta), with lovely views of the village from its hillside perch.

Lunch: In Kropa, *see below*.

Afternoon: Backtrack out of the village to reach **Radovljica**. A dreary modern town conceals historic kernel Linhartov trg, where colourful Gothic and Renaissance buildings testify to the wealth of medieval merchants. The Baroque stucco Thurn Manor is now home of the Museum of Apiculture (Čebelarski muzej; *open May–Oct Tues–Sun 10–1 and 3–6; Mar–April and Nov–Dec Wed, Sat, Sun 10–12 and 3–5; adm*), which tells the story of Slovenian beekeeping. Renaissance older sister Šivčeva House has a Gothic interior used as a gallery, and the church of St Peter (Cerkev sv. Petar) features a Baroque altar by Ljubljana cathedral architect Angelo Pozzo. Continue north to **Lake Bled**.

Dinner and Sleeping: In Bled, *see below*.

Day 1

Lunch in Kropa

Gostilna Pr' Kovač, Kropa 30, t (04) 533 63 20 (*moderate*). A taste of tradition in a snug inn near the museum: start with bean soups, then tuck into two-person meat-feast *kovaška plošča* (blacksmith's plate).

Pri Jarmu, Kropa 2, t (04) 533 67 50 (*cheap*). Pizzas and light bites in a bar-cum-pizzeria, whose welcome is not nearly as gruff as its patrons would have you believe.

Dinner in Bled

Okarina, Riklijeva 9, t (04) 574 14 58 (*expensive–moderate*). Quietly classy dining in a culinary aristocrat of Bled whose talented chef does inventive things with Slovene dishes. There's also excellent Indian cuisine and a vegetarians menu.

Ribič, Cesta Svobode 27, t (04) 576 83 20 (*moderate*). Reserve a terrace table for lake and castle views in a speciality fish restaurant – expect a haul of Adriatic fishes plus salmon and trout with figs and almonds.

Pri Planincu, Grajska cesta 8, t (04) 574 16 13 (*cheap*). Just downhill, this ever-busy bar-restaurant serves pub-grub in vast portions.

Sleeping in Bled

Grand Hotel Toplice, Cesta svobode 12, t (04) 569 10 00 (*expensive*). Five-star comforts and yesteryear opulence unite in a hotel which recalls roots as a *fin-de-siècle grande dame*.

Villa Bled, Cesta Svobode 26, t (04) 579 15 00 (*expensive*). President Tito would recognize the marble walls and 1950s furnishings of his lakeside retreat southwest of the centre, now a Relais & Chateaux luxury hotel.

Penzion Mayer, Želeška 7, t (04) 574 10 58 (*inexpensive*). Cosy, homely rooms in an alpine-style house above the lake. Its restaurant (*moderate; closed Mon*) is one of Bled's finest with a menu of exquisite national dishes.

Day 2: Around Lake Bled

Morning: A placid glacial lake, a church romantically sited on an island, a medieval castle and the backcloth of the Alps elevate **Bled** to Slovenia's premier tourist resort. Begin your exploration in the nation's oldest castle (Blejski grad), a fairytale vision on a cliff whose first incarnation in 1004 as a stronghold of the Bishops of Brixen founded Bled. Largely rebuilt in the 16th century, then renovated in Baroque, it houses a so-so museum (*open daily May–Oct 9–8; Nov–April 9–5; adm*), with jaw-dropping views, which evokes feudal high-living in weaponry and furniture. Don't miss its lovely Gothic chapel whose frescoes salute Heinrich II and wife Kunigunde, saintly donors of the estate to the bishops, before you succumb to the Baroque Church of the Assumption (Cerkev Marijinega Venbovzetja) on an islet reached by gondolas (return 2,400 SIT) or rowing boats (*see* below), with lovely Gothic frescoes and foundations of the first Romanesque church seen through glass.

Lunch: In and around Lake Bled, *see* below.

Afternoon: Pootle on or beside the lake: Bled tourist agency Kompass (Ljubljanska 4) hires bikes (*2,200 SIT/half-day*); rent a rowing boat at the swimming area of Castle Baths (*2,300 SIT*); or take a horse-drawn carriage round the lake (*4,500 SIT*). Alternatively, drive 4km north to Podham then follow signs to the **Vintgar Gorge** (*open daily April–Oct 8–7; adm*); a 1.6km walkway clings to ravine walls above the Radovna river and twists 1.6km to the Šum waterfall. Explorers can follow trails to cave Pokljuka Luknja in the magnificent **Pokljuka Gorge** (Krnica, 7km west of Bled, right at bus station, then signs to Pokljuška soteska); the tourist office (Cesta svobode 11) stocks hiking maps. Return to Bled then go west to Lake Bohinj for the night.

Dinner and Sleeping: In Bela and/or Ribčev Laz, *see* below.

Day 2

Lunch in Bled

Park Hotel Café, Cesta Svobode 15, **t** (04) 579 30 00 (*cheap*). Pastas and cold platters plus the usual pork and trout (and famous cream cakes) on the best terrace in town – wait rather than suffer the cafeteria-style interior.

Lunch in Podham

Gostilna Vintgar, Podham 62, **t** (04) 572 52 62 (*moderate*). Fill up before a stroll in the Vintgar Gorge on fresh trout stuffed with buckwheat or mushrooms in a streamside alpine-style charmer before the walkway.

Dinner in Bela

Rot Bohinjska, Bela 34, **t** (04) 572 00 72 (*moderate*). Bled locals wax lyrical about the Slovene cuisine of this traditional *gostilna* 4km west on the Bohinj road. Excellent trout comes straight from the tank and there's a

tasty goulash venison, or choose farmer's platter *kmečka pojedino*, a huge plate of ham, pork, sausages, potatoes and cabbage.

Dinner and Sleeping in Ribčev Laz

Dining is in hotels of main village Ribčev Laz; lovely village alternatives are listed in Day 3.

Bellevue, Ribčev Laz 65, **t** (04) 572 33 33 (*moderate*). The fact that rooms are not the most modern just adds to the fuzzy yesteryear nostalgia of the secluded hotel where Agatha Christie stayed; refuse to be palmed off with adjacent Savica Annexe.

Jezero, Ribčev Laz 51, **t** (04) 572 91 00 (*moderate*). More comfortable is this central four-star with a pool and good restaurant. Category I rooms are modern and bright; category II are rather dated but cheaper.

Kristal, Ribčev Laz 4a, **t** (04) 577 82 00 (*inexpensive*). A cheerful *pension* at the village entrance whose chef prepares tasty Slovene fare; try stewed veal with cranberries.

Day 3: Lake Bohinj: A Mystery Retreat?

Morning: Crowd-puller Bled preserves the allure of brooding **Lake Bohinj** to the west; Agatha Christie dodged deadlines and dreamed up dastardly plots here, although she refused to tarnish in fiction a lake 'too beautiful for a murder'. Alongside natural beauty, the lake is famous for the fabulously frescoed church of St John (Cerkev sv. Janeva Krstnika) in principal village **Ribčev Laz**. Take your time to digest its Gothic narrative whose plot wanders from the decapitation of its patron to include Cain and Abel, St George and his dragon and the apostles. If it's locked, the tourist office (Ribčev Laz 48) has the key. Then stroll 1.5km east to the village of **Stara Fužina**, where the Alpine Dairy Museum (Planšarski muzej; *open July–Aug Tues–Sun 11–7; Sept–Oct and Jan–June 10–12 and 4–6; adm*) tells the story of Slovenia's lushest dairy region. The next village, **Studor**, has Oplen House (Oplenova hiša; *same hours; adm*), a time-capsule of peasants' lives during the industry's late-1800s heyday.

Lunch: In Stara Fužina or **Srednja Vas**, *see* below.

Afternoon: Return to the lake. For a stroll, follow a footpath which ambles along the tranquil, wooded north bank. Otherwise drive along the south bank to the village of **Ukanc** where a cable car (*open daily summer 8–8; winter 9–4*) hums up to ski runs at 1,535m/5,036ft. Take the road away from the lake to reach the 200ft plume of the **Savica waterfall** (Slap Savica; *open daily July–Aug 9–6, April–June, Sept–Oct 9–5; adm; Nov– Mar adm free*). Backtrack to Bled and turn north towards Jesenice to pick up the road to **Kranjska Gora**. Chalet Liznjek House (Liznejekova Hiša; *Borovška cesta 63; open Tues–Fri 10–5, Sat–Sun 10–4; closed April and Nov; adm*) is a snapshot of traditional life-styles now vanished in an alpine village reinvented as a ski resort.

Dinner and Sleeping: In Kranjska Gora, *see* below.

Day 3

Lunch in Stara Fužina

Planšar, Stara Fužina 179, no tel (*cheap*). A taste of the traditions you've learned about in the Dairy Museum, with tangy soft cheeses plus yesteryear dairy delights curd pie and sour milk. Fatten up for a walk on herder's choice cereal-based dishes.

Mihovic, Stara Fužina 118, no tel (*cheap*). A good old *gostilna* that's a credit to its breed; robust pork fillets and steaks are rustled up in a country inn with a pleasant terrace.

Lunch in Srednja Vas

Gostilna Rupa, Srednja Vas 87, 3km east of Studor, t (04) 572 34 01 (*moderate*). Trout plucked from the lake is grilled with parsley and garlic or in breadcrumbs and in summer (*on Thurs*) there's spit-roast suckling pig in the the Bohinj region's most charming *gostilna*, twee and rustic. *Closed Mon*.

Dinner and Sleeping in Kranjska Gora

Lipa, Koroška cesta 14, t (04) 582 00 00 (*moderate*). Steaks are laced with truffles, there's game goulash, and venison comes with doughy potato dumplings in the classy restaurant of a family *pension* with quietly classy rooms (*moderate*).

Gostilna Cvitar, Borovška cesta 83, t (04) 558 36 00 (*cheap*). Locals' choice for a good-value feed, with surprisingly classy décor in dining rooms and a terrace on the central square.

Miklič, Vitranška 13, t (04) 588 16 35 (*moderate*). A friendly family *pension* – bright rooms are modern and cheerful – with one of Kranjska Gora's finest restaurants (*expensive*). Upmarket rustic flavours such as venison with wild berries and mushrooms star, but there are also Adriatic fishes.

Prisank, Borovška 99, t (04) 588 41 00 (*moderate*). Not as characterful, perhaps, but four-star creature comforts in a smart hotel with spa and pool.

Day 4: Into the Julian Alps and to Kobarid

Morning: Now for the full jaw-dropping splendour of the Julian Alps. Fifty hairpin bends twist up, up and over the **Vršič Pass** on Slovenia's most scenic drive. In winter double-check conditions with Kranjska Gora locals before climbing a link-road dug in horrific conditions by 10,000 Russian prisoners of war. They erected the Russian Chapel to lament comrades killed by an avalanche in March 1916 and saluted fallen brothers in arms in a military graveyard (after bend 21). Park at a hostel-restaurant at 1,525m/5,000ft to explore footpaths in the shadow of Mojstrovka (2,366m/7,762ft) and Prisojinik (2,547m/8,356ft), or continue over the 1,611m pass to gawp at tiers of mountains as you descend. Sidetrack off bend 49 to the **source of the Soča river**, which gushes from a magical pool in a cleft and tumbles down to the Adriatic.

Lunch: Around the Vršič Pass or around the source of the Soča, *see* below.

Afternoon: Continue downhill on the main road past alpine botanic garden **Alpinum Juliana** (*open May–Sept 8.30–6.30*) to the village of **Trenta**, renowned for mountain guides celebrated in a museum of fauna and ethnology (*open daily April– Oct 10–6; adm*) in the Triglav National Park. Follow the china-blue Soča beloved by white-water rafters (*1½hr trips in Bovec, April–Oct, c. 7,500 SIT; kayak hire 4,600 SIT/ half-day*) past the **Boka waterfall**, a 350ft curtain 6km south of Bovec, to lovely **Kobarid**. Hemingway's 'little white town with a campanile in a valley' (*A Farewell To Arms*) mourns the horrific trench warfare between Italy and Austria on the Soča Front broken by the world's first *Blitzkrieg* (24 October 1917) in the moving Kobarid Museum (Kobariški muzej; *open April–Sept Mon–Fri 9–6, Sat–Sun 9–7; Oct–Mar Mon–Fri 10–5, Sat–Sun 9–6; adm; ask about audiovisual presentation in English*).

Dinner and Sleeping: In Kobarid or Staro Selo, *see* below.

Day 4

Lunch at the Vršič Pass
Tičarjev Dom na Vršiču, Vršič Pass, no tel (*cheap*). The menu of the hostel on the pass is stolid hikers' stuff, but, oh, the views – a panorama of peaks beyond a valley. It's closed late Oct to mid-April, when you can tuck into soups and sausages in lodge Erjavčeva Koča na Vršiču before the pass.

Lunch around the Source of the Soča
Kekčeva Domačija, Trenta 76, t (05) 381 10 88 (*moderate*). A lovely chalet in a picture-post-card valley, where authentic Slovene rustic fare is served in a folksy dining room. Spend a day pottering alpine paths and it can offer four homely apartments (*moderate*). A gem.

Dinner and Sleeping in Kobarid
Breza, Mučeniška ulica 17, t (05) 389 00 41 (*moderate*). Delicious home cooking –

sausages, venison and goulash – in an enjoy-ably old-fashioned place behind the Hvala.
Hvala, Trg Svobode 1, t (05) 389 93 00 (*moderate*). Kobarid's premier address is a stylish modern number, designer in style without showing off, with a gourmet fish restaurant, **Topli Val** (*expensive*); try the daily specials or treat yourself to a nibble of every-thing on a house-special fishy platter.
Koltar, Trg Svobode 11, t (05) 389 11 10 (*inexpensive*). Excellent value, modern rooms and top-notch seafood (*expensive*) served in a characterful restaurant hung with sails.

Dinner and Sleeping in Staro Selo
Hiša Franko, Staro Selo, 1.3km west of Kobarid, t (05) 389 41 20 (*moderate*). Slick streamlined style is softened by a sigh of romance in this classy boutique hotel where a gourmet chef dreams up daring international dishes too beautiful to eat; faced with such abundance, a €41 tasting menu is a godsend.

Day 5: Mercury and Old Lace

Morning: After the museum, now for the real thing – the Kobarid Historical Tour embarks from the north side of Trg Svobode to tour Italian defences plus the Middle Ages foundations of Tonocov Grad, a hill fort occupied since the Stone Age, and an impressive waterfall, all to a backcloth of the Alps. Your guide is a free leaflet from the Kobarid Museum. Even reluctant walkers should stroll to the first stop, the Italian Charnel House, where lie the bones of over 7,000 soldiers listed on green-grey slabs beneath Baroque St Anthony's Church. Then leave Kobarid and drive east to **Tolmin**, with a regional museum (Tolminski muzej; *open Tues–Fri 9–4, Sat–Sun 1–5; adm*) of twee rustic furniture and serious archaeology from prehistory to the early Middle Ages, then drive 2km north (signposted or maps from tourist informa-tion, Petra Skalarja 4, **t** (05) 381 00 84) to explore footpaths through the ravines of the **Tolminska Gorge** (Tolminska korita).

Lunch: In Tolmin or nearby **Zatolmin**, *see below*.

Afternoon: Allow an hour to drive east to **Idrija**, famous for mercury-mining and for exquisite lace. It was the former which elevated Idrija to second national town after Ljubljana and filled the coffers since 1500, when the first shovelful of earth was dug from Anthony's Main Road Mine (*open Mon–Fri 10–3, Sat–Sun 10, 3, 4; adm*); descend into tunnels braced with tree trunks and which squirrel away their own chapel. For claustrophobes, a town museum (Mestni muzej; *open daily 9–6; adm*) in the jaunty Renaissance Gewerkenegg castle details the mercury obsession and celebrates local lacemaking in bobbins and bravauras at the Lace School (Čipkarska šola; *open Mon–Fri 8–3; adm*). A gallery opposite the museum sells dainty samplers.

Dinner and Sleeping: In Idrija, Spodnja Idrija or Razpotje, *see below*.

Day 5

Lunch in Tolmin

Krn, Mestni trg 3, **t** (05) 388 19 11 (*moderate*). Forgive the dreary décor of this hotel restau-rant; come for the Slovene cuisine of its chef, who adds neat touches of truffles and wine sauces and prepares a delicate Soča trout.

Rutar, Mestni trg 1, **t** (05) 380 05 00 (*moderate*). Be prepared to wait for a table in Tolmin's favourite Italian. Yes, there are pastas for light bites, but the chef truly enjoys himself when preparing creamy *carne* and *pesca*.

Lunch in Zatolmin

Zatolmin, Zatolmin 4, 2km north of Tolmin via Gregorčičeva ulica on central crossroads, **t** (05) 388 25 33 (*moderate*). A local star, always busy – snaffle a conservatory table for a lazy lunch. An expansive menu features a herd of steak and flock of turkey dishes.

Dinner and Sleeping in Idrija

Pra Škafarju, Ulica sv Barbare 9, **t** (05) 377 32 40 (*cheap*). There are the usual steaks and horse fillets, but cartwheel-sized pizzas pack 'em into this central *gostilna*. *Closed Tues*.

Gostišče Barbara, Kosovelova 3, **t** (05) 377 11 62 (*inexpensive*). Book ahead to secure Idrija's only accommodation, a simple but comfy enough inn above the Anthony Mine.

Dinner and Sleeping in Spodnja Idrija

Kendov dvorec, Na griču 2 **t** (05) 377 25 100 (*expensive*). Backtrack 4km on the Tolmin road for a night of antiques and lace linen in a romantic Relais & Chateaux traditional 14th-century mansion; *reservation essential*.

Dinner and Sleeping in Razpotje

Fortuna, Idršek 1a, **t** (05) 37 79 149 (*inexpensive*). Alternatively, turn off at signs for Žiri for a modest family three-star, serving up home cooking with produce from the family farm.

Italy:
Travel, Practical A–Z and Language

12

Travel

Entry Formalities

Passports and Visas

You need a valid passport. EU, US, Canadian and Australian nationals do not need a visa to enter Italy for stays of up to 90 days. You must register with the police within 8 days of your arrival; a hotel will do it for you.

Customs

EU nationals over the age of 17 can now import a limitless amount of goods for their personal use. Arrivals from non-EU countries have to pass through Italian Customs. For more information, US citizens can look at *www.customs.gov*.

Getting Around

By Train

Trenitalia t 892 021; www.trenitalia.com

Italy's national railway, now repackaged as Trenitalia, is well run and often a pleasure to ride. There are also several private rail lines.

There is a strict hierarchy of **trains**. Faster trains often carry an obligatory seat reservation requirement and usually require a supplement. The *Eurostar* is the fastest, followed by the *Eurocity* and *Intercity* trains, then the *Diretto* or *Interregionale*, and then the humble *Regionale*.

Train **fares** have increased greatly over the last couple of years. There are several Trenitalia Passes for non-Italians, in versions for individuals, under-26s and groups of up to five.

On Friday nights, weekends and in the summer, **reserve a seat** in advance (*fare una prenotazione*). **Tickets** may be purchased at the station or at many travel agents;. Do check when you buy your ticket in advance that the date is correct; tickets are only valid the day they're bought unless you specify otherwise.

Always remember to **stamp your ticket** (*convalidare*) in the yellow machine at the head of the platform before boarding. If you get on a train without a ticket you can buy one from the conductor. Be sure you ask which **platform** (*binario*) your train will come into; the boards are not always correct.

Details on tickets, discount passes and advance reservations are available at:

Rail Europe, UK: 178 Piccadilly, London W1, **t** 08705 848 848, *www.raileurope.co.uk*; USA and Canada: *www.raileurope.com*.

Ffestiniog Travel, t (01766) 512400, *www.fest travel.co.uk*. Can book Eurostars, intercity trains throughout Europe, rail-sea-rail journeys and every kind of rail pass.

Trains Europe, *www.trainseurope.co.uk*.

By Coach and Bus

Inter-city coach travel is sometimes quicker than train travel, but also a bit more expensive. You will find regular coach/bus connections only where there is no train.

Coaches almost always depart from the vicinity of the train station, and tickets usually need to be purchased before you get on, from a booth or one of the nearby bars. If you can't get a ticket before the coach leaves, get on anyway and ask the driver.

By Car

While virtually all the day trips we propose are accessible by public transport, you may decide to hire a car if you plan to follow the touring itineraries suggested in this guide.

Signposting is generally good, roads are well maintained, and for touring a car gives immeasurable freedom. Buy a good road map (the Italian Touring Club series is excellent). The **Automobile Club of Italy** (ACI, *www.aci.it*) is a good friend to the foreign motorist. They can be reached from anywhere by dialling **t** 116 – also use this number to find the nearest service station.

Petrol (*benzina*: unleaded is *benzina senza piombo*, and diesel *gasolio*) is still expensive in Italy (around €1/litre). Many petrol stations close for lunch in the afternoon, and few stay open late at night, although you may find a 'self-service' where you feed a machine nice, smooth notes. Services can be hard to find in remote areas and are generally closed all afternoon. **Motorway** (*autostrada*) **tolls** are quite high, but rest stops and petrol stations along the motorways stay open 24hrs.

Third-party **insurance** is a minimum requirement in Italy. Extend your cover if necessary to ensure you are fully covered for driving in Italy, and keep your documents to hand as proof. Also get hold of a **European Accident**

Statement form, which may simplify things if you are unlucky enough to have an accident. Always insist on a full translation of any statement you are asked to sign.

Speed limits (generally ignored) are officially 130kph on motorways, 110km/hr on main highways, 90kph on secondary roads and 50kph in built-up areas. Speeding **fines** may be up to €250, or €50 for jumping a red light.

Hiring a Car

Hiring a car (*autonoleggio*) in Italy is simple but not particularly cheap. Some companies require a deposit amounting to the estimated cost of the hire. A small car (e.g. Fiat Punto) with unlimited mileage and collision damage waiver, including tax, will cost around €40 per day although, for longer rentals, this will decrease slightly pro rata. The minimum age limit is usually 25 (sometimes 23) and the driver must have held their licence for over a year – this must be produced, along with the driver's passport and credit card, when hiring the car. It is probably easiest to arrange your hire with a domestic firm before you depart and to check out fly-drive discounts.

Car hire firms are listed for the larger towns in this book, and most major rental firms have offices in airports or main train stations.

Practical A–Z
Crime and the Police

Police **t** 113

In Italy, there is a fair amount of petty crime – purse-snatchers, car break-ins, etc. – but violent crime is rare. Be careful in crowded places and stations, don't leave valuables in hotel rooms and don't carry too much cash.

There are three types of **police** in Italy: the national, quasi-military *Carabinieri*, clad in black; the more local *Polizia Urbana*; and the *Vigili Urbani*, who are mainly concerned with directing traffic and handing out fines.

Disabled Travellers

Recent access-for-all laws in Italy have improved the once dire situation: the number of ramps and stair lifts has increased probably a hundredfold in the past few years, and

nearly every hotel has one or two rooms with facilities for the disabled – although the older ones may not have a lift, or not one large enough for a wheelchair. Local tourist offices are helpful.

Thanks to the efforts of **Venice**'s Institute for Architecture and its *Veneziapertutti* (Venice For All) campaign launched several years ago, the labyrinth opened up a little for visitors with disabilities or limited access. The city's 407 bridges still present the major obstacle in getting around, but by judicious use of the *vaporetti* a good proportion of the city becomes accessible. The tourist office's Venice–Lido map no.1 indicates the parts of the city easily accessible by wheelchair.

Electricity

Your electrical appliances will work if you adapt them to run on 220v AC with two round prongs on the plug. American appliances need transformers as well.

Embassies and Consulates

Italian Embassies Abroad

UK: 38 Eaton Place, London SW1 8AN, **t** (020) 7235 9371; 32 Melville St, Edinburgh EH3 7HA, **t** (0131) 226 3631, *www.embitaly.org.uk.*
USA: 690 Park Ave, New York, NY, **t** (212) 737 9100, *www.italconsulnyc.org*; 12400 Wilshire Bd, Suite 300, Los Angeles, CA, **t** (310) 820 0622, *www.conlang.com.*
Canada: 136 Beverley St, Toronto M5T 1Y5, **t** (416) 977 1566, *www.italconsulate.org.*

Foreign Embassies in Italy

UK: Piazzale Donatori di Sangue 2/5, Venice-Mestre, **t** 041 505 5990, *www.britain.it.*
USA: Via V. Veneto 119a, Rome, **t** 06 46741, *www.usembassy.it.*
Canada: Via Zara 30, Rome, **t** 06 445 981, *www.canada.it.*

Health and Insurance

Ambulance (ambulanza) **t** 113
Fire **t** 115

In an **emergency**, call an ambulance or ask for the nearest hospital (*ospedale*). Less serious problems can be treated at a *pronto soccorso* (casualty department) at any hospital clinic (*ambulatorio*), or at a local health unit (Unità Sanitariale Locale – USL). Airports and major train stations also have **first-aid posts** and pharmacists are trained to advise on minor ills. Dispensing **chemists** (*farmacie*) are usually open 8.30–1 and 4–8. Big towns will have a 24hr *farmacia*; others take turns to open overnight (the address rota is posted in the window).

EU citizens who carry their **E111 form** (to be replaced by a card from December 2005) are entitled to reciprocal health care on Italy's National Health Service and a 90% discount on prescriptions. The E111 should cover you for emergencies, but does not cover all medical expenses (e.g. no repatriation costs and no private treatment). If you have to pay for any treatment, make sure you get a receipt, so that you can claim for reimbursement later.

Non-EU citizens should check that they have adequate insurance for any medical expenses plus the cost of returning home. Sporting accidents are rarely covered by ordinary insurance.

Money and Banks

The **euro** is the official currency in Italy. Euros come in denominations of €500, €200, €100, €50, €20, €10 and €5 (banknotes) and €2, €1, 50 cents, 20 cents, 10 cents, 5 cents, 2 cents and 1 cent (coins).

Most **ATMs** (*Bancomats* – automatic cash dispensers) will spout cash with your bank card and PIN – for a significant commission – but check with your bank first. They also take Eurocheque cards and **credit cards**. Large hotels, shops and car-hire firms will accept plastic as well; smaller places may not. Visa, American Express and Diner's are more widely accepted than MasterCard (Access).

The major **banks and exchange bureaux** licensed by the Bank of Italy give the best exchange rates for currency or traveller's cheques. Hotels, private exchanges in resorts and FS-run exchanges at train stations usually have less advantageous rates, but are open outside normal banking hours. In addition there are exchange offices at most airports.

For the latest exchange rates, see *www.xe.com/ucc*.

National Holidays

1 Jan New Year's Day
6 Jan Epiphany
Easter Monday
25 April Liberation Day
1 May Labour Day
2 June
15 Aug Assumption, or *Ferragosto*, the climax of the Italian holiday season
1 Nov All Saints' Day
8 Dec Immaculate Conception
25 Dec Christmas Day
26 Dec *Santo Stefano*, St Stephen's Day

Opening Hours

Although it varies between regions, most of Italy closes down at 1pm until 3 or 4pm. Afternoon hours are from 4–7, often 5–8 in the summer. Some cities close down completely during August. Don't be surprised if a place is unexpectedly closed (or open).

In general, Sunday afternoons and Mondays are dead periods for the sightseer.

Banks: Open Mon–Fri 8.30–1 and 3–4.
Shops: Open Mon–Sat 8–1 and 3.30–7.30. Some supermarkets and department stores stay open all day. Hours vary according to season.
Museums: Italy has a hard time financing the preservation of its cultural heritage, so it's wise to check at the tourist office on exactly what is open and what is 'temporarily' closed before setting off. Entrance charges vary widely; major sights may be €6 or more, others may be free.
Churches: All churches, except for the biggest cathedrals and basilicas, close in the afternoon at the same hours as the shops, and the little ones tend to stay closed. If there's no caretaker to keep an eye out, churches are usually locked. If you've come for the art, don't come during services, always keep some small change for the light machines (in case the work you want to see needs to be illuminated).

Post

La posta italiana is one of the most expensive and slowest **postal services** in Europe. Offices are open Mon–Sat 8–1; in cities 8–6/7.

Stamps (*francobolli*) are available in post offices or at tobacconists (*tabacchi*, identified by blue signs with a white T). Prices fluctuate.

Price Categories

Hotels
Hotel prices are for a double room with bath/shower in high season.

luxury over €230
very expensive €150–230
expensive €100–150
moderate €60–100
inexpensive under €60

Restaurants
Restaurant categories are for set menus or a two-course meal for one without wine.

very expensive over €45
expensive €30–45
moderate €20–30
cheap under €20

Telephones

Most **phone booths** now take either coins or phone cards (*schede telefoniche*), costing €3, €5 or €10; the latter are available at tobacconists and news-stands – snap off the small perforated corner or they won't work. In smaller villages you can usually find *telefoni a scatti*, with a meter attached, in at least one bar (usually charging a small fee).

To make a reverse charge call (*a erre*), you need to go to the offices of Telecom Italia. To **call Italy from abroad**, the international dialling code is 39.

For **international calls** from Italy, dial 00, then dial the country code (UK 44; USA and Canada 1; Ireland 353), then the local code (minus the 0) and number. The area code must always be dialled even within the region.

Calls within Italy are cheapest after 10pm; international calls after 11pm.

Time

Italy is on Central European Time, one hour ahead of Greenwich Mean Time and 6hrs ahead of Eastern Standard Time. From the last weekend of March to the end of September, Italian Summer Time is in effect – i.e. clocks go forward one hour in March.

Tipping

When you eat out, mentally add to the bill (*conto*) the bread and cover charge (*pane e coperto*, €2–4), and a 15% service charge. This is often included in the bill (*servizio compreso*); if not, it will say *servizio non compreso* and you'll have to do your own arithmetic. Additional tipping is at your own discretion, but never do it in family-run places as you may offend.

Tourist Information

Known as EPT, APT or AAST, information booths provide hotel lists, town plans and information on local sights and transport. Nearly every city and province has a web page.
UK, Italian State Tourist Board, 1 Princes Street, London W1R 8AY, **t** (020) 7408 1254, **f** (020) 7493 6695, *www.italiantourism.com*.
USA, 630 Fifth Ave, Suite 1565, New York, NY 10111, **t** (212) 245 5095/4822, **f** (212) 586 9249; 12400 Wilshire Blvd, Suite 550, Los Angeles, CA 90025, **t** (310) 820 1898/9807, **f** (310) 820 6357; 500 N. Michigan Ave, Suite 2240, Chicago 1 IL 60611, **t** (312) 644 0996, **f** (312) 644 3019, *www.italiantourism.com*.
Canada: 175 Bloor St E, Suite 907, South Tower, Toronto M4W 3R8, **t** (416) 925 4882, *www.italiantourism.com*.

Language

Italians are not especially adept at learning other languages. However, at most hotels and restaurants there will be someone who speaks some English.

Pronunciation

Italian words are pronounced phonetically. Every vowel and consonant except 'h' is sounded. **Consonants** are the same as in English, with the following exceptions:
The **c**, when followed by an 'e' or 'i', is pronounced like the English 'ch' (*cinque* thus becomes cheen-quay). Italian **g** is also soft

before 'i' or 'e' as in *gira*, or jee-rah. *Z* is pronounced like 'ts'. The consonants *sc* before the vowels 'i' or 'e' become like the English 'sh', as in sci, pronounced 'shee'. The combination *ch* is pronouced like a 'k', as in *Chianti*, 'kee-an-tee'. The combination *gn* is pronounced as 'nya' (thus *bagno* is pronounced ban-yo). The combination *gli* is pronounced like the middle of the word million (so *Castiglione* is pronounced Ca-steel-yoh-nay).

Vowel pronunciation is as follows:
A is as in English *father*.
E when unstressed is pronounced like 'a' in *fate* (as in *mele*); when stressed it can be the same or like the 'e' in *pet* (*bello*).
I is like the 'i' in *machine*.
O, like 'e', has two sounds, 'o' as in *hope* when unstressed (*tacchino*), and usually 'o' as in *rock* when stressed (*morte*).
U is pronounced like the 'u' in *June*.

The **stress** usually (but not always!) falls on the penultimate syllable. Accents indicate if it falls elsewhere (as in *città*). Also note that in the big northern cities, the informal way of addressing someone as you, *tu*, is widely used; the more formal *lei* or *voi* is commonly used in provincial districts, *voi* more in the south.

Useful Vocabulary

yes/no/maybe *sì/no/forse*
I don't know *Non (lo) so*
I don't understand (Italian) *Non capisco (l'italiano)*
Does someone here speak English? *C'è qualcuno qui che parla inglese?*
Speak slowly *Parla lentamente*
Help! *Aiuto!*
Please *Per favore*
Thank you (very much) *Grazie molte/mille*
You're welcome *Prego*
It doesn't matter *Non importa*
All right *Va bene*
Excuse me/I'm sorry *Permesso/Mi scusi/ Mi dispiace*
How are you? *Come sta?*
Well, and you? *Bene, e Lei?/e tu?*
Hello *Salve or ciao (both informal)*
Good morning *Buongiorno (formal hello)*
Good afternoon, evening *Buonasera*
Goodnight *Buona notte*
Goodbye *Arrivederci/Ciao (informal)*
What?/Who?/Where? *Che?/Chi?/Dove?*

When?/Why? *Quando?/Perché?*
How? *Come?*
How much (does it cost? *Quanto (costa)?*
I am sorry *Mi dispiace*
Leave me alone *Lasciami in pace*

Days, Months and Time

Monday *lunedì*
Tuesday *martedì*
Wednesday *mercoledì*
Thursday *giovedì*
Friday *venerdì*
Saturday *sàbato*
Sunday *doménica*

January *gennaio*
February *febbraio*
March *marzo*
April *aprile*
May *maggio*
June *giugnio*
July *luglio*
August *agosto*
September *settembre*
October *ottobre*
November *novembre*
December *dicembre*

weekdays *feriali*
morning/afternoon *mattina/pomeriggio*
evening *sera*
yesterday/today *ieri/oggi*
tomorrow *domani*

Numbers

1 *uno/una*
2/3/4 *due/tre/quattro*
5/6/7 *cinque/sei/sette*
8/9/10 *otto/nove/dieci*
11/12 *undici/dodici*
13/14 *tredici/quattordici*
15/16 *quindici/sedici*
17/18/19 *diciassette/diciotto/diciannove*
20 *venti*
21/22 *ventuno/ventidue*
30/40/50 *trenta/quaranta/cinquanta*
60/70/80/90 *sesanta/settanta/ottanta/novanta*
100 *cento*
101 *centuno*
200 *duecento*
1,000 *mille*
one million *un milione*

Italy:
Food and Drink

13

There are those who eat to live and those who live to eat, and then there are the Italians, for whom food has an almost religious significance. For the visitor this culinary obsession is an added bonus – along with Italy's sights, and the warm sun on your back, you can enjoy some of the best tastes and smells the world can offer.

Eating Out

Breakfast (*colazione*) in Italy is an early morning wake-up shot to the brain: a *cappuccino* (*espresso* with hot foamy milk), a *caffè latte* (white coffee) or a *caffè lungo* (a generous *espresso*), accompanied by a croissant-type roll (*cornetto* or *briosca*). Breakfast in most Italian hotels seldom represents great value. **Lunch** (*pranzo*), served around 1pm, is the most important meal of the day, with a minimum of a first course (*primo piatto* – any kind of pasta dish, broth or soup), a second course (*secondo piatto* – a meat dish, with a *contorno* or side dish), followed by fruit or dessert and coffee. You can begin with a platter of *antipasti*. *Cena*, the **evening meal**, is much the same as *pranzo* although lighter, without the pasta: a *pizza* and beer, eggs or a fish dish.

The various terms for types of **restaurants** – *ristorante*, *trattoria* or *osteria* – have been confused, so that a *trattoria* or *osteria* can be just as elaborate as a restaurant, though a *ristorante* is rarely as informal as a *trattoria*. Invariably the least expensive eating place is the *vino e cucina*, serving simple cuisine for simple everyday prices. Eating out in Italy is not the bargain it used to be, but in many places you'll find a choice of set menus which are cheaper than eating *à la carte*. A *menu turistico* offers full, set meals of usually meagre inspiration for a reasonable set price; a *menu degustazione* is the gourmet option. Bars often double as *paninotecas* (serving sandwiches or *tramezzini*, little sandwiches), and *pizza* by the slice (*al taglio*) is common in cities.

Regional Specialities

In Northern Italy, look for heavier dishes prepared with butter and cream. *Pasta all'uovo* and *risotto* are favourite first courses, while game dishes, liver, *bollito misto* (mixed boiled meats), *fritto misto* (mixed fried meats), sausages and seafood appear as main courses. In the Veneto, a typical seashore meal might include oysters or *sarde in saor* (marinated sardines) followed by *risi e bisi* (rice and peas, cooked with Parma ham and Parmesan) or Venice's favourite pasta, *bigoli in salsa* (thick spaghetti, served with a piquant onion, butter and anchovy sauce). *Secondi* range from *fegato alla veneziana* (liver and onions) to *seppie alla veneziana* (cuttlefish in its own ink). I

Seafood is prominent in the Marches (around Ancona), along with a fancier version of lasagne called *vincisgrassi* and stuffed fried olives. The Abruzzo (around Pescara) is a region known for its game dishes, sheep cheese, saffron and its quality pasta. The further south you go, the spicier things get, and the richer the puddings and cakes. Southern Italy is the land of home-made pasta, vegetables and superb seafood; its specialities are often seasoned with capers, anchovies, lemon juice, olives and fennel.

Italy is a country where everyday wine is cheaper than Coca-Cola or milk. There is a bewildering array of regional wines, many of which are rarely exported because they are best drunk young. Unless you're at a restaurant with an exceptional cellar, do as the Italians do and order the local wine (*vino locale* or *vino della casa*).

Italy: Trieste, Venice and the Northern Adriatic Coast

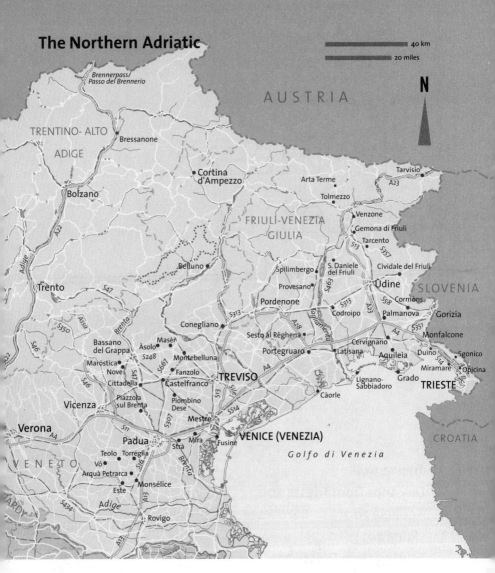

The Northern Adriatic

40 km
20 miles

N

AUSTRIA

TRENTINO- ALTO
ADIGE

Brennerpass/
Passo del Brennerio

Bressanone

Bolzano

Cortina
d'Ampezzo

Arta Terme

Tarvisio

A23

Tolmezzo

FRIULI-VENEZIA
GIULIA

Venzone

Gemona di Friuli

Tarcento

S13

S357

Belluno

Spilimbergo

S. Daniele
del Friuli

Cividale del Friuli

Trento

S47

Provesano

Udine

SLOVENIA

Pordenone

Codroipo

Cormòns

S58

Palmanova

Gorizia

Conegliano

Sesto al Règhena

S38

A23

A4

S351

Monfalcone

Bassano
del Grappa

Àsolo

Masèn

Cervignano

Portegruaro

Latisana

Aquileia

Duino

Sgonico

S248

Marostica

Montebelluna

Nove

Fanzolo

TREVISO

A4

Lignano-
Sabbiadoro

Miramare

Grado

Opicina

Cittadella

Castelfranco

Càorle

TRIESTE

Vicenza

Piazzola
sul Brenta

Piombino
Dese

Verona

Mestre

A4

Padua

Mira

Strà

Fusine

VENICE (VENEZIA)

CROATIA

Teolo

Torréglia

Vó

Golfo di Venezia

Arquà Petrarca

Monsélice

Este

Adige

Rovigo

VENETO

Trieste

Once it was the main seaport of the Austro-Hungarian Empire, but two world wars left Trieste a woebegone widow of the Adriatic. With the fall of the Berlin Wall, however, it became a very merry widow, quick to regain its old cosmopolitan lustre. Streets and shops bubble with a babel of Slovene, Czech, German, Serbo-Croat and Hungarian, and an exotic bouquet of car licence plates clog up the straight, central European, 19th-century streets. Don't come to Trieste for art or beautiful buildings: the city's capitalist swag has been firmly invested in banks, shipping-lines and stocks. Come to sense the energy of a city shaking off decades of nostalgic sloth and picking up from where it left off, in the vibrant days just before the First World War.

Along the Port to Piazza dell'Unità d'Italia

Across from the station, the **Galleria Nazionale d'Arte Antica** (*Piazza della Libertà 7; open Mon–Sat 9–1; adm*) offers some second division 15th–19th-century Italian paintings. Corso Cavour, meanwhile, leads into the **Borgo Teresiano**, Trieste's business hub, laid out with ruler-straight streets and planted with neoclassical architecture. Just across the **Canale Grande**, an inlet with moorings for small craft, stands the city's oldest coffee house, **Caffè Tommaseo** (1830), restored with its Belle Epoque fittings.

Next along the waterfront opens Trieste's whale of a heart, **Piazza dell'Unità d'Italia**, framed by a hefty **Palazzo del Comune**, topped by two Moors who ring the bell over the clock, and the **Palazzo del Governo** glowing in its bright skin of mosaics.

Trieste keeps its chief art collections a few blocks south of Piazza Unità d'Italia, around **Piazza Venezia**. The **Museo Revoltella** (*Via Diaz 27, t 040 675 4350, www. museorevoltella.it; open 9–1.30 and 4–7, tours at 9, 10.30, 12, 3 and 6; closed Tues and Sun; adm*), in a house full of original furnishings, contains 18th- and 19th-century paintings by Triestine artists that evoke the city's golden days, as well as works by Morandi, De Chirico and Canova. On Largo Papa Giovanni XXIII, the **Museo Sartorio** (*closed until early 2006; call t 040 301 479*) offers another glimpse into 19th-century bourgeois life, with works by Paolo Veneziano and Giambattista Tiepolo, ceramics and a wonderful collection of miniatures in some surprising poses.

The Capitoline Hill

Trieste has its very own Capitoline Hill (*bus 24 from the station/Piazza dell'Unità*), the nucleus of the Roman and medieval city. In the 5th century the Triestini raised the first of two basilicas here to their patron San Giusto. An adjacent 11th-century basilica was linked to the earlier church in the 14th century, thus giving the **Cathedral of San Giusto** (*closed 12–3*) its curious plan. The doorway is framed by the fragments of a Roman sarcophagus, with six funerary busts gazing solemnly ahead like a board of directors. Inside, there are some beautiful mosaics, especially the 13th-century *Christ with SS. Giusto and Servulus*. Buried on the right is Don Carlos, the Great Pretender of Spain's Carlist Wars, who died as an exile in Trieste in 1855.

Outside, the view over Trieste is marred by a 1933 **war memorial** extolling the principal Fascist virtues of strength, brutality and vulgarity. The 15th-century **Castello di San Giusto** (*open daily until sunset*) offers better views from its ramparts and a small **Museo Civico** (*closed for restoration at the time of writing; contact tourist office for reopening date*), full of armour and weapons.

Down the lane from the cathedral, the **Civico Museo di Storia ed Arte e Orto Lapidario** (*Via Cattedrale 15; open Tues–Sun 9–1; adm*) houses intriguing finds from Roman Tergeste and a famous 5th-century deer's-head silver drinking vessel from Greek Tarentum (Taranto). Down the hill, stop to look at the **Roman Theatre**, built during the reign of Trajan and remarkably intact.

More *Caffè* and Museums

Trieste's famous Grand Cafés, once filled with cross-cultural conversation, ideas and spies, still serve delicious pastries as well as dollops of nostalgia. Irish author James

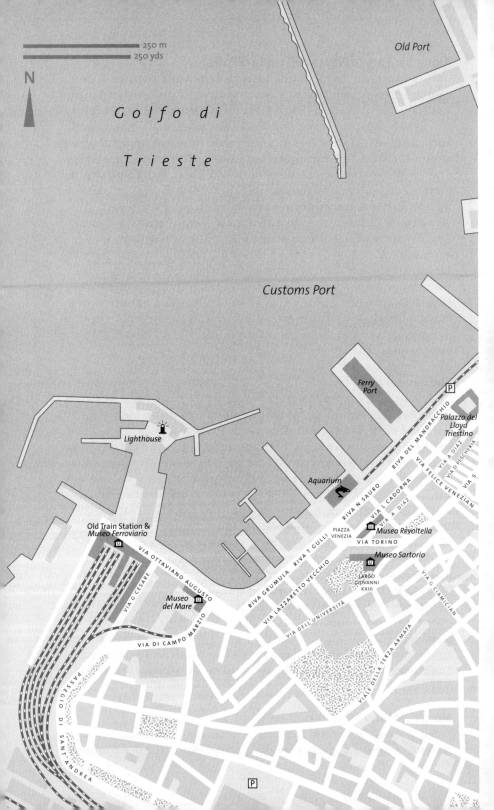

N

250 m
250 yds

Golfo di

Trieste

Old Port

Customs Port

Ferry Port

Lighthouse

Aquarium

Palazzo del Lloyd Triestino

Old Train Station & Museo Ferroviario

Museo Revoltella

PIAZZA VENEZIA

VIA TORINO

Museo Sartorio

Museo del Mare

LARGO GIOVANNI XXIII

VIA G. CESARE

VIA OTTAVIANO AUGUSTO

RIVA N SAURO

RIVA GRUMULA

RIVA T GULLI

RIVA LAZZARETTO VECCHIO

VIA DI CAMPO MARZIO

VIA DELL'UNIVERSITÀ

VIALE DELLA TERZA ARMATA

VIA DEL MANDRACCHIO

VIA L CADORNA

VIA A. DIAZ

VIA FELICE VENEZIAN

VIA A. DIAZ

VIA D PESCHERIA

VIA G. CIAMICIAN

PASSEGGIO DI SANT'ANDREA

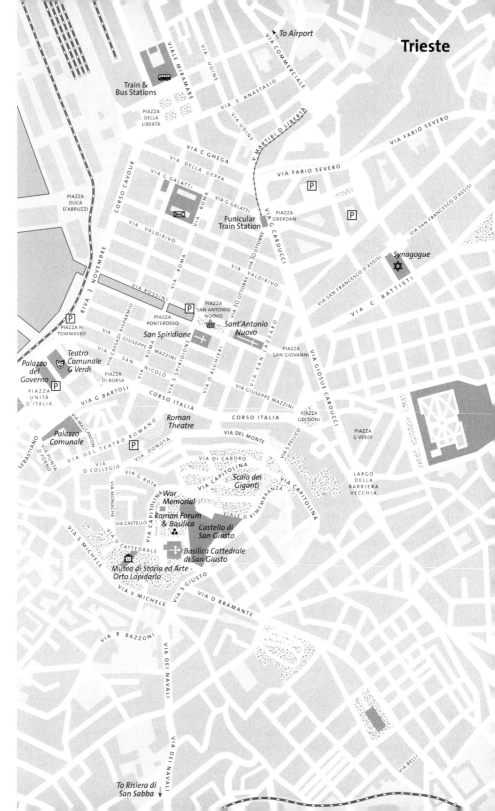

Getting There

See **Getting There**, pp.3–8.

Getting from the Airport

Trieste's Ronchi dei Legionari airport (**t** 0481 773 224) is 35km north near Monfalcone; APT **buses** (**t** 0481 593 511) run to and from Trieste's main bus station in Piazza della Libertà (every 30mins or so), taking 50mins–1hr (tickets €3.50 from the airport bar or post office). A **taxi** to the centre will cost about €50.

Getting Around

Trieste's long, straight Habsburger streets mean that finding one's way around on foot is relatively simple, although use the crossings carefully; these streets make even Rome appear pedestrian. **City buses** (**t** 040 77951) are frequent, and most routes run from or by the main bus station. A **funicular railway** (*tranvia*) runs every 22mins from Piazza Oberdan to Villa Opicina. The train station, **Stazione Centrale**, is on Piazza della Libertà. The **bus station** (**t** 040 425 020) is in front of it.

Cars have been banished from the centre and parking can be diabolical; surrender your *macchina* to one of the car parks. For a **taxi**, call **Radio taxi, t** 040 307 730.

To Slovenia and Croatia

The *Marconi* ship links Trieste Wed–Sun, late May–Sept, with Lignano and Piran in Slovenia, and Umag, Porec, Rovinj and Pula in Croatia.

There are now no car ferries from Trieste – only **passenger ships**. Lines are run by SAMER, Molo Bersagliere 3/H, **t** 040 303 540, *www. adriatica.it*.

The main **bus** station at Piazza della Libertà, **t** 040 425 020, *www.autostazionetrieste.it*, has services to Ljubljana in Slovenia, and Pula and Zagreb in Croatia.

Car Hire

Avis, Piazza della Libertà, **t** 0481 421 521; at the airport, **t** 0481 777 085.
Budget, at the airport, **t** 0481 779 166.
Europcar, Stazione Marittima, **t** 040 322 0820; at the airport **t** 0481 778 920.
Hertz, Piazza della Libertà, **t** 040 322 0098; at the airport, **t** 0481 777 025.
Sixt, Stazione Marittima, **t** 040 322 6533; at the airport, **t** 0481 774836.

Tourist Information

Trieste: Via San Nicolò 20, **t** 040 67961, and Piazza dell'Unità d'Italia 4/C, **t** 040 347 8312, *www. triesteturismo.com (open daily 9–7.30).*

Market Days

Piazza Ponterosso, next to the Canale Grande, is the site of the daily market.

Shopping

Trieste's shopping streets are the **Corso Italia** and the **Via Carducci**. The single most famous Friulian comestible is *prosciutto di San Daniele*, which rivals Parma's famous hams.

Where to Stay

Trieste ✉ 34100
★★★★Duchi d'Aosta, Piazza dell'Unità d'Italia 2, **t** 040 760 0011, *www.magesta.com* (*luxury*). Trieste's finest hotel is on its finest square, in a neo-Renaissance palace now owned by the CIGA chain. It exudes a dignified Belle Epoque ambience; upstairs, the luxurious rooms are fitted with every comfort and it has an excellent restaurant, **Harry's Grill**.
★★★Novo Hotel Impero, Via S. Anastasia 1, **t** 040 364 242, *www.fenicehotels.it* (*very*

Joyce was a habitué of the **Caffè Pirona** (*Largo Barriera Vecchia 12*), south of the Piazza Goldoni, during his stay here, while, on the other side of the piazza, **Caffè San Marco** contains Venetian murals that betrayed the owner's pro-Italian sentiments. One street away, Europe's largest **synagogue** (*open only to groups;* **t** *040 371 466*), built in 1910 on ancient Syriac models, is decorated with copper and black and white marble. At Via Romagna 6 the **Ipanema Rovis** (*t 040 308 686 for opening hours*) is a treasure trove of minerals and fossils, the collection of a former coffee importer from Istria.

expensive). Near the train station and the centre; some rooms are cheaper.

★★★**San Giusto**, Via C. Belli 3, **t** 040 762 661, *www.hotelsangiusto.it* (*very expensive*). By the historic hill, a modern hotel with all you need.

★★★**Milano**, Via Ghega 17, **t** 040 369 680, *www.hotel-milano.com* (*expensive*). A comfortable hotel near the station.

★★★**Nuovo Hotel Daneu**, Via Nazionale 11, **t** 040 214 214, *www.hoteldaneu.com* (*expensive*). If you don't like the hurly-burly of a big city, take the tram up to Opicina where this hotel has a good restaurant and indoor pool.

★★**Hotel James Joyce**, Via dei Cavazzeni 7, **t** 040 311 023, *www.hoteljamesjoyce.com* (*moderate*). Newly opened, cosy and popular with 12 rooms, a couple of minutes' walk from Piazza dell'Unità d'Italia.

There are many less expensive choices in the centre of Trieste – look around Via Roma, Via della Geppa, or Via XXX Ottobre.

★**Alabarda-Flora**, Via Valdirivo 22, **t** 040 630 269, *www.alabarda.it* (*moderate–inexpensive*). A clean, comfortable, good-value hotel.

Eating Out

Slovenian and Hungarian influences are strong and Trieste is a good place to eat dumplings. A famous *primo* is *jota*, a bean, potato and sauerkraut soup, or *kaiserknödel* (bread dumplings with grated cheese, ham and parsley). For *secondo*, there's a wide variety of fish, such as tasty sardines, served fried or marinated, or the popular goulash, roast pork and *stinco* (veal knuckle). The Middle European influence, however, is most noticeable in the desserts: strudels, *gnocchi di susine* (plums) or *zavate*, a warm cream pastry.

Al Cantuccio, Via Cadorna 14a, **t** 040 300 131 (*expensive*). A haven for lovers of creative

food, located right by the seafront. Try the scallops with pine nuts and balsamic vinegar, the risotto with prawns and prosecco, or the chicken with black grapes, then delicious zabaglione with bitter chocolate. *Closed Sun.*

Antica Trattoria Suban, Via Comici 2, **t** 040 54368 (*expensive*). The place to partake of *cucina Triestina* is this wonderful old inn in the suburb of San Giovanni (take a taxi), maintaining much of its old feel and fine views over Trieste. They offer a famous *jota*, *sevapcici* (Slovenian grilled meat fritters), sinful desserts and good wines. Check when you book, however, that the regular chef is on duty; if not, wait till he is. *Closed Mon lunch, Tues, part of Jan and Aug.*

Città di Cherso, Via Cadorna 6, **t** 040 366 044 (*expensive–moderate*). Convenient to Piazza dell'Unità d'Italia, serving delicious seafood Friulian-style, topped off with heavenly desserts. *Closed Tues, and Aug.*

Re di Coppe, Via Geppa 11, **t** 040 370 330 (*moderate–cheap*). The waiters still write the orders on the tablecloths at this restaurant, where you can find a classic *jota* and boiled meats. *Closed Sat, Sun and mid-July–mid-Aug.*

Buffet da Pepi, Via Cassa di Risparmo 3, **t** 040 366 858 (*cheap*). Founded in 1903 and has been thriving ever since, serving up Trieste's specialities. *Closed Sun and half of July.*

Birreria Forst, Via Galatti 11, near Piazza Oberdan, **t** 040 363 486 (*cheap*). Another old favourite, serving goulash and lots of beer. *Closed Sun.*

Entertainment

The **opera** season at Trieste's Teatro Comunale Verdi runs Nov–Mar (*www.teatroverdi-trieste. com*); in summer the theatre and the Sala Tripcovich in Pza. della Libertà see an **International Operetta festival** (**t** 040 672 2500, **f** 040 672 2249).

In sombre counterpoint, at the southern extreme of the city stands the only concentration camp in Italy to be used for mass exterminations, the **Risiera di San Sabba** (*bus 8; open Tues–Sun 9–1*), now housing a small museum.

On a far lighter note, the **Museo Ferroviario** (*Via G Cesare 1, in the old train station in the Campo Marzio; currently closed, call for a visit by appointment, **t** 040 379 4185*) runs summer excursions in period trains: three-hour electric train journeys around the city, and day-long steam train excursions around the region and neighbouring countries.

Short Excursions from Trieste

Miramare: Habsburg Folly by the Sea

*t 040 224 143, www.castello-miramare.it; 7km from Trieste; bus 36 from Piazza Oberdan/Stazione Centrale; open daily 9–7 (ticket office closes at 6.30pm); adm exp. **Park** open daily in summer 8–7, winter 8–5; adm free.*

Towering on its own little promontory overlooking the sea, the castle of Miramare hides a dark history behind its white 19th-century façade, having acquired the ominous reputation of laying a curse on anyone who slept within its walls. Once he built his pleasure palace, the Habsburg archduke Maximilian allowed himself to be conned into leaving it, only to face a firing squad; later, the archduke Franz Ferdinand stayed here on his way to assassination in Sarajevo. The whole sad story is retold in a **sound and light show** (*in Italian on Mon, Tues and Wed at 9.30 or 10.45 pm in July, Aug and Sept; call t 040 679 6111 for possible English performances*). The palace interior retains its overblown Victorian-era décor, some rather cosy rooms designed like ship's cabins and 1920s furnishings. The magnificent **park** was designed by Maximilian; the gardens and coastal waters shelter the rare Stella's otter and marsh harriers.

Grotta Gigante

t 040 327 312; bus 42 departs every 30mins from Piazza Oberdan; open Mar and Oct 10–4; Nov–Feb 10–12 and 2–4; April–Sept 10–6; closed Mon except in July and Aug; adm exp.

The famous stalactite **Grotta Gigante**, near Opicina, is the largest cavern in the world open to visitors; its main hall could swallow Rome's basilica of St Peter whole and is graced by a pair of record-breaking 346ft stalactites. The ceiling is so high that drops of water disintegrate before reaching the floor, forming curious leaf-shaped stalagmites; you can follow a path past a belvedere over a vertiginous 360ft drop.

The cave is in Sgonico, also the site of a beautiful botanic garden, the **Carsiana** (*open May–mid-Oct Tues–Fri 10–12, Sat, Sun and hols 10–1 and 3–7*).

Day Trips from Trieste

Aquileia

Aquileia is unique in that it was the only great Roman city in Italy to die on the vine; once the proud capital of the X Legio Venetia et Histria, it has dwindled from 200,000 to 3,500 inhabitants. No longer receiving emperors, they now tend to vineyards, and to tourists who flock to see the most important archaeological site in northern Italy.

The city's magnificent **Basilica** (*open April–Sept 8.30–7; Oct–Mar 8.30–12.30 and 2.30–5.30*) and its campanile are a landmark for miles around. It was founded in 313 by the Aquileia's first Patriarch, Theodore, and when Patriarch Poppone rebuilt it in 1023 he covered the floor, nicely preserving it for its rediscovery in 1909. At 837 sq yards, this

Getting There

The simplest way from Trieste to Aquileia is to take the **train** to **Cervignano** (35mins), then catch a **bus** from outside the station 7km to Aquileia (10mins). Trains leave Trieste roughly hourly, with regular bus links in Cervignano.

Tourist Information

Aquileia ✉ **33051**: Piazza Capitolo, **t** 0431 910 087 (*open April–Nov*).

Eating Out

La Colombara, Via Zilli 42, **t** 0431 91513 (*moderate*). A family-run restaurant which specializes in fish and seafood, and all sorts of recipes involving asparagus; there's a choice of menus. *Closed Mon*.

*Aquila Nera, Piazza Garibaldi 5, **t** 0431 91045 (*moderate–cheap*). An old hotel with a traditional and homely restaurant, serving good *gnocchi* and basic meat dishes. *Closed Mon*.

is the largest Palaeochristian mosaic in the west, a vivid carpet of portraits, animals and geometric patterns mingling with Christian and pagan scenes. Frescoes from 1031 survive in the apse, showing Patriarch Poppone dedicating the basilica. Next to the left wall of the nave, the 11th-century marble Santo Sepolcro marks the entrance to the **Cripta degli Scavi**, containing more mosaics from 313, sandwiched in between Roman mosaics and others from the 8th century. The crypt under the altar is adorned with 12th-century Byzantine-style frescoes (*one adm for both crypts*).

Down the road opposite the church, the **Museo Archeològico** (*open Mon 8.30–1.45, Tues–Sun 8.30–7.30; adm*) houses artefacts from pre-Christian Aquileia. There is a fine set of warts-and-all Republican portrait busts (Tiberius and Trajan among them), as well as amber and gold, glass, coins, a rare, intact Roman chandelier, and a thousand and one household items that breathe life into ancient Aquileia.

A circular walk, beginning on the Via Sacra behind the basilica, takes in what remains of the ancient city, passing **Roman houses** and **Palaeochristian oratories** (some with mosaics), then the considerable ruins of the **harbour**: in the 1st century AD this was a bustling commercial port. Continue straight and bear right after the crossroads on Via Gemina to the **Palaeochristian Museum** (*open daily 8.30–1.45*), with reliefs, sarcophagi and a walkway over the mossy mosaics of a 4th-century basilica. Return by way of Via Gemina to Via Giulia Augusta; to the right you can see the old Roman road and, to the left, the **Forum** with its re-erected columns. Just off a fork to the right, the **Grand Mausoleum** (1st century AD) was brought here from the suburbs. The meagre ruins of the amphitheatre, baths and **Sepolcreto** (five Roman family tombs) are on Via XXIV Maggio and Via Acidino, north of Piazza Garibaldi.

Ùdine

Ùdine, the culture capital of Friuli, is a charmer, and not half as well known as it deserves to be. Its old streets are interwoven with little canals. Venice left its handprint on the architecture, while Giambattista Tiepolo brightened many of the walls, thanks to his patron Patriarch Dionisio Delfino who kept him here between 1726 and 1730, when he took up the brilliant colours that became his trademark.

The heart of Ùdine, **Piazza della Libertà**, has been called 'the most beautiful Venetian square on the *terra firma*', adorned by its striking, candy-striped **Loggia del**

Getting There

Trains to Ùdine from Trieste run roughly every 30mins (taking 1hr 15mins); **buses** (t 040 425 020) may take slightly longer (1hr30mins). Ùdine's **train station** is on Viale Europa Unità. The **bus station** is not far away on the other side of the same street, t 0432 506 941.

Tourist Information

Ùdine ✉ 33100: Piazza 1 Maggio 7, t 0432 295 972, f 0432 504 743, arpt1.ud@adriacom.it.

Eating Out

★★★La' di Moret, just north of the centre at Viale Tricesimo 276, t 0432 545 096, *www. ladimoret.it* (*expensive*). With one of the region's best restaurants, featuring seafood Friuli-style. *Closed Sun eve and Mon lunch.*

Vitello d'Oro, Via Valvason 4, t 0432 508 982, f 0432 508 982 (*expensive*). A historic inn serving traditional specialities; the emphasis is on fish. *Closed Mon lunch, Wed; plus Sun in June–Aug.*

Vecchio Stallo, Via Viola 7, t 0432 21296 (*moderate*). A charming restaurant and the best value; good food, and wine by the glass. *Closed Wed and 3 weeks in Aug.*

Lionello, and the **Loggia di San Giovanni** (1533), with its clock tower and bell rung by Venetian-style Moors. The **Municipio**, all in white, is a bravura piece of Art Deco by Raimondo d'Aronco (1910–31) that manages to blend right in with all the rest.

Palladio's rugged **Arco Bollari** (1556) is the gateway to the sweeping **portico**, built to shelter visitors to the **Castello**. This now houses the **Civici Musei** (*open Tues–Sat 9.30–12.30 and 3–6, Sun 9.30–12.30; closed Mon; adm, free Sun*) with sections on archaeology, designs and prints – by Tiepolo and Dürer, among others – and a notable collection of paintings, beginning in the Salone del Parlamento with its frescoes by Pomponio Amalteo and Giovanni Battista Grassi. Among the highlights are works by Carpaccio, Tiepolo and a bird's-eye view of Ùdine by local boy Luca Carlefarijs (1662–1730).

Just east of Piazza della Libertà, the oft-altered **Duomo** has a charming 14th-century lunette of the *Coronation of the Virgin and Saints* over the door. The interior, a digni-fied Baroque symphony of grey and gold, contains frescoes by Tiepolo in the first two altars on the right and in the Cappella del Sacramento. In the heavy-set campanile, the small **Museo del Duomo** (*open Tues–Sat 9–12 and 4–6, Sun 4–6*) is adorned with excellent frescoes of 1349 by Vitale da Bologna. Tiepolo never forgot Ùdine, and in 1759 he returned to decorate the adjacent **Oratorio della Purità** (1680) with a masterful, partly frescoed, partly painted and recently restored *Assumption* on the ceiling, and an altarpiece of the *Immaculate Conception*; the frescoes on the walls are by his son.

The Tiepolo trail continues in the Piazza Patriarcato, where he frescoed an entire gallery with Old Testament scenes in the **Museo Diocesano** (*open Wed–Sun 10–12 and 3.30–6.30*). More recent art (Arturo Martini, Severini, De Chirico, De Kooning, Segal, Lichtenstein, Dufy and works by the local brothers Afro, Mirko and Dino Basaldell) is on display in the excellent **Galleria d'Arte Moderna** (*bus 2; open Tues–Sat 9.30–12.30 and 3–6, Sun 9.30–12.30; closed Mon; adm, Sun free*), on the northern fringes of the old town. The new **Museo Friulano di Storia Naturale** (*Via Grazzano 1; closed until further notice*) offers a mixture of natural history and Friuli culture, showing how the people have developed customs and traditions from the land.

Touring from Trieste

Day 1: Karst and Wines of the Collio

Morning: Leave Trieste by the S58, and at Villa Opicina follow signs northeast for **Sgonico**. Trieste province is known as the Carso, after its limestone karst, pocked with caves and resurgent rivers, and covered with sumac; learn more about it at Sgonico's Carsiana botanical garden (*open 24 April–15 Oct Tues–Fri 10–12, Sat, Sun and hols 10–1 and 3–7; closed Mon*). Continue northwest to the seaside resorts of **Sistiana** and **Duino**, on two pretty bays. In the latter's 15th-century Castello Nuovo, poet Rainier Maria Rilke wrote his *Duino Elegies*; follow his favourite 2km path, the Rilke walk, around the promontory. Just above Duino, visit the winsome Romanesque church of San Giovanni in Tuba, where the River Timavo resurfaces in a lush setting.
Lunch: In Duino, *see* below.
Afternoon: Head northeast to the frontier city of **Gorízia**, with a medieval Castle of the Counts of Gorizia (*open Oct–Mar Tues–Sun 9.30–6; April–Sept Tues–Sun 9.30–1 and 3–7.30; adm*). Just below, the Museo Provinciale (*open Tues–Sun 9–7; adm*) has histor-ical and art exhibits, while the adjacent Museo delle Guerre (*open Tues–Sun 9–7; same ticket as Museo Provinciale*) has fascinating displays on the First World War. From Gorízia, explore Friuli's most prestigious wine district, the hilly and pretty **Collio**; go tasting at the Cantina Prodottori Vini del Collio (*closed Sun*) in medieval **Cormòns**.
Dinner and Sleeping: In or around Cormòns, *see* below.

Day 1

Lunch in Duino

Duino has fashionable seafood restaurants, so prices here tend to be over the odds. If you don't feel like indulging, pack a picnic lunch before leaving Trieste.
Dama Bianca, t 040 208 137 (*expensive*). By the old castle walls, overlooking Duino's bijou port. Highly rated for its absolutely fresh fish, beautifully prepared in pasta dishes and the main course, where the menu depends on the day's catch. Great wine list. *Closed Wed exc summer.*
Ai Cavalluccio, next door to the Dama Bianca, t 040 208 133 (*expensive*). Zuzana Hornakovar's restaurant also has lovely fish (try the sea bass baked in salt), besides Collio wines and great desserts. *Closed Tue*s.

Dinner and Sleeping in or around Cormòns

***Felcaro, Via Giovanni 45, t 0481 60214, f 0481 630 255 (*expensive*). The nicest place

to sleep in the Collio. It began life as an Austrian villa and is spread out among several buildings, with a pool as well as a fine restaurant, specializing in game dishes to set off its enormous wine list (*expensive*).
La Subida, Monte 22, t 0481 60531, f 0481 61616, *www.lasubida.it* (*moderate*). In a charming rural setting on a hill, with a handful of rooms, many of which sleep up to five; there's an outdoor pool and riding avail-able, too. The hotel's restaurant, **Il Cacciatore (*very expensive*), is famed for its excellent regional dishes, with borrowings from nearby Slovenia: the cold breast of pheasant in mushroom cream is a popular summer dish. Excellent Collio wines. *Open for dinner only Wed–Fri, lunch and dinner Sat and Sun.*
Il Giardinetto, Via Matteotti 54, t 0481 60257, f 0481 630 704, *www.jre.it* (*very expensive*). Twin chefs have put this restaurant firmly on the gastronomic map with their innova-tive Friulian dishes, such as *millefoglie di polenta* and gnocchi with crinkly cabbage and game sauce. *Closed Mon, Tues and July.*

Day 2: Dark Age Wonders and Carnia Foothills

Morning: Take the S356 north to **Cividale del Friuli**, a city founded by Julius Caesar that caught the fancy of the invading Lombards, who made it their capital in 568. The **Duomo** has a great 12th-century altarpiece and two wonderful 8th-century Lombard works, the Baptistry of Callisto and the Altar of Ratchis, in the Museo Cristiano (*open summer 9.30–12 and 3–7; winter 9.30–12 and 3–6*). Other Lombard artefacts, along with Roman ones, fill the adjacent Museo Archeològico Nazionale (*open summer Tues–Sat 9–7; winter Tues–Sun 8.30–7.30*). Walk down to the river to see the lofty Ponte del Diavolo (1442) spanning the turquoise Natisone; just up the river is the marvellous Tempietto Longobardo (*open summer 9–1 and 3–6.30; winter 9.30–12 and 3–7; adm*), where a lovely sextet of princesses and female saints in high relief are the finest 8th-century works in Italy, a love letter from the Dark Ages.

Lunch: In Cividale del Friuli, *see* below.

Afternoon: Head for the hills – take the S356 to **Tarcento**, then cross over west to the S13 for **Gemona del Friuli**; its fine 13th-century cathedral has a remarkable portal. Continue north on the S13 to **Venzone**, a double-walled town that had to be rebuilt, twice: after the Second World War and after the 1967 earthquake. North of here, leave the S13 to turn west for **Tolmezzo**, once a great producer of damasks; visit the great ethnographic collection of the Carnia Mountains at the Museo Carnico delle Arti Popolari (*open Tues–Sun 9–1 and 3–6*), in a 16th-century palace. If you need a dose of mountain scenery, drive to **Lake Verzeghis**, 5km south of Tolmezzo.

Dinner and Sleeping: In Tolmezzo or nearby **Arta Terme**, *see* below.

Day 2

Lunch in Cividale del Friuli

Alla Frasca, Via di Rebeis 8a, **t** 0432 731 270 (*moderate*). A restaurant with a charming Renaissance atmosphere and tasty Friulian dishes, including a *menu di funghi* that offers truffles and mushrooms with everything. In winter, game dishes rule the menu. All year round, though, save room for the many home-made desserts. *Closed Mon.*

Al Fortino, Via Carlo Alberto 46, **t** 0432 731 217 (*moderate*). Another pleasant place for lunch, featuring home-made pasta dishes and typical Friulian fare. *Closed Tues.*

Dinner and Sleeping in Tolmezzo

★★★Roma, Piazza XX Settembre 14, **t** 043 346 8031, **f** 043 343 316 (*rooms moderate, restaurant expensive – 20% discount for residents*). Smack in the heart of town, where Friuli's top chef, Gianni Cosetti, used to hold forth before his death in 1999. The new owners are doing their best to honour Cosetti's name, and serve local, seasonal food – polenta, mushrooms, truffles and game. *Closed Sun eve and Mon.*

Dinner and Sleeping in Arta Terme

Arta Terme is just 7km north of Tolmezzo.

★★★Poldo, up in Piano d'Arta, Arta Terme, **t** 043 392 056, **f** 043 392 577 (*moderate*). Enjoys a peaceful setting in the trees, with an exotic garden and views down into the valley. You may want to come back: it's also a spa centre, specializing in the treatment of obesity and dietary disorders.

★★Salon, Via Peresson 70, **t** 043 392 003, **f** 043 392 9364, *www.albergosalon.it* (*rooms moderate, restaurant moderate*). This hotel has more basic rooms, but an excellent restaurant, serving traditional Carnican dishes, where mushrooms and fresh herbs are plentiful; in summer crêpes with courgette flowers are a speciality. Don't miss the selection of mountain cheeses. *Closed Nov–April; restaurant closed Tues exc in season.*

Day 3: Prosciutto, Frescoes and a Really Big Villa

Morning: Retrace your way south, picking up the S463 near Gemona for **San Daniele del Friuli**, the ochre-tinted 'Siena of Friuli', where you can try to buy its famous sweet-cured hams. Don't miss the church of Sant'Antonio Abate, containing the finest fresco cycle in Friuli, the masterpiece of Pellegrino di San Daniele, painted between 1498 and 1522. To the right of the Duomo, the Biblioteca Guarneriana (*open Tues–Sun 9–12*) was established in 1466 by a canon of Aquileia and has lovely medieval manuscripts. Then drive south and cross the River Tagliamento for **Spilimbergo**, a historic town with plenty of churches and a 12th-century castle with exterior frescoes and a mosaic school (*open Mon–Sat 9–12 by appointment, t 0427 2077, f 0427 3903*).

Lunch: In Spilimbergo, *see* below.

Afternoon: Drive south to **Provesano** to see the fine frescoes (1496) inside its church, by Gianfrancesco da Tolmezzo, then turn east for **Codroipo**, where the the last Doge, Ludovico Manin, built the **Villa Manin** (1738) (*open summer Tues–Sun 10–7; winter 10–6; times vary, call t 0432 906 657; adm free*), the biggest villa in all Venetia. Besides rooms of frescoed fluff, there's a museum of carriages and a handsome park. From here backtrack west to **San Vito**, for the 16th-century frescoes by Pompeo Amalteo in Santa Maria dei Battuti. Continue west to **Pordenone**, where the Duomo and Museo Civico d'Arte (*open Tues–Sat 3–7, Sun 10–1 and 3–7; adm*) contain works by the famous Renaissance painter named after the town.

Dinner and Sleeping: In or around Pordenone, *see* below.

Day 3

Lunch in Spilimbergo

La Torre, Piazza Castello, **t** 0427 50555 (*expensive*). Dine in the castle on the likes of ravioli, filled with pumpkin in mushroom sauce, and strudels. If you love wine, you'll have a field day with its packed cellar. *Closed Sun eve and Mon.*

Osteria Al Bachero, Via Pilacorte 5, **t** 0427 2317 (*cheap*). The furniture may be simple and wooden, but here you'll find the authentic taste of Friuli. Try the *baccalá con polenta* (salt cod with polenta) or other local dishes, and dine around an open fire. They have one menu in English but you won't have to wait for it. *Closed Sun, and Mon eve.*

Dinner and Sleeping in and around Pordenone

★★★★Villa Ottoboni, Piazzetta Ottoboni 2, **t** 0434 208 891, **f** 0434 208 148, *www.getour hotels.com* (*moderate*). An elegant hotel right near the centre, offering fully furnished rooms; the dining room dates from the late 15th century.

★★★Park, Via Mazzini 42, **t** 0434 27901, **f** 0434 522 353, *www.bwparkhotel-pn.it* (*moderate*). Modern, comfortable rooms in the centre.

Antica Trattoria La Primula, Via San Rocco 47, San Quirino, **t** 0434 91005, **f** 0434 919 280 (*expensive*). For something special, drive 9km north of Pordenone to San Quirino. Here six generations have served up the best food in the province, classic and simply prepared, from the *antipasti* through the fresh seafood to the elegant desserts. It has seven rooms as well, but you'll need to book ahead to nab one. The same talented family also runs the adjacent, frescoed **Osteria Alle Nazioni**, serving simpler delights at prices that are kinder on the pocket. *Closed Sun eve, Mon, part of Jan and July.*

Alla Cantina, Piazza Cavour 3, **t/f** 0434 520 358 (*cheap*). This is easy to find in the centre. There'll be no surprises, but it's a good bet for well-prepared Italian classics, served in rather opulent surroundings. *Closed Tues.*

Day 4: Romans, a *Pala d'Oro* and Beaches

Morning: Speed south on the A28 to **Sesto al Règhena**, a quaint medieval village built around Santa Maria in Silvis (*open 8–8*), an abbey founded by the Lombards. The Romanesque Byzantine basilica dates from the 11th century and has some fine and unusual frescoes, including one of Christ crucified on a pomegranate tree. Continue 9km south to **Portugruaro**, a seductive old town of porticoed streets, palm trees and canals. It has a striking 14th-century Loggia Comunale (the Municipio) and the Museo Nazionale Concordiese (*open daily 9–8; adm*) is full of bronzes, coins and finds from the Roman glass-and-arrow manufacturing colony of **Concordia Sagittaria**, located just south of Portugruaro. Here you'll find a Romanesque cathedral sitting next to a ruined basilica of 380, and a frescoed Byzantine baptistry of 1089, as well as a museum (*open Tues–Sun 9–12 and 3.30–6.30; closed Mon; times vary, call t 0421 270 442*) with more archaeological finds. Next, drive south towards **Càorle**.

Lunch: In **San Giorgio di Livenza** or Càorle, *see* below.

Afternoon: Visit Càorle – its landmark church lighthouse on an isthmus; its cathedral, vintage 1028, with a radiant Venetian Pala d'Oro (12th–14th centuries) on the altar; and go out watching birds in its inner lagoon. Then head eastwards, crossing the flatlands; stop in **Latisana** to see Veronese's *Baptism of Christ* (1567) in the cathedral, then drive south to **Lignano-Sabbiadoro**, the fastest-growing resort on the whole of the Adriatic, to relax on its long sandy beach and/or birdwatch in the Laguna di Marano.

Dinner and Sleeping: In Lignano-Sabbiadoro, *see* below.

Day 4

Lunch in San Giorgio di Livenza

Al Cacciatore, Corso Risorgimento 35, **t** 0421 80331 (*expensive*). Ten km before Càorle, near the Livenza river. A popular family-run restaurant of long standing, featuring the freshest of fish and tasty mushroom dishes in the autumn. *Closed Wed and some of Aug.*

Lunch in Càorle

Duilio, at the Hotel Diplomatic, Via Strada Nuova 19, **t** 0421 81087, **f** 0421 210 089 (*moderate*). In a charming setting overlooking a little port, famed for the heavenly seafood served in the *antipasti*, with the pasta, and as the main course. A huge wine list and reasonably priced menus are added attractions. *Closed Mon and Jan.*

Dinner in Lignano-Sabbiadoro

Bidin, Via Europa 1, **t** 0431 71988 (*expensive*). A small, convivial restaurant, with a separate *menu degustazione* featuring either fish or meat to accompany the fine bottles in its tremendous wine cellar. *Closed Wed except in summer.*

Al Bancut, Via Friuli 32, **t** 0431 71926 (*expensive*). In the centre of town, a popular restaurant with a woodsy seaside décor featuring tasty grilled fish, traditionally prepared, followed by delightful home-made desserts. *Closed Mon eve and Tues.*

Sleeping in Lignano-Sabbiadoro

★★★★Miramare, Calle Mendelssohn 13, **t** 0431 71260, **f** 0431 428 992, *www.miramare.com* (*moderate*). A fashionable hotel in Lignano Riviera, enjoying perhaps the most beautiful setting in the whole area and offering lovely rooms, a heated pool and much more. *Open mid-Mar–end Sept.*

★★★Etna, Viale Miramare 24, **t** 0431 720 640, **f** 043 172 1649, *www.albergoetna.com* (*moderate*, including breakfast). A tasteful hotel near the sea with well equipped rooms; it's also one of the few that remains open all year.

Day 5: New Towns, Old Towns and Sand Cures

Morning: Have a last swim in Lignano, and then head east for **Palmanova**. In the Renaissance, despite all of its theories on planning, only a handful of new towns ever saw the light of day, and this was one of them, built in 1593 by the Venetians as a bulwark against the Austrians and Turks. Perhaps because it was never actually needed, Palmanova remains intact, a perfect example of an 'ideal' radial military plan: a nine-pointed star with a hexagonal piazza in the centre; learn all about it in the **Museo Storico** at Borgo Udine (*open Thurs–Tues 10–12 and 3–6; closed Wed*). Then drive south to **Cervignano del Friuli**.

Lunch: In Cervignano del Friuli, *see* below.

Afternoon: Stop in ancient **Aquileia** (*see* p.200), just south, then continue to **Grado**, Aquileia's old port. In the narrow lanes of the old town, the Castrum Gradense, look for the Basilica of Sant'Eufemia, once the seat of the 6th-century Patriarch of Nova Aquileia, as he fashioned himself. Inside it has its original 6th-century mosaic floor, an 11th-century domed pulpit and a silver *pala* donated by the Venetians in 1372; also visit the adjacent baptistry and Basilica of Santa Maria delle Grazie, both from the 5th century. You might fancy a swim, either at the town beach or at the pine-fringed Pineta; or you could take the 'sand cure' (get buried up to your neck in benevolent warm sand, full of curative minerals and micro-organisms) at the Thermal Bath and Theraputic Department (*t 0431 899 309*); or simply watch birds in Grado's lagoon.

Dinner and Sleeping: In Grado, *see* below. In the morning, jump on the *autostrada* back to Trieste.

Day 5

Lunch in Cervignano del Friuli

Hotel Internazionale Rotonda, Via Ramazzotti 2, t 0431 30751 (*expensive*). An elegant hotel restaurant on the Trieste–Venice road, with keen attention to detail. Top billing goes to seasonal vegetables and seafood, but everything is delicious, including the exquisite desserts. Excellent wine list, too. *Closed Sun eve, Mon and half of Aug.*

Chichibio, Via Carnia 2, t 0431 32704 (*cheap*). A big, busy place on the Grado crossroads, serving up delicious meat or seafood menus, as well as top-notch pizzas. *Closed Wed.*

Dinner in Grado

All'Androna, Calle Porta Piccola 4, t 0431 80950 (*very expensive*). In the winding streets around the cathedral, with a summer garden and a daily-changing menu of fresh fish, home-made bread and pasta. If it's on the menu, try the *zuppette di frutti di mare* or the *ravioli di scampi in brodo. Closed Tues out of season and Dec–Mar.*

De Toni, Piazza Duca d'Aosta 37, t 0431 80104 (*expensive*). A characteristic little restaurant overlooking the Roman excavations, offering fresh fish prepared in a variety of local styles with garden vegetables. A long wine list is another bonus, and excellent desserts round things out very nicely indeed. *Closed Wed and Dec.*

Sleeping in Grado

★★★★Antica Villa Bernt, Via Colombo 5, t 0431 82516, f 0431 82517, *www.hotelbernt.it* (*very expensive*). There are lots of nice hotels in Grado, but only a couple stand out. Right in the centre of town, this one is a refurbished villa from the 1920s with 22 lovely rooms, equipped with all mod cons. *Open April–Oct.*

★★★Ambriabella, Riva Sant Andrea, t 0431 81479, f 0431 82257 (*expensive–moderate*). A pleasant little place with six rooms, and welcome personal touches that are sometimes missing from Grado's larger hotels.

Venice (Venezia)

In a world racked by stress, Venice is *la Serenissima*, a fairytale city on the sea, a lovely mermaid with the gift of eternal youth. Founded in mud flats by refugees fleeing Attila the Hun, on the surface she is little changed from the days when she dazzled the world with her wealth and pageantry, her magnificent fleet and luminous art, her silken debauchery, and her decline and fall into a seemingly endless carnival. Credit for this unique preservation goes to the Lagoon, the formaldehyde that has pickled her more thoroughly than many more venerable mainland cities.

The Grand Canal

There's no finer introduction to Venice than a vaporetto ride (no.1) down her bustling main artery. The Grand Canal has always been Venice's status address and along its looping banks the patricians of the Golden Book, or *Nobili Homini*, built a hundred marble palaces, framed by peppermint-stick posts where they moored their watery carriages. Halfway along, Antonio da Ponte's **Ponte di Rialto** (1592) spans 157ft in an audacious single arch while holding up two rows of shops. Guarding the southern entrance to the Canal is the **Dogana di Mare**, crowned by a weathervane of Fortune; a little beyond, on the north bank, is the landing-stage of San Marco.

Piazza San Marco

Napoleon described this asymmetrical showpiece as 'Europe's finest drawing-room' and, no matter how often you've been there, its charm never fades. Lining the piazza and its two flanking *piazzette* are the long, arcaded **Procuratie Vecchie** (1499) and **Procuratie Nuove** (1540), filled with jewellery, embroidery and lace shops, and graced by Venice's rival 18th-century grand cafés: **Caffè Quadri** and **Florian's**.

St Mark's Basilica

Open to visitors Mon–Sat 9.30–5, Sun and hols 2–4.30. No shorts; women must cover their shoulders and show a minimum of décolletage; the queue can be diabolically long in season. Separate adm for many of the smaller chapels and individual attractions; different sections frequently closed for restoration. Ramp access from Piazzetta dei Leoncini.

This was the holy of holies of the Venetian state, built to house the relics of its patron saint, the evangelist St Mark, whose winged lion symbol became the city's own. A law decreed that all merchants trading in the East had to bring back an embellishment for the basilica, and the result is a glittering robbers' den. The present structure was consecrated in 1094. Five rounded doorways, five upper arches and five round Byzantine domes are the essentials of the **exterior**, all frosted with a sheen of coloured marbles, ancient columns and sculpture. Ready to prance off the façade, the controversial 1979 copies of the **horses of St Mark** masquerade well enough from a distance. The **interior** dazzles with the intricate splendour of a thousand details: golden mosaics on New Testament subjects cover the domes and atrium; ancient columns, sawn into slices of rich colour, line the lower walls; the 12th-century pavement is a magnificent mosaic of marble, glass and porphyry. The 14th-century **baptistry** (*ask a caretaker to show you the 'Ufficio Technico'*) is famous for its mosaics on the life of John the Baptist, with a Salome who could probably have had just as many heads as she pleased. You can't visit the relics of St Mark, safe in the **sanctuary** (*open Mon–Sat 9–5, Sun 2–4; adm*), but you can see the altar's retable, the fabulous, glowing Pala d'Oro, a masterpiece of medieval gold and jewel work. Before leaving, climb up to the **Museo Marciano, Galleria and Loggia dei Cavalli** (*open same hours as the church*) to see the original ancient Greek bronze horses, and get a better view of the dome mosaics from the women's gallery, along with a visit to the loggia, where you can inspect the replica quadriga and look down on the swarming piazza below.

The Campanile, the Torre dell'Orologio and Piazzetta San Marco

St Mark's 332ft **bell tower** (*open April–Sept daily 9.30–30mins before sunset; Nov– Mar daily 9.30–3.30; adm*) can seem rather alien, a Presbyterian brick sentinel in the otherwise delicately wrought piazza. But it has been there since 912; when it gently collapsed in 1902, the Venetians felt its lack so acutely that they constructed an exact replica. Another famous ornament, at the head of the Procuratie Vecchie, is the **Torre dell'Orologio** (*under scaffolding*), built in 1499 and crowned by two bronze 'Moors' who sound the hours. Of elaborate astronomical clocks, none is as beautiful as this; according to rumour, the Council of Ten blinded the builders to prevent them from creating such a marvel for any other city.

To the south of the basilica, the **Piazzetta San Marco** was the republic's foyer, where ships would dock under the watchful eye of the doge. One of its pair of Egyptian columns bears an ancient Assyrian or Persian winged lion, under whose paw the Venetians adroitly slid a book to create the symbol of St Mark. The columns frame the famous view out to the Lagoon towards the islet of **San Giorgio Maggiore**, crowned by Palladio's church of the same name. Built according to his theories on harmonic proportion, it seems to hang between the water and the sky.

Piazza San Marco Museums and the Biblioteca Marciana

One ticket will get you into the Museo Correr, the Biblioteca Marciana, the Museo Archeològico and Ducal Palace (*entrance to all except the Palazzo Ducale is via the Museo Correr*). The **Museo Correr** (*facing the basilica in the corner of the piazza; open April–Oct daily 9–7; Nov–Mar daily 9–5; last tickets 1hr before closing; adm to all museums €10*) contains an engaging collection of Venetian memorabilia, and many fine Venetian paintings upstairs. These include Carpaccio's *Courtesans* (or Ladies – in Venice it was hard to tell) and his *Visitation*; there are also works by Antonello da Messina, Cosme Turà, Bellini, Canova and Il Civetta.

Opposite the Doges' Palace stands Sansovino's superb **Biblioteca**, where scholars with permission can examine such treasures as the 1501 *Grimani breviary*, Homeric *codices* and Marco Polo's will. Next to the library, the **Archaeology Museum** has an excellent collection of Greek sculpture, including a violent *Leda and the Swan* and ancient copies of the *Gallic Warriors of Pergamon*. By the waterfront, the **Zecca**, or Old Mint, once stamped out thousands of gold *zecchini*, giving English the word 'sequin'.

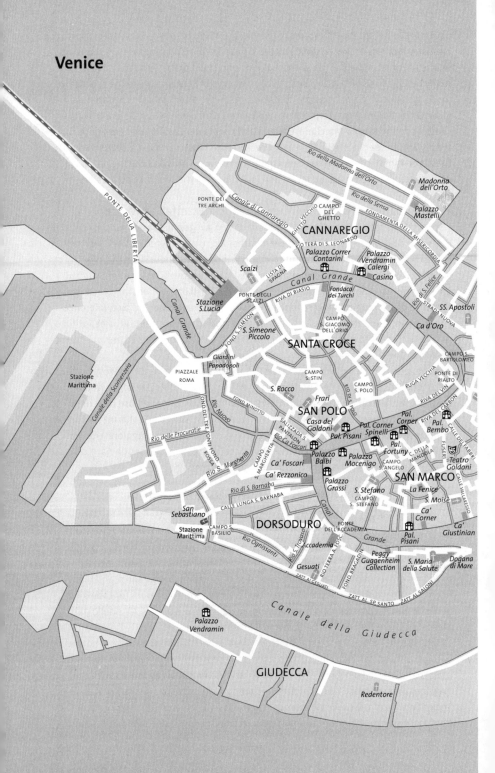

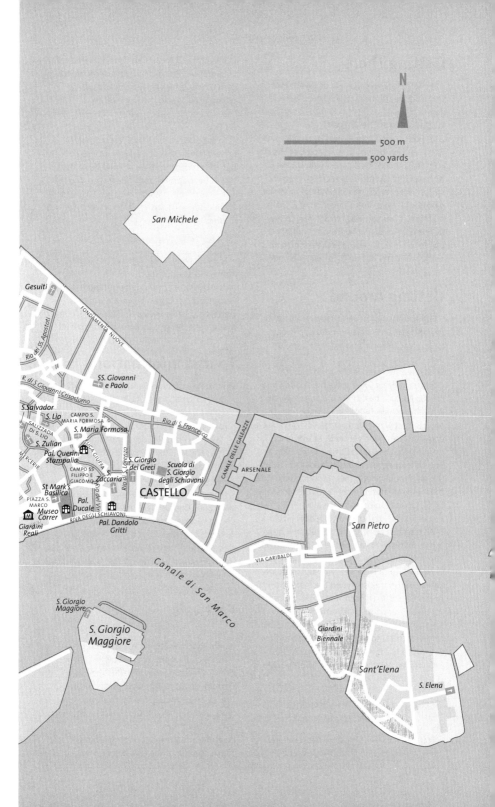

Getting There

See **Getting There**, pp.3–8. Be aware that some budget flights actually fly to Treviso.

Getting from the Airport

Venice's Marco Polo airport (**t** 041 260 9260, *www.veniceairport.it*) is 13km north of the city near the Lagoon. It is linked to Venice by **water-taxi** (**t** 041 541 6363/**t** 041 595 1402 at airport) for over €80 (to San Marco); or by *motoscafi* (taking 1hr 10mins, hourly, 4.50am–midnight; **t** 041 541 5084) to San Marco. Buy **tickets** (€9) on board. There is also an **ATVO bus** to the Piazzale Roma (€3), taking 25mins, or the **ACTV city bus** no.5 (€2), every 30mins.

Getting Around

Public transport in Venice means by water, by *vaporetti*, or the faster *motoscafi* (**t** 041 2424, *www.hellovenezia.it*). Most lines run until midnight; there is also an all-night line. Schedules are listed in the free guide, *Un Ospite di Venezia*. They serve the Grand Canal, the Rio Nuovo, the Canale di Cannaregio and Rio dell'Arsenale. Between them, you must rely on your feet; Venice is so small you can walk across it in an hour. *Vaporetti* tickets (valid for 90mins) for the Grand Canal routes (Nos. 2 and 82) cost €5; other routes are €3.50. **Tickets** (€3.50) should be bought and validated in the machines at landing-stages; it's best to stock up at *tabacchi* (blocks of 10 available). There are also passes: **24hrs** (€10.50), **3 days** (€22).

Water-taxis work like taxis, but their fares are de luxe. Stands are at the station, Piazzale Roma, Rialto, San Marco, Lido and the airport. They hold up to 15 passengers, and fares are set for destinations beyond the historic centre, or pay €73/hr. In the centre the minimum fare for up to four people is €73; there are also surcharges for extra people, baggage, holidays or service after 10pm, and for using a **radio taxi** (**t** 041 522 2303 or **t** 041 723 112).

Gondolas now operate frankly for tourists (€73/50mins; €91 after 8pm).

Getting to Croatia and Slovenia

By Boat

From May to Oct, Venezia Lines (**t** 041 522 2568, *www.venezialines.com*) runs services from Venice to the Istrian Peninsula (including Umag, Porec, Rovinj and Pula) and down to Mali Losinj. Ferries leave from San Basilio where there is also the ticket office.

By Bus

Two coaches a day leave Venice for the Istrian Peninsula (each takes a different route but they both terminate at Pula). They are run by Fils (*www.fils.hr*) and SAF (*www.saf.udi.it*). They leave from outside the Brusatti office in Piazale Roma; Brusatti sell tickets and give out information (**t** 041 520 5530).

Car Hire

The following have branches at Piazzale Roma and at the airport.
Avis, **t** 041 523 7377, *www.avisautonoleggio.it*.
Europcar, **t** 041 523 8616, *www.europcar.it*.
Hertz, **t** 041 528 4091, *ww.hertz.it*.
Maggiore, **t** 041 935 300, *www.maggiore.it*.

Tourist Information

Venice: Palazzina dei Santi, Giardini Reali, Vaporetto Vallarosso, **t** 041 522 5150, *www.turismovenezia.it*. Branches at Venice Pavilion, the train station and the bus station in Piazzale Roma offer accommodation services. There are also offices on the Rotonda Marghera, at Marco Polo Airport, and on the Lido at Gran Viale 6.

Many churches now belong to an association called **Chorus** (**t** 041 275 0462, *www. chorus.venezia.org*), and a collective ticket for all these churches costs €8 (individually €2.50). Tickets are available from the churches, from VELA ticket offices, and from the Venice Pavilion tourist office.

Festivals

Venice is one of Europe's top cities for exhibitions: the **Biennale**, the world's most famous contemporary art show, is held in even-numbered years in early June in the Giardini Pubblici. The other great cultural junket is the **Venice Film Festival** (*late Aug–Sept*). Venice's famous **Carnival**, first held in 1094, attracts huge crowds, but dressing up in costume and taking each other's picture is as much as most of the revellers now get up to.

The most spectacular festival is **Il Redentore** (*3rd Sun of July*), with its bridge of boats. On the Saturday before, Venetians row out for a picnic on the water, manoeuvring for the best view of the fireworks.

Shopping

Venice is a fertile field for shoppers, whether you're looking for tacky bric-a-brac (walk down the Lista di Spagna) or the latest in Italian design – but be warned that bargains are hard to find. The area around Campo San Maurizio, near Campo Santo Stefano, has the largest concentration of antique shops. Most of Venice's designer boutiques are in the streets to the west of Piazza San Marco; **Emilio Ceccato**, Sottoportico di Rialto, S. Polo, is the place for typically Venetian gondoliers' shirts. The greatest name in Venetian leather is Vogini, S. Marco 1300, Via XXII Marzo.

The best place to find Venetian lace is on **Burano**, but **Jesurum**, Piazza S. Marco 60/61, has Venetian lace and linen of all kinds. **Codognato**, S. Marco 1295, Calle dell'Ascensione, is one of the oldest jewellers in Venice; at **Missiaglia**, Piazza S. Marco 125, you can see pieces produced by Venetian gold and silversmiths working today.

Anyone seeking unusual gifts will find plenty in Venice, though prices may need to be handled with care. For an overview, the **Consorzio Artigianato Artistico Veneziano**, S. Marco 412, Calle Larga, has a fair selection of hand-made Venetian crafts. The most renowned of Venice's ancient crafts is, of course, Venetian glass. **Murano** is still the place to go, but in the city try **Paolo Rossi**, S. Marco 4685, Campo S. Zaccaria.

Where to Stay

Wherever you stay in Venice, expect it to cost around a third more than it would on the mainland. Booking is near-essential April–Oct and for Carnival; many hotels close in winter.

*******Danieli**, Castello 4196, Riva degli Schiavoni, t 041 522 6480, f 041 520 0208, *www.starwood.com/italy* (*luxury*). The most famous hotel in Venice, in the most glorious location, overlooking the Lagoon next to the Palazzo Ducale. Formerly a Gothic *palazzo*, it has been a hotel since 1822; Dickens, Proust, George Sand and Wagner checked in here. Nearly every room has silken walls, Gothic stairs, gilt mirrors and oriental rugs. The new wing is comfortable but lacks the stories.

*******Gritti Palace**, San Marco 2467, Campo Santa Maria del Giglio, t 041 794 611, f 041 520 0942, *www.luxurycollection.com/ grittipalace* (*luxury*). A 15th-century Grand Canal palace preserved as a true Venetian fantasy and elegant retreat. All the rooms are furnished with Venetian antiques.

*****Accademia**, Dorsoduro 1058, Fondamenta Bollani, t 041 521 0188, f 041 523 9152 (*luxury*). A generous dollop of slightly faded charm in a 17th-century villa with a garden, off the Grand Canal. Its 26 rooms are furnished with a menagerie of antiques. Book well in advance. Off-season discounts.

*****Do Pozzi**, San Marco 2373, Via XXII Marzo, t 041 520 7855, f 041 522 9413, *www.hotel dopozzi.it* (*very expensive*). With 29 rooms on a charming little square where tables are set out for breakfast or a drink.

*****La Calcina**, Dorsoduro 780, Fondamente delle Zattere, Dorsoduro, t 041 520 6466, f 041 522 7045. *www.lacalcina.com* (*very expensive*). Overlooking the Giudecca canal, this was Ruskin's *pensione* in 1877. Totally refurbished with all mod cons, and a beautiful floating terrace restaurant.

*****CasaVerardo**, Castello 4765, Campo SS Filippo e Giacomo, t 041 528 6138, *www. casaverardo.it* (*very expensive*). A few minutes walk from Piazza San Marco, this newly refurbished hotel is tucked away down a narrow *calle*. There is a cool, calm reception hall, a pretty courtyard garden, and a flower-filled terrace off the elegant salon where breakfast is served.

****San Fantin**, San Marco 1930A, Campiello Fenice, t/f 041 523 1 401 (*expensive*). Just around the corner from La Fenice in a quiet little *campo*, this simple hotel is out of a time-warp, with a reception area a bit like your granny's parlour, dated in a rather refreshing way. 14 rooms, two without bath.

****Hotel Iris**, San Polo 2910A, Calle del Cristo, t 041 522 2882, *www.irishotel.com* (*expensive*). The clean, pleasant rooms here have been recently redecorated; one has a pretty ceiling fresco and is really quite elegant. All rooms have phone and TV. *Closed Jan.*

*San Samuele, San Marco 3358, Salizada San
Samuele, t/f 041 522 8045, *www.albergo
sansamuele.it* (*moderate*). A delightful little
budget hotel with flower-filled window-
boxes overlooking the *salizada*. Clean, sunny
and homey rooms and very friendly staff
make this one of the best one-star places in
Venice. Single rooms have bathrooms in the
corridor. No credit cards.

*Casa Boccassini, Cannaregio 5295, Calle del
Fumo, t 041 522 9892 (*inexpensive*). In a quiet
neighbourhood well away from the crowds;
the basic but clean-as-a-whistle rooms have
the odd antique piece to add character, and
there is a pleasant breakfast room and
sitting area, and a delightful garden.

Eating Out

Antico Martini, San Marco 1983, Campo San
Fantin, t 041 523 7027, *www.anticomartini.
com* (*very expensive*). A Venetian classic, all
romance and elegance. A Turkish coffee-
house in the early 18th century, but now
better known for seafood. The intimate
piano bar-restaurant stays open till 2am.

Da Fiore, San Polo 2202A, Calle del Scaleter,
t 041 721 308 (*very expensive*). People 'in the
know' believe this to be the best restaurant
in Venice. Food is taken seriously here; the
atmosphere is sober without any preten-
tious frills. *Closed Sun and Mon, Jan and Aug.*

Harry's Bar, S. Marco 1323, Calle Vallaresso,
t 041 523 5777 (*very expensive*). A favourite of
Hemingway, this is a Venetian institution for
its celebrity atmosphere. Avoid the food and
flit in to sample the justly famous cocktails
(a Bellini, Tiziano or Tiepolo). *Closed Mon.*

Vecio Fritolin, Santa Croce 2262, Calle della
Regina, t 041 522 2881, *www.veciofritolin.com*
(*expensive*). A calm, civilized restaurant with
a delightful owner, Irina. The day's catch is
cooked without fuss and beautifully
presented. *Closed Sun eve and Mon.*

L'Incontro, Dorsoduro 3062, Rio Terrà Canal,
t 041 522 2404 (*expensive*). An unusual
restaurant for Venice: the food is Sardinian,
and there's no fish, just succulent meat
dishes and a choice of Sardinian pasta.

Bancogiro: Osteria da Andrea, San Polo 122,
Campo Giacometto, t 041 523 2061 (*expensive*). This modern *osteria* enjoys a fabulous

position overlooking the Grand Canal. In the
street-level bar, excellent wines and snacks
are served; above, those who have booked
can choose creative dishes such as fish salad
with apple and mandarin. Booking essential.
Closed Sun eve and Mon.

Ca d'Oro–Alla Vedova, Cannaregio 3912, Ramo
Ca d'Oro, t 041 528 5324 (*expensive*). This
atmospheric old *bacaro* serves both *cicheti*
at the bar and sit-down meals. The atmosphere is cosy and welcoming and the food is
good and not too expensive. Try the lasagne
with artichokes. *Closed Thurs.*

Anice Stellato, Cannaregio 3272, Fondamenta
della Sensa, t 041 720 744 (*expensive*). New-
generation, family-run *bacaro/trattoria* near
the remote church of Sant'Alvise. Booking
advised. *Closed Mon and 3 weeks Aug/Sept.*

Ai 4 Feri, Dorsoduro 2754, Calle Lunga San
Barnaba, t 041 520 6978 (*expensive*). *Osteria*
run along traditional lines, with *cicheti* and
full meals at honest prices: pumpkin soup,
spaghetti with artichokes and shrimps,
grilled fish. No cards. *Closed Sun.*

Gam-Gam, Cannaregio 1122, Sottoportico di
Ghetto Vecchio, t 041 715 284, *www.jewish
venice.org* (*moderate*). A modern kosher bar
and restaurant by the ghetto with tables on
the canal. No cards. *Closed Sat.*

The classic **cafés** face each other across
Piazza San Marco: **Florian's** and **Quadri**, both
beautiful, and both exorbitant. For ice cream,
head to tiny **Boutique del Gelato** on Salizada
San Lio, or **Paolin**, on Campo Santo Stefano.

Entertainment and Nightlife

The main source in English on any current
events is the fortnightly *Un Ospite di Venezia*,
free from tourist offices and hotels. The local
papers *Il Gazzettino* and *Nuova Venezia* both
have listings of films, concerts, etc. Venice's
music programme is heavily orientated to the
classical. **La Fenice**, t 041 786 511, *www.teatro
lafenice.it*, has now reopened; for tickets,
contact the Cassa di Risparmio, Campo
S. Luca, t 041 521 0161. Sadly, life after dark is
notoriously moribund; do as most people do –
just wander about. The hotblooded may go
on to bars and discos in Mestre, Marghera or
the Lido.

The Palace of the Doges (Palazzo Ducale)

Open 15 April–Oct 9–7; Nov–Mar 9–5; adm exp – includes entry to the Museo Correr. Ticket office (closes 6pm summer, 4pm winter) through Porta della Carta and in the courtyard.

What St Mark's is to sacred architecture, the **Doges' Palace** is to secular – unique and audacious, an illuminated storybook of Venetian history and legend. Its weight is partly relieved by the white and red diamond pattern on the façade, which from a distance gives the palace its wholesome, peaches-and-cream complexion. Some of Italy's finest medieval sculpture crowns the columns of the lower colonnade. Beautiful sculptural groups adorn the corners, most notably the 13th-century *Judgement of Solomon*, near the grand **Porta della Carta** (1443), a Gothic symphony in stone by Giovanni and Bartolomeo Bon. Just within the Porta, don't miss Antonio Rizzo's delightful courtyard and his **Scala dei Giganti**. Visitors enter the palace via Sansovino's **Scala d'Oro**. The first floor is used for special exhibitions (*separate adm*), while the golden stairway continues up to the Secondo Piano Nobile, from where the Venetian state was governed. After a fire, Veronese and Tintoretto were employed to paint the newly remodelled chambers with mythological themes and scores of allegories and apotheoses of Venice. Among the highlights are the **Sala del Consiglio dei Dieci**, where the Council of Ten deliberated under Veronese's ceiling, and the magnificent **Sala del Maggior Consiglio**, capable of holding the 2,500 patricians of the Great Council. By the entrance is Tintoretto's *Paradiso*, the biggest oil painting in the world, from which all the Blessed look up at Veronese's great *Apotheosis of Venice* on the ceiling. At the end the **Bridge of Sighs** (Ponte dei Sospiri) takes you to the 17th-century **Palazzo delle Prigioni**, where those to whom the Republic took real exception were dumped into uncomfortable *pozzi*, or 'wells'. Celebrities like Casanova, meanwhile, got to stay up in the rather cosier *piombi* or 'leads', just under the roof. These, and the rooms where the real nitty-gritty business of state took place, can only be seen on the 1½-hour **Itinerari Segreti** (*guided tours in English at 9.55 and 11.35; 20 people only; book at least a day in advance, or call **t** 041 520 9075; adm exp*).

San Marco to Rialto

The streets between the piazza and the famous Rialto bridge are the busiest in Venice, especially the **Mercerie**, lined with some of the city's smartest shops. The Mercerie continue past two churches in which Sansovino had a hand: **San Zulian**, with a façade most notable for Sansovino's statue of its pompous benefactor; and **San Salvatore**, containing his monument to Doge Francesco Venier. An 89-year-old Titian painted one of his more unusual works for this church, the *Annunciation*, which he signed with double emphasis *Titianus Fecit* – '*Fecit*' because his patrons refused to believe that he had painted it. Humming, bustling **Campo San Bartolomeo** has for centuries been one of the social hubs of Venice, and still gets packed daily with after-work crowds. Follow the signs up to the **Ponte di Rialto**, the geographical heart of Venice. The city's central morning markets have been just across the bridge for a millennium, divided into sections for vegetables and for fish.

San Marco to the Accademia

Following signs 'To the Accademia' from Piazza San Marco, the first *campo* belongs to Baroque **San Moisè** (1668), Italy's most grotesque church. Detour up Calle Veste to see **La Fenice** (1792;), Venice's renowned opera house, now finally reopened after devastation by fire, which saw the premières of Verdi's *Rigoletto* and *La Traviata*. Back en route to the Accademia, the signs lead past the fancy façade (1680) of **Santa Maria Zobenigo** to the **Campo Santo Stefano**, one of the most elegant squares in Venice; at one end, a gravity-defying campanile leers over the church of **Santo Stefano**, which has a striking wooden ceiling like the keel of a ship.

Just over the Grand Canal stands the **Accademia** (*open Mon 8.15–2, Tues–Sun 8.15–7.15; adm exp; arrive early; only 300 visitors at a time*), the grand cathedral of Venetian art, ablaze with light and colour. The collection is arranged chronologically, beginning with fine altarpieces, including Giovanni Bellini's *Pala di San Giobbe*, one of the key works of the *quattrocento*. The next rooms are small but, like gifts, contain the best things: works by Mantegna, Giovanni Bellini and Piero della Francesca. The climax of the Venetian High Renaissance comes in Room X, with Veronese's *Christ in the House of Levi* (1573), its ghostly imaginary background in violent contrast to the rollicking feast in front. Here, too, is *La Pietà*, Titian's last painting (at age 90); he intended it for his tomb, and smeared the paint on with his fingers. Alongside several Tintorettos, the following few rooms mainly contain work from the 17th and 18th centuries. Canaletto and Guardi are represented in Room XVII, and the final rooms house more luminous 15th-century painting by Alvise Vivarini, Giovanni and Gentile Bellini, Marco Basaiti and Crivelli. There's a compelling *Cycle of S. Ursula* by Carpaccio and, in the last room, Titian's striking *Presentation of the Virgin* (1538).

Dorsoduro

The Accademia lies in the *sestiere* of Dorsoduro, which also boasts the **Peggy Guggenheim Collection** (*open Wed–Mon 10–6; April–Oct also Sat 10–10; adm exp*), an impressive quantity of brand-name 20th-century art: Bacon, Brancusi, Braque, Calder, Chagall, Dali, De Chirico, Duchamp, Max Ernst (her second husband), Giacometti, Gris, Kandinsky, Klee, Magritte, Miró, Moore, Mondrian, Picasso, Pollock, Rothko and Smith. From here it's a short stroll to the elegant, octagonal basilica of **Santa Maria della Salute** (*1631–81; open daily 9–12 and 3–5.30, until 6.30 in summer*), the masterpiece of Baldassare Longhena, with its snow-white dome and marble jelly rolls. The interior is a relatively restrained Baroque, and contains the *Marriage at Cana* by Tintoretto and several works by Titian. Almost next to the basilica stands the distinctive **Dogana di Mare**, the Customs House. The long **Fondamenta delle Zattere** skirts the Canale della Giudecca (*or vaporetto no.5 to San Basegio*) to the church of **San Sebastiano**, embellished with magnificent ceiling frescoes and illusionistic paintings by Veronese. Back towards the Grand Canal to the north is the delightful **Campo Santa Margherita**, traditionally the marketplace of Dorsoduro; it's also a good spot for restaurants and cafés. A red campanile marks the 14th-century church of the **Carmini**, next to the **Scuola dei Carmini** (*open summer Mon–Sat 9–6, Sun 9–4; winter daily 9–4; adm; also open for concerts*), which has one of Tiepolo's best and brightest ceilings, *The Virgin in Glory*.

San Polo and Santa Croce

From the Ponte di Rialto, the yellow signs lead through the pretty **Campo San Polo** to a venerable Venetian institution: the severe medieval brick **Frari** (*open Mon–Sat 9–6, Sun and hols 1–6; adm*), celebrated for its paintings, especially the most overrated painting in Italy, Titian's *Assumption of the Virgin* (1516–18). Marvel at the revolutionary use of space and movement, but the Virgin herself has as much artistic vision as a Sunday school holy card. His less theatrical *Madonna di Ca' Pésaro*, in the north aisle, had a greater influence on Venetian composition. In the sanctuary is the beautiful Renaissance **Tomb of Doge Nicolà Tron** (1476) by Antonio Rizzo. Titian is buried here too, as is composer Monteverdi. Next to the Frari, the extraordinary **Scuola Grande di San Rocco** (*open 9–5.30, until 4 in winter; adm*) holds one of the wonders of Venice – or rather, 54 wonders – all painted by Tintoretto between 1562 and 1585.

East of San Marco to Castello

From Piazzetta San Marco, the ever-thronging **Riva degli Schiavoni** curves east beyond the Palazzo Ducale. Northeast, the tiny **Scuola di San Giorgio degli Schiavoni** (*open Tues–Sat 9.30–12.30 and 3.30–6.30, Sun 9.30–12.30; adm*) is decorated with the most beloved art in all Venice: Vittore Carpaccio's frescoes on the lives of Dalmatian patron saints, among them George charging a petticoat-munching dragon in a landscape strewn with maidenly leftovers from lunch. Further east lies the first of all arsenals, the **Arsenale**, founded in 1104; today it is occupied by the Italian military, but up until the 17th century these were the greatest dockyards in the world. Nearby, Venice's glorious maritime history is the subject of the artefacts and models in the **Museo Storico Navale** (*open Mon–Fri 8.45–1.30, Sat 8.45–1; closed Sun; adm*).

North of San Marco

Through the web of alleys north of San Marco is Campo San Zanipolo and **SS. Giovanni e Paolo** (*open Mon–Sat 7.30–12.30 and 3.30–7, Sun 3–6; adm*), the pantheon of the doges. Some 25 of them lie here in Gothic and Renaissance tombs; the finest is that of Doge Andrea Vendramin, by Tullio and Antonio Lombardo (1478). From here, Largo G. Gallina leads to the Renaissance church of **Santa Maria dei Miracoli** (*open Mon–Sat 10–5, Sun and hols 1–5; adm*), an exquisite jewel box built by Pietro Lombardo in the 1480s. Further north, the enchanting Gothic fantasy **Ca' d'Oro** houses the **Galleria Franchetti** (*open Mon 8.15–2, Tues–Sun 8.15–7.15; adm*); among its artistic treasures are Mantegna's *St Sebastian* and Guardi's series of Venetian views, as well as Renaissance bronzes and medallions by Pisanello and Il Riccio. Due north, near the Fondamenta Nuove, stands the unrestored church of the **Gesuiti** (*open daily 10–12 and 4–6*), a Baroque extravaganza from 1714–29, full of *trompe-l'œil* of white and green-grey marble draperies.

Cannaregio

Crumbling, piquant Cannaregio is the least visited *sestiere* in Venice and here, perhaps, you can begin to feel what everyday life is like behind the tourist glitz. This was Tintoretto's home base, and he is buried in the beautiful Venetian Gothic **Madonna dell'Orto** (*open Mon–Sat 10–5, Sun and hols 1–5; adm*), alongside several of his jumbo masterpieces. Here, too, was the cramped **Ghetto**, with its five synagogues; all Jews were confined here in 1516, in part for their own protection, surrounded by a moat-like canal. In contrast, towards the station to the north runs the **Lista di Spagna**, Venice's famous tourist highway, lined with restaurants, hotels and souvenir stands.

The Lagoon and its Islands

Pearly and melting, iridescent blue or murky green, a sheet of glass in the dawn or leaden, opaque grey: Venice's Lagoon is a wonderful, desolate 'landscape'.

Nearest to the centre, next to the little islet of San Giorgio Maggiore (*vaporetto 82*), the string of eight islands that make up **La Giudecca** (*vaporetti 41, 42, 82, N*) is seldom visited. Those who can afford it come to rub shoulders with the rich and famous at the luxurious **Cipriani Hotel**; others to visit Palladio's best church, **Il Redentore** (*open Mon–Sat 10–5, Sun 1–5; adm*), its temple front providing a fitting backdrop for one of the most exciting events on the Venetian calendar, the *Festa del Redentore* (*see p.213*).

The **Lido**, with its 12km of beach, was the pinnacle of Belle Epoque fashion, and it's still Venice's playground today, with its bathing concessions, riding clubs, tennis courts, golf courses and shooting ranges. The free beach (**Spiaggia Comunale**) is on the north side, a 15-minute walk from the *vaporetto* stop at San Nicolò.

Murano (*vaporetti 41 and 42 from Ferrovia or Fondamenta Nuove; 71 and 72 from Piazzale Roma, Ferrovia, S. Zaccaria and F. Nuove – summer only; DM line from Ferrovia and Piazzale Roma*) has been synonymous with glass ever since all the forges in Venice were relocated there in 1291. Can you visit them? You bet! There's the inevitable tour of the 'Museum Show Rooms', but it's free and there's not much pressure to buy. The **Museo dell' Arte Vetrario** (*open April–Oct Thurs–Tues 10–5; Nov–Mar Thurs–Tues 10–4; included in San Marco museums adm*) has a choice collection of 15th-century Murano glass. Nearby, a marvellous mosaic incorporating ancient Murano glass paves the floor of **Santi Maria e Donato** (*open daily 8.30–12 and 4–6*).

In supremely photogenic **Burano** (*LN line from Fondamente Nuove and San Marco, which also calls at Torcello and Burano*), all the buildings are painted with a Fauvist sensibility in brightly coloured miniature. Traditionally the men fish and the women make Venetian point, 'the most Italian of all lace work'. You can see it being made at the **Scuola dei Merletti** (*open April–Oct Wed–Mon 10–5; Nov–Mar 10–4; adm*).

Birthplace of Venice, quiet **Torcello** is now overgrown with vegetation, but its **Cathedral of Santa Maria Assunta** (*open April–Oct 10.30–6.30; Nov–Mar 10–5; adm*) contains Venice's finest mosaics. All are by 11th- and 12th-century Greek artists, from a wonderful floor to a spectacular *Last Judgement* and the heart-rending *Teotoco*.

Day Trips from Venice

Padua (Padova)

Padua refuses to be overshadowed by Venice, and can rightly claim a place among Italy's most interesting and historic cities. It's a short walk from the station to the jewel in Padua's crown: Giotto's extraordinary frescoes (1304–7) in the **Cappella degli**

Getting There

Padua is easily reached by **train** from Venice (40mins). There are also **buses** from Venice every half-hour, arriving at Padua's **bus station** in the Piazzale Boschetti (**t** 049 820 6844), a 10-minute walk from the train station.

Tourist Information

Padua: at the station, **t** 049 875 2077; Galleria Pedrocchi, **t** 049 876 7927; *www.turismo padova.it, www.provincia.padova.it*. If you plan to visit several attractions, a **Padova Card** is a wise investment for €14.

Eating Out

Bastioni del Moro, Via Bronzetti 18, **t** 049 871 0006 (*expensive*). Delicious gnocchi beyond Padua's western walls (take Corso Milano). The tourist menu is cheap, though prices soar if you order fish. *Closed Sun.*

Godenda Winebar, Via F Squarcione 4, **t** 049 877 4192 (*moderate*). A stylish, informal wine bar just behind Piazza delle Erbe; fine foods arrive daily from all over Italy. *Closed Sun.*

Scrovegni (*open 9–7, museum closed Mon; adm exp, inc. museum and chapel; visits to the chapel timed, book in advance, **t** 049 8204 551*). In sheer power and inspiration, the cycle was as revolutionary as Michelangelo's Sistine Chapel: a fresh, natural, narrative composition, with three-dimensional figures solidly anchored in their setting. In the adjacent convent, Padua's vast **Museo Civico** (*same hours and ticket*) combines archaeology with acres of fine art. Here you'll find Giotto's *Crucifixion*, works by Guariento, founder of the medieval Paduan school, and others by nearly every Venetian who ever applied brush to canvas. Next to the museum, the church of the **Eremitani** (1306; *open Mon–Sat 8.30–12.30 and 3.30–6, Sun 10–12.30 and 4–6; same ticket as the Cappella degli Scrovegni*) was shattered in a Second World War air raid, but what could be salvaged of the frescoes has been painstakingly pieced together, most importantly Mantegna's remarkable Ovetari chapel (1454–7).

A short walk from the Eremitani takes you to **Piazza Cavour**, the historic heart of Padua. Here, the Palazzo del Bo' was the seat of the **University of Padua**, where Galileo delivered his lectures from an old wooden pulpit. To the west are the bustling market squares of **Piazza delle Erbe** and **Piazza delle Frutta**, separated by the massive **Palazzo della Ragione** (*open Feb–Oct Tues–Sun 9–7; Nov–Jan Tues–Sun 9–6; closed Mon; adm*). A little further west, Padua's **Duomo** is rather neglected, but the **baptistry** (*open 10–6; adm*) was beautifully frescoed by Florentine Giusto de' Menabuoi in the 1370s.

Below the commercial heart of Padua, an exotic, fantastical cluster of seven domes rises up around a lofty cupola, two campanili and two minarets: this is the **Basilica di Sant'Antonio**, begun in 1232, the same year that St Anthony was canonized. Inside, pilgrims queue patiently to press their palm against his tomb; no one pays much attention to the 16th-century marble reliefs lining his chapel, but they are exquisite: the fourth and fifth are by Sansovino, the sixth and seventh by Tullio Lombardo, and the last by Antonio Lombardo. The high altar is the work of Donatello and his helpers (1445–50), while the great Paschal Candelabrum is the masterpiece of Il Riccio. In the ambulatory, don't miss the treasury of gold reliquaries, one containing Anthony's tongue and larynx, found intact when his tomb was opened in 1981.

Touring from Venice: Villas and Gardens

Day 1: La Malcontenta and a Fiendish Maze

Morning: From Venice, take the S11 to **Mestre**. South of Mestre, the S11 follows the **Brenta Canal** west towards Padua, sprinkled along its length with 16th-century villas of Venetian patricians. Start at the east end of the S11, between Fusina and Oriago, at Palladio's celebrated **La Malcontenta** (1560) (*open April–Oct Tues and Sat 9–12 or call* **t** *041 520 3966; guided tours; adm*), a vision begging for Scarlett O'Hara to sweep down the steps – numerous American plantations were modelled on it. Inside are delicate frescoes, including the sad lady to whom the villa owes its name. Take the S11 west, past **Oriago**'s Villa Gradenigo, and stop for lunch in **Mira**, or beyond, in **Dolo**.

Lunch: In Mira or Dolo, *see below*.

Afternoon: Take a look at Mira's post office, the Palazzo Foscarini, where Byron lived (1817–1819) while working on *Childe Harold*. Then drive on to **Strá** to see the grandest villa in the Veneto: the **Villa Nazionale** (1760) modelled on Versailles (*open Nov–Mar Tues–Sun 9–4; April–Oct Tues–Sun 9–7; advisable to book ahead in summer,* **t** *041 271 9019; adm*). Tackle the fiendish maze in the park, and don't miss Giambattista Tiepolo's shimmering *Apotheosis of the Pisani Family* in the ballroom. Continue west to Padua, and take the S16 south to **Monsélice**, spilling like an opera set down the slopes of the Euganean Hills.

Dinner and Sleeping: In Monsélice or **Este** (9km west on the S10), *see below*.

Day 1

Lunch in Mira
Nalin, Via Nuovissimo 29, **t** 041 420 083 (*expensive*). One of the traditional places to round off an excursion along the Brenta Canal, with a lovely poplar-shaded veranda. The emphasis is on Venetian seafood, finely grilled. *Closed Sun eve, Mon and Aug.*

Lunch in Dolo
Locanda alla Posta, Via Ca' Tron 33, **t** 041 410 740 (*very expensive*). This restaurant has been around a long time. You'll be offered great fish, delicately prepared, alongside other creative versions of local dishes. *Closed Mon.*

Dinner in Monsélice
La Torre, Piazza Mazzini 14, **t** 0429 73752 (*expensive*). An elegant place where *funghi* fiends can head for gratification. *Closed Sun eve, Mon, and part of July and Aug.*

Sleeping in Monsélice
★★★Ceffri Villa Corner, Via Orti 7, **t** 0429 783 111, **f** 0429 783 100 (*expensive*). A modern hotel, with a swimming pool and well equipped rooms, plus a good restaurant featuring home-made pasta and an economical tourist menu.

Venetian Palace Hostel, 'Città di Monsélice', Via Santo Stefano Superiore 33, **t** 0429 783 125 (*inexpensive; no breakfast*). For somewhere rather more stylish, try this hostel, which was once used by the dukes of Padua as a guest house. It now offers comfortable rooms fitted with modern conveniences.

Dinner and Sleeping in Este
★★Hotel Beatrice d'Este, Via le Rimembranze 1, **t** 0429 600 533, **f** 0429 601 957 (*moderate*). This hotel has a lovely little trattoria attached, serving all the standard dishes of the Veneto.

Day 2: Euganean Musings and Grandiose Gardens

Morning: Explore the citadel of **Monsélice**, and look at the superb medieval and Renaissance arms and antiques in Ezzelino da Romano's Castello Monsélice (*open 20 Mar–30 Nov; tours 9–12 and 3–6; adm*). Zig-zag your way up the Via Sacra delle Sette Chiese past the sumptuous Villa Nani, the Duomo, seven chapels by Scamozzi (frescoed by Palma Giovane), and the elegant Villa Duodo. Then visit Monsélice's old rival, **Este** (9km west down the S10), bristling with the towers of the 1339 castle. Next door, the Museo Nazionale Atestino (*open 9–8; adm*) covers the Paleoveneto civilization from the 10th century BC up to Roman times; don't miss the outstanding bronze vase, the *Situla Benvenuti*. Muse over the **Villa De Kunkler**, where Shelley, as Byron's guest, penned *Lines written among the Euganean Hills*. Drive up into the hills themselves to have lunch in the medieval gem of **Arquà Petrarca**.

Lunch: In Arquà Petrarca, *see* below.

Afternoon: Visit Petrarch's villa, the charming **Casa del Petrarca** (*open Mar–Oct Tues–Sun 9–12 and 3–6.30; Nov–Feb Tues–Sun 9–12 and 2.30–5; adm*), with many of its 14th-century furnishings. Then continue north some 9km to the **Villa Barbarigo** at **Valsanzibio** (*www.valsanzibiogiardino.it; open daily Mar–Nov 10–1 and 2–sunset; adm exp*) for the grandest gardens in the Veneto, laid out with fountains, waterfalls and another wicked maze. From here, wiggle your way north to **Torreglia**, where a road leads west to **Teolo**, Livy's birthplace. The Museo di Arte Contemporanea (*open Tues, Thurs and Sun 3–7*) has works from many of Italy's finest living artists.

Dinner and Sleeping: Torréglia's the spot to dine, but return to sleep in Teolo; *see* below.

Day 2

Lunch in Arquà Petrarca

La Montanella, Via Costa 33, **t** 0429 718 200 (*expensive*). Near the centre, with a garden and views; exquisite risottos and duck with fruit. *Closed Tues eve, Wed, 2 weeks each in Aug and Jan.*

*Roncha, Via Costa 132, **t** 0429 718 286 (*moderate*). Just down from La Montanella; serves local specialities. *Closed Mon–Wed.*

Dinner in Torreglia

Join the hungry Paduans at their favourite country restaurants in Torreglia, 9km east.

Da Taparo, Via Castelletto 42, **t** 049 521 1685 (*moderate*). This restaurant has a beautiful terrace overlooking the hills to match its delicious Veneto cuisine. *Closed Mon.*

Antica Trattoria Ballotta, Via Carromatto 2, **t** 049 521 2970, **f** 049 521 1385 (*moderate*). One of the oldest restaurants in Venetia (since 1605), with fine dining either inside or out in the garden. *Closed Tues.*

Rifugio Monte Rua, Via Mone Rua 29, **t** 049 521 1049 (*moderate*). Come here for a panoramic location and a seasonal menu. *Closed Tues.*

Sleeping in or around Teolo

*Lussana, V. Chiesaeolo 1, **t** 049 992 5530, **f** 049 992 5530, *www.villalussana.com* (*moderate*). A charming Art Nouveau villa in Teolo, with bright rooms and lovely views over a terraced garden.

Bacco e Arianna, 5km west in Vò, **t** 049 994 0187 (*inexpensive*). A delightful bed and breakfast in the middle of a vineyard.

Praglia Abbey, 9km east, near S. Biagio, **t** 049 999 9300. If you call ahead you can stay in this Benedictine abbey (*free, but make a donation*), founded in 1117 but given the Renaissance treatment by Tullio Lombardo, Montagna and others (*tours every half hour, 3.30–5.30 in summer, 2.30–4.30 in winter; closed Mon*). There's a dormitory for men, and another for both sexes in the grounds. Their famous Gregorian Mass is on Sun at 11am, Tues–Sat 8am, daily 6pm.

Day 3: A Holy Hill, More Villas and Human Chess

Morning: Drive west out of Teolo to pick up the S247 north to **Vicenza**, aiming for its holy hill, **Monte Bérico**, just south of the city. Take the pilgrims' way up the half-mile-long **Portici** to the **Basilica di Monte Bérico** (*currently closed for restoration*), where the refectory has paintings by Bartolomeo Montagna and Veronese. On your way back down, pause by Via M. D'Azeglio; just down on the right is an alley to the **Villa Valmarana** (*open 5 Mar–5 Nov Wed–Sun 10–12 and 3–6; Tues and Fri just 10–12; adm exp*), adorned with stone dwarves and Tiepolo's sumptuous frescoes. Five more minutes along the Stradella Valmarana brings you to Palladio's most famous creation, the **Villa Rotonda** (*gardens open April–Oct Tues–Sun 10–12 and 3–6; interior open Wed only; adm exp*): a circle in a cube.

Lunch: In Vicenza, *see* below.

Afternoon: Drive east along the S11 to Padua, turning left after Torri di Quartieri towards **Camisano Vicentino**, from where a road leads east to **Piazzola sul Brenta**. Here, visit the imposing **Villa Contarini** (*villa and garden open Mar–Oct daily 9–7; Nov–Feb Tues–Sat 11–4, Sun 10–5; adm*), especially notable for its elaborate interior featuring Music Rooms with excellent acoustics. Follow the Brenta north to **Nove** (just before Bassano), brimful of colourful ceramics; it's only 4km west to **Maròstica**, enclosed in 13th-century walls, a perfect setting for its fairytale human chess match (*second weekend in Sept in even-numbered years*), played in medieval costume on a 72sq ft board. You can see the finery in the **Museo dei Costumi** (*ask at Pro Loco; adm*).

Dinner and Sleeping: In or around Maròstica, *see* below.

Day 3

Lunch in Vicenza

Nuovo Cinzia & Valerio, Piazzetta Porta Padova, **t** 0444 505 213 (*expensive*). For perfectly prepared seafood: tagliatelle with salmon, cuttlefish risotto or grilled sole, followed by home-made ice cream and crisp biscuits. *Closed Sun eve, Mon and Aug.*

Antica Casa della Malvasia, Contrà delle Morette 5, near Piazza dei Signori, **t** 0444 543 704 (*cheap*). Basic, lively and very popular, with real home cooking. *Closed Mon.*

Antica Offelleria della Meneghi, Contrà Cavour 18. For something sweet and stylish, Vicenza has two historic *pasticcerias* near the Basilica: this one, and **Sorarù**, Piazzetta Palladio 17.

Dinner and Sleeping in or around Maròstica

Look out for Maròstica's famous cherries and a rather unusual dish, *paetarosta col magaragno*, young turkey roasted on a spit and served with pomegranate sauce.

Be sure to try some of the local firewater while you're here; Bassano, just 7km east, is a major *grappa* producer. It can be drunk unaged and white, or aged in oak barrels, where it takes on a rich, amber tone.

★★★Europa, Via Pizzamano 19, **t** 0424 77842, **f** 0424 72480 (*moderate*). In Maròstica proper. An up-to-date place to stay, its restaurant serving not only Italian but Spanish dishes – one of your few chances for paella in the region.

★★★La Rosina, 2km north in Valle San Florian, Contrà Narchetti 4, **t** 0424 470 360, *www.la rosina.it* (*moderate*). In a superb hilltop setting, this has modern, comfortable rooms, and a restaurant with a talented chef. *Closed Aug.*

Ristorante al Castello, **t** 0424 73315 (*moderate*). In a renovated upper castle; there are lovely views and food to match, with an emphasis on fresh local ingredients (asparagus and mushrooms in season). Top the meal off with a *caffè corretto*, 'corrected' with one of a score of different *grappas*.

Day 4: Masèr and the View of a Hundred Horizons

Morning: Drive east through Bassano along the S248 towards Montebelluna, taking a left fork at **Casella** (just south of Àsolo) to **Masèr**. Visit the lovely **Villa Barbaro** (*open Mar–Oct Tues, Sat, Sun and hols 3–6; Nov–Feb Sat, Sun and hols 2.30–5; adm exp*), begun in 1568 for brothers Daniele and Marcantonio Barbaro and a unique synthesis of two great talents: Palladio and his friend Veronese. Palladio taught Veronese about space and volume, and nowhere is this so evident as in these ravishing, architectonic *trompe-l'œil* frescoes, featuring the villa's original owners and their pets. Signora Barbaro and her sons gaze down from painted balconies; painted windows offer views of imaginary landscapes; the huntsman in the far bedroom is Veronese, gazing at his mistress. Behind the villa, the nymphaeum is guarded by giants sculpted by Marcantonio himself.

Lunch: Near Masèr, *see* below.

Afternoon: Drive to the old walled hilltown of **Àsolo**, and succumb to the charms that inspired both Pietro Bembo's dialogues on love, *Gli Asolani*, and Robert Browning's last volume of poems, *Asolando*. Some people never get beyond Àsolo's perfect piazza with its 16th-century Fontana Maggiore, but every passing celebrity has had a drink at the historic Caffè Centrale (*Via Roma* 72), and you should too, for it's a great place to watch the world go by. Stroll to the Castello with its watch tower, and step inside the Duomo to see its works by Lotto, Jacopo da Bassano and Vivarini. Finally, for the famous view of 'a hundred horizons', climb (or drive) up to the Rocca.

Dinner and Sleeping: In Àsolo, *see* below.

Day 4

Lunch near Masèr

Al Ringranziamento, Via S. Pio X 107, t 0423 543 271 (*very expensive*). Just north in Cavaso del Tomba, the chef at this romantic restaurant is a master at concocting delicious dishes. *Closed Mon, Tues lunch and some of Aug.*

Da Bastian, Via Cornuda, t 0423 565 400 (*moderate*). Just up the road from Palladio's villa; dine in enchanting surroundings, where the pâté, risotto, Venetian-style snails and desserts are renowned. *Closed Wed eve, Thurs and some of Aug.*

Dinner in Àsolo

Hosteria Ca' Derton, Piazza D'Annunzio 11, t 0423 529 648 (*expensive*). In one of Àsolo's oldest houses, featuring traditional specialities. *Closed Sun eve and Mon.*

Ai Due Archi, Via Roma 55, t 0423 952 201 (*moderate*). Wood-panelled, intimate, elegant and antique, with delicious polenta in various guises. *Closed Wed eve and Thurs.*

Sleeping in Àsolo

Àsolo is a wonderful place to spend a night in style, but it doesn't do cheap; if you'd prefer somewhere more reasonable, **Castelfranco Veneto** is just 15km south (*see* 'Day 5').

*****Villa Cipriani, Via Canova 298, t 0423 523 411, f 0423 952 095 (*luxury*). One of Italy's most charming and evocative hotels, in a house dating from the 16th century that belonged to Robert Browning, decorated with Persian carpets owned by Eleonora Duse. Overlooking a paradise of hills and cypresses, it has an enchanting garden.

****Al Sole, Via Collegio 33, t 0423 951 332, f 0423 951 007, www.albergoalsole.com (*very expensive*). Also in the *centro storico*, this celebrated hotel is both very comfortable and very charming, whispering with memories of famous past guests. It has an agreement with the local country club.

***Duse, Via Browning 190, t 0423 55241, f 0423 950 404 (*expensive, but the cheapest in town*). Overlooking Àsolo's central piazza, with a little garden behind it.

Day 5: Masonic Codes and Big George

Morning: Take the road south of Àsolo via San Vito and Riese to join the S667 to
Castelfranco Veneto. Then continue south on the S307 towards Padua, turning left
at Resana for **Piombino Dese**, a Palladiophile must-see for its **Villa Cornaro** (*villa and
garden open May–Sept Sat 3.30–6; rest of year by appointment only, t 049 936 5017*)
of 1553. This is one of the master's most innovative structures, the first with a double
loggia. It's also the only one to preserve much of its original cladding and tile floors.
See what you make of the frescoes (1716) by Bortoloni; Cornaro eschewed the usual
allegories for biblical scenes, but they may have been a vehicle to smuggle in a
forbidden message: those on the east wall of the main room abound with Masonic
symbols. Puzzle them on your way to lunch, either in Castelfranco itself, or just west
down the S53 in **Galliera Veneto**.

Lunch: In or near Castelfranco, *see* below.

Afternoon: Castelfranco basks in the glory of having given the world Giorgione, in 1478,
and the Duomo holds the masterpiece he gave the town in return: the *Castelfranco
Madonna* (1504). There's more Big George next door in the Casa del Giorgione (*open
Tues–Sun 10–12.30 and 3–6.30; adm*), which keeps copies of all his works. If you're not
villa-ed out, nip up the road to **Fanzolo** (5km northeast), for another of Palladio's
finest: **Villa Emo** (*open April–Sept Mon–Sat 3–7, Sun and hols 10–12.30 and 3–7; Oct–
Mar Sat and Sun only 2–6; adm exp*), containing bright mythologies by Zelotti.

Dinner and Sleeping: In Castelfranco or Fanzolo, *see* below. In the morning, the S245
leads back via Piombino Dese to Venice.

Day 5

Lunch in or near Castelfranco Veneto

Alle Mura, Via Preti 69, **t** 0423 498 098
(*expensive*). An elegant place situated next
to the walls in Castelfranco, with well-
prepared seafood dishes and a garden.
Closed Thurs.

Palazzino, Via Roma 29, **t** 049 596 9224
(*expensive*). In Galliera Veneto, on the road
between Castelfranco and Cittadella, with a
former patrician hunting lodge serving as its
setting. A great place to try Renaissance
dishes such as pheasant stuffed with truffles. *Closed Tues eve, Wed and Aug.*

Dinner in Castelfranco Veneto

Barbesin, at the Hotel Ca' delle Rose, on the
Circonvallazione Est at Salvarosa, **t** 0423 490
446 (*moderate*). At this famous restaurant,
the setting is as idyllic as the cuisine, based
entirely on fresh, seasonal ingredients; the
veal with apples melts in your mouth. You
can also stay here. *Closed Wed eve and Thurs.*

Dinner and Sleeping in Fanzolo

★★★Villa Emo, Via Stazione 5, **t** 0423 476 414,
f 0423 487 043 (*very expensive*). There's fine
dining to be had in the restaurant at
Palladio's villa. If you wish, you could even
stay in one of the wings, where a handful
of elegant rooms and suites come with a
pool; quiet guaranteed. *Closed Mon and
Tues lunch.*

Sleeping in Castelfranco Veneto

★★★★Fior, Via dei Carpani 18, **t** 0423 721 212,
f 0423 498 771 (*expensive*). In the same area,
occupying an old villa and park, with tennis,
pool and sauna.

★★★Roma, Via Fabio Filzi 39, **t** 0423 721 616,
f 0423 721 515 (*moderate*). Situated outside
the fortifications but offering a good view
of them; all rooms have TV and a/c.

★★★Al Moretto, Via S. Pio X 10, **t** 0423 721
313, **f** 0423 721 066 (*inexpensive*). In the
centre of Castelfranco Veneto, set in a
17th-century palace.

Italy: Ancona, Pescara, Bari and the Central Adriatic Coast

Ancona

A patch of mountains on an otherwise pancake coast provides the mid-Adriatic's biggest port with a splendid crescent-shaped harbour under the steep promontory of Monte Guasco. Ancona never had the leisure to blossom in the style of Italy's other maritime republics: it was too busy battling rival Venice and various emperors; then the 20th century thought to inflict it with a rash of bombings, earthquakes and even a landslide, causing the abandonment of parts of the old town. But, for all its troubles, Ancona (pop. 101,000) has come up smiling. The port is prospering, and the city is now devoting its attention to restoring the historic centre.

Around the Port

Most of Ancona's monuments have survived the recent misfortunes. At its western end, the long curve of the port is anchored by the fortress-like **Mole Vanvitelliana**, a pentagonal building designed in 1733 by the Neapolitan Luigi Vanvitelli, which now

Getting There

See **Getting There**, pp.3–8.

Getting from the Airport

Ancona's Raffaello Sanzio airport (**t** 071 28271 or **t** 071 282 7491), is 12km north of the city at Falconara. Airport **buses** run to Piazza Cavour. **Trains** also run from Castelferretti station, outside the airport, to the station at Piazza Rosselli. A **taxi** into the centre (**t** 071 918 221) takes only 10mins and costs about €20–25.

Getting Around

You can get around town on foot, but Ancona has a network of buses/trams that also serve the Cònero Riviera. **Tickets** (€0.80) are available from *tabacchi*, from machines in the stations, and on board (more expensive). Ancona's **train** station is west of the port on Piazza Rosselli (bus no.1 or 3 to or from Piazza Repubblica near the port). A few trains go on to Ancona Marittima station on the port itself.

By Sea to Croatia

Car ferries to Croatia are run by four lines:
Adriatica di Anvigazione (**t** 041 781 611, *www.adriatica.it*) goes to Split.
Jadrolinija (**t** 071 204305) goes to Split and Zadar; there is a service to certain islands in the summer.
SMC (**t** 071 204 090) goes to Split and Hvar.

SNAV (**t** 071 207 6116, *www.snav.it*) to Split and Zadar; service to islands in the summer.

All these companies have offices at the Stazione Marittima (the port). For information on all routes, look at the port authority's website (*www.autoritaportuale.ancona.it*). The journey from Ancona to Split takes 7–8hrs. *See* also *www.traghetti.com*.

Car Hire

Avis, Via Bruno 1, or at the airport, **t** 071 44241.
Europcar, Piazza Rosselli 16, **t** 071 203 100, or at the airport, **t** 071 916 2240.
Hertz, Via Flaminia 16, **t** 071 41314, or at the airport, **t** 071 207 3798.
Maggiore Budget, Via Marconi 215, **t** 071 42624, or at the airport, **t** 071 918 8805.

Tourist Information

Ancona: Via Thaon de Revel 4, **t** 071 358 991, **f** 071 358 0592. Branches at the train station (no tel); in the port, **t** 071 201 183.

Market Days

Markets are held on Corso Mazzini (*Tues and Fri*) and on Piazza Medaglie d'Oro (*Wed and Sat*).

Shopping

Look out for *beccute* (biscuits with nuts and raisins), and don't miss the wines: celebrated holds temporary exhibitions. At the other end of the port, the tall, graceful **Arco di Traiano** was built in AD 115 in honour of Trajan, Ancona's imperial benefactor; nearby, Pope Clement XII had Vanvitelli erect an **Arco Clementino** (1733) to himself, as papal benefactor (he declared the city a duty-free port). At the heart of the port, the elegant 15th-century Venetian Gothic **Loggia dei Mercanti** recalls Ancona's maritime heyday.

Piazza della Repubblica and Via Gramsci

Just in from the Loggia, the 19th-century **Teatro delle Muse** and the church of **Santissimo Sacramento** dominate Piazza Repubblica. From here, Corso Garibaldi leads east to Piazza Cavour and Ancona's business district, while Via Gramsci climbs to the oldest quarters of Ancona. On the right, under the Renaissance arch of the handsome **Palazzo del Governo** (1484), the elongated **Piazza del Plebiscito** extends to the church of **San Domenico** (*open daily 8–12 and 3–7.30*), worth a step inside to see Titian's *Crucifixion* (1558) on the high altar, and Guercino's *Annunciation*, to the left. Below the

---

Verdicchio, a delicate white born to wash down *stocco*, and **Rosso Cònero**, a full-bodied red.

Where to Stay

Ancona ✉ **60100**
★★★★**Grand Hotel Palace**, Lungomare Vanvitelli 24, **t** 071 201 813, **f** 071 207 4832, *www.alberghiancona.it* (*very expensive*). Ancona's finest hotel, near the Arco di Traiano. Comfy and small, in a 17th-century palace, with a roof garden and magnificent views over the port, but no restaurant.
★★★★**Grand Hotel Passetto**, Via Thaon de Revel 1, **t** 071 31307, **f** 071 32856, *www.hotel passetto.it* (*very expensive*). Similar; central but modern, with a pool in summer.
★★★**Fortuna**, Piazza Rosselli 15, **t** 071 42663, **f** 071 42662, *www.hotelfortuna.it* (*moderate*). The nicest place near the station; convenient and comfortable.
★★**Viale**, Viale della Vittoria 23, **t** 071 201 861 (*moderate*). Tranquillity and lower prices nearly a kilometre out of the centre.
★★**Gino**, Via Flaminia 4, **t/f** 071 42179, *hotel. gino@tiscalinet.it* (*inexpensive*). A straight-forward place, but the restaurant (*moderate*) has excellent fresh seafood. *Closed Sun*.
★★**Dorico**, Via Flaminia 8, **t/f** 071 42761 (*inexpensive*). On the same road, near the station, with simple rooms, with or without bath.

Eating Out

The dish to try is *stoccafisso all'anconetana*, dried cod exquisitely prepared in a casserole with tomatoes, potatoes and marjoram, or *brodetto*, a soup made with a variety of fish.
Passetto, Piazzale IV Novembre, **t** 071 33214 (*very expensive*). An excellent seafood place with a seaside terrace, offering a set menu with meat dishes. *Closed Sun eve, Mon and last 2 weeks in Aug*.
La Moretta, Piazza Plebiscito 52, **t** 071 202 317 (*expensive*). This is a long-established local favourite for excellent *stoccafisso all'anconetana* and *spaghetti agli scampi*. *Closed Sun*.
Al Rosso Agontano, Via Marconi 3, **t** 071 207 5279 (*expensive*). A simple yet elegant little restaurant which is highly rated locally for its imaginative fish dishes (such as fusilli with artichokes and salt cod, shrimp kebabs with spinach and ginger, seared tuna fillet) and excellent wines. *Closed Sun*.
Osteria del Pozzo, Via Bonda 2, **t** 071 207 3996 (*cheap*). In the middle of the port, this is elegant but absurdly cheap; try the mixed fry or pasta of the day. *Closed Sun and Aug*.
La Cantinetta, Via Gramsci, **t** 071 201 107 (*cheap*). A popular, atmospheric place near the port and handy for the ferry, full of Greek seamen fingering worry beads, and famed for its *stoccafisso*, its nightly fish fry, *vincisgrassi* and lemon sorbet. *Closed Mon*.

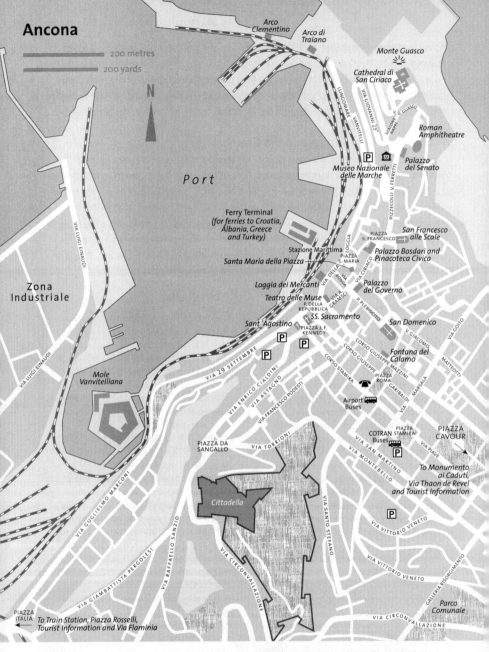

church, on Corso Mazzini, Ancona is proud of its pretty **Fontana del Calamo** with its 13 spouts designed by Pellegrino Tibaldi in 1560.

Off the continuation of Via Gramsci, the 13th-century church of **Santa Maria della Piazza** (*open 7.30–7*) has a great late Romanesque façade, carved with musicians, soldiers and strange animals by a 'Master Phillippus'. Under the pavement are the ruins of the church's predecessors, from the 5th and 6th centuries. To the left of the church, the late Renaissance **Palazzo Bosdari** houses a small **Pinacoteca Comunale** (*Via Pizzecolli 17; open Mon 9–1, Tues–Sat 9–7, Sun 3–7; adm*), with a masterly *Madonna col Bambino* by the eccentric Carlo Crivelli, the tidiest of all Renaissance painters, complete with his trademark apples and cucumbers hanging overhead. Other *Madonnas* include one by Lorenzo Lotto (a good one), and one by Titian, floating smugly on a cloud.

On Monte Guasco

Further up towards Via del Guasco is the area hardest hit by the earthquake and landslide; bits of decorative brickwork from Roman Ancona's **theatre** peek out between the ruined buildings. In the ripe interior of a 16th-century palace, the **Museo Archeologico Nazionale delle Marche** (*Via Feretti 6; open Tues–Sun 8.30–7.30; closed Mon; adm*) has a rich archaeological collection, including some exceptional Greek vases and metalwork, beautiful Etruscan bronzes, gold and amber from Gaulish and Piceni tombs, and an extensive collection of Roman finds. Crowning the ancient Greek acropolis of Monte Guasco is the pink and white **Cattedrale di San Ciriaco** (*open autumn and winter 8–12 and 3–6; spring and summer 8–12 and 3–7*), facing out to sea on the site of a famous temple of Venus. Beyond the fancy Gothic porch, the marble columns of the interior come originally from the temple, some topped by Byzantine capitals; there's also an elaborate 12th-century altar screen in the right transept.

Day Trips from Ancona

Portonovo

The same arm of the Apennines that shelters Ancona's port also creates a short but uniquely beautiful stretch of Adriatic coast south of the city. The cliffs of Monte

Getting There

Portonovo is only 30mins from Ancona city centre. RENI **buses** to the Cónero Riviera depart from Piazza Cavour, t 071 804 6430. CONERO bus no.94 serves Portonovo from Piazza Rosselli, t 071 280 2092, with around 10 buses each way daily.

Where to Stay and Eat

Portonovo ✉ 60020

★★★★Fortino Napoleonico, t 071 801 450, f 071 801 454, *www.hotelfortino.it* (*very expensive–expensive*). An award-winning hotel incorporating part of a fortress built in the Napoleonic Wars; set apart, quiet and modern, it has its own beach and swimming pool. Its restaurant (*very expensive*) is one of the Marches' finest, with two beautiful dining rooms. Eight superb courses include sole stuffed with spinach, cream and smoked salmon, shrimps with fennel and orange, gnocchi with caviar, and more.

★★★★Emilia, Collina di Portonovo, t 071 801 145, *www.hotelemilia.com* (*very expensive*). Luxurious accommodation in a lovely setting. Artists stay free in exchange for a painting. The place is covered with pictures, including one by Graham Sutherland.

Il Laghetto, near Portonovo's lake, t 071 801 183 (*expensive*). A great place to feast on fish and *frutti di mare*, prepared in some unusual ways. *Closed Mon and mid-Jan–end Feb.*

★★★Internazionale, Via Portonovo 149, t 071 801 001, f 071 801 082 (*moderate*). A sturdy stone building in the trees, with ravishing views, its own beach and a good restaurant.

Around Ancona

20 km
10 miles

N

To Ravenna · Rimini · Verrúcchio · Torello · S. Marino · Novafeltria · S. Leo · S. Agata Feltria · Pennabilli · M. Carpegna · Carpegna · Macerata Feltria · Piandimeleto · Sassocorvaro · Sestino · Urbino · Urbania · Acqualagna · Sansepolcro · M. Petrano · Cagli · Citta di Castello · Sassoferrato · Genga · Scheggia · Grotte di Frassassi · Umbertide · Gubbio · Fabriano · Fossato di Vico · Perugia · Assisi

Montefeltro · VIA FLAMINIA

Pesaro · Fano · Senigallia · Falconara Marittima · ANCONA · Portonovo · Monte Conero · Sirolo · Numana · Jesi · R. Esino · Loreto · Civitanova Marche · Fermo

Adriatic Sea

THE MARCHES

Gabicce Mare

Conero (1,876ft) plunge steeply into the sea, isolating a number of beautiful beaches and coves that are often packed out in summer. From Ancona, the Conero road threads the narrow corniche between sea and mountain; tucked under the cliffs is Portonovo, the most beautiful place for a swim in these parts, its pebble beach clean and unspoiled despite its proximity to the city. Besides the beach, there's a lovely church of the 1030s, built in the style of Ancona cathedral. The recently restored **Santa Maria di Portonovo**, with the same blind arcading around the roofline and a distinctive cupola in the centre, is one of the better Romanesque churches in the north, mentioned as 'the House of Our Lady on the Adriatic coast' in the 21st *canto* of Dante's *Paradiso*. Portonovo's fortress, the **Fortino Napoleonico** (*see* 'Where to Stay and Eat', p.229), has a watch-tower built by Pope Clement XII in 1716 – even at that late date, pirates were a menace. Much earlier, some of the local pirates hung out at the nearby **Grotta degli Schiavi**, facing a sheltered cove popular with divers.

Jesi

The busy Valle dell'Esino is named for the hill town of **Jesi** ('Yea see'), set on a narrow ridge with houses built on and over its walls. The *centro storico* evolved around a necklace of theatrical squares: in 1194, the uppermost was thrust into the limelight when Constance de Hauteville, passing through on her way to Sicily, found herself assailed

Getting There

Several **trains** a day on the Ancona–Rome line stop at Jesi. CONERO **buses** (**t** 071 919 8623 or 071 280 2092) to Jesi leave from Piazza Cavour; many stop at the train station.

Tourist Information

Jesi: Piazza Repubblica 11, **t** 0731 59788, **f** 0731 58291, *www.comune.jesi.an.it/proloco*.

Eating Out

Hostaria Santa Lucía, Via Marche 2/b (500yds from centre; ask for directions), **t** 0731 64409 (*very expensive*). Delectable seafood classics, simply prepared. Book ahead. *Closed Mon and some of Aug; winter open eves only.*

Tana Liberatutti, Piazza Baccio Pontelli I, **t** 0731 59237 (*moderate, expensive with truffles*). Set in a pretty medieval building with a garden. *Closed Sun and part of Aug.*

Da Antonietta, Via Garibaldi 19, **t** 0731 207 173 (*cheap*). The best kind of simple, Italian home cooking. *Closed Sun and eves.*

by labour pains; she promptly pitched her tent and gave birth then and there to the future Emperor Frederick II *Stupor Mundis*. The square was renamed **Piazza Federico II** and the exact spot of the tent marked by an obelisk. Further down, in Piazza Colocci, the elegant **Palazzo della Signora** has a clock tower, and wears Jesi's proud *stemma* over the portal: a giant lion rampant, paws up, ready to box all comers.

Besides the most extraordinary of medieval emperors, Jesi also gave birth to the composer Giambattista Pergolesi in 1710, who, although he died aged only 26, managed to produce some perennial favourites of the Italian repertoire: the *Stabat Mater*, the *Frate 'nnammorato* and *La Serva Padrona*. Next door to the late 18th-century **Teatro Pergolesi**, the **Sale Pergolesiane** exhibits odds and ends relating to his life and works (*theatre and 'sale' open late June–late Sept Tues–Sun 10–8; rest of year Tues–Sat 10–1 and 4–7, Sun 10–1 and 5–8*).

Jesi's real treasure, however, is the **Pinacoteca e Musei Civici** (*same hours as Teatro Pergolesi; adm*) in Via XV Settembre, housed in the Palazzo Pianetti. This has a delightful rococo gallery – 230ft of exuberant stuccoes on the 'human adventure in time and space' – a catch-all for lobsters, drums, camels and anything else its creator Placido Lazzarini felt like throwing in. Pride of place goes to a set of paintings by Lorenzo Lotto, including a strange, beautifully lit *Annunciation* (1526) and a luxurious *Sacra Conversazione*. A small **Museo Civico** holds Renaissance sculpture, ceramics and archaeological finds, and a modern art gallery which is mainly an excuse to see more frescoed ceilings. Outside the walls, the church of **San Marco** (*open winter daily 9–11am; summer daily 9–11 and 4–7*) has exceptional 14th-century frescoes in the manner of Giotto.

Loreto

Loreto, a small but concentrated dose of fine art from the Renaissance, has been one of the most popular pilgrimage sites in Europe since the 1300s, when Mary's house from Nazareth – site of the Annunciation – miraculously flew across the sea and landed in the laurel woods (*loreti*) south of Ancona. Doubting Thomases are referred to the Hebrew-Christian graffiti on its walls, similar to that in the Grotto of Nazareth. Corso Boccalini, lined with the inevitable souvenir stands, leads from the town centre up to the **Santuario della Santa Casa** (*www.santuarioloreto.it; Basilica open daily*

Getting There

After 11am, there are around two **trains** hourly to Loreto from Ancona, taking 20mins. COTRAM **buses** (**t** 071 202 766) also operate a frequent service to Loreto from Piazza Cavour (taking about 45mins). Local buses link Loreto station with the town centre.

Tourist Information

Loreto: Via Solari 3, **t** 071 970 276, **f** 071 970 020, *iat.loreto@regione.marche.it* (*open summer Mon–Sat 9–1 and 4–7, Sun 9–1 only; winter Mon–Fri 9–1 and 3–6, Sat 9–1*).

Where to Stay and Eat

Loreto ✉ **60025**

The best places are outside the centre.

★★★★**Villa Tetlameya**, Via Villa Costantina 187, Loreto Archi, **t** 071 978 863, **f** 071 976 639, *www.loretoitaly.com* (*expensive*). An elegant 19th-century villa, with the most comfortable rooms and one of the best restaurants in the area, Zi Nene (*moderate*), specializing in classic seafood and historical *marchigiano* recipes. *Closed Mon.*

★★★**Blu Hotel**, Via Villa Costantina 89, Loreto Archi, **t** 071 978 501, *www.cssg.it* (*moderate*). Simple but pleasant rooms. *Closed Xmas.*

★★★**La Vecchia Fattoria**, Via Manzoni 19, **t** 071 978 976 (*moderate–inexpensive*). A hotel with restaurant that's a local favourite for weddings and banquets.

★★★★**Casa del Clero Madonna di Loreto**, Via Asdrubali 104, **t** 071 970 298 (*inexpensive*). In the centre of town, the hotels are clean, quiet and respectable, and have a crucifix above every bed. Many are run by religious orders as accommodation for pilgrims. This is a typical example, with 32 rooms with bath.

Andreina, Via Buffolareccia 14, **t** 071 970 124 (*moderate*). This place has been here for donkey's years, continuing to serve wonderful grilled meats and *marchigiano* specialities. *Closed Tues and some of July.*

6.45am–7pm (*8pm in summer*); *Santa Casa closed 12.30–2.30*), which materializes in all its glory when you turn a corner and enter the Piazza della Madonna. The understated façade is typical early Roman Baroque (1587): one of the best features is the series of reliefs on the bronze doors; another is the circle of radiating brick apses on the east end, turreted like a Renaissance castle. The only unfortunate element is the ungainly neoclassical campanile, topped with a bronze-plated garlic bulb and designed to hold a 15-ton bell.

Chapels line the walls inside, embellished by the faithful from nations around the world. Under the dome you'll see the object of the pilgrims' attention: the **Santa Casa**, a simple brick room with traces of medieval frescoes, sheathed in marble by Bramante to become one of the largest, most expensive sculptural ensembles ever attempted – the better to make the flying house stay put. Its decoration includes beautiful reliefs by Sansovino, Sangallo, della Porta and others, showing scenes from the *Life of Mary*. The reliefs on the back show the airborne house-removal that made Loreto's Virgin the patroness of the airline industry. A good deal of Loreto's art was swiped by Napoleon, but the **sacristies** on the right aisle have fine frescoes by Luca Signorelli and Melozzo da Forlì, and the **Sala del Tesoro** (1610) has a ceiling frescoed with the *Life of Mary* by Pomarancio. Upstairs in the Apostolic palace, the **Museo-Pinacoteca** (*open April–Oct Tues–Sun 9–1 and 4–7; Nov–Mar Sat and Sun 10–1 and 3–6; mid-June–mid-Sept also Thurs and Fri 9–11pm; contribution requested*) has excellent, dramatic late paintings by Lorenzo Lotto, Flemish tapestries from cartoons by Raphael and a superb collection of ceramics.

Touring from Ancona

Day 1: The Medieval Towns of Fabriano and Gubbio

Morning: Take the N16 north from Ancona, turning left at Falconara Marittima on to the S76. This winds up past rolling vineyards and castles before the looming mountains are sliced by a dramatic gorge, the **Gola della Rossa**. In medieval **Fabriano** stroll through the beautiful, arcaded Piazza del Comune and visit the 14th-century Cattedrale Basilica di San Venanzio, containing frescoes by Allegretto Nuzi, one of Fabriano's 14th-century school of painters. Discover the art of papermaking at the Museo della Carta e della Filigrana (*open Tues–Sat 10–6, Sun 10–12 and 2–5; closed Mon; adm*). Take the S76 west to Fossato di Vico, then the S219 northwest to **Gubbio**.

Lunch: In Gubbio, *see* below.

Afternoon: Wander through Gubbio's resolutely medieval lanes, and discover the local ceramics, a craft inherited from the 16th-century Mastro Giorgio. Gubbio also produced a master painter, Ottaviano Nelli; step into the church of San Francesco to see his 15th-century frescoes in the left apse. Hovering over a steep drop is the magnificent Piazza della Signoria, where Gattapone's beautiful Palazzo dei Consoli, now the Museo Civico (*open April–Oct daily 10–1 and 3–6; Nov–Mar daily 10–1 and 2–5; closed 13–15 May, 25 Dec and 1 Jan; adm*) houses a unique treasure: the bronze Eugubian Tablets, the most important inscriptions ever found in the old Umbrian language. From the Porta Romana, a *funivia* (*open winter 10–1 and 2.30–5; summer 8.30–7.30*) lifts you up to the sanctuary of San Ubaldo, for more spectacular views. Take the S298 northeast of Gubbio to Scheggia, turning north on to the S3, before eventually turning off at Acqualagna to **Urbino**.

Dinner and Sleeping: In Urbino, *see* below.

Day 1

Lunch in Gubbio

Taverna del Lupo, Via Ansidei 21a, t 075 927 4368 (*expensive*). An atmospheric medieval setting, with excellent traditional fare, as well as delicious pasta and *frico*, a local dish of mixed meats with cress. *Closed Mon.*

Funivia, on Monte Ingino, t 075 922 1259 (*moderate*). Offering fabulous views on a clear day, as well as delicious pasta and tasty *secondi. Closed Wed and Nov–Feb.*

San Francesco e Il Lupo, Via Cairoli 24, t 075 927 2344 (*cheap*). Local products – among them porcini and truffles – or you can order the cheaper pizza. *Closed Tues.*

Dinner in Urbino

Vecchia Urbino, in the historic centre at Via Vasari 3/5, t 0722 4447 (*expensive–moderate*). An elegant option which will treat you to a feast in the autumn/winter *tartufi* and porcini season. *Closed Tues in winter. See also* Day 2, 'Lunch'.

Sleeping in Urbino

Urbino's few hotels can be busy; book ahead.

★★★★Bonconte, Via delle Mura 28, t 0722 2463, f 0722 4782, www.viphotels.it (*moderate*). Sitting on the walls of the city, this is the most luxurious place in town. Lovely views.

★★★Italia, Corso Garibaldi 32, t 0722 2701, f 0722 322 664, www.albergo-italia-urbino.it (*moderate*). Good and central, one block from the Ducal Palace.

★★★Tortorina, northeast of the centre at Via Tortorina 4, t 0722 308100, f 0722 308 372, www.hotel-tortorina.it (*moderate*). Has a large panoramic terrace and rooms furnished with antiques.

Day 2: Renaissance Urbino and San Leo's Alcatraz

Morning: A lively university town, **Urbino** is a Renaissance monument combining elegance, learning and intelligent patronage. Here Raphael was born; here there are beautiful frescoes to be sought out in the churches; but the crown jewel is Duke Federico's twin-towered Palazzo Ducale (*open Tues–Sun 8.30–7, Mon 8.30–2; visits every 15mins in winter; adm*), famed for its amazing art collection and wonderful interior décor embellished by Piero della Francesca, Paolo Uccello and Botticelli.

Lunch: In Urbino, *see* below.

Afternoon: Follow signs northwest of Urbino to **Sassocorvaro**; the roads grow increasingly scenic as you approach the town, topped by the striking 15th-century Rocca Ubaldinesca (*open Oct–Mar Sat and Sun 9.30–12.30 and 2.30–6; April–Sept daily 9.30–12.30 and 3–7; adm*), with exhibits on country life. Continue west past Macerata Féltria towards the majestic **Monte Carpegna** (4,641ft), in a natural park noted for its rare wild orchids and falcons. From **Carpegna**, detour up a track below the summit for grandiose views. Backtrack and take the road north to **San Leo**. Dante slept and St Francis preached in San Leo, but for all that, it is tiny, a huddle of stone houses balanced on the gentle slope of the stupendous crag. Visit the most extraordinary of all the area's extraordinary castles, the Rocca di San Leo (*open Mon–Sat 9–6, Sun 9–6.30; adm*), which became the Alcatraz of its day; inside you can see Renaissance weapons, illustrations from Dante's *Inferno*, and the cell where the popes kept one of their most famous prisoners, Count Cagliostro, until he went mad and died. San Leo's churches are also worth a look: the Pieve (*open daily 9–12.30 and 3–7*) is one of the oldest in the Marches; the ciborium over the altar has an inscription from the year 882. In the Palazzo Mediceo (*open Mon–Sun 9–6; adm*) the Museo d'Arte Sacra displays 14th- to 18th-century artworks.

Dinner and Sleeping: In San Leo, *see* below.

Day 2

Lunch in Urbino
L'Angolo Divino, Via Sant'Andrea 14 (off Via Battisti), **t** 0722 327559 (*cheap*). Occupies a pretty room in an old palace and specializes in old Urbino specialities – pasta with chickpeas, bacon, lamb or breadcrumbs, and tasty *secondi* from the grill; some vegetarian dishes. *Closed Sun eve and Mon lunch. See also* Day 1.

Dinner and Sleeping in San Leo
Locanda San Leone, Strada Sant'Antimo 102, **t** 0541 912 194, **f** 0541 912 348 (*expensive*). There are some rooms here as you head towards Sant'Igne; but the farm restaurant (*expensive, open to all*) serves lovely pasta with eggs and other home-grown ingredients. *Restaurant closed Mon–Wed and Jan.*

La Lama, Strada per Pugliano 4, **t** 0541 926 928 (*moderate*). At the foot of San Leo, this charming *agriturismo* is run personally by the Conte Nardini; rooms are individually decorated with wrought-iron beds, and the restaurant (*moderate; closed Mon; book*) uses ingredients grown on site; dine on pasta with truffles, roast meats, game and cheeses, all washed down by fine wines. Horse-riding is also available.

Castello, Piazza Dante Alighieri 11–12, **t 0541 916 214, **f** 0541 926 926 (*moderate*). The most comfortable place to sleep; made all the better by its excellent restaurant.

La Quercia, Via Leontina, **t** 0541 916 282 (*cheap*). Offers *tagliatelle al ragù* and other typical dishes. *Closed Tues.*

Day 3: San Marino, Rimini and Beaches

Morning: Drive north to **Villanova**, take the S258 towards Verúcchio for 3km, then turn right to San Marino, a mecca for duty-free shopping. From Borgo Maggiore, take the funicular up to the citadel of San Marino, a steep medieval village preserved in aspic, with wonderful views over the coast. Then drive down the S72 to **Rimini**, Italy's biggest resort, with a colourful fishing port and, tucked behind the beachfront, a genuine old city possessing one first-rate Renaissance attraction: the tyrant Sigismondo Malatesta's Tempio Malatestiano (*open Mon–Sat 8–12.30 and 3.30–7; Sun 9–1 and 3.30–7*). This eclectic, thoroughly mysterious work is full of indecipher-able sculptural allegories. Most famous are the sculptural reliefs by Agostino, on blue backgrounds, depicting angels and musicians, the Arts and Sciences, St Michael, putti, Sigismondo himself and the Triumph of Scipio. Some of the best are allegorical panels of the planets and signs of the zodiac. Note the tombs of Sigismondo and Isotta, adorned by their omnipresent monograms S and I, together with elephants, the Malatesta symbol.

Lunch: In Rimini, *see* below.

Afternoon: Drive back towards Ancona down the coast along the S16; for the best views, opt for the corniche road hugging the coast from Gabbice Mare. South of Pésaro, the string of resorts continues; break off at **Fano**, not merely a seaside play-ground but a fine old town retaining a perfect provincial Roman town plan. Stroll along its long, broad beach, or visit the 15th-century Castello Malatestiano (*open only for special exhibitions; call tourist office, **t** 054 151 331 for information*), with a lovely crenellated courtyard and mullioned windows, and a picture gallery starring Michele Giambono and Guercino. Look into the church of Santa Maria Nuova, decorated with stuccoes and altarpieces by Perugino and Giovanni Santi.

Dinner and Sleeping: In Fano, *see* below.

Day 3

Lunch in Rimini

Dallo Zio, Via S. Chiara 16 (*expensive*). An excel-lent seafood palace in the old town, offering marine lasagne, fishy vol-au-vents and other surprises; popular with locals and tourists alike. *Closed Mon.*

4 Moschetteri, Via S. Maria al Mare, just off Piazza Ferrari, **t** 0541 56496 (*moderate–cheap*). The practically perfect *trattoria* in the centre, with excellent pizza and pasta and a menu of Romagna favourites that changes every day.

Dinner and Sleeping in Fano

Ristorantino (Giulio), Viale Adriatico 100, **t** 0721 805 680 (*expensive–moderate*). A reliable favourite, serving tasty, fresh seafood; try the local shrimp. *Closed Tues and Nov.*

Pesce Azzurro, near the port at Viale Adriatico 48, **t** 0721 803 165 (*cheap*). This was founded by the local fishermen's cooperative to promote the glories of 'blue fish' – a variety of sardines, anchovies, mackerel and other small fish, all very tasty! At this self-service restaurant you can try them in three courses. *Closed Mon and Oct–mid-April.*

★★★★Augustus, Via Puccini 2, **t** 0721 809 781, **f** 0721 825 517, *www.hotelaugustus.it* (*moderate*). A central, family-run hotel, which has had a recent facelift; the restau-rant serves fish as well as some more creative dishes. *Restaurant closed Mon.*

★★Mare, Viale C. Colombo 20, **t/f** 0721 805 667 (*full board; inexpensive*). This place just off the beach is like a homely *pensione* of 20 years ago, where *mamma* Anna cooks up some of the best, most affordable seafood in Fano. *Restaurant (cheap) closed Sun eve.*

Pescara

Pescara wears many hats: it is Abruzzo's biggest city and its most popular resort, its most prosperous town, a fishing port and provincial capital. In ancient times it was a modest port, but Pescara never made much of itself until 1927, when the government

Getting There

See **Getting There**, pp.3–8.

Getting from the Airport
City bus 38 connects Liberi airport (t 085 432 421) to Pescara Centrale station every 10mins (5.30am–11pm; journey 15mins). Buy **tickets** (€1) from the airport news-stand or bar.
A **taxi** to the centre will cost about €15.

Getting Around

The centre of Pescara is easily tackled on foot, but there are also local **buses**. The main **train station**, Pescara Centrale, is on Piazza delle Stazione; the **bus station** is close by. For a **taxi**, call **CO.TA.PE**, t 085 421 1870/ 085 422 4379.

By Sea to Croatia
Daily fast catamaran car ferries are run by **SNAV** (t 071 202 6116, *www.snav.it*) between late June and mid-Sept and go to Split (about 4½hrs) and Hvar (3½hrs). They leave from the Porto Canale commercial port. For information and tickets visit the Sanmar shipping agency (t 085 451 0873, *www.sanmar. it*), whose office is inside the Stazione Marittima.

Car Hire
The following have branches at the airport:
Avis, t 085 421 2442.
Europcar, t 085 421 1022.
Hertz, t 085 53900.
Maggiore, t 085 389 167.

Tourist Information

Pescara: Via Paolucci 3, t 085 421 9981, and Corso Vittorio Emmanuele 301, t 085 429 001; *www.abruzzoturismo.it*.

Market Days
There's a weekly market in **Via Pepe** (*Mon*).

Shopping

It's probably most fun to browse around the fish market, but Pescara is also a good place to pick up a bottle of the region's famous red wine, Montepulciano d'Abruzzo. Abruzzo is also well known for its ceramics.

Where to Stay and Eat

Pescara ✉ **65100**
★★★★Carlton, Viale Riviera 35, t 085 373 125, f 085 421 3922 (*very expensive*). A very comfortable resort palace on the sea, with a private beach that almost absorbs the noise.
★★★Bellariva, Viale Riviera 213, t/f 085 471 2641 (*moderate*). This is unpretentious, and a good, friendly place to stay for families.
★★★Salus, Lungomare Matteotti 13/1, t 085 374 196, f 085 374 103 (*moderate*). Offers good standard rooms and a private beach.
Guerino, Viale della Riviera 4, t 085 421 2065 (*very expensive*). Elegant, with a seafront terrace, this is the city's best seafood restaurant: the Adriatic speciality – fillets of John Dory (*pesce San Pietro*) with *prosciutto* – go down especially well. *Closed Tues.*
Duilio, Via Regina Margherita 11, t 085 378 278 (*very expensive*). Serves delicately prepared dishes, most of which feature seafood. *Closed Sun eve, Mon and Aug.*
Taverna 58, Corso Manthoné 46, t 085 69 0724 (*moderate*). A delightful trattoria serving seasonal traditional food with some unusual variations; try the spaghetti with pesto of courgette and almonds, or spring chicken (*pollastrello*) with honey and thyme. There's a good wine list too. *Closed Sat lunch, Sun and hols.*
Dieci Tavoli, Via Trento 86, t 085 295 374 (*cheap*). Tucked away, this is a good place for hearty Abruzzese cooking and fresh, local dishes. It's very popular with locals, and the menu changes daily. *Closed Sun, Mon lunch.*

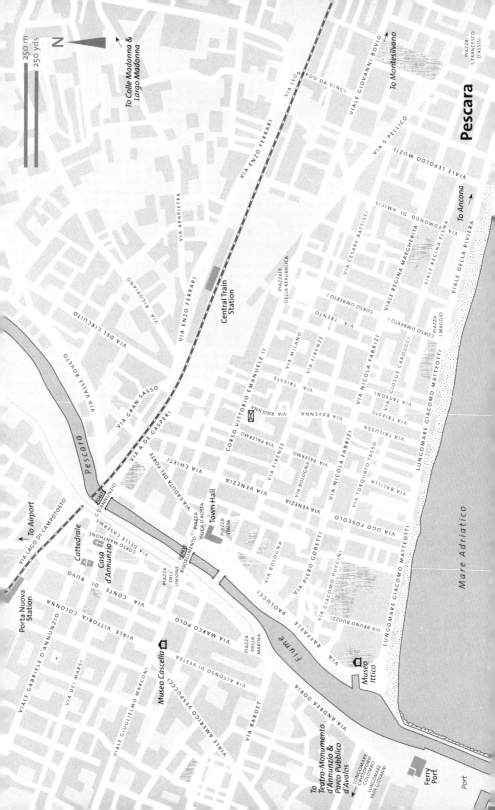

Pescara

**To Colle Madonna &
Largo Madonna**

PIAZZA
S FRANCESCO
D'ASSISI

To Montesilvano

To Ancona

Mare Adriatico

VIA LEONARDO DA VINCI

VIALE GIOVANNI BOVIO

VIA S PELLICO

VIALE LEOPOLDO MUZII

VIA EDMONDO DI AMICIS

VIA ARAPIETRA

VIA ENZO FERRARI

Central Train
Station

PIAZZALE
DELLA REPUBBLICA

VIA CESARE BATTISTI

VIALE REGINA MARGHERITA

VIALE REGINA ELENA

VIALE DELLA RIVIERA

VIA ENZO FERRARI

VIA RICOPIANO

VIA DEL CIRCUITO

VIALE ROVETO

VIA TRENTO

CORSO UMBERTO I

CORSO UMBERTO I

PIAZZA
I MAGGIO

VIA GRAN SASSO

VIA A DE GASPERI

VIA MILANO

VIA FIRENZE

VIA GIOSUE CARDUCCI

Pescara

VIA CHIETI

VIA TRIESTE

VIA RAVENNA

VIA NICOLA FABRIZI

VIA TASSONI

VIA TRIESTE

To Airport

CORSO VITTORIO EMANUELE II

VIA RAVENNA

VIA PALERMO

VIA TRILUSSA

VIA CADUTA DEL FORTE

VIA FIRENZE

VIA PALERMO

VIA NICOLA FABRIZI

VIA TORQUATO TASSO

VIA BALILLA

Town Hall

VIA VENEZIA

VIA BOLOGNA

LUNGOMARE GIACOMO MATTEOTTI

VIA LACO DI CAMPOTOSTO

VIALE GABRIELE D'ANNUNZIO

G D'ANNUNZIO

PIAZZA
DUCA D'AOSTA

PIAZZA
ITALIA

VIA VENEZIA

VIA UGO FOSCOLO

Porta Nuova
Station

Cattedrale

Casa
d'Annunzio

CORSO MANTHONE

VIA DELLE CASERME

PONTE
RISORGIMENTO

PIAZZA
DELL'
UNIONE

VIA BOLOGNA

VIA PIERO GOBETTI

VIA GIACOMO MATTEOTTI

VIA CONTE DI RUVO

PIAZZA
DELLA
MARINA

VIA GIACOMO MATTEOTTI

VIALE VITTORIA COLONNA

VIA MARCO POLO

VIALE CIUGLIELMO MARCONI

VIA BRUNO BUOZZI

VIA DEI MARSI

Museo Cascella

VIA ALFONSO DI VESTEA

VIA RAFFAELE PAOLUCCI

LUNGOMARE GIACOMO MATTEOTTI

VIALE AMERICO VESPUCCI

VIA BARDET

Museo
Ittico

VIA ANDREA DORIA

Fiume

**To
Teatro-Monumento
d'Annunzio &
Parco Pubblico
d'Avalos**

LUNGOMARE
CRISTOFORO
COLOMBO

LUNGOMARE
PAPA GIOVANNI

Ferry
Port

Port

250 m
250 yds

N

20 km
10 miles

N

Ascoli Piceno

Civitella
del Tronto   Giulianova

Téramo   Roseto degli Abruzzi

S. Maria
S. Clemente

Parco Nazionale   R. Vomano   Atri

Gran Sasso d'Italia

Castelli   Penne
Campo Imperatore   Loreto
Aprutino

Assergi   Gran Sasso
Camarda

A B R U Z Z O

L'Aquila

Caporciano
Bominaco   Guardiagrele

R. Aterno

Parco

Nazionale

Albe   Celano   della Maiella

Avezzano   Piano del Fucino   Sulmona

Montesilvano
Marina

PESCARA

Ortona

Chieti

Lanciano

San Giovanni in Venere
Fossacésia Marina

Vasto

Térmoli

Adriatic

Sea

merged the sleepy little fishing village with the equally inconsequential Castellamare Adriatica across the River Pescara, and started pumping money into it. Such efforts were largely due to the influence of the city's most famous son, Gabriele D'Annunzio, who was born here in 1864. Today Pescara is the metropolis of the central Adriatic, with a population of 120,000. It isn't the most charming of cities, but its splendid Lungomare and miles of broad beaches make up for the monotonous streets behind.

Pescara's golden egg is its 16km stretch of sandy **beach**, broad and safe for the youngest child, almost solid with hotels, cafés and fish restaurants between the River Pescara and Montesilvano to the north. Any old buildings it had were decimated during the Second World War. Still, this is no Rimini; if you need excitement, there are riding stables, go-kart tracks, tennis courts, fishing and, for some real thrills, the pescatorial **Museo delle Meraviglie Marine** (*currently closed, with no projected opening date*) in the bustling **fish market** on Lungofiume Paolucci, offering aquariums and fossils. Close by, and facing the sea, the new **Museo d'Arte Moderna 'Vittoria Colonna'** (*open daily 9–1 and 3.30–8.30*) hosts temporary exhibitions of modern art. From here Via Paolucci follows the river to **Piazza Italia**, Pescara's Mussolinian, somewhat uninspiring civic centre.

The original fishing village of Pescara lies on the southern bank of the river, now spoilt by an elevated motorway. Here, the **Museo delle Genti d'Abruzzo** (*Via delle Caserme 22; open Mon–Sat 9–1, Tues and Thurs Mon–Sat 9–1 and 2.30–5, Sun 10–1; adm*) has a comprehensive collection dedicated to everyday life and traditions in the Abruzzo over the centuries. The **Casa Cascella** (*Via G Marconi 45; open Tues–Sat 9–1, also Tues and Thurs 4.30–6.30; adm*) features sculptures, ceramics and other works of art by three generations of the Cascella family. One of them made *The Nave*, the ship fountain along the Lungomare at Piazza 1 Maggio.

This otherwise resolutely normal town must have a bit of kryptonite in it to have produced Gaetano Rapagnetto, the son of a local merchant. He left Pescara for Rome and France, only to re-emerge as the 'Angel Gabriel of the Annunciation', Gabriele D'Annunzio, and went on to become the greatest poet of his generation. Decadent, deeply political and deeply passionate, he was an inspiration to many of his fellow Italians. You can see where he got his start in life, at the **Casa d'Annunzio** (*Corso Manthonè 101; open Mon–Sat 9–1, Sun 9–12.30; adm*), housing memorabilia of the poet.

Day Trips from Pescara

Chieti

For something a bit weightier than gills and beachballs, head up to **Chieti**, some 13km up the River Pescara. Another provincial capital, Chieti was the Roman town of Theate Marrucinorum, and its star attraction is the **Museo Nazionale Archeologico di Antichità** (*Villa Comunale; open Tues–Sun 9–7; adm*), the chief repository of pre-Roman and Roman artworks unearthed in the Abruzzo region. These include the shapely 6th-century BC **Warrior of Capestrano**, accompanied by an inscription in the language of the Middle Adriatic Bronze Age culture; items found in Bronze Age tombs; Hellenistic and Roman sculptures; plus portraits, coins, jewellery and votive offerings, many of which were discovered in Alba Fucens, in the Parco Nazionale d'Abruzzo, and Amiternum, near L'Aquila. The documentation of material from Abruzzo's many Upper Palaeolithic caves is displayed with ancient ceramics and artefacts from Italic necropolises.

Out of doors, Chieti's best feature is its lovely views, stretching from the sea to the Gran Sasso and Maiella Mountains. However, it also retains a dramatic 12th–14th-century Gothic **cathedral** and a couple of traces of old Theate Marrucinorum: the ruins of three little temples on Via Spaventa, and, in the eastern quarters of town, the **Terme Romane** (*closed for restoration; to visit ask at the Museo Archeologico*), with a mighty cistern.

Getting There

Trains run from Pescara Centrale to Chieti roughly every hour (more in the middle of the day) taking 10–15mins. **ARPA buses** (t 085 421 5099) and **SATAM buses** (t 085 421 0733) also connect Chieti with Pescara several times a day; buy bus tickets from Piazza Repubblica.

Tourist Information

Chieti ⊠ **66100**: Palazzo INAIL, Via B. Spaventa 29, t 0871 63640.

Eating Out

Nonna Elisa, Via Per Popoli 265, Località Brecciarola (near the motorway exit), t 0871 684 152 (*moderate*). Offers a delicious, strictly Abruzzese experience. *Closed Mon, Nov and one week in July.*

Venturini, Via de Lollis 10, t 0871 330 663 (*moderate–cheap*). For a fairly priced, fairly cooked meal, try this local institution, whose speciality is mushroom risotto with mozzarella. *Closed Tues.*

Bari

The second city of the Mezzogiorno is a bustling town full of sailors and fishermen, and can also boast a university and a long heritage of cultural distinction. Yet Bari will be a disappointment if you come here expecting Mediterranean charm and medieval romance. If, on the other hand, you'd like to see a southern city that has come close to catching up with the rest of Italy economically, Bari will be just the place. It has oil refineries, a busy port and a new suburban business centre of glass skyscrapers called the Baricentro. The newer districts, with their smart shops and numb boulevards jammed with noisy traffic, exhibit a thoroughly northern-style glitter, and the good burghers who stroll down the Corso Cavour for their evening *passeggiata* are among the most overdressed in Italy. Bari has also become one of the Italian cities most often visited by international rock music tours. Be warned, though – the city has one of the highest street-crime rates in the country.

Getting There

See **Getting There**, pp.3–8.

Getting from the Airport

Bari's airport, **t** 080 583 5230, is about 9km west of the city at Palese. There is a bus to the airport, leaving from the central train station.

By Sea to Croatia

Adriatica di Navigazione, *www.adriatica.it*, and **Jadrolinija**, *www.jadrolinija.hr*, run ferries to Dubrovnik (*summer only*). All ferries leave from the Stazione Marittima on the Mole San Vito, at the opposite end of the city from the main FS rail station (connected by bus 20). For ferry information try CTS, Via Fornari 7, **t** 080 521 3244, a helpful travel agent in town.

Getting Around

Bari's central **FS** station is on Piazza Aldo Moro. Nearby is the **Ferrovia Bari-Nord** station. Bus services to coastal towns north of Bari operate from Piazza Eroi del Mare. **SITA** buses (Largo Sorrentino behind the FS train station) go to inland and southern towns. The bright orange city buses run from 5.30am to 11pm.

Tourist Information

Bari: Piazza Aldo Moro 33/A, **t** 080 524 2361, situated to the right of the FS station (*open Mon–Fri 9–1, Tues and Thurs also 3–5*).

Where to Stay

Bari ✉ 70100

The city is full of bad hotels at bad prices.

****Villa Romanazzi Carducci, Via Capruzzi 326, **t** 080 542 7400, **f** 080 556 0297 (*luxury*). One upmarket hotel that is not a total rip-off.

***Albergo Moderno, Via Crisanzio 60, **t** 080 521 3313, **f** 080 521 4718 (*moderate*). A third of the price of the above, and quite pleasant.

***Costa, Via Crisanzio 12, **t** 080 521 9015, **f** 080 521 0006 (*moderate*). Another unremarkable but pleasant hotel at comparatively reasonable prices.

Albergo Giulia, **t 080 521 6630, **f** 080 521 8271 (*moderate*). In the same building as the Costa; one of the best budget choices.

Eating Out

Murat de l'Hotel Palace, Via Lombardi 13, **t** 080 521 6551 (*expensive*). The adventurous should try this highly rated restaurant. *Closed Sun and 2wks Aug.*

Al Pescatore, Via Federico II di Svevia 6, **t** 080 523 7039 (*expensive*). Excellent fresh, local fish in informal surroundings. *Closed 1–15 Jan.*

Taverna Verde, Largo Adua 19, **t** 080 554 0870 (*moderate*). A few steps down the road, this is a popular place for fish and beer. *Closed Sun, last 2 weeks of Aug, and 24 Dec–6 Jan.*

Terranima, Via Putignani 213, **t** 080 521 9725 (*moderate*). Arguably the best trattoria in town. *Closed Sun eve and Aug.*

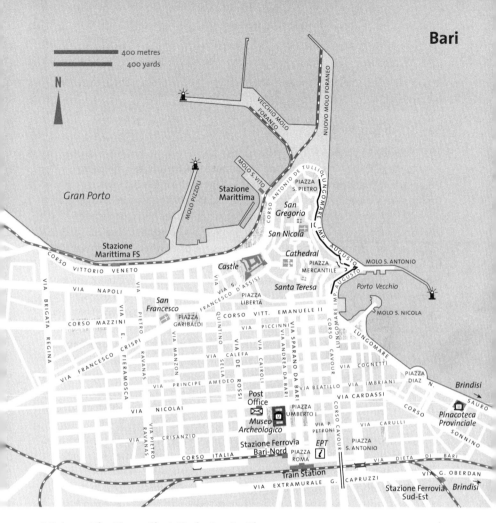

History: The Town that Stole Santa Claus

Bari can trace its history back to before the Romans, but it only began to make a name for itself in the 10th century. As an important trading city and seat of the nominally independent Byzantine governor, Bari was sometimes a rival of Venice, though more often its ally. Robert Guiscard and his Normans, who took the city in 1071, favoured Bari and helped it become the leading town of Puglia. Sixteen years later in 1087, a fleet of Barese merchantmen in Antioch got word that some of their Venetian counterparts were planning a little raid on Myra, on what is now the southern coast of Turkey. Their intention was to pinch the mortal remains of St Nicholas, Myra's 4th-century bishop, canonized for his generosity and good deeds. Relic-stealing was a cultural imperative for medieval Italians, and the Baresi sneaked in by night and beat the Venetians to their prey. The Greek Christians of Myra were disgusted by the whole affair, but the Baresi had them outmatched, and so St Nicholas went west (his sarcophagus was too heavy to move, and so you can still see it today in the museum at Antalya, Turkey). Every year on 8 May the Baresi celebrate their cleverness with a procession of boats in the harbour, and an ancient icon of the saint is held up to receive the homage of the crowds on shore, recreating the scene of Nicholas' arrival 900 years ago.

Basilica di San Nicola

Open daily 7–1 and 4–8 and for daily Mass.

To provide a fitting home for such an important saint, Bari almost immediately began to construct the Basilica di San Nicola at the centre of the old town. Unfortunately the original ambition over-reached the ability of succeeding generations to finish the job. The two big towers remain unfinished and much of the decorative scheme was abandoned, giving the church a dowdy, barn-like appearance. Still, this is the first of the great Puglian churches, the place where the style was first translated from Norman French to southern Italian. Inside, the only surprise is the **tomb of Bona Sforza**, Queen of Poland and Duchess of Bari. The daughter of a 16th-century Duke of Milan, she inherited Bari on her mother's side and as a teenager was packed off to marry Sigismund, one of Poland's greatest kings. She survived him, and had a brief but eventful career as a dowager queen before retiring to sunny Puglia in her last years. Near the main altar, note the wonderful 11th-century **bishop's throne**, one of the greatest works of medieval sculpture in Puglia. Its legs, carved into the figures of men groaning as if they were supporting some unbearable burden, must have been a good joke on any fat bishop over the centuries.

Down in the crypt, you can pay your respects to St Nicholas. There will nearly always be somebody down there, praying or conducting a service; Nicholas' tomb has always been one of the south's most popular places of pilgrimage. The church is also home to a centre for ecumenical studies, as the Baresi try to make amends after nine centuries. One of Nicholas' tricks is to exude gallons of a brownish liquid the faithful call *manna*, to which all sorts of miracles are attributed. Most of the visitors are local, but an Orthodox chapel has been added to accommodate pilgrims from Greece and Russia.

Around the Old Town

South of San Nicola is the **cathedral** (*open 8.30–1 and 5–7*), which is difficult to distinguish from San Nicola, although it was begun almost a century later. The plan is the same, as is the general feeling of austerity broken by small areas of richly detailed carving around some of the doors and windows. Unlike San Nicola, the cathedral still has its original beam ceiling, interrupted only by an octagonal cupola, and much more suited to its Romanesque plainness. Two unusual features of the church are the stone baldachin over the main altar and the *trullo*, the large round building adjacent to the north wall that once served as the baptistry.

Old Bari, as we have said, is a bit drab for a medieval historic centre. There is a reason for this, in that Bari has had more than its share of trouble. The Normans levelled it once after a revolt. A plague in the 1650s wiped out most of the population, and the port area was heavily bombed in the Second World War. As a result, old Bari in some parts has the air of a new town. But although the buildings in the old centre may be all rebuilt or restored, at least the labyrinthine old street plan survives – it's famous, in fact, for being one of the easiest places in all Italy to get lost. There will be no trouble, however, finding the **castle** (*open Thurs–Tues 9–7; adm*), just across the Piazza Odegitria from the cathedral. The Normans began it, Frederick II completed it, and later centuries added the polygonal bastions to deflect cannonballs. Inside, some sculpted reliefs and windows survive from Frederick's time, along with bits of sculpture and architectural fragments from all over Puglia. Excavations have revealed parts of Roman Bari, which lies directly underneath.

Modern Bari

On your way up towards the railway station, you will be crossing the Corso Vittorio Emanuele – site of both the city hall and Bari's famous fish market, and also the boundary between the old city and the new. When Bari's fortunes began to revive at the beginning of the 19th century, Joachim Murat's Napoleonic government laid out this broad rectilinear extension to the city. It has the plan of an old Greek or Roman town, only with wider streets, and it fits Bari well. Many streets have a view to the sea. Via Sparano di Bari and Corso Cavour are the choicest shopping streets.

Bari's two museums are in the new town. The **Pinacoteca Provinciale** (*open Tues–Sat 9–1 and 4–7, Sun 9–1; adm*) is in the Palazzo della Provincia on Lungomare Nazario Sauro, and has a good selection of south Italian art. Few Neapolitans are represented, although there is a genuine Neapolitan *presepio* (crib).

The **Museo Archeologico** occupies a corner of Bari University's sprawling, crowded palace on the Piazza Umberto I, near the railway station. As is usual in southern museums, the star exhibits are classical ceramics: there are painted vases from Attica, including one very beautiful figure of the *Birth of Helen* from Leda's egg, and also several Puglian copies, some as good as the best of the Greek work. Much of the rest of the collection is devoted to the pre-Greek Neolithic cultures of Puglia.

Day Trips from Bari: *Trullo*-hunting

Southeast of Bari is a small but attractive region of little towns in an extraordinary, unique man-made landscape, given its character by one of the oldest forms of building in Italy still in regular use – the whitewashed, dome-roofed houses known as *trulli*. White arches and steps climb the hillsides, topped with Baroque churches.

The **Valle d'Itria**, between the towns of Putignano and Martina Franca, is the best place to see *trulli*. **Alberobello**, the *trulli* capital, has over a thousand of them – and nearly as many souvenir stands and craft shops – in two adjacent neighbourhoods called the Rione Monti and the Ala Piccola. Even the modern church of Sant'Antonio has been built *trullo*-fashion. There is a small museum next door.

Trulli look pretty out in the countryside too, and particularly so around **Locorotondo**, a gleaming white town with views around the valley, topped not with *trulli* but tidy rows of distinctive gables. The street plan, from which the town takes its name, is neatly circular, built around an ancient well dedicated to St George. Nearby, at the top of the town, the pretty church of **Santa Maria Graecia** has a carved altarpiece, bits of frescoes, and valley views. For a more heady diversion, pay a visit to the **Cantina del Locorotondo** (*Via Madonna della Catena 99*, **t** *080 431 1644*), a modern winery with a *trullo* that produces some of the best vintages in southern Italy.

Martina Franca, the highest town in Puglia, has a garland of Baroque monuments including the old **Palazzo Ducale**, a number of other palaces and a **cathedral** at the top, which towers over the city like a castle. In July and August, Martina Franca becomes an important point on the Puglian cultural map when it hosts the **Valle d'Itria Festival** (**t** *080 480 5100*) – an international music festival that attracts opera, classical and jazz performers from around the world.

Getting Around

The Ferrovia Sud-Est **rail** line between Bari and Taranto or Lecce stops at Putignano, Alberobello, Locorotondo and Martina Franca, where the Lecce and Taranto lines divide. The FSE also operates **bus** services to the area from Tàranto and Bari.

Tourist Information

Martina Franca: Piazza Roma 9, **t** 080 480 5702. *Open Mon–Fri 9–1 and 5–7.30, Sat 9–1.*

Where to Stay and Eat

Alberobello ✉ 70011

★★★★★**Hotel dei Trulli**, Via Cadore 32, **t** 080 432 3555, *www.hoteldeitrulli.it* (*very expensive*). A group of *trulli* cottages, set in a garden. Each cottage has its own patio and is beautifully furnished. There is also a pool. *Closed Jan, Feb.*

Il Poeta Contadino, Via Indipendenza 21, **t** 080 432 1917 (*very expensive*). 'The Peasant Poet' is another one of Puglia's fine 'creative' restaurants. *Closed Mon and 3wks Jan.*

Trullo d'Oro, Via Cavallotti 27, **t** 080 432 1820 (*moderate*). Good, sophisticated cuisine. You could try the Puglian-style *spiedini*. *Closed Mon and most of Jan.*

Locorotondo ✉ 70010

Centro Storico, Via Eroi di Dogali 6, **t** 080 431 5473 (*moderate*). The owner's love of food is obvious in the care taken with the cooking at this intimate trattoria. *Closed Wed winter.*

Martina Franca ✉ 74015

★★★**Dell'Erba**, Via dei Cedri 1, **t** 080 430 1055, **f** 080 430 1639 (*moderate*). This place has a garden, pool and an excellent restaurant.

Main page references are in **bold**. Page references to maps are in *italics*.